D1613129

Patricians and Parvenus

Patricians
— AND —
Parvenus

*Wealth and High Society
in Wilhelmine Germany*

Dolores L. Augustine

Oxford / Providence, USA

Published in 1994 by
Berg Publishers, Ltd.
Editorial offices:
150 Cowley Road, Oxford OX4 1JJ, UK
221 Waterman Street, Providence, RI 02906, U.S.A.

© 1994 Dolores L. Augustine

Library of Congress Cataloging-in-Publication Data
A CIP catalog record for this book is available from the Library of
Congress.

ISBN 0 85496 397 9

This book is dedicated to my parents,
Reginald and Yolanda Augustine, and to my sister,
Nancy Augustine.

Table of Contents

CHAPTER 1

Profile of the Wilhelmine Wealth Elite

CHAPTER 2

Marriage

CHAPTER 3

Family Life and Power Relations within the Family

CHAPTER 4

Family Solidarity, Youthful Rebellion, and the Sons' Choice of Profession

CHAPTER 5

Residential Patterns, Villas, and Landed Estates

CHAPTER 6

Wealthy Business Families in High Society

Contents

List of Tables

❀

Acknowledgments

This study is a revised version of my dissertation, "Die wilhelminische Wirtschaftselite: Sozialverhalten, Soziales Selbstbewußtsein und Familie," accepted as a doctoral dissertation at the Free University of Berlin in 1991, and translated into English by my father, Reginald C. Augustine. My mother, Juno Yolanda Augustine, assisted in preparing the manuscript. I would like to express my deepest gratitude to my mentor, Prof. Hartmut Kaelble, now at Humboldt University, Berlin, for the intellectual guidance, moral support, and devoted attention that not only I, but all his graduate students received. An especially warm thanks goes out to my friends in Prof. Kaelble's doctoral colloquium – Christoph Conrad, Ruth Federspiel, Thomas Golka, Rüdiger Hohls, Oliver Janz, Hasso Spode (whose computer expertise was of great help), Armin Triebel, and Gudrun Wedel – who with wide-ranging knowledgeability, meticulous care, patience, and humor critiqued every chapter of this book, some sections more than once. I also thank my second reader, Prof. Jürgen Kocka, for his suggestions and words of encouragement. I am also grateful to the German Women's History Study Group of New York – Bonnie Anderson, Maria Baader, Barbara Bari, Renate Bridenthal, Jane Caplan, Belinda Davis, Katharina Feil, Atina Grossmann, Amy Hackett, Deborah Hertz, Marion Kaplan, Claudia Koonz, Jan Lambertz, Molly Nolan, and Nancy Reagin – for their comments and criticism on chapters 2, 3, and 6. I also received suggestions and encouragement from many other scholars and friends, among them Detlef Bald, Richard Evans, Bernd Faulenbach, Gerald D. Feldman, Horst Handke, Karin Kaudelka, Toni Pierenkemper, Julius Posener, Dirk Schumann, Hannes Siegrist, Lili Sprecher, Alan Steinweis, and Hartmut Zwahr. Several private persons, most of them descendents of businessmen in my study, provided me with information that I would not otherwise have had access to. These include Gerhart Gilka, Countess Sibylle von Hardenberg, Peter Hecker, Friedrich August Nebelthau, Ernst-Ludwig Raab, Franz Lerner, Werner Pfeiffer, Hermann Segnitz, Else Stinnes, and Ingrid Wilke. The assistance provided by the personnel of the archives I visited was invaluable, and here I would like to make special mention of Friedrich Wilhelm Euler, the head of the *Institut zur Erforschung historischer Führungsschichten* in Bensheim, and Carl-Friedrich Baumann, the head of the Thyssen Archive. Finally, a special word of gratitude goes out to my father, who awakened my interest in history and European cultures, to both my parents for the years of emotional support for my project, and to my husband, Claude LeBrun, for the large dose of patience and love he gave me while I was preparing the manuscript of this book for publication.

This study was made possible by the generous financial support provided in 1985/86 by the Berlin Senate (*Stipendium nach dem Nachwuchsförderungsgesetz*) and in 1988/89 by the Berlin Airlift Foundation. My three-month research stay in the G.D.R. was supported by a grant from the International Research & Exchanges Board (IREX), with funds provided by the National Endowment for the Humanities and the United States Information Agency. None of these organizations is responsible for the views expressed in this book.

I thank the Archive of the Thyssen AG for granting permission to use a photograph of August Thyssen in this book and the Econ-Verlagsgruppe (Econ Publishing Group) for allowing me to use a photograph of Hans Fürstenberg from one of their publications.[1] I also thank Ingrid Wilke for the use of a family photo of Conrad Niethammer's house. I have used various sentences and passages out of my article "Arriving in the upper class: the wealthy business elite of Wilhelmine Germany"[2] in Chapters 5 and 6. I thank Routledge for permission to use these passages.

---

1. H. Fürstenberg, *Erinnerungen.*
2. Augustine, "Arriving."

❀

Introduction

Krupp and Siemens, Bleichröder and Ballin – these are names that for many represent the triumphs, tragedies, and sins of the business elite of imperial Germany. An older school of biographers tended to view such businessman as unique individuals – pioneers or geniuses who braved the rough waters of the business world, alone or as part of an unusual family. Other biographers placed their subject in the context of the larger questions of German history – the aristocracy's supposed eclipse of the bourgeoisie; anti-Semitism; the rise of corporate capitalism; or war aims in the First World War. Empirical research on businessmen as a group – as an elite or as a segment of the bourgeoisie – was long left to political and economic historians. Social historians were primarily concerned with the working class or with the lower middle class. Only in the last few years has the focus of research shifted to the bourgeoisie, or *Bürgertum*. It should be noted that, in German, the term *Bürgertum* carries with it a whole range of connotations and historical references that cannot be translated into English. It is a class with a history of its own, with values and lifestyles that distinguished it from other classes. In eighteenth- and nineteenth-century Germany, "*Bürger*" meant citizen, ideally a "free" individual in the sense of the Enlightenment, endowed with the rights of citizenship, including *Bürgerrechte* or civil rights. Together, these citizens formed the *bürgerliche Gesellschaft*, or civil society. During the course of the nineteenth century, the terms *Bürger* and *bürgerlich* took on negative connotations as well, which were linked to criticism of bourgeois society.[1] The term *Mittelstand*, which originally embraced what we would call the

1. See Kocka, introduction to *Burger und Burgerlichkeit*, pp. 7–20; also, see Haltern, *Bürgerliche Gesellschaft*.

1

"middle class," came during the course of the nineteenth century to stand for the lower portion of the middle class, which included some segments that in present-day America would be considered to be "middle-middle class."[2] This group could at best call itself "*Kleinbürgertum*," but was increasingly excluded from the concept "*Bürgertum*," translated in the present study as "bourgeoisie." The latter in turn broke down into the propertied bourgeoisie (*Besitzbürgertum*)[3] and the educated bourgeoisie (*Bildungsbürgertum*), consisting of university-educated professionals. In the present study, the term "middle class" will be understood to include both the lower middle class and the bourgeoisie proper, which, however, increasingly straddled the line between the middle and upper classes.

It is in this context that the recent upsurge of interest in the bourgeoisie among German scholars should be seen. An international group of scholars from various fields came together at the Center for Interdisciplinary Studies of the University of Bielefeld in 1986/87 to discuss and conduct research on "The Bourgeoisie, Bourgeois Identity and Civil Society: A Comparative Study of Nineteenth Century Europe."[4] A series of longer-term projects on the bourgeoisie are being carried out at this university as part of an interdisciplinary *Sonderforschungsbereich* (Special Research Group) on the "Social History of the Modern Bourgeoisie: Germany in International Comparison." Research on the bourgeoisie is also taking place in other places. These endeavors have contributed to the formulation of broader and more precise lines of inquiry and have placed German social history within a European context. The present study, a prosopography of the wealthiest businessmen of Wilhelmine Germany, is intended as a contribution to this body of research.

The group under study consists of the wealthiest businessmen of the Wilhelmine period up to the First World War (1890–1914).[5] Not only owners were included, but also top corporate managers

---

2. However, comparisons are very difficult because present-day definitions of class are often based on income, whereas the present study makes use of historical terms based on profession, and that have a strong historical-cultural component.

3. In the present study, "wealthiest businessmen," "wealthy business elite," "business elite," and "wealthy propertied bourgeoisie" are used as synonyms.

4. Jürgen Kocka (in collaboration with Ute Frevert) edited a three-volume study with this title, in which the results of empirical research on various aspects of the subject were brought together: *Bürgertum*. English edition: Kocka and Mitchell, *Bourgeois Society*. In addition, four symposia were held and the papers published.

5. Due to the fact that social history generally moves in long waves, it has not always been possible to adhere strictly to this time frame.

and members of the board of directors. Industrialists, bankers, merchants, and entrepreneurs in other commercial enterprises and services, such as shipping, were all considered businessmen, while landowners were not (unless also active in the industrial or services sector). The present study is somewhat unusual in that it does not focus on one region, one industry or sector, one ethnic or religious group. The scope is national and the selection criterion is wealth. This somewhat unorthodox approach seeks to measure the impact of wealth on social behavior, while allowing quantitative and non-quantitative analysis of regional, industrial and sectoral, ethnic and religious differences, as well as differences between corporate managers and owners. Comparisons will also be made between businessmen who received titles of nobility and those who did not.[6] The main themes of this study are the feudalization thesis, the social history of the bourgeoisie, family history and the related fields of women's history and the history of childhood and youth, and German-Jewish history. Other topics will be touched upon as well: the rise of the corporate manager, social mobility and elite recruitment, businessmen's participation in politics, the architectural history of the bourgeois "villa," and the development of residential suburbs.[7] It is hoped that from these various perspectives will emerge a coherent view of the social world of the wealthy business elite of Wilhelmine Germany and a better understanding of how the social, economic, and political roles of this group fit together.

Themes and Debates

Historians were long convinced that Germany in the nineteenth and early twentieth centuries was set apart from Western countries by traditions, outlooks, institutions, and decisions that contributed to a deviant path of development, or *Sonderweg*, which ultimately led to the failure of democracy in Germany and the rise of National Socialism. The failure of the German bourgeoisie to fulfill its "historic mission" was seen as one of the major reasons why a liberal-

---

6. Since this study focuses on aristocratization and the history of the bourgeoisie, businessmen of the older nobility – though not entirely absent – are largely ignored.

7. The subject of this study is not the origin of great fortunes but rather the effect of wealth upon social behavior. It therefore cannot contribute to research on the sociological prerequisites for the successful development of capitalism. Among the topics neglected here are factory paternalism, social policy, charity work, art patronage, and bourgeois attempts to serve as a model for the "lower" orders of society. Some of these topics are very well researched, others were omitted due to lack of material.

ization and democratization of society, the political culture, and the constitution did not take place in Germany. The traditional theory was that Germany, unlike England or France, ostensibly, did not experience a "bourgeois revolution," so that power was left in the hands of the traditional, aristocratic elite. The defeat of the liberal-nationalist movement in the Revolution of 1848, the Prussian Constitutional Conflict of 1859–66, and the unification of Germany through a war fought by the militaristic, monarchical Prussian state in 1870–71 (rather than through a popular uprising) had a decisive impact on the political attitudes and behavior of the German middle classes, greatly weakening their will for reform and paving the way for a political coalition with the old agrarian elite. The specter of proletarian revolution was a further important factor pushing the German bourgeoisie into the arms of the landed aristocracy. This reorientation then came to fruition in the political alliance between "rye and iron" (the great agricultural landowners and the great industrialists). According to the feudalization thesis, political capitulation was accompanied – or in fact caused – by the downfall of that sense of self-esteem that had allowed middle-class values and lifestyles to flourish in the early nineteenth century.[8]

This approach to German history has fallen into disfavor in some quarters in recent years, as a generation of historians attuned to both the continuities and discontinuities of German history and given to empiricism has come to the helm. David Blackbourn and Geoff Eley unleashed a heated debate on the *Sonderweg* thesis, arguing that the German path to modernity was indeed tied to the rise of the bourgeoisie.[9] Because of the hostility of the working class, the *Mittelstand* and peasantry, the bourgeoisie did not try to attain a position of overt political predominance. This was unnecessary in any case, for the German state, far from being the defender of the old order, carried out a true "revolution from above" and promoted what the bourgeoisie saw as progress in many areas: German unification, state interventionism to promote economic

---

8. On the *Sonderweg* thesis, see Bruggemeier, "Der deutsche Sonderweg," pp. 244–49; Kocka, "Der 'deutsche Sonderweg'". 365–79. The feudalization thesis, as formulated before the First World War, was usually applied to other European nations as well as to Germany. See Kaelble, "Das aristokratische Modell," pp 14–15. For early formulations of the feudalization thesis, see Michels, *Umschichtungen*, p. 50; Sombart, *Die deutsche Volkswirtschaft*, pp. 469–70; Weber, *Gesammelte politische Schriften*, pp. 109–10; and comments on Weber in Blackbourn and Eley, *Peculiarities*, p. 229. Ralf Dahrendorf's reformulation of the *Sonderweg* thesis became a new orthodoxy for a generation of historians seeking explanations for the rise of National Socialism in Germany. See Dahrendorf, *Gesellschaft*, esp pp. 62–64.

9. See Blackbourn and Eley, *Peculiarities*.

growth, the rule of law, and – one might add – imperialism. The monarchical system served as a bulwark against revolution in the country with the largest and best-organized labor movement in the world. Moreover, bourgeois values came to predominate in many areas of German society: the rise of the merit principle and the decline of privilege, the belief in efficiency, rationality and progress, the spread of materialism, professionalization, the rise of the public sphere, and fashion. Here, cultural pessimism, the narrow perspective of professional and employers' associations, and factory paternalism are interpreted not as signs of the persistence of the old order, but as negative side effects of industrialization.[10]

The élan of myth-destroying has given way to careful empiricism. Major weaknesses in the feudalization thesis have gradually come into focus.[11] Though some studies have found evidence of feudalization, it has often been rather unclear how the group under study was defined and how representative the findings were. This is particularly the case with older works, such as Friedrich Zunkel's pioneering study on businessmen in the Rhineland and Westphalia in the period from 1834 to 1879.[12] In later studies, though newer quantitative methods have been used, the number of cases has often been too small, and Rhineland-Westphalia was overly favored.[13] Hans-Konrad Stein[14] came to the conclusion in a study on business families with new titles of nobility that the bourgeoisie was "sucked up into the old aristocracy," not realizing that the newly ennobled were most atypical in their social orientation and behavior.[15] These problems have been overcome in two exemplary new dissertations – one by Dirk Schumann on businessmen in five Bavarian towns, and one by Karin Kaudelka-Hanisch on holders of the title "Commercial Councillor" in Westphalia and Düsseldorf.[16]

10. The reinterpretation of various German "peculiarities" in the area of social and economic history as the product of modernization rather than as remnants of traditional structures did not begin with Blackbourn and Eley. See Crew, *Town*.

11. On the following discussion, see Kaelble, "Wie feudal," pp. 148–71.

12. Zunkel, *Der rheinisch-westfälische Unternehmer*.

13. See Gerhard Adelmann, "Führende Unternehmer," pp. 335–52; Faulenbach, "Die Herren," pp. 76–88; Henning, "Soziale Verflechtung," pp. 1–30; Spencer, "West German"; and Teuteberg, *Westfälische Textilunternehmer*. Wilhelm Stahl, in his study on businessmen listed in the *Neue Deutsche Biographie* (*Der Elitenkreislauf*), defined his group too broadly, including all born in the eighteenth and nineteenth centuries and all "ethnic" Germans (such as the Swiss, Austrians, and Sudeten Germans). Wolfgang Zapf presented data that were too aggregated to test the feudalization model. (Zapf, *Wandlungen*)

14. Stein, *Der preußische Geldadel*.

15. See the results of my study below.

16. Kaudelka-Hanisch, "Preußische Kommerzienräte" and Schumann, "Bayerns Unternehmer."

Studies that are international in scope have shown that the German bourgeoisie was not as "peculiar" in its relationship to the aristocracy as has sometimes been asserted. The volume growing out of research conducted at the Bielefeld Center for Interdisciplinary Studies has made a major contribution here.[17]

Empirical research has called into question the interpretation of a whole range of phenomena as indicators of feudalization. The older view that factory paternalism was indicative of the continued influence of feudal values[18] has given way to interpretations that look for explanations within the context of capitalist development in Germany.[19] Ute Frevert has shown how dueling was reinterpreted in the context of a bourgeois code of honor.[20] Close ties between the bourgeoisie and the state – previously thought to be indicative of feudalization – have been reinterpreted by various scholars. They remind us that though the top administrative positions in government remained in the hands of the nobility (especially in Prussia), the state played a particularly active role in social and economic development in Germany – to the benefit not only of the traditional elites, but also of the rising middle classes. This resulted in a more intense interchange between bureaucracy and society and greater prestige for civil servants than in other countries. The bourgeoisie became accustomed to appeal to the state when seeking solutions to problems and to see the state bureaucracy as a model in various areas. Symptomatic of this process (termed by some "social bureaucratization") was the awarding of titles and decorations, which was based to a growing extent on loyalty to the monarchical system and ties of friendship, marriage, and kinship to civil servants.[21]

17 See Kocka, *Burgertum*, especially the articles by Youssef Cassis, Werner Mosse, and Hartmut Kaelble. Unlike other authors, Mosse remains faithful to the feudalization model. Also, see Mayer, *Persistence*. Mayer concludes that in all of Europe, the bourgeoisie was lacking in self-esteem vis-à-vis the pre-industrial elite, and did not become the dominant class in the economic, political, cultural or social life until after the First (or perhaps even the Second) World War. See also Blackbourn and Eley, *Peculiarities*, pp. 229–231; Kaelble, *Nachbarn am Rhein*, chapter 3; Kaeble, "Wie feudal," pp. 159–63.

18. Ascher, "Baron v. Stumm," pp. 271–85.

19. See Blackbourn and Eley, *Peculiarities*, pp. 48–49, 107–11; Crew, *Town*, pp. 145–48; Faulenbach, "Die Preußischen Bergassessoren," pp. 236–37, Fridenson, "Herrschaft," pp. 65–91, Newby, "Paternalism," pp. 59–73.

20. See Frevert, *Ehrenmänner* and "Bourgeois honour."

21. See Blackbourn and Eley, *Peculiarities*, pp. 232–33, Kaelble, "Wie feudal," pp. 163–66, Kaelble, "Sozialstruktur," 132–79: Kaudelka-Hanisch, "Preußische Kommerzienräte"; Schumann, "Bayerns Unternehmer," pp. 330–60. On the predominant role of the bureaucracy in Germany, see Niethammer et al., *Burgerliche Gesellschaft*

In still another area, the true meaning of the indicators must be rethought: namely, conspicuous consumption and social life. By 1900 wealthy businessmen were not only making regular appearances in the most exclusive circles of high society, but were also beginning to shape social life in these illustrious environs and to adopt the forms and norms associated with them, including ostentatious display and social snobbery. These changes have often been measured against the frugal, unpretentious way of living and (supposedly) sincere friendships of the early nineteenth century. But is this not a false yardstick? In the era before the take-off of the German economy, capital was scarce and risk great. Therefore, business families were forced to save much and spend little. This behavior was reinforced, not only by religious values, but also by the urge to counter the nobility's claims of birthright with middle-class claims of moral superiority (based on hard work and lack of materialism). The few very wealthy business families in the early nineteenth century did not conform to these middle-class values[22] – nor did they need to – and by the end of the century, there were even more entrepreneurial families that were in a position to challenge the social predominance of the nobility head on, using the time-honored strategy of imitation. Our definition of what is bourgeois must therefore not be static, but must take into account changes in social norms over time. But where do shifts in bourgeois values end and where does aristocratization begin? It is only possible to decide this question within the framework of careful, contextualized analysis.

The present study will examine "feudalization," in the sense of a general social and political capitulation to the nobility, and "aristocratization,"[23] which will be understood in the much more limited sense of imitating aristocratic models of behavior and forming ties of marriage and friendship with the nobility. A series of "classic" indicators of aristocratization will be empirically examined. These include the granting of titles and decorations, marriage patterns, the sons' choice of profession, friendships, entertainment and

---

22 See Kaelble, *Berliner Unternehmer*, pp. 166–71; Kaelble, "Wie feudal," p 153; Zwahr, "Zur Klassenkonstituierung," esp pp 102–03 and 118.

23. It has been pointed out that the process supposedly described by the term "feudalization" actually has nothing to do with feudalism as a social, economic, military, and political system. The terms "aristocratization" or, where appropriate, "aristocratic model" are preferable. (See Kaelble, "Wie feudal," p. 150.) However, the latter terms do not really convey the theoretical implications of the feudalization thesis. Since I question the validity of the feudalization thesis, I see no problem in employing the faulty term "feudalization" in connection with this overarching interpretation of the history of the German bourgeoisie.

social networking, consumption, and residential style (choice of neighborhood, type of home, furnishings, grounds). But the analysis cannot stop here: the indicators themselves must be problematized and reevaluated.

Previous studies, which have focused mainly on middle-scale businessmen, have not in any way corroborated the feudalization theory. However, it could be argued that feudalization would be most likely to occur among the wealthiest or most successful businessmen, who could most easily afford an aristocratic life style and who would be the most likely to be accepted as equals by the nobility. Very wealthy businessmen would be particularly susceptible to the temptations of a life of luxury and leisure. Moreover, it was big businessmen that allied themselves politically with agrarian conservatism. Did a "feudal-capitalistic ruling class" – to employ an expression that has found favor with a number of historians – actually exist?[24] The present study sets out to demonstrate it did not, that feudalization was in fact very limited in scope in precisely the group of businessmen in which it could be expected to be strongest: its wealthiest segment.

A contribution can also be made to the history of the bourgeoisie that, going beyond the feudalization model, places the wealthy business elite within the class system as a whole and focuses in particular on its position within the bourgeoisie, its ties with the educated bourgeoisie (*Bildungsbürgertum*), the lower middle class, and other classes. Were the richest businessmen still a part of the bourgeoisie or did they rise into the ruling class? Did they cut themselves off from the middle and lower classes? If so, how did social distinction manifest itself? Was the business elite socially isolated? What were typical career patterns and how did they compare with those of other professional groups?[25] We must also deal with the elusive question of class identity and values. Historians have generally discussed the question of social orientation in terms of the bourgeoisie. Lothar Gall sees the ideal of individual success and the "idea of the classless society of *Bürger*" (in the sense of both

24. This conception is to be found in the writings of Eckart Kehr and in more recent writings by Marxist historians. See Kehr, "Zur Genesis," pp. 492–502 and "Das soziale System," pp. 253–74. These and other essays in English translation in Kehr, *Economic Interest*. Also, see Handke, "Einige Probleme," pp. 261–88, esp pp. 281–84. For a non-Marxist use of the conception, see Mosse, "Die Juden," pp. 58–59, in Mosse, *Juden*.

25. For two recent attempts at broad synthesis, see Pilbeam, *Middle Classes*; and Niethammer et al , *Bürgerliche Gesellschaft*. Also, see Henning, *Das westdeutsche Bürgertum*, vol. 1; Henning, "Verflechtung"; Kocka, *Bürgertum*; Kaelble, "Sozialstruktur", Kaelble, "Wie feudal," pp. 168–69; Haupt, "Männliche und weibliche," pp. 143–60.

bourgeois and citizen) as central to the bourgeois identity of the business elite, represented in his recent study on the Bassermann family.[26] He interprets the changes of the late nineteenth century as signs of decline, or even crisis – the economic decline and professional failure of many family members, the loss of economic and political independence due to the rise of corporate capitalism and mass political organizations, growing social exclusivity, and the increasing geographic and professional dispersion of the family. The problem with this approach is not only that it romanticizes the bourgeoisie of earlier eras and makes its way of life out to be an eternal ideal, but also that it does not ask whether other bourgeois groups and elites came to the fore that had their own distinct way of being bourgeois. The bourgeoisie of the pre-war era was fragmented, and we must analyze the nature and consequences of this fragmentation. Did the wealthiest businessmen and their families perceive themselves as a social, political, or economic elite? Or were they so diverse in their social or political predilections (as opposed to economic interests) that they never thought of themselves as part of a larger entity, of a business elite? The present study shows that a business elite did exist that surmounted regional, ethnic, and other divisions, an elite with a strong sense of its identity and its power, but an elite whose values could not sweep aside those of traditional society because of the deep divisions within the bourgeoisie and within the upper class, to which this business elite now belonged.

A discussion of class relations presents special problems relating to terminology and categorization.[27] In the present study, the bourgeoisie is divided into the propertied bourgeoisie (*Besitzbürgertum*) and the educated bourgeoisie (*Bildungsbürgertum*), which includes the upper echelons of the professions, teaching, political offices, the ministry, and upper (university-educated) civil servants (aside from the *Landrat*[28]). Some quantitative data distinguish upper civil servants from the rest of the educated, or profes-

26. See Gall, *Bürgertum*. Despite the title, this is essentially a history of the Bassermann family. See review: Ute Frevert, "Literaturbericht."

27. The class model and categorization of professions used here is based on: Lundgreen, Kraul, and Ditt, *Bildungschancen*, vol. 2, pp. 319–64. I have modified this model for my purposes. On specific professions, see my dissertation: "Die wilhelminische Wirtschaftselite," pp. 326–27. Following Lundgreen, Kraul, and Ditt's somewhat unorthodox class model, I included the upper middle class in the upper class and termed the lower middle class "middle class" in the tables of my dissertation. This practice will not be followed in the present study.

28. On the ties of the *Landrat* to the pre-industrial elite, see Witt, "Der preußische Landrat," pp. 205–19

9

sional bourgeoisie.[29] (Though technically civil servants through much
of German history, teachers, professors, and ministers were not
counted as such.[30]) The pre-industrial, traditional elite consists here
of large landowners, members of the high nobility (where no profession is known), those holding court posts, officers, diplomats, and
civil servants holding the office of *Landrat*). This group is largely
identical with the aristocracy. The lower middle class includes small-
scale businessmen (including master craftsmen and the petty bourgeoisie), farmers, middle-grade civil servants (who had no university
degree), white-collar workers, factory foremen, non-commissioned
officers, Catholic priests, rabbis, artists, and writers. The lower class
includes the blue-collar professions, craftsmen below the master, soldiers, low-grade civil servants, and poor or landless peasants.

German-Jewish history constitutes a third focus of the present
study. A major theme – if not *the* major theme – of research in this
field is Jewish assimilation.[31] It is, understandably, a very emotional
theme for some, who have categorically condemned Jewish assimilation in Germany. Criticism has focused on wealthy German Jews,
who have been accused by Gershom Sholem (among others) of
near-complete self-abnegation.[32] Harboring a strong collective
inferiority complex, they are said to have blindly sought the acceptance of a society that would always remain deeply anti-Semitic.
True assimilation was in any case impossible, according to Sholem
and Werner Mosse, because of the existence of a "distinctive
Jewish psyche," a concept that goes back to Freud.[33] Fritz Stern
has done much to create the image of the "pariah merchant
prince," a Jewish banker whose apparent conquest of the pinnacle
of Prussian society was nothing but a tragic illusion.[34] Similarly,
Lamar Cecil has asserted that wealthy Berlin Jews lavishly courted

29. The ranks of university-educated civil servants contained some members of the nobility,
who were part of the pre-industrial elite. They were concentrated in the highest offices, especially in Prussia, and were distinguished from bourgeois civil servants by their aristocratic lineage. However, the bulk of civil servants were bourgeois in origin and social orientation. See
Henning, *Das westdeutsche Bürgertum*, passim.
30. This decision was based not so much on the Anglo-American conception of the free professions as on the real social cleavages within the educated bourgeoisie. See ibid., passim.
31. See Herzig, "Juden," pp. 108–32.
32. See Sholem, "Social Psychology," pp. 9–32.
33. Mosse, *German-Jewish*, pp. 158–59. The full quotation is as follows. "The ethnic and
social divides frequently coincided with a cultural chasm. Sigmund Freud goes further in posit-
ing the existence of something like a distinctive Jewish psyche." See also Sholem, "Social
Psychology," p 14.
34. See Stern, *Gold and Iron* David Landes contrasts the Bleichröders with the Rothschilds
in "Bleichroders."

the very Junkers who despised them, while turning their backs on less prominent Jewish circles and denying their true religious and political identity.[35] Looking at Jewish intellectuals from business families, Hans Dieter Hellige came to the conclusion that "Jewish self-hatred" was widespread among the children of Jewish businessmen in imperial Germany and Austria.[36] Raised in an authoritarian climate, they reacted to anti-Semitism by rebelling against their fathers, whom they saw as overwhelmingly powerful, so as to escape their authority and at the same time the stigma of their Jewishness. They denied their identity and identified with the anti-Semitic pre-industrial elites, adopting the latter's anti-capitalist arguments and aristocratic mentality.

Marion Berghahn has demonstrated that a false understanding of what assimilation is underlies the approach of Sholem and others.[37] She points out that until fairly recently, the "melting pot" theory dominated sociological thought concerning assimilation: it was believed that where different groups lived side by side, a fusion had to take place. Once the institutions and traditions that formed the basis of ethnic identity – Jewish religious traditions, for example – started changing in any way, total assimilation, i.e., submersion in the dominant culture, was thought to be inevitable. In the 1960s, the growing value attached to the preservation of separate ethnic identities forced sociologists to recognize that ethnic identity was more than just a transitional stage leading to assimilation. Berghahn sees assimilation or, to use a better term, acculturation as a process in which the ethnic minority reinterprets the dominant culture according to its own values. A new culture emerges that incorporates elements of the original ethnic culture and of the dominant culture. Complete non-assimilation is impossible, but the degree to which a minority opens itself to the majority culture depends on the attributes of the minority and the majority. Jews felt an affinity for German culture of the eighteenth and nineteenth centuries, and by the late nineteenth century most had come to define themselves as "German Citizens of the Jewish Faith," a concept that denied allegiance to a Jewish nation while affirming Jewish ethnicity.[38]

35. See Cecil, "Jew and Junker," pp. 47–58.
36. See Hellige, "Generationskonflikt," pp. 476–518.
37. See Berghahn, *Continental Britons*, pp. 11–44.
38. ". . . it is probably true to say that the Jews in Germany were among the first to attempt – both consciously and unconsciously – the transition from a national to an ethnic minority within a plural society. They thus represented an early case of ethnic consciousness as reflected in the 'hyphenated' identity more commonly associated with ethnic groups in the 20th century." Ibid., p. 36.

There are many signs that Jews did not become "just like Germans." This is particularly true of middle-class Jewish women who, as Marion Kaplan has shown, kept Jewish traditions alive in the home and maintained social contacts with Jewish friends and relatives, while at the same time helping their families to acculturate and to achieve bourgeois respectability.[39] Shulamit Volkov also argues that a unique German-Jewish identity came into existence, though she neglects traditional and cultural aspects of ethnicity, stressing instead that Jews were more middle class and more "modern" than other Germans (in the limitation of the size of their families and in their stress on education).[40] Werner Mosse, in his comprehensive two-volume study on the social and economic history of the German-Jewish business elite, finds strong evidence of the survival of Jewish ethnicity, particularly in the social cohesion and economic solidarity of Jews, Jewish intellectualism, and the talent for certain kinds of business enterprises.[41] He finds attempts to shed Jewish identity and assimilate with the pre-industrial elite only in a small group. Nevertheless, Mosse does not seem to perceive German-Jewish ethnic identity as a new synthesis (rather than merely the breakdown of an older Jewish ethnic identity), and he appears to subscribe to the theory of "over-assimilation" and to the idea that assimilation was "false" because German society would never really accept Jews.[42]

Was assimilation really a false path? As Marion Berghahn has pointed out, the terms assimilation/acculturation and integration have all too often been blurred, and acculturation (a natural process of re-definition) condemned because integration ultimately failed.[43] Integration of Jews into German society was an ongoing process whose successful outcome seemed likely in 1900 or 1914. Peter Gay has written: "For German Jews anxious to live and work in peace, as Germans, the persistence of exclusive organizations,

39. See Kaplan, *Making*.
40. See Volkov, "Jüdische Assimilation," pp. 331–48 Volkov's analysis is too narrow. She demonstrates a good understanding of "structures," but a poor understanding or lack of interest in culture.
41. See Mosse, *Jews*, esp. pp. 1–2, 271–95, 380–403; and *German-Jewish*, esp. pp. 132, 158–9.
42. See Mosse, *German-Jewish*, pp. 89, 151, 351–55 He writes of Jews "who painfully sought an entry into a society to which they did not and could not belong" (p. 151). See also Mosse, "Die Juden in Wirtschaft und Gesellschaft," in Mosse, *Juden*, pp. 83–92. Here, Mosse divides Jewish businessmen into three "types": the "Jewish-bourgeois," "normal-ennobled," and "feudal-assimilatory." Around 1900, most belonged to the second group, which he refers to as "modern *Schutzjuden* (court Jews)."
43. See Berghahn, *Continental Britons*, p. 35.

outbursts of hostility, and anti-Semitic publicists appeared as depressing survivals. The centers of darkness and animosity still scattered across the social landscape seemed so unpleasant precisely because so much had happened in the way of liberalization and enlightenment. But the main point was that much *had* happened."[44]

Mosse's findings are also interesting from the point of view of business history. Ethnic identity, along with historical factors such as pre-Emancipation legal restrictions of economic activity and the rise of the Jewish court bankers, helped create what Mosse called a "Jewish sector of the economy."[45] A 1989 conference held at the Friedrich Naumann Foundation in Königswinter was devoted to "Jewish businessmen in Germany in the nineteenth and 20th centuries."[46]

Family history and the related fields of women's history and the history of childhood and youth – all rapidly growing areas of research[47] – constitute a fourth perspective. This area is important not only in its own right, but also because it deepens and enriches our understanding of the *mentalité* of the wealthy businessmen, "feudalization," and the position of the bourgeoisie in Wilhelmine society. With the rise of the bourgeoisie in Europe, a new family form emerged that supplanted the earlier "*ganzes Haus*" or "whole household" (a household including not only a couple and their offspring, but also their servants, journeymen, and other outsiders, all subject to the authority of the father). While the "whole household" had been a working unit that tended to define relationships in terms of division of labor, production was moved out of the bourgeois family.[48] The family came to be seen as the "private sphere," a haven in a harsh world, untouched by the struggle of economic endeavor.

This development was accompanied by the rise of the ideology of "separate spheres," according to which the public sphere was

44. Gay, *Freud*, p. 93. Gay argues that a fusion took place between Jews and Germans. As a cultural historian, he disputes the existence of a "Jewish spirit " He writes, "Jewish assimilation into German society was not a theoretical matter. It was practical. And, increasingly, in occupations in which Jews found a welcome . . German Jews thought and acted like Germans" (p 95).
45. Mosse, *Jews*, p. 403; see pp 380–403 Also, see Barkai, *Jüdische Minderheit*.
46. The papers appeared in. Mosse and Pohl, *Jüdische Unternehmer*.
47. For a survey of publications up to the early 1980s, see Gay, *Bourgeois Experience*, vol. 1, pp. 501–5 For an overview of more recent research on women's history, see Bock, "Geschichte," pp 364–91; and Frevert, "Bewegung "
48. See Frevert, *Women*; Gerhard, *Verhältnisse*, Rosenbaum, *Formen*.

the man's sphere, while the private sphere was the domain of the woman, who could find her greatest fulfillment as wife and mother.[49] As gender roles rigidified, women were confined more and more to the home and induced to give up gainful employment in the marketplace. In the upper middle class, it was no longer socially acceptable for the woman to work, even in a family business. The idleness of the wife, which became an important status symbol, was for most a myth. Lower-middle-class families could not afford this luxury, and allowed women to work. In some families, the pretense of ladylike idleness was preserved, while the wife took in work, hidden from society's watchful eye. In addition, most bourgeois women had to do a fair amount of housework. Though this work was unpaid, performed "out of love," it too was shamefully concealed.[50]

Only in the wealthiest of families could enough servants be employed to free the lady of the house from this burden. Were the wives of very wealthy German businessmen able to utilize the opportunities that leisure afforded them or did they have other, different, burdens? Were they more confined than other middle-class women or freer to move about in public spaces? Were their various roles purely a function of their husband's needs or were they able to live according to values that were distinctly their own to any degree? Bourgeois women were long depicted as passive recipients of a pre-ordained, highly proscribed role. Leonore Davidoff has shown, however, that in Britain, women exercised considerable power as arbiters of high society.[51] Bonnie Smith demonstrates that in the Northern French wealthy bourgeoisie, women helped shape their gender roles and tried to place the stamp of female values on society (most aggressively through social work). This gave them a sense of power, but, according to Smith, was not truly emancipating because women retreated into an irrational world dominated by traditional female values and religion.[52]

At the same time that a new family type became prevalent in the middle classes, related changes were taking place in the internal dynamics and emotional life of the family. The middle class certainly regarded love as the element that held families together and as a central characteristic of bourgeois family life. Marriage for love

49. See Davidoff and Hall, *Family Fortunes*; Niethammer, Lutz et al., *Bürgerliche Gesellschaft*; Hausen, "Die Polarisierung," pp. 363–93; Rang, "Zur Geschichte," pp. 194–205.
50 See S. Meyer, *Das Theater.*
51 See Davidoff, *Best Circles.*
52. See Smith, *Ladies*

14

– proclaimed by the German Romantic Movement – became part of bourgeois ideology, as did motherly love. But did the ideal correspond to reality? Philippe Ariès has described a social revolution in family life that has been dubbed the "discovery of childhood."[53] In traditional (pre-bourgeois) society, children were not valued for themselves, but rather for the work they performed. Child-rearing was a rather haphazard affair. Small children were neglected, and older children sent off to work as soon as they could fend for themselves. They were constantly with adults, forced to live like adults to a large degree. They grew into adult roles through observation and imitation. These patterns began to undergo great changes in the eighteenth century. Parents – especially mothers – became more emotionally attached to their offspring, of whom they took far better care than in earlier times. It was recognized that children needed to be educated and nurtured, and that they needed a sphere of their own – a bed of their own, but also clothing, toys, and schooling designed for children. Ariès is not explicit here, but clearly the conditions, both in terms of resources and motivation, were most favorable in the middle class. This transformation was part of a more general "intimization of family life," described by Edward Shorter in a controversial study.[54] Shorter must resort to a rather contorted line of argumentation to explain his findings that love and sexuality first became the basis for partner selection in the lower classes (particularly servants, peasants, and cottage workers), while emotional bonding between mothers and children first appeared in the petty bourgeoisie (shop owners and craftsmen). Shorter argues that the ultimate cause of both developments was the rising standard of living and growing individualism brought about by the spread of capitalism. The nature of middle-class marriage in the nineteenth century has been the subject of heated debate. Some point out that in the business class, marriages were often economically motivated. Nonetheless, Peter Gay has done much to inject an element of passion into our image of the Victorian marriage.[55]

It is no doubt impossible to understand the nineteenth-century business family without looking at the economic role of the family – a subject of some relevance to business history as well. In his article on "Family, Businessmen and Capitalism," Jürgen Kocka shows

53. See Ariès, *L'Enfant*. See Heidi Rosenbaum's comments in Rosenbaum, *Formen*, pp 277–83

54. See Shorter, *Making* See also critique in Rosenbaum, *Formen*, pp. 225–27.

55. See Gay, *Bourgeois Experience*

what a central role the family played in the early period of industrialization.[56] One of the motivating factors in the founding or expansion of a business was the idea that the sons and grandchildren of the founder would continue to head it. For their sake the founder made sacrifices and avoided risky deals, no matter how enticing they might be, and avoided the diversion of capital for purposes of consumption. Sacrifices were required of other family members as well – often women.[57] In addition, the socialization of a future generation of businessmen was best accomplished inside a businessman's family. The relatives of businessmen often performed important functions, for example, in the formation of a cartel or in the recruitment of top management personnel. The eldest son usually had to suppress his own desires if his professional inclinations went in a different direction, but sometimes a younger son or son-in-law or a nephew took the place of the eldest. Kocka points out that family solidarity and the economic role of the businessman's family gradually declined. With the rise of the joint stock company in the late nineteenth century, the importance of inheritance and marriage as ways of accumulating capital and transferring control over a company decreased. However, Kocka's thesis is not entirely irrelevant to this later period.

The decline of the economic role of the business family is directly related to the decline of the family-run firm and the rise of corporate capitalism, an important theme in business history.[58] During the Industrial Revolution, capital ownership and management were generally united in one person or family. These two functions grew apart in the era of corporate capitalism. Often there was a transitional phase. Families such as the Siemens were able to retain a majority interest in their company after its conversion into a corporation and to continue to occupy the top positions. Though at first in control of long-range planning and strategic decisions, the entrepreneurial family lost control over day-to-day operations. Over time, capitalist families tended to withdraw entirely from management. To an ever-growing extent, the true entrepreneur was a manager. As a result, education, personal achievements, and connections became more important to an entrepreneurial career than wealth. (Though top corporate management tended to

56. See Kocka, "Familie." Conditions in Britain and France were not dissimilar. See Bergeron, "Familienstruktur", and Davidoff and Hall, *Family Fortunes*, esp pp. 209–28

57. See Haupt, "Männliche und weibliche," pp. 158–59

58. See Chandler and Daems, introduction to *Rise*, pp. 5f.; Kaelble, "Sozialstruktur," pp 150–60 (references in fn. 15, p. 151); Kocka, *Unternehmer*.

acquire wealth.) How far did this development progress before the First World War? Did it open up top careers in business to social newcomers, men whose social and political attitudes distinguished them from the "establishment"? Only partial answers can be given in a study on very wealthy businessmen, a group that is skewed in favor of owners.

Sources

A two-pronged methodological approach was taken that combines quantitative and non-quantitative methods. Literary sources were not exploited, first of all because excellent studies along these lines already exist,[59] second, because of the methodological difficulties that arise when three different types of sources (in this case, novels, autobiographical and biographical sources, and quantitative data) are used. On the qualitative side, approximately two hundred auto-biographies and biographies,[60] along with letters, newspaper clippings and other private papers were utilized. Where available, quantitative data was used to help determine how representative this material was. The question of reliability is more complex. Those biographies were eliminated from consideration that did not make adequate use of primary sources, or that appeared to be more works of fiction than fact. Autobiographies present a special set of problems,[61] but nonetheless contain fascinating material on many areas, family and social life in particular. Quantitative data can put some autobiographical evidence in perspective. In other cases, the autobiographies of various members of a family can be compared with one another. Otherwise, plausibility plays a key role in analysis: how probable is it that recollections regarding a particular subject were falsified? How accurate are the childhood memories of the middle-aged and elderly? Two very sensitive areas – and at the same time those most subject to falsification – are relationships within the family and lifestyle. Here, we often encounter stereotypes regarding "exemplary family life" and "the simple way of life."[62] The specific

59. See Niemann, *Bild*; Bramsted, *Aristocracy*
60 Approximately 600 of such works were examined. Material for this study was to be found in only about 200.
61. For a theory-oriented discussion of the use of German autobiographies, see Goodman, *Dis/Closures*; Sloterdijk, *Literatur*; Vogt, *Autobiographik*
62. One author wrote, for example, of the Rhenish-Westphalian industrialists "These men are possessed by a drive for creative work . . . Rest, high living and pleasure are unknown to the true captains of industry They live and work under the simplest imaginable circumstances" (Brinckmeyer, *Hugo Stinnes*, p 9). Many examples that contradict the assertion made here regarding consumption and lifestyle will be presented in chapter 4.

situation and the subjective point of view of the author were taken into account. For example, the description "love marriage" was not taken at face value if applied to a marriage with a wealthy heiress. For the quantitative part of this study,[63] we are very fortunate to possess a unique source, the history of which merits closer attention. The nineteenth-century belief in science as a vehicle of human progress created a tremendous enthusiasm for statistics in the "educated classes." One of the countless popular statistical works that appeared before the First World War, the *Yearbook of Millionaires of Germany* (*Jahrbuch der Millionäre Deutschlands*[64]), is the source of the list of the wealthiest businessmen of the Wilhelmine period that was used to compile the quantitative data for the present study. The second edition of the *Yearbook* was used. Published by Rudolf Martin in 1912/14, it was based on the official tax statistics of the individual German states for the years 1910 to 1912. In the *Yearbook* Martin attempted to assign names to the numbers in the various tax categories, listing all living millionaires in Germany in 1912/14, be they great landowners, businessmen, rentiers, or members of any other professional or social group, along with their addresses and the size of their fortunes. He provided additional information on the wealthiest among them in brief biographies. The volumes of the *Yearbook* for all the provinces of Prussia, the Hanseatic cities, Wurttemberg (including Hohenzollern), Bavaria, and the Kingdom of Saxony appeared before the First World War. Planned volumes for Baden, the Grand Duchy of Hesse, Alsace-Lorraine, the Thuringian states, and some of the minor principalities were never published.[65] A first edition of the *Yearbook*, which included only the millionaires of Prussia and was compiled on the basis of the wealth and income tax records for the year 1908, had appeared in 1911.[66] The regular, even annual, publication of the *Yearbook* was planned,[67] but could not be carried out after the outbreak of war.

63. The data were processed by computer at the Free University of Berlin. In my dissertation, the quantitative material was presented in 117 tables, five of which are contained in the present work. Material presented in the text is taken from those tables. If not otherwise indicated, the data are based on my own research, the sources of which are to be found in sections 1–3 of the bibliography.

64. Martin, *Das Jahrbuch der Millionare Deutschlands.*

65. Statistics of the Grand Duchy of Hesse indicate that there were hardly any persons there with wealth of more than six million marks. In 1907 there were 233 persons assessed for wealth of one million marks or more, their combined wealth was 557 million marks. Cf. *Statistisches Handbuch*, p. 213.

66. Martin, *Das Jahrbuch des Vermogens und Einkommens der Millionare in Preußen.*

67. Martin, *Jahrbuch*, 1912–14, vol. 1, p. III.

18

The group under study consists of 502 businessmen who according to Martin possessed fortunes of six million marks or more. This figure has no special significance, and there is no assumption that it constitutes a threshold figure. It was chosen, rather, because approximately 500 of the businessmen listed by Martin possessed wealth of this amount. (If, for example, one lowers the minimum wealth to five million marks, the size of the group approximately doubles.) For practical reasons it seemed advisable not to investigate substantially more or less than 500 people.[68] The breakdown according to size of fortune is provided in order to help determine to what extent differences in size of fortune may have influenced social behavior. In cases where research has been carried out by others, the data for those other groups of businessmen are compared with the data compiled for this study. The question of representativeness is not of great significance since the 502 businessmen examined here unquestionably constitute an important elite in and of themselves. The definition of "businessman" employed in this study is a broad one based on position.[69] All people were included who were holding, or had previously held, a position that implied activity as a businessman, such as owner or co-owner of a private firm or mining company, chief executive of a corporation, or chairman or member of the board of directors. Since it is of special significance in the study of aristocratization to include members of the wealthy bourgeoisie who were withdrawing from business activity, this study includes some retirees and people with other primary professions, provided that they were at least members of a board of directors. Twenty-two businessmen fall into this "gray area." They include four members of boards of directors who were essentially rentiers,[70] twelve sons-in-law and brothers-in-law of businessmen whose fortunes were inherited from their father-in-law or brother-in-law and who followed another profession in addition to that of businessman,[71] and

68. The number of cases without backup data increases disproportionately and would be excessively high if 1,000 or more cases were to be included. A group smaller than 500 would also not be desirable since there would be too few cases in each category to reach any valid conclusions if two or more variables were to be applied.

69. Regarding the use of this definition, see Pierenkemper, *Die westfälischen Schwerindustriellen,* pp. 22–24.

70. This applies especially to those people who held no higher position than that of member of a board of directors. Examples are Moritz von Stetten, who in 1914 was a pensioner and member of the board of directors of the Dresdener Bank, Paul Schottländer, Walter Naumann, and Freiherr Hugo von Mayer. All four were sons of significant businessmen. As representatives of important families of the business elite, they are clearly of interest to this study.

71. All of these were at least deputy chairmen of boards of directors, co-owners of companies, or the like.

six businessmen who retired before the age of fifty. The group under study includes those landowners who had investments in industry, commerce, or banking in the amount of at least six million marks.[72] These were usually members of the nobility who operated mines on their own lands.

Some information about Martin's objectives can be found in the prefaces to the individual volumes. He wrote: "The secrecy which has heretofore been maintained regarding wealth and income is a remnant of the ignorance and superstition of the Middle Ages. Anyone who favors the advancement of learning must also favor enlightenment in the areas of wealth and income. . . . The social and economic conflicts of the present day demand edification concerning the wealth and income of rich people, as do the political conflicts." Martin seems to have had social reform and democratization in the back of his mind. He reminds the reader: "According to a higher and rational principle private wealth is only a part of the national wealth and is only a possession held in trust." Martin was not a revolutionary, however: "The power of publicity protects the moneyed magnates of today. . . . The power of publicity protects us from cabinet wars, palace revolutions, legal murders, and revolutions and assures internal and external peace. False perceptions lead to misunderstandings. Accurate perceptions, even in the area of private finances, will contribute the most to the securing of internal peace."[73] Martin wanted to provide the bureaucracies of states without property taxes with statistics that could be used in connection with the introduction of such taxes.[74] Martin also wanted to provide the basis for a more general discussion of the taxation of large fortunes. He was not concerned with more theoretical matters, however.[75]

In the official tax statistics, the number but not the names of taxpayers in the various tax brackets were given. The data were, however, quite detailed with reference to the differentiation of the upper tax brackets and to the geographic breakdown. Martin, a former civil servant,[76] used information gleaned during the course of his duties, published reference works, and information gained

72. Inexact data in the sources make estimates necessary.

73 Martin, *Jahrbuch*, 1911, p. VII–VIII.

74. Martin, *Jahrbuch*, 1912–14, Bd. 10, p V–XII, XXII–XXV.

75. Such as theoretical discussions of the development of income. See Nitschke, *Einkommen*.

76. From 1897 to 1905, Martin was a trainee at the Interior Ministry in the production statistics section of the Economic Committee for the Preparation of Customs Duties and Commercial Treaties. Later, he had a regular upper civil service position (as councillor) in the Interior Ministry. See Martin, *Jahrbuch*, 1911, p. XV.

through contacts with wealthy families to match the figures up with known persons. This project must have been a lifelong hobby, if not an obsession.

Due to differences in tax laws, different kinds of statistics were available to Martin for different regions: on income taxes for Hamburg, Lubeck, Bremen, and Wurttemberg, on capital gains taxes for Bavaria. Only Prussia and Saxony had taxes on wealth, which in Prussia applied to land and mine ownership, plants and equipment, though not to furniture, household equipment, and other mobile durable goods. Unlike income taxes, Prussian taxes on wealth did not involve a compulsory declaration. In those cases where the taxpayer did not voluntarily provide information about his property, an assessment committee fixed the amount of the tax on the basis of the income tax declaration. The taxpayer had the right of appeal.[77] It can be assumed that property values were systematically underestimated. Martin was of the opinion, for example, that the wealth of August Thyssen was pegged at too low a value by the assessment committee. Although the Deutscher Kaiser Mining Company made an unusually high net profit, this was not paid out as a dividend but was reinvested, so that August Thyssen paid no tax on income from that mining company, probably leading to an underestimation of his wealth.[78] Others undoubtedly employed less-than-legal methods in order to evade property taxes. Kurt Nitschke was of the opinion that around the turn of the century there was substantial tax evasion in Germany.[79] He showed on the basis of cases contested by the tax authorities that in the period from 1897 to 1899 one-third of the taxpayers had underdeclared their income by about 25 percent. However the government initiated investigations only in cases where the prospects of winning were good. Nitschke estimated that on the average, those declaring incomes of over 3,000 marks actually earned 15 percent to 20 percent more. The Berlin police chief also believed that tax evasion was widespread among Berlin industrialists and bankers. The banker Ludwig Delbrück was one such suspect.[80] Prior to the tax reform of 1892, tax evasion was more prevalent among capitalists than landowners.[81] Capital goods presumably could be more easily concealed than land.[82] However, the relation between

77. See Heckel, "Vermogenssteuer," p. 267; and Leesch, *Geschichte*.
78. Martin, *Jahrbuch*, 1912–14, vol 9, pp. 145–146.
79 Nitschke, *Einkommen*, pp 24–26.
80 Polizeipräsident Berlin an Handelsministerium, 1912, StA Potsdam, Pr.Br Rep. 30 Berlin C Tit. 94 Nr. 9650.
81. Nitschke, *Einkommen*, p. 23
82. On tax evasion by owners of large estates, see Witt, "Der preußische Landrat," pp. 205–19.

21

landed and non-landed wealth is of minor importance in the present study. More importantly, Martin's data are not based on the records of the tax authorities, but on his personal knowledge of where the wealth was. It is therefore more relevant to ask how accurate Martin's estimates were.

A comparison with the official Prussian statistics[83] shows that Martin came close to accounting for and naming all taxpayers in Prussia with fortunes of over two million marks. Martin lists 2,691 persons with fortunes of two to six million marks, while there were 2,783 taxpayers in this category according to the official statistics. Thus Martin is missing 92 cases (3.3 percent of the taxpayers in this category). The figures for the next two categories coincide almost exactly.[84] Under intergovernmental agreements the German sovereigns (including the emperor and the Prussian princes) were exempt from income taxes. Martin listed these rulers and members of ruling families in his *Yearbook* and estimated their fortunes,[85] and therefore in the highest category Martin has two more cases than are found in the official statistics. The discrepancies in the lower categories are partly attributable to death and bankruptcy.[86] It is also possible that Martin did not possess a sufficient knowledge of certain regions to fill in all the spaces. However, this hardly occurred except in the case of millionaires with fortunes of less than six million marks, who are not of interest to the present study.

Martin's estimates can in some cases be compared with the official records on individuals. The files on people being considered for a title or decoration in Prussia sometimes note the actual size of the fortune, as listed in government tax records.[87] Such information could be found for fifty-seven of the 502 businessmen under study. In only seven cases were Martin's estimates right on the mark. He was relatively accurate in eighteen additional cases.[88]

83. *Statistik*, pp XXIX–XXX.

84. According to Martin, there were 621 millionaires with fortunes in the six to fifty million mark range and sixteen with fortunes of over fifty million marks. The official statistics show 629 and fourteen taxpayers in these respective categories.

85. Martin, *Jahrbuch*, 1912–14, vol. 10, pp. VII–VIII

86. Martin writes: "But I do not search for a name at any cost. When I am convinced that the statistical records have incorrectly assigned a place to an individual, I do not fill in that space, for example when the individual concerned had fallen into bankruptcy." Martin, *Jahrbuch*, 1911, p. X.

87. These files were examined at the Central State Archives of the G.D R., Merseburg: Zentrales Staatsarchiv, Dienststelle Merseburg (Ministerium für Handel und Gewerbe, 2.2.1. Nr. 1018 bis 2536 und Rep. 120 A IV) and at the State Archive, Potsdam: Landeshauptarchiv Potsdam (Polizeiprasidium Berlin, Rep 30 Berlin C Tit 94)

88. This category includes the fortunes of over five million marks which he over– or underestimated by 1.1 to fifteen million marks and the fortunes of over fifteen million marks which he overestimated by five to ten million marks

There were relatively large discrepancies in the remaining thirty-two cases. Martin tended to err on the plus side. One or two examples suffice to illustrate the sources of these miscalculations. By far the largest involves Eduard Beit von Speyer, whose wealth Martin estimated at eighty-eight million marks, though official records set his fortune at fourteen million marks. The official figure is surprisingly low when one considers that Beit von Speyer had been a co-owner of the banking firm Lazard Speyer-Ellissen, the largest private bank in Frankfurt, since 1896, and that he had inherited the substantial fortunes of both his father, the banker Ferdinand Beit, and his mother, who was of the wealthy Ladenburg banking family. It is conceivable that this large fortune was more widely split up among family members than Martin assumed. Particularly James and Edgar Speyer, co-owners of the bank, come into question. Special inheritance provisions may also be involved in this case. In any case, it is clear that in choosing Eduard Beit von Speyer, Martin placed one of the most important Frankfurt bankers close to the top of his list. A second interesting case is that of the above-mentioned Ludwig Delbrück. If the police's suspicion that Delbrück was guilty of tax evasion is correct, then Martin's estimate of 13.5 million marks is perhaps more accurate than the official estimate of 6.2 million marks. In reading through the names of millionaires whose wealth was one to five million marks but was estimated higher by Martin, it strikes one that these were for the most part very prominent men in the business world.[89] Martin's estimates could not be expected to be completely accurate. He did not have at his disposal complete information about inheritance and dowry arrangements, short-term and largely speculative business deals, and similar factors that could have influenced the amount of wealth significantly at the time of the tax assessment. He based his projections more on the reputation of the businessman concerned. Thus he was probably in a better position than the tax authorities to estimate the long-term ranking of many of the fortunes.

It becomes clear through a third means of verification that Martin's list actually contains many top businessmen. The busi-

---

89. They include Edwin and Karl Bechstein, the important Berlin publisher Georg Büxenstein, the co-owner of the Mendelssohn Bank Arthur Fischel, the brandy distillery owner Albert Gilka, the Berlin construction magnate Georg Haberland, whose firm constructed the Bavarian Quarter and Tempelhof Field, Georg Liebermann from the well-known textile industry family, the director of the Darmstädter und Nationalbank Jakob Riesser, and Georg Wertheim, co-owner of the well-known department store.

nesses headed or owned by the 502 businessmen in this study were checked against a list of the 200 largest German corporations in 1913 and another of the 100 largest industrial enterprises 1907.[90] Of the 502, 219 were active in at least one of the largest firms. The proportion would probably have been 50 percent or higher if private banks had been included. The group under study thus represents a significant cross section of the Wilhelmine economic elite.

The biographical information contained in the *Yearbook of Millionaires* is unfortunately full of gaps. Supplementary data were taken from other published sources, including reference works such as the *Neue Deutsche Biographie* (New German Biography), the *"Gothaer"* (a listing of noble families), autobiographies, and biographies.[91] Extensive material was found in public and private archives in the German Federal Republic and the German Democratic Republic. Particularly useful for the quantitative investigation were, first, the genealogical collection of the *Institut zur Erforschung historischer Führungsschichten* (Institute for Research on Historical Ruling Classes) in Bensheim, under the direction of Friedrich Wilhelm Euler, and second, files on people being considered for a title or decoration in Prussia, which were at that time to be found in the *Staatsarchiv Potsdam* (the State Archives in Potsdam) and in the *Deutsches Zentralarchiv* (German Central Archives) in Merseburg. Further information was acquired through correspondence with genealogists, the descendants of multimillionaires, archives, and scholars.[92]

In spite of this abundance of sources, there was a relatively large

---

90. The lists of the largest enterprises come from the following studies: Weder, "Die 200"; Kocka and Siegrist, "Die Hundert," pp. 55–112.

The Schichau-Werft (shipyard) is a firm of this size and has been counted in this study as one of the largest enterprises of the period from 1907 to 1913, although Kocka and Siegrist missed it. These two lists do not cover all types of businesses. Private companies and corporations in the following areas are missing: the construction industry, banking, commerce, transportation, and other service industries. A slight distortion results from the fact that Weder includes all corporations with stock of twelve million marks or more, whereas Kocka and Siegrist have also included firms with ten million marks of stock in their list. Perhaps more serious is the fact that the two studies did not use the same base year: the Kocka-Siegrist list is for the year 1907, the Weder list for the year 1913. The slight recession that occured between these years was not of great importance. However, differences in growth rates between different industries and sectors during this period lead to distortions: The study for the year 1907 tends to underestimate the significance of the "growth industries," to the extent that they were organized as private companies.

91. The company *Festschrift* – or commemorative publication – turned out to be less useful (most contain little information on the "private lives" of owners and managers).

92. For complete bibliographical data, see bibliography. These sources will henceforth not be cited in connection with the tables and the examples drawn from such sources.

number of cases in which no information was available. The most successful and respected family members are more likely to appear in the sources than others. Marriages and friendships with the illustrious were undoubtedly considered to be more noteworthy than ties with the middle and lower ranks of society. Thus, we cannot know as much about links with the lower and lower middle classes as about those with the upper and upper middle classes.[93]

Finally, a word concerning the organization of the book. Chapter 1 introduces the wealthiest businessmen in Wilhelmine Germany as a group. Data on age, region, area of economic activity, wealth, size of the company, type of enterprise and entrepreneur, and religion will be presented. Their position in public life and relationship to the state will be sketched in sections on titles and other honors and on participation in politics and associational life. Two final sections on social origins and education and training round out this profile of wealthy businessmen. The next three chapters deal with the family: marriage, procreation and raising of children, family life and power structures within the family, and the children's choice of profession and marriage partner. Intertwining themes of social history and family history will stand in the forefront: ties with other classes versus social isolation (choice of marriage partner and choice of profession of the sons) and the tension between patriarchal structures and growing individualism (as reflected in the decision to marry or not to marry, marriage age, patterns of courtship and marriage preliminaries, the socialization of children, and the sons' choice of a profession). Chapters 5 and 6 deal with important aspects of social life, lifestyle and residential style. Here we will have the opportunity to think about the true meaning of the new styles – often called "aristocratic" – in clothing, furnishings, architecture and entertaining around the turn of the century. Social networks will be examined: circles of friends, acquaintances, and neighbors.

93 However, this is not true in the case of the "*Gothaer*," in which information on an individual's profession is distinctly colored by aristocratic values For example, a businessman who was also the owner of a nobleman's estate would often be listed only as the latter There is no indication of a bias towards either bourgeois or aristocratic professions in the other sources used

Chapter 1

Profile of the Wilhelmine
Wealth Elite

A Group Portrait in Numbers: Age, Region, Economic Activity, Wealth, and Religion

The top business multimillionaires of Wilhelmine Germany were not the superannuated group one might expect. Though about forty percent were over sixty-one years of age in 1911, roughly one-fourth each were in the 42-to-51 and 52-to-61 age brackets. Young men were to be found among the wealthiest businessmen of Wilhelmine Germany as well: nine percent were under forty-two. This age spread is quite advantageous for the purposes of analysis because it allows a fairly detailed breakdown by cohort.

What was the political and economic climate of the years in which these plutocrats were growing up? Only one percent of the multimillionaires in this study were twenty-one years of age or older in 1848. Four-fifths were born in 1840 or later. Thus, for most, the unification of Germany was the first major political experience, while many in fact had no memory at all of the pre-unification era. Their political consciousness was molded by Bismarck. These are the generations in which feudalization is supposed to have taken place. As far as economic development is concerned, most of the men in the present study entered professional life after Germany's economic take-off, a period of dynamic growth, marred though it was by economic crisis (notably the depression of the 1870s). This was also the era of "organized capitalism," a period of decline for family-run enterprises. It remains to be seen whether the theories developed by Kocka for the period of early industrialization have any relevance for this later period.

Significant regional differences in economic and social life persisted after 1871, and so it is fortunate that three major regions are well represented in the present study: Greater Berlin and Potsdam, with twenty-three percent of the cases, the western provinces of Prussia (the Rhine Province, the Saar, and Westphalia), with twenty-four percent of the cases, and the Hanseatic cities (Hamburg, Bremen and Lübeck), with fourteen percent of the cases.[1] The Province of Hesse (primarily Frankfurt) and the two Saxonies (the Prussian province and the kingdom) each account for about ten percent of the cases. Only about five percent of the businessmen in the study were active in each of three other areas, Bavaria, Silesia, and the southwest (consisting of Baden, Wurttemberg and the Palatinate). Other regions are hardly represented. This regional distribution is typical by and large for the distribution of wealth generated by business in those areas covered by Martin's *Yearbook*. The picture would not have to be radically revised if Martin had published the planned volumes for Baden, the Grand Duchy of Hesse, Alsace-Lorraine, Thuringia, and some of the minor principalities.

It has often been thought that there were two societal models at work in Wilhelmine society, the dominant, "feudalized" one represented by Prussia, Berlin and the western provinces[2] in particular. The Hanseatic cities (Hamburg, Lübeck, and Bremen), along with the south and particularly the southwest, seem to symbolize bourgeois society as it might have been in Germany as a whole: self-assured, liberal and anti-aristocratic. Baden, Württemberg, and Bavaria, lacking a powerful nobility of the Prussian variety, had liberal traditions that continued to play a role after German unification. With respect to Hamburg, historians are generally in agreement with Richard J. Evans in his assertion that "neither the economic activity nor the social world nor finally the political beliefs and actions of the Hamburg merchants corresponded to anything that has ever been defined, however remotely, as 'feudal.'"[3] Berlin, on the other hand, was dominated by the Imperial Court and the Junkers, who, it is said, seduced and fatally weakened the business elite of the capital.[4] The present study asks if there really were basic differences between Berlin and Hamburg, or between the southwest and Rhineland-Westphalia, pointing to parallel developments

1. Martin's regional breakdown was based on the place of residence for tax purposes, whereas I have taken the main place of economic activity.
2. Zunkel, *Der rheinisch-westfälische Unternehmer*; Spencer, "West German", Faulenbach, "Die Herren."
3. Evans, *Death*, p. 559.
4. See esp. Cecil, "Jew and Junker."

and calling into question the idea that some regions followed a "feudal model," others a "bourgeois model."[5]

Table 1 shows the distribution of the 502 millionaires by the industry, commercial activity, or service in which they were primarily active.[6] The categorization of businesses was adapted from the *Betriebszählung* (business census) of 1907.[7] Roughly half of the multimillionaires were industrialists, with the other half in the services sector. The two largest single groups are the bankers and the wholesale merchants. The traditional lines of business predominate. Department store owners, with eight cases, constitute only a very small percentage of all merchants. In the industrial sector, the three largest categories – heavy industry (including mining); the textile, leather, and clothing industries; and the food, drink, and tobacco industries – were all older industries. Other older branches of industry, namely the metal products industry, construction, printing and publishing, the precision instruments industry, and the "miscellaneous industries" (paper, stone, and earth and wood industries), make up another twelve percent of the cases. The newer growth industries – chemicals, machinery, and electrical engineering and equipment -- together make up only ten percent of the cases. This demonstrates that there was a noticeable time lag in the conversion of economic success into wealth. Otherwise the distribution of types of business corresponds roughly to the overall structure of the German economy.

Rubinstein's study of British millionaires provides an interesting basis for comparison.[8] Among the 843 British millionaires and half-millionaires in business who died between 1900 and 1939, the percentage of heavy industrialists was lower (nine percent) than among the German multimillionaires (twelve percent). There were slightly more machinery industrialists among British businessmen (five percent), but slightly fewer chemical industrialists (three percent).

5. Ideally, regional analysis would take into account a whole range of factors. the system of government and political traditions, individual political events such as the French Revolution and the Revolution of 1848, and the influence of other countries (especially that of France in southwest Germany); the position of nobility in society, economy, and government, especially differences in the numerical strength of the nobility, its ownership of land, its business activity, its role in the officer corps and in the bureaucracy of the various states, and the significance of the local court; the time frame of industrialization and its stage of development; the structure of the economy; and the significance of the labor movement.

6. Only where it could not be determined in which company the businessman was primarily involved was the case assigned to the category "Industry: 2 types" or " Service/industry: 2 types" or "2nd and 3rd sectors "

7 *Statistik*, vol. 218, section VI.

8. Calculation based on Rubinstein, *Men of Property*, pp. 62–65.

Table 1. The Wealthiest Businessmen by Branch and Sector (in %)

Primary sector (commercial nurseries only)	0.2

Industrial sector

Heavy industry (mining, metallurgy)	12.4
Metal products	2.8
Textiles, clothing, and leather	8.0
Food, drink, and tobacco	6.6
Construction	1.6
Printing and publishing	4.6
Chemicals	5.8
Machinery, except electrical	3.4
Precision instruments	1.0
Electronics, electrical equipment, and machinery	1.0
Other industries	1.6
Two or more industries	0.8
Industry, branch unknown	0.2
Industry: Total	49.8

Services Sector

Banking	27.3
Department stores	1.6
Commerce (without department stores)	12.8
Transportation	1.4
Other services	0.4
Services: more than one branch	3.4
Services: Total	46.9

Activity in industry and services	3.2
Total	100.1
Total (absolute)	501
Information not available (absolute)	1

Textile industrialists alone constitute nine percent of the British group, whereas among the Germans the textile, clothing, and leather industrialists together account for eight percent. There were more publishers among the wealthy German businessmen (five percent) than among their British counterparts (two percent). A substantial difference can be observed in the food, drink and tobacco industry, in which seventeen percent of the British millionaires were involved as against only seven percent of the Germans. Other industries constitute eleven percent of all cases among the Germans in my study and five percent of all cases in Rubenstein's study. Bankers are much more strongly represented among the German multimillionaires (twenty-seven percent as against fifteen percent in the British group). Wholesale merchants make up nineteen percent of the British and fourteen percent of the German group. Miscellaneous service industries claim a substantially larger share of the British businessmen, namely fifteen percent, as against five percent for the Germans. This difference is probably attributable to the greater significance of shipping in the British economy.

The regional concentrations of economic activities in my study follow predictable patterns. Food, drink, and tobacco is the leading industry among the twenty-six Bavarian businessmen (eleven cases). The Berlin group includes thirty-four industrialists, fifty-three bankers and twenty merchants; six of the seven department store owners operated primarily in Berlin. Among the seventy-one multimillionaires of the Hanseatic cities, there are practically no industrialists, but fifteen bankers, thirty-two wholesale merchants, five businessmen in transportation, and five in two branches of the service sector. Among sixteen Hessian industrialists there are seven in the chemical industry. There is a preponderance of bankers in Hesse (twenty-eight cases), concentrated in Frankfurt, but only five wholesale merchants. Heavy industrialists, textile-leather-and-clothing industrialists and bankers, with thirty-nine, twenty, and seventeen cases respectively, constitute the majority of the businessmen in Rhineland-Westphalia. There are twelve Saxon businessmen in the textile, leather, and clothing industries, eleven in printing and publishing, and seven in banking. The Silesians are predominantly heavy industrialists (sixteen cases). The twenty-four businessmen of the southwest are scattered over a number of different lines of business.

Historians have tended to assume that the West German heavy industrialists were the representatives *par excellence* of feudalization, particularly since they played a leading role in the "coalition of rye and iron" and in the conservative Central Association of German Industrialists (*Centralverband deutscher Industrieller*).[9]

9. See section below entitled "Participation in Public Life: Political Activity and Membership in Associations." In the back of some historians' minds is probably also the (albeit hotly debated) role of heavy industry in the rise of National Socialism.

The growth industries (chemicals, electrical engineering and equipment, and machinery) have been thought to be bastions of "modernity," partly because these were new industries supposedly run by social newcomers, partly because these were exported-oriented industries wary of an alliance with agrarian conservatism and the *Centralverband*.[10] This thesis will be put to the test in this study.

The extremely wealthy elite under study here was not a homogeneous group with regard to wealth. The lower half had fortunes of between 6.0 and 9.4 million marks. In the upper quarter were those with wealth of over fourteen million marks, and in the upper ten percent those with wealth of over twenty-five million marks. At the apex of the wealth pyramid stands Bertha Krupp von Bohlen und Halbach (whose husband actually headed the firm) with 283 million marks. The greatest fortunes were concentrated in the western provinces, the Hanseatic cities, Berlin, Silesia and Hesse, and in heavy industry and the chemical industry.

A total of 219 of the 502 businessmen in this study were actively involved in at least one of the 200 largest corporations or one of the 100 largest industrial firms of the pre-war period.[11] Of that number, seventy-nine were active in two to four of such firms, and twenty-two were active in five or more. As one might expect, wealth went hand in hand with a powerful position: two-thirds of those with fortunes of over twenty-five million marks headed one of the largest firms of the Wilhelmine period. The businessmen who were in heavy industry and the growth industries were especially powerful in the business world (seventy-six percent and sixty-three percent of them, respectively, headed at least one of the largest firms). Of the bankers in this study, just over half were actively involved in the largest enterprises, a figure that would surely be higher if we had a list of the largest private banks.[12]

Nonetheless, family firms were certainly not absent from this elite. The data on the legal form of the companies that were headed by the businessmen in this study show that almost two-thirds headed private firms. An additional twelve percent headed either a mining company (*bergwerkliche Gewerkschaft*), a limited liability company (*G.m.b.H.*), a limited partnership (*Kommandit-*

10. For a important critique of the whole idea of industrial factionalism, see Hayes, "Industrial Factionalism."

11. See Introduction, fn. 90.

12. The acquisition of seats on boards of directors was substantially more frequent among bankers than among other businessmen. See Eulenburg, "Die Aufsichtsrate," pp. 105–6.

gesellschaft), or companies in two or more of these categories. Only nineteen percent headed a joint stock company or a joint stock company plus a company with a different legal form.

Turning now to the types of entrepreneurs, we find that at most nineteen percent of the 502 millionaires (including unclear cases) were salaried managers of their companies. This is not surprising, since the managers shared less in the company's profits. Almost three-quarters were owners.[13] Those businessmen who headed a corporation that was effectively owned by a family or group of relatives may be termed "entrepreneurs."[14] Surprisingly, this group, which represents a transitional stage between the era of the family enterprise and the corporate age, makes up only five to nine percent of the total. The traditional figure of the owner who ran his own company clearly predominated among the wealthiest businessmen in the *Yearbook of Millionaires*.

Scholars have engaged in extensive debates on the role of Calvinism (Max Weber) and Judaism (Werner Sombart, among others) in the rise of capitalism.[15] Data from the *Yearbook of Millionaires* study seem to indicate that there was a strong correlation between religious affiliation or ethnicity and the accumulation of great wealth. Of the 482 businessmen whose religious affiliation is known, 287, or almost sixty percent, were Lutherans (including Evangelical Lutherans and United Protestants), which roughly corresponds to the percentage of that denomination in the population at large.[16] Other Protestants made up only four percent of all cases. Catholics, with nine percent, were inordinately underrepresented in comparison with their percentage in the population at large. Counting baptized Jews and Christians from originally Jewish families,[17] one-

13. This includes owners of private firms and the heads of limited partnerships (*Kommanditgesellschaft*), limited liability corporations (*G.m.b H.*), and mining companies (*bergwerkliche Gewerkschaft*), provided that they or their families owned more than fifty percent of the stock.

14. See Chandler and Daems, introduction to *Rise*, pp. 5f.

15. See Weber, *Die protestantische Ethik*, Sombart, *Die Juden*; Sombart, *Der Bourgeois*. These writings concern themselves with the origins of the "capitalist spirit," primarily prior to the nineteenth century. The present study also does not deal with the origins of the great fortunes of the Wilhelmine period. Mosse treats this aspect of economic history in *Jews*. See also: Prinz, *Juden*.

16. In 1910, about 61.7 percent of the population of the German Empire was Lutheran (including Evangelical Lutherans and United Protestants), 36.7 percent Roman Catholic, and 0.5 percent belonged to other Christian denominations, while about 1.0 percent of the population was Jewish.

17. This definition is highly controversial because it unfortunately bears a resemblance to the racist National Socialist definition of Jewishness. In theory, it would be desirable to define Jewishness in terms of self-identity. However, in a quantitative study it is hardly possible to determine in individual cases whether a baptized Jew still considered him- or herself Jewish.

fourth of the 502 millionaires were Jewish. Thus, Jews were very strongly overrepresented.

A few studies offer possibilities for comparison. Wilhelm Stahl compiled data on the religion of the businessmen of German-speaking areas listed in the *Neue Deutsche Biographie* (New German Biography).[18] He found that roughly two-thirds of the businessmen born in the nineteenth century were Lutherans. Ten percent of the owners and six percent of the top corporate managers belonged to other Protestant denominations. Sixteen percent of the owners and twenty-two percent of the managers in his study were Catholic. Jews and baptized Jews made up nine percent of the owners and seven percent of the managers. The percentage of Catholics is thus higher than among the wealthy businessmen in the *Yearbook of Millionaires*, and the percentage of Jews is lower.[19] However, a comparison is made difficult Stahl's inclusion of German-speaking areas which were not part of Germany.[20]

Dirk Schumann, in his study on Bavarian businessmen, shows that even in this predominantly Catholic state, Protestants were overrepresented among the businessmen.[21] Out of 419 businessmen operating in five Bavarian cities in 1870, fully one-half were Protestants, thirty-eight percent Catholics and about ten percent Jews. Stahl arrives at similar results for Franconia and Baden-Württemberg, though on the basis of a very small sample.[22] Friedrich Zunkel pointed out that Protestants and Jews were overrepresented among the nineteenth-century businessmen of Rhineland-Westphalia relative to their percentage in the population at large, though he had no statistics.[23] In a

---

Werner E Mosse takes a pragmatic approach, considering Jews, baptized Jews, and Christians whose ancestors were predominantly Jewish as a group. His argues that these groups were up against the same kinds of limitations, resulting in a peculiarly Jewish pattern of economic activity for all three groups. Central to his definition is also a Jewish ethnicity based not primarily on religion, but on ancestry, endogamy, extended family relationships, and common customs and traditions. See Mosse, *Jews*, pp. 1–2. In my own quantitative study, the number of cases was for the most part too small to distinguish between Jews, baptized Jews, and Christians of Jewish ancestry. All three were counted as Jews, first because all three tended to be regarded as such by anti-Semitism, which undoubtedly had an impact on social behavior. Second, the autobiographies and biographies indicate that baptized Jewish businessmen and Christian businessmen of Jewish ancestry only slowly lost their ties with the Jewish community

18. See Stahl, *Der Elitenkreislauf*, pp. 208, 218.

19. Stahl did not count Christians whose families were originally Jewish as Jews. Between seventeen and twenty-two percent of the people in my study were Jewish by this more limited definition.

20 10.9 percent of the businessmen in his study were active in Switzerland, Austria, or the Sudetenland.

21. See Schumann, "Bayerns Unternehmer," esp. p. 209. Also, see Schumann, "Herkunft," pp. 295–304.

22. See Stahl, *Elitenkreislauf*, pp. 221–22.

23. See Zunkel, *Der rheinisch-westfälische Unternehmer*, pp. 29–32.

study on Berlin businessmen in the period of early industrialization, Hartmut Kaelble found that Jews made up half of his sample.[24]

Rubinstein collected data on the religion of the British and Irish millionaires and half-millionaires born between 1840 and 1879 who were actively engaged in business.[25] As in Germany, both the (non-Calvinist) established church (Church of England) and the Calvinist denominations were represented roughly in proportion to their share of the total population. (Whereas the other Protestant denominations constitute a tiny minority in Germany, they were of some significance in Great Britain.) Catholics were underrepresented in both countries, though more pronouncedly among the British millionaires. The disadvantaged political situation of Ireland played a role here. The percentage of Jews (in this case only Jews and baptized Jews) is about as high in the small group that Rubinstein examined as among the 502 businessmen in my study. However, this finding is quite atypical for Great Britain.

Jews – the most important ethnic minority in this study – were concentrated in certain cities and sectors of the economy. Very wealthy Jewish businessmen were to be found primarily in Berlin (making up a majority of the Berlin businessmen in this study), and in Frankfurt.[26] Of the Christian businessmen, fifty-nine percent were industrialists, whereas almost three-fourths of the Jews under study were active in the services sector. Given the historical role of Jews as money-lenders and court financiers, it is not surprising that fifty-nine percent of the wealthiest Jewish businessmen in the *Yearbook of Millionaires* were bankers, while only seventeen percent of the non-Jewish businessmen were. On the other hand, the percentage of millionaires engaged in commerce – another sector thought to be typically Jewish – was about the same (roughly fourteen percent) for Christians and Jews. In the industrial sector, Jewish activity was concentrated in the growth industries. This corroborates Mosse's theory that there was a "Jewish sector" in the German economy.[27]

Jews were heavily concentrated in the upper quarter of the

24. See Kaelble, *Berliner Unternehmer*, p. 79. For further quantitative studies, see Kocka, *Unternehmer*, pp. 36–37, esp. fn 35.

25. See Rubinstein, *Men of Property*, pp. 147, 150.

26. However, Jews made up only 4.3 percent of the population of Berlin and 6.3% of the population of Frankfurt in 1910. See Monika Richarz, introduction to *Jüdisches Leben*, vol. 2, p. 21.

27. However, Mosse's data on merchants diverge from mine. among the businessmen in the *Yearbook of Millionaires*, he finds a higher percentage of Jews than of non-Jews occupied as wholesale merchants (Mosse, *Jews*, p 205). This is attributable first to his inclusion of landowners – who were exclusively non-Jews – and second to his data applying only to Prussia, so that the Protestant wholesale merchants of the Hanseatic cities are missing. On Jewish forms of economic activity, see also pp. 380–403; and Richarz, *Jüdisches Leben*, esp p. 30.

wealth pyramid. Protestants were more strongly represented in the lower half. Whereas half of the Jews sat on the board of directors of one of the largest corporations or were owners of one of the largest companies of that period, this was true of only forty-two percent of the non-Jews. The data on the legal form of the enterprises and on type of entrepreneur show only slight differences between Jews and Christians. Concerning the role of Jews in the joint stock companies, Mosse writes: "The adaptation of men of Jewish origin to the corporate age of high (organized) capitalism is a striking phenomenon. . . . Contrary to what is sometimes asserted, the role of Jews in corporate economic activity in Germany was scarcely, if at all, inferior to the part they had played in the days of earlier industrialization, of private banking houses, and of individual entrepreneurship."[28]

Titles, Decorations, and Other Honors[29]

The title craze in imperial Germany was regarded by Zunkel and others as an aspect of the feudalization of the bourgeoisie.[30] They argue that the government introduced the granting of titles and decorations in order to establish control over the bourgeoisie, make it dependent on the state, and strengthen the predominance of the pre-industrial elite. Karin Kaudelka-Hanisch modifies and refines this thesis in a recent study on Prussian Commercial Councillors.[31] According to Kaudelka-Hanisch, the granting of the title of Commercial Councillor truly honored economic achievement in the early years. Up until the turn of the century wealth was also an important criterion: a Commercial Councillor had to have a

28. Mosse, *Jews*, pp. 218–19.

29. The phenomenon of the bourgeois reserve officer cannot be dealt with in this study because the sources used in my quantitative study seldom contain information on this subject. It was possible to ascertain that forty-six of the 484 non-aristocratic businessmen were reserve officers. Twenty-seven others were officers in the *Landwehr* or *Seewehr* (second-line army or navy reserves). Eighteen others were not reserve officers. There was no information to be found on the remaining 403. The files on titles and decorations in Prussia and Bavaria only occasionally contain information on military service because this was not considered an important criterion for the granting of titles (see Schumann, "Bayerns Unternehmer," p 345; Kaudelka-Hanisch, "Preußische Kommerzienräte," p 108). The autobiographies and biographies are also largely silent on this subject, as they are on attitudes toward militarism

30. See Böhme, *Deutschlands Weg*, pp. 580–81; Sombart, *Die deutsche Volkswirtschaft*, pp 469–70; Stegmann, "Linksliberale Bankiers," pp. 26–28; Stern, "Prussia," p. 56, Zunkel, *Der rheinisch-westfälische Unternehmer*, pp. 107, 119–20.

31. Kaudelka-Hanisch, "Preußische Kommerzienrate." See also Kaudelka-Hanisch, "Titled Businessman," pp. 87–114.

fortune of at least 500,000 marks. (In Berlin the minimum was one million marks.) Other important criteria for the granting of titles were active membership in professional societies, the holding of honorary political offices, volunteer work in charitable institutions, and accomplishments in the area of employee welfare. But the granting of titles also served as a means of establishing control over businessmen. Thus, political reliability was an important prerequisite, though this was interpreted rather liberally.[32] According to Kaudelka-Hanisch the granting of titles and decorations in Germany served primarily to achieve the "political pacification and social integration of the bourgeoisie."[33]

It should be noted, however, that in the late nineteenth century the granting of titles had partially lost its power as an instrument of control because it was becoming possible to a growing extent to purchase titles.[34] They were granted primarily to men who financially supported civic and charitable causes. There are cases, however, in which the title was crassly purchased through a professional middleman. On this point Schumann wrote: "Thus the granting of titles was more and more divested of its original character: An act of monarchical grace turned into an act of mediated and concealed self-service. . . . In this respect the grantors as well as the seekers of titles, the state as well as the businessmen actively engaged in the process of social bureaucratization."[35]

"Social bureaucratization" should not be equated with aristocratization. Hartmut Kaelble argues that the enthusiasm for decorations and titles was above all indicative of the close attachment of

32. See Kaudelka-Hanisch, "Preußische Kommerzienrate," pp. 54–59, 62–63, 140, 258–60. See also Mosse, *Jews*, pp. 73–79.

33. Kaudelka-Hanisch, "Preußische Kommerzienrate," p. 408. She further notes on p. 410: "Instead of adapting the political system to advanced economic development, instead of pushing forward the stalled transition to a parliamentary government and thus taking greater account of the existing socio-economic power relationships at the political level, the government, as a cheap substitute, offered among other things a system of government titles and decorations which on the one hand promoted, as a social model, the internal cohesion among Commercial Councillors and at the same time accelerated the process of internal differentiation within the economic bourgeoisie. On the other hand it reinforced the pre-modern orientation of the dominant classes of Prussian-German society without detracting from their economic modernity."

34. When the title of Commercial Councillor was introduced in Bavaria in 1880, the most important criteria for its bestowal were the size of the company, the businessman's entrepreneurial achievements, his company's social policy, his reputation in the business world, and the holding of local honorary offices, and political reliability. Gradually, however, there was a tendency to reward large contributions through the Commercial Councillor title. The number of titles granted rose rapidly. See Schumann, "Bayerns Unternehmer," pp. 330–57, 359–60. Also, see Kaudelka-Hanisch, "Preußische Kommerzienräte," pp. 71–79

35 Schumann, "Bayerns Unternehmer," pp. 356, 360.

the bourgeoisie to the state and not the subjection of the bourgeoisie to the nobility.[36] Schumann points out in his study on Bavarian businessmen that the title of Commercial Councillor "suggested social equality with the academically trained government official"[37] and strengthened the orientation of the businessman toward officialdom. Bavaria presents an interesting case, because here the nobility played a significantly lesser role in the bureaucracy than it did in Prussia. In conferring titles and other honors on businessmen, the state was not so much trying to tie businessmen into the rigid pre-industrial social hierarchy as it was to compensate them for the sacrifices foisted upon them by state social policy, and thereby to insure their continued political loyalty.

What significance did titles and decorations have for wealthy businessmen of the Wilhelmine era? The mania for titles is well documented. According to Hans-Joachim Flechtner, the biographer of Carl Duisberg (who was the general director of the Bayer pharmaceutical corporation), "He (Duisberg) rejoiced over every sign of recognition, yes, one can safely say that he collected marks of honor and hung all the many diplomas and documents on the walls of the 'hall of fame' in the basement of Villa Duisberg. There were also visiting cards on which his offices and titles, including eventually nine doctor degrees, were listed."[38]

Many businessmen were totally unscrupulous in their quest for a title or decoration. It was presumed that the brewery owner Georg Haase of Breslau obtained his Commercial Councillor title through fraud. He is said to have used a middleman to establish contact with the government official Baron von Broich. Haase guaranteed a mortgage on a home for convalescents in which von Broich had an interest. However, an investigation against the middleman was dropped due to lack of evidence.[39] It was also rumored that the heavy industrialist Fritz von Friedländer-Fuld paid for a decoration.[40]

The case of Siegmund Aschrott is an especially flagrant one. As a military contractor in 1870/71 he apparently accumulated a great fortune through unsavory business methods. Although rumors of

36. See Kaelble, "Wie feudal," pp. 164–66. Also, see Kocka, "Bürgertum," p. 75.

37. Schumann, "Bayerns Unternehmer," p. 359, see also p 360

38. Flechtner, *Carl Duisberg*, p. 264.

39. "Abschrift aus den Akten der Staatsanwaltschaft bei dem Königlichen Landgericht I zu Berlin und Verf.5 F J.93.01/15" (undated), StA Potsdam, Pr.Br.Rep. 30 Berlin C Tit 94 Nr. 10699.

40. Gustav Liebig, "2. Nachtrag zum Testament vom 15.11 1891," StA Potsdam, Pr.Br Rep.30 Berlin C Tit. 94, Nr. 9940.

stolen goods and usurious deals circulated and were partly confirmed in military reports, he was not prosecuted. Thirty years later Aschrott still did not have a good reputation in business circles. For this reason and also because Aschrott contributed little to civic projects, the president of the senior directorate of the Berlin merchants' association, R. Herz, advised against granting a title to Aschrott. However, he won the favor of the head of the government of the city of Kassel and of the provincial president of Hesse-Nassau through gifts of land to the government in Kassel and other "meritorious services to the city of Kassel." Apparently on their initiative, he was granted a succession of decorations and titles, including the title of Commercial Councillor (in 1900), the Order of the Crown (1905), and the Order of the Red Eagle, Third Class (1908). Haase, Jandorf, Meyer, and Aschrott had at least one thing in common: none of them belonged to the social elite of his city. Not only Aschrott but Jandorf as well, whose department store (KaDeWe) specialized in cheap goods for the masses, were regarded as men who had accumulated their wealth by not entirely respectable means. Meyer and Haase were relatively insignificant as businessmen. In these cases, an attempt to overcome social ostracism was the motivating force behind the scramble for titles and decorations. However, this explanation is not applicable to Friedländer-Fuld, whose social ambitions did not arise from a position of inferiority, but rather from a driving desire to conquer the heights of Wilhelmine society.[41]

Many businessmen, however, displayed considerable reserve with respect to the acquisition of titles and decorations.[42] This was in reaction to contemporary criticism of title-chasing. Many doubtless feared that it might be assumed that they had "bought" one of these honors, or had obtained it through connections. Businessmen who accepted such an honor often wanted to show that they had not sought it. The banker Rudolf von Koch offers a good example of this.[43]

Wilhelm Merton, a prominent metal industrialist, did not attend

---

41. Central State Archives of the G.D R., Merseburg: Zentrales Staatsarchiv, Dienststelle Merseburg, Geheimes Zivilkabinett, 2.2.1. Nr. 1594 Bl. 20a–20o StA Potsdam, Pr.Br. Rep. 30 Berlin C Tit. 94, Nr. 8795 passim

42 See Anonymous, *Carl Funke*, p 11; Art'l, *Richard Roesicke*, pp. 63–64; Ehrhardt, *Hammerschlage*, pp. 54–56; Hoffmann, *Wilhelm von Finck*, p. 185; Klotzer, "Wilhelm Daniel Weismann," p. 255; Kohlschutter, *Ein Genie*, p. 37, Matschoß and Diesel, *Robert Bosch*, pp 9–10; Solmssen, *Gedenkblatt*, p. 20, H. Wallich, *Aus meinem Leben*, p. 157.

43. Hauptgeschäftsstelle Außendienst an Polizeipräsident Berlin, 24.8.1918, StA Potsdam, Pr.Br. Rep. 30 Berlin C Tit. 94, Nr. 11075.

the opening ceremonies of the Academy of Social and Commercial Studies in Frankfurt in 1901, knowing that he would be honored, but fled to his vacation house in Italy. Afterwards, he seemed pleased with the imperial decoration (*Wilhelmsorden*) that had been bestowed upon him.[44] The banker Carl Fürstenberg received few honors because he did not seek them. According to a report from the office of the chief of police, "I have learned in confidence that he would not like to be honored with the title of Commercial Councillor; that in 1888, before the Order of the Crown (*Kronenorden*) was to be conferred, he expressed himself negatively to the Imperial Chancellor Prince Bismarck with respect to the granting of this title and enjoyed the satisfaction that he had nonetheless been considered worthy of this distinction. Moreover, he is generally addressed as 'Herr Fürstenberg' because he does not like titles such as Director, etc."[45]

For many businessmen, it was not just a question of upholding their bourgeois honor, but of real distress at the prospect of receiving a title or decoration, the reasons for which cannot always be determined. In many cases it was probably a question of not wanting to accept a decoration that was primarily intended for government officials or nobles. For others, it may be that the honor was not sufficiently significant or the timing of the bestowal was regarded as inappropriate. Herbert von Meister, director of the Höchster Farbwerke (a major corporation of the chemical industry), refused to accept the Order of the Red Eagle (*Roter Adlerorden*), Fourth Class. He wrote that he would have considered it a genuine recognition of his entrepreneurial achievements

44. This comes through in the draft of a letter: "Herewith enclosed I am returning the certificate of receipt for the *Wilhelmsorden* which my wife sent me and which incidentally pleases me greatly, although I am not yet certain whether it will be good for me or might not sometimes bring me into a state of vanity and conceit " Quoted in Achinger, *Wilhelm Merton*, p. 240. Merton's wife and children were very proud of the decoration, see pp. 226–43. Merton was co-founder of the Academy. There is a similar incident in Arnst, *August Thyssen*, p. 69.

45. Polizeipräsident Berlin an Handelsministerium, 22.1.1901, StA Potsdam, Pr Br. Rep. 30 Berlin C Tit. 94, Nr. 9929. Fürstenberg wrote in his memoirs on this subject: "My personal stand on titles of any kind contributed in no small measure, in pre-war times, to the suspicion that I was putting on some sort of a show of originality. I consider myself to be completely innocent in this regard, for I have absolutely never been able to bring myself to hang a designation of rank onto my name. I recall that even so serious a man as Emil Rathenau once reproached me for my negative attitude. But this neither harmed nor helped me when I went around completely untitled and so to speak undressed among a bunch of Privy Commercial Councillors, Privy Government Councillors, Privy Government Architects and Privy Councillors of Justice. In imperial Germany it was only natural for a person to accept with thanks a decoration when it was handed out." C. Fürstenberg, *Lebensgeschichte*, pp. 198–99; see also pp 395, 483 Also, see H. Fürstenberg, *Erinnerungen*, 1968, p. 7

and of his charitable activities if, for example, he had been honored on the emperor's birthday. However, he considered it "an insult to me personally and a disparagement of the respect I enjoy as a member of the board of directors"[46] that he should be decorated precisely on the jubilee of the Höchster Farbwerke. Georg Haberland tried in vain to obtain the title of Privy Commercial Councillor for his father, who founded a major construction corporation. The father, decorated with the Order of the Crown (*Kronenorden*), refused to wear it.[47]

Many businessmen were unenthusiastic about the Commercial Councillor title because it was associated with trade.[48] Werner Mosse conjectures that this attitude is related to the growing enthusiasm for technology and to the reputation of the technical university (*Technische Hochschule*). He also argues that the inflation and depreciation of the Commercial Councillor title in the late nineteenth century caused big businessmen increasingly to seek ennoblement or some other title, Government Councillor (*Regierungsrat*), for example.[49]

Quantitative data on the wealthiest businessmen in the *Yearbook of Millionaires* show, however, that this attitude was atypical, that the title of Commercial Councillor was still the most important distinction in the business elite. Whereas only nineteen percent of businessmen who were of bourgeois birth were ennobled after 1870, about forty-one percent were granted the title of Commercial Councillor. Of these, 107 (twenty-two percent of all cases) were further elevated to Privy Commercial Councillor.[50] Non-commercial privy councillor titles (which were generally intended

46. Central State Archives of the G.D.R., Merseburg: Zentrales Staatsarchiv, Dienststelle Merseburg, Geheimes Zivilkabinett, 2.2.1. Nr. 1836, Bl. 112–15

47 See Haberland, *Aus meinem Leben*, pp. 69–72.

48 Examples include Werner Siemens, Heinrich Ehrhardt, a munitions manufacturer, and chemical industrialist Carl Alexander von Martius. On Siemens, see W. Siemens, *Lebenserinnerungen*, pp. 276–77. On Ehrhardt, see Ehrhardt, *Hammerschlage*, p. 55. On Martius, see Central State Archives of the G.D.R., Merseburg: Zentrales Staatsarchiv, Dienststelle Merseburg, Preußisches Ministerium für Handel und Gewerbe, Rep. 120 A IV, Nr 5a, Bd. 4, Bl. 64. Wholesale merchant James Simon "renounced, as he expressly declared, nomination as a Commercial Councillor, since this title was not in accord with his inclinations." (Polizeipräsident Berlin an Handelsministerium, 1902, StA Potsdam, Pr Br. Rep. 30 Berlin C Tit. 94, Nr. 13190, Bl. 29–30.) Neither was he pleased with the title of Acting Privy Councillor (*Wirklich Geheimer Rat*). He was granted the Imperial Order (*Wilhelmsorden*). See Feder et al., "James Simon," p. 7.

49 See Mosse, *Jews*, pp. 73–79.

50. In Prussia, a Commercial Councillor normally had to wait ten years before being designated Privy Commercial Councillor. See Kaudelka-Hanisch, "Preußische Kommerzienräte," p 5.

for other professional groups) were far less common in this group: only thirty-one of these businessmen had such a title.[51]

There were significant regional differences in the distribution of the title of Commercial Councillor. Of the twenty-six Bavarian businessmen included in my study, eighty-eight percent held the Commercial Councillor title. This illustrates the extent of the wave of title-granting in Bavaria before the First World War.[52] Another explanation lies in the fact that competition for this title in this less industrialized state was not as great as in other regions of the empire. Variations within Prussia were also not insignificant: fifty-four percent of the 116 businessmen in the western provinces were Commercial Councillors, but only forty percent of the 114 Berlin businessmen. This difference can probably be traced to the preference given by the authorities to Rhineland-Westphalia,[53] but also to discrimination against Jewish businessmen.[54] There were hardly any Commercial Councillors to be found among the businessmen of the Hanseatic cities because Hamburg, Bremen, and Lübeck did not grant Commercial Councillor titles. Titles in general played a lesser role there than elsewhere. Hamburg senators were not permitted to accept titles and decorations, not even those conferred by the King of Prussia. Titles had traditionally been rejected by Hamburg patricians and wholesale merchants.[55] In the late nineteenth century there was a change of attitude in this regard, which resulted in the proliferation of titles of nobility. This will be discussed below.

Commercial Councillors and Privy Commercial Councillors were to be found as frequently among the Jewish businessmen in my sample as among the non-Jewish. However, if one considers the fact that very few of the (primarily non-Jewish) Hanseatic businessmen held such a title, it becomes clear that in the other states Jews were discriminated against in the granting of titles, especially since an overproportionately large number of Jews headed companies

---

51. The titles involved were the following: Councillor of Justice/Privy Councillor of Justice, Court Councillor/Privy Court Councillor, Government Architect/Privy Government Architect, Truly Confidential Councillor (which conferred upon its recipient the right to the form of address "excellency"), Economic Councillor, Privy Government Councillor.

52. See Schumann, "Bayerns Unternehmer," pp. 351–58.

53. See Mosse, *Jews*, p. 84.

54. Kaudelka-Hanisch states that it occurred more frequently in Berlin than in Westphalia and Dusseldorf that a businessman himself applied for a Commercial Councillor title; such applications were usually rejected. In five out of nineteen cases the applicant was a Jewish businessman. See Kaudelka-Hanisch, "Preußische Kommerzienrate," p. 296.

55. See Evans, *Death*, pp. 33–35, Hauschild-Thiessen, *Burgerstolz*, pp. 97–105.

that were among the largest in Germany (and thus more likely to be honored). Werner Mosse points out that the Jewish share decreased in the new nominations made after 1890.[56] This points up the importance of government initiative (as opposed to the inclinations of the grantees) in the pattern of granting the title of Commercial Councillor.

One hundred sixty-six of the millionaires under study (excluding the noble landowners) received a decoration.[57] The most important of these decorations were those of the Order of the Crown and the Order of the Red Eagle, both of which were conferred by the Prussian king.[58] In Prussia decorations were often bestowed upon younger businessmen who then later received the title of Commercial Councillor, which was considered more significant in the business community. There were also cases in which businessmen, for whom the Commercial Councillor title was out of the question, received decorations. In Bavaria decorations could also serve an additional purpose: since the title of Commercial Councillor had depreciated in value to some extent, the authorities increasingly bestowed decorations on the leading businessmen who were already Commercial Councillors so as to emphasize their prominent positions.[59]

Honorary official appointments were granted to 133 businessmen. The most common was that of consul or vice-consul. Honorary degrees or other honors were granted by universities to sixty-four of the 502 businessmen. The honorary degree was a coveted distinction that technically placed the honorary doctor on the same level as the university-educated bourgeoisie of the free professions and the civil service. By way of comparison, Kaudelka-Hanisch found that only twenty-one of the 673 Commercial Councillors in Westphalia and Düsseldorf achieved this distinction, which was also quite rare in the Bavarian economic bourgeoisie.[60] On the other hand, two-fifths of the top industrialists in Kaelble's

56. See Mosse, *Jews*, p. 84.

57. On the history of the most important decorations, see Kaudelka-Hanisch, "Preußische Kommerzienrate," pp. 398–403.

58 Before 1918 Prussian decorations were the equivalent of imperial decorations. See Geeb, Kirchner, Hermann, and Thiemann, *Deutsche Orden*, p. 22.

59 See Schumann, "Bayerns Unternehmer," pp 331–36, 346, 350 Kaudelka-Hanisch, "Preußische Kommerzienrate," pp 261, 403–4. Out of 673 Westphalian Commercial Councillors, 145 received a Order of the Red Eagle, and seventy-five an Order of the Crown. Bavarian decorations were much less frequently granted to businessmen than Prussian decorations.

60 See Schumann, "Bayerns Unternehmer," p. 330; Kaudelka-Hanisch, "Preußische Kommerzienrate," p. 261.

study were conferred a university honor.[61] Thus, the business elite
– whether defined in terms of position or in terms of wealth – had
an unusually close relationship with the universities, and thus with
the university-educated professional and academic bourgeoisie.

One-fourth of the businessmen in the present study held a title
of nobility, including eight percent who held an older title (granted before 1871) and eighteen percent who were newly ennobled
or who held non-hereditary titles. Of those who were commoners
up until 1871, nineteen percent were elevated to the nobility in
the imperial period (including those with non-hereditary titles).
Other studies indicate that this represents an unusually high concentration of ennoblements. Among the 225 Westphalian textile
industrialists in Hans-Jürgen Teuteberg's study, there was only one
nobleman. Only three of the 248 Westphalian heavy industrialists
in Toni Pierenkemper's sample were granted titles of nobility.
According to Wilhelm Stahl, the percentage of aristocrats among
the businessmen in the "*NDB*" was about five percent.[62] In Great
Britain, on the other hand, a relatively large number of businessmen gained entrance to the aristocracy. W.D. Rubinstein ascer-
tained that fifty-three of 162 wealthiest non-agrarian British millionaires who died between 1920 and 1929 were raised to the
nobility.[63] Forty-one of them received a hereditary title.

Among the businessmen in the present study, the new titles were
very unevenly distributed as far as wealth goes. Whereas one-tenth
of the businessmen in the lower half of the wealth pyramid were
elevated to the aristocracy, just over one-third of the richest businessmen (upper tenth of the pyramid) were so honored. The differences are even more pronounced if one counts only those of
bourgeois birth (that is, omits the older nobility), so that the percentages of the newly ennobled become ten and forty-four percent
respectively.

One can get an idea of the status value of a title of nobility for
many businessmen from the fact that they in some cases paid substantial sums to secure such a title. Some established a landed entail,[64]

61. See Kaelble and Spode, "Sozialstruktur," p. 148

62. See Teuteberg, *Westfälische Textilunternehmer*, p. 38; Pierenkemper, *Die westfalischen
Schwerindustriellen*, p. 73; Stahl, *Elitenkreislauf*, p. 247.

63. See Rubinstein, *Men of Property*, p. 170.

64. Case of chemical industrialist Carl Scheibler discussed in Central State Archives of the
G.D.R., Merseburg: Zentrales Staatsarchiv, Dienststelle Merseburg, Geheimes Zivilkabinett,
2.2.1. Nr. 1048, Bl. 1–20; and Hauschild-Thiessen, *Bürgerstolz*, p. 97. Case of heavy industrialist Hugo von Gahlen discussed in Central State Archives of the G.D.R., Merseburg: Zentrales
Staatsarchiv, Dienststelle Merseburg, Geheimes Zivilkabinett, 2.2.1. Nr. 1340, Bl 5–12.

which was an absolute prerequisite for the title of baron, while others actually purchased their titles (a million marks seems to have been the going price).[65]

The Hamburg banker and merchant Baron John von Berenberg-Goßler had established a landed entail in order to become *Freiherr* (baron).[66] One son was to inherit the estate, another was to inherit the father's company. The father approached the authorities with the request that he be allowed to hand down his title of baron to the son who was to become his successor in the business. He thought it important that his son not be inferior in rank to the heads of two banking houses in Hamburg who also were barons.[67] The father asked the ministry to grant his son the baronial title in connection with the establishment of a financial entail instead of the usual landed entail. He offered to invest the sum in the public debt. The request was approved, however with the proviso that in the next generation the financial entail be transferred into land.[68]

While some haggled and finagled their way into the ranks of the nobility, others were offered a title of nobility and turned it down.[69] According to the provisions of a family endowment fund established by the Kiel banker Wilhelm Ahlmann, any member of the family was required to withdraw from this venture if he or she were to ". . . accept an elevation of class and thereby rise above the bourgeoisie."[70] Banker Paul von Schwabach made no use of his title. Chemical industrialist Walther vom Rath did not change his name to von Rath after being ennobled.[71]

A regional breakdown of the data on ennoblement is in some respects difficult to interpret. An unusually high percentage of the

65 Fritz von Friedlander-Fuld and Oskar von Caro are rumored to have done this. See Vierhaus, *Das Tagebuch*, p. 456.

66. This was a prerequisite for the granting of the title of baron in Prussia.

67. He was referring to the banking families Schroder and Jenisch.

68. Central State Archives of the G.D.R., Merseburg: Zentrales Staatsarchiv, Dienststelle Merseburg, Geheimes Zivilkabinett, 2.2.1. Nr. 1048, Bl 1–20. See Hauschild-Thiessen, *Burgerstolz*, p. 97.

69. The latter group includes Friedrich Alfred Krupp, Heinrich Ehrhardt, the Hamburg banker Max Warburg, the Lorraine industrialist Gustav Adt, the owner and director of the Henschel Works Sophie Henschel, the owner of the Schichau Shipyards Carl Ziese, the publisher Rudolf Mosse, Carl Furstenberg, heavy industrialist August Thyssen, and Emil Kirdorf, the prominent heavy industrialist. See Adt, *Aus meinem Leben*, p. 146; Bacmeister, *Emil Kirdorf,* pp. 151–52; Baumann, "August Thyssen," p. 22; Ehrhardt, *Hammerschlage*, p. 55; C. Furstenberg, *Lebensgeschichte*, p. 199; Martin, *Jahrbuch*, vol. 16, p. 29; Mosse, "Rudolf Mosse," p. 250; Raphael, *Krupp et Thyssen*, p. 72, Treue, "Henschel & Sohn," p 21; Vagts, "M.M. Warburg," p. 294.

70. Letter from Werner Pfeiffer to the author, dated 30 May, 1987.

71. See Stein, *Der preußische Geldadel*, pp. 61–62.

richest Bavarian businessmen (thirty-five percent, or nine out of twenty-six cases) was granted a title of nobility. In most cases, it was non-hereditary. According to Dirk Schumann, hereditary nobility was granted only once to a businessman during the three decades preceding the First World War in the five largest Bavarian industrial cities. Non-hereditary nobility was also not conferred very often in those cities.[72] An explanation for the surprising data on the Bavarians in my study may well lie in the fact that in this less industrialized economic area there were fewer businessmen who could be considered for such an honor. We have earlier observed a similar phenomenon with regard to the Commercial Councillor title. The percentages for the millionaires in three areas of Prussia – Berlin, the western provinces, and Silesia – are close to one another (fifteen percent, eighteen percent, and seven percent[73] respectively).

It is noteworthy that eleven percent of the wealthiest businessmen in the Hanseatic cities were raised to the nobility. There was a general increase in the number of titles granted to (and accepted by) Hamburg patricians in this period.[74] The efforts of the leading banking families to acquire the title of baron reflect this trend. Richard J. Evans sees a sign here that the bourgeois-republican independence of the Hamburg patrician class had begun to crumble, especially after the turn of the century. According to Evans, this growing similarity to the bourgeoisie in other regions of Germany (Prussia in particular) came about first because Hamburg businessmen increasingly had business connections outside the Hanseatic cities; second because wealthy businessmen from other parts of Germany moved to Hamburg; third because of an increase in many kinds of ties between Hamburg and other regions; and fourth because interregional politics played a growing role in Hamburg.[75]

Nonetheless, Evans is of the opinion that the process of aristocratization never made much headway there. Renate Hauschild-Thiessen also argues that ennobled citizens of Hamburg remained true to the traditions of their city: "They were all proud of their new dignity; but at the same time they considered themselves to be

72. Schumann, "Bayerns Unternehmer," pp. 338, 358–59.

73. Two percent of the Berlin businessmen, one percent of the businessmen of the Hanseatic cities, but sixty-four percent of the Silesian businessmen were members of older aristocratic families (i.e , families whose titles pre-dated 1870).

74 See Rohrmann, *Max von Schinckel*, p 289; Stein, *Geldadel*, p 68.

75 See Evans, *Death*, pp. 560–62

loyal Hamburg citizens, tied to their city by family and company tradition."[76] Essentially, a reinterpretation of the meaning of titles of nobility took place. It is telling that Berenberg-Goßler's primary motivation in trying to secure a title of baron for his son was the promotion of his company's interests.

There were considerable differences in the percentage of ennoblements between different areas of economic activity. The largest concentration (at twenty-nine percent) of "true" aristocrats – i.e., members of the old, landed nobility – was to be found among heavy industrialists, who often got into business by opening mining operations on their own lands. Banking, a reputedly patrician activity, was especially conducive to ennoblement. Of the bankers, twenty-two percent were of the newer nobility. Most of the bankers with older titles, who made up nine percent of all bankers, were from older ennobled banking families and did not originate in the landed or bureaucratic aristocracy.

The percentage of ennoblements in the growth industries (chemical, machinery, and electrical industries) was especially high. There are two possible explanations. First, the government was undoubtedly anxious to reward the entrepreneurial accomplishments of these businessmen in a special way. Second, it is possible that as parvenus, these businessmen pursued social recognition with particular energy. On the other end of the scale, only one-tenth of the businessmen in the textile, clothing, and leather industries, as well as in the "miscellaneous" industries, were granted titles.

Ethnic and religious differences were remarkably small, especially those between Protestants and Jews.[77] These findings certainly do not confirm the thesis that Jews were more socially ambitious. Many representatives of the German-Jewish elite, such as Carl Fürstenberg, showed no interest in a title of nobility. One reason might be that bourgeois pride was as strong in the Jewish economic elite as among the wealthy non-Jewish businessmen. Another explanation may be found in the fact that Jews, when they accepted a title of nobility, often had to renounce their religion. In Prussia, conversion to Christianity was usually a requirement for a title of nobility. Baron Max van Goldschmidt-Rothschild was the only unbaptized Jew to be elevated to the aristocracy in Prussia.

76. Hauschild-Thiessen, *Burgerstolz*, p. 97. Also, see Schramm, *Neun Generationen*, vol. 2, p. 426. For a contrary example, see Rohrmann, *Max von Schinckel*, esp pp. 269–71.

77 Religious differences were primarily noted in connection with the older titles of nobility (A significant percentage of the Catholic businessmen were big industrialists of the older nobility.)

To be sure, a Prussian Jew could seek a title of nobility in another German state.

More weighty was the question of whether one could be a Jew and an aristocrat at the same time. There were disagreements in the Mendelssohn Bartholdy family when a branch of the family was granted a title of nobility.[78] Franz Mendelssohn received this honor in 1888 in recognition of his achievements as a banker. However, Ernst Mendelssohn-Bartholdy and Otto Mendelssohn Bartholdy[79] had to purchase their titles of nobility through contributions to the emperor's pet projects. As a result, Otto Georg Oppenheim refused for months to talk to his grandson Otto Mendelssohn Bartholdy. Albrecht Mendelssohn Bartholdy, who belonged to the artistic and scholarly branch of the family,[80] attacked Otto von Mendelssohn Bartholdy, with whom he had a close relationship, in a letter. Albrecht argued that the army officers and government officials in Potsdam (where Otto lived) would never fully accept his family socially, in spite of their title, because their name was still Jewish. In the second place, he expressed the opinion that Otto should not turn his back on his ancestors – above all Moses Mendelssohn: "It is my feeling that a place in the Prussian nobility cannot be reconciled with proper reverence for our origin, with fitting pride in your great-grandfather and his emergence from the lowest level of the Jewry of that time, and with the bearing of his name; and the compulsion you place upon your children to make such a reconciliation appears to me to entail severe conflicts for them."[81] Did ennoblement lead to a genuine assimilation into the nobility? This question will be explored in detail in later chapters.

What conclusions can be drawn from the findings presented here regarding titles and decorations? These honors were genuinely popular among the wealthiest businessmen of the Wilhelmine period. Probably not all who desired the title of Commercial Councillor received one, and this would certainly explain why Jews and the heads of less significant companies were passed over more than others. However, it was above all the businessman who felt insecure in his social status who spent a great deal of time and energy pursuing such honors. Many businessmen were anxious to

78. See Gantzel-Kress, "Noblesse," pp. 163–81.
79. One branch of the family used the hyphen in its name, the other did not.
80. This branch was not on good terms with the branch that headed the banking house.
81. Gantzel-Kress, "Noblesse," p 180. Also, see Gilbert, *Lehrjahre*, p. 17; Gilbert, *Bankiers*, p. XLV.

make it clear that they had not bought their titles or decorations. A few self-confidently asked the government authorities for a mark of distinction different from the one they had received. These findings confirm Schumann's thesis that the businessmen took an active part in the re-definition of the relationship between the bourgeoisie and the state that was going on here. The special significance of honorary university degrees shows that the monied elite was also strongly oriented toward the educated bourgeoisie.

An atypically high percentage of the 502 wealthiest businessmen belonged to the newer nobility. An astonishing forty-four percent of the forty-one richest businessmen of bourgeois birth were ennobled. In the following chapters it will be shown that tendencies toward aristocratization appeared primarily in this group, which constitutes a minority within the highly exclusive stratum of the 502 richest businessmen. While a decoration or bourgeois honor of any sort was seldom turned down, a number of multimillionaires refused titles of nobility. These included Jews, and Jews were not overproportionately represented among the ennobled businessmen.

Participation in Public Life: Political Activity and Membership in Associations

Much has been written about the relationship between business and politics in Wilhelmine Germany. It is not my intention to make an original contribution here, but rather merely to give a general impression of the political orientation of the wealthiest businessmen in the *Yearbook of Millionaires*. Roughly one-quarter held a public office,[82] fifty-nine percent of which were at the local or district level. There were only eleven Reichstag representatives in the group under study. The businessmen born after 1850 were substantially less often politically active then the older members. This is in line with Kaelble's findings on top industrialists in 1907, a seventh of whom held political offices on the national or state level and twenty-eight percent of whom held offices on the local level.[83]

82. Heavy industrialists with older titles of nobility are not included in this figure. In view of the abundance of sources, it can be assumed that the businessmen on whom no information could be found were not politically active. Very similar findings for the heads of the largest companies were noted in Horst Handke, "Soziale Annaherung und Verbindung von Adel und Burgertum am Ende des, 19 Jahrhunderts," (unpublished manuscript, East Berlin, 1987), p. 19 About one half of the 673 Commercial Councillors in Kaudelka-Hanisch's study held a local honorary office. See Kaudelka-Hanisch, "Preußische Kommerzienrate," p 221.

83 See Kaelble and Spode, "Sozialstruktur," p. 148

It has been established in several studies that, first, during the imperial period German businessmen held political offices primarily at the local level because the decisions that most directly affected them were made at that level,[84] and second, that political commitment declined after 1870.[85] Friedrich Zunkel draws the conclusion that "The business community renounced its own political emancipation in order to be able to promote industrial development and halt the emancipation of the working class."[86] This thesis hardly applies to the economic elite, which had direct access to the emperor and other top decision-makers. Political office-holding was least frequent in Berlin, where informal influence on policy through personal contacts was most widespread.

Almost thirty percent of the Protestant and Catholic businessmen, but only twelve percent of the Jewish businessmen, held political office. Anti-Semitism hurt Jews and converted Jews in party caucuses and at the electoral polls. According to Peter Pulzer, only thirteen Jews and baptized Jews can be found among the Reichstag representatives for the years 1881 to 1893, and only eighteen among the members of the parliaments of the individual states. From 1893 to 1918, twenty-six Jews and baptized Jews had seats in the Reichstag (seventeen of them as Social Democrats), fifty-three in the parliaments of the individual states (among them thirteen Social Democrats).[87]

The files on people being considered for a title or decoration in Prussia often contain information on political affiliation or even on the voting record.[88] About one-third of the 114 businessmen on whom information was available supported the National Liberal Party, one-sixth were Conservative, and five percent Free Conservative. For one-fifth, we find characterizations along the lines of "loyal to the king." Only one-sixth could be counted as leftist liberals. Thus, the majority was not politically apathetic, but rather part of the broad anti-reformist, nationalistic alliance that first coalesced in 1879. The political swing to the right was observable in the entire population, but was greater in the economic

---

84. On businessmen's influence on local politics, see Gall, *Stadt*

85. See Adelmann, "Die wirtschaftlichen Fuhrungsschichten," p. 191; Croon, "Die wirtschaftlichen Fuhrungsschichten des Ruhrgebiets in der Zeit von 1890 bis 1933," p. 154, Croon, "Die wirtschaftliche Fuhrungsschicht des Ruhrgebiets 1850–1914," p 221; Jaeger, *Unternehmer*, passim; Pierenkemper, *Die westfalischen Schwerindustriellen*, pp. 62–70, Schumann, "Herkunft," pp. 305–14; Teuteberg, *Westfalische Textilunternehmer*, pp. 35–37.

86. Zunkel, *Der rheinisch-westfalische Unternehmer*, p. 251

87. See Pulzer, "Die jüdische Beteiligung," pp. 143–239, esp pp. 159, 176–77.

88 In at least some cases the Berlin Chief of Police looked at the Prussian election records.

elite.[89] Out of a total of nineteen leftist liberal businessmen on whom information could be found, fourteen were ethnically Jewish. By contrast, only five of the twenty-three Conservative or Free Conservative businessmen were Jewish. These results confirm the thesis that Jewish businessmen fell farther to the left in the political spectrum than did non-Jewish businessmen.[90]

The businessmen in the present study were more active in lobbies and other associations than in politics. Of the 484 non-aristocratic businessmen, 171 (a good third) were members of at least one association.[91] Did these businessmen attempt to gain broad political and economic influence through their membership in an association?[92] Certainly not through chambers of commerce (one-third of all memberships), which as state-sponsored organizations could take no initiative to promote the economic and political interests of businessmen. The associations for specific industries or specific regions were rather diverse, on the other hand. Some concerned themselves almost exclusively with the narrow technical or organizational problems of one industry or region. Others, such as the Association of German Iron and Steel Industrialists and the "Langnam" Association, focused on broad economic questions.

Clearly, the large national organizations played a prominent role in representing the political and economic interests of the business world. Of particular importance was the Central Association of German Industrialists (*Centralverband deutscher Industrieller*), which accounts for about one-fifth of all memberships covered by this study. This organization was dominated by forces friendly to agrarian conservatism, favoring protective tariffs and cartels, and pushing a hard line in social policy. It was the real representative of big industry.[93] On the other hand, the League of Industrialists (*Bund der Industriellen*) and the Hanseatic League (*Hansa-Bund*),

89. Karın Kaudelka-Hanisch came to similar conclusions. See "Preußische Kommerzienrate," p. 252.

90. See Mosse, *German-Jewish*, p. 340; Richarz, *Jüdisches Leben*, vol. 2, p. 45, Toury, *Die politischen Orientierungen*, passim.

91 In view of the abundance of sources it can be assumed that at least all those who sat on the executive committee of an association were covered. By comparison, 254 (thirty-eight percent) of the 673 Commercial Councillors researched by Kaudelka-Hanisch were members of chambers of commerce; sixty-nine Commercial Councillors were members of business lobbying associations See Kaudelka-Hanisch, "Preußische Kommerzienrate," pp. 223–24.

92. Toni Pierenkemper asserts that this was not the case with the Westphalian heavy industrialists, since they were involved primarily in technical associations and chambers of commerce. See Pierenkemper, *Die westfälischen Schwerindustriellen*, pp. 62–66.

93. See Kaelble, *Industrielle Interessenpolitik*; Nussbaum, *Unternehmer*, Stegmann, *Die Erben*.

50

which followed a more liberal line, were of hardly any signifi-cance.[94] Cartels and nationalistic associations (three and five per-cent, respectively, of all memberships) also sought broad economic and political influence. Businessmen who headed social service organizations (about six percent of all cases) were seeking to docu-ment their commitment to the promotion of public welfare but also to gain influence over social policy. Employer associations (five percent of all cases) were concerned with social policy and labor conflicts. All in all, participation in associations by the businessmen in this study was widely dispersed, but not politically irrelevant. For some of the richest businessmen, activity in associations was a sub-stitute for political activity. This is particularly true of industrialists and non-Jews.

Social Origins

It has been shown in several recent studies that the top positions in the business world during the periods of high and late industrial-ization were no longer open to "any qualified person."[95] My find-ings confirm this thesis. Among the 407 businessmen in this study on whom information was available, the rate of self-recruitment was very high.[96] Forty-five percent were the sons of big business-men, and an additional thirty-nine percent the sons of businessmen whose socio-economic status is unclear.[97] The overwhelming majority of the largest fortunes in industry, banking, and com-merce were not accumulated within a single generation. An espe-cially high percentage of owners of businesses were sons of busi-nessmen (eighty-seven percent). But this was also the background of over three-quarters of the men running corporations. Although the recruitment of top management was becoming increasingly bureaucratic and performance-oriented, the rise of corporate capi-talism hardly improved the chances of joining the ranks of the very

94. The League of Industrialists represented primarily small- and medium-scale industry. The Hanseatic League (founded in 1909) sought to bring together commerce, the trades, and industry. It also tried to attract businessmen, employees, and the middle class. It was supported by representatives of banks, wholesale trade, and overseas commerce. See Ullmann, *Der Bund*; Mielke, *Der Hansa-Bund*.

95. For a general introduction to research on social mobility, see Kaelble, *Social Mobility*; Schüren, *Soziale Mobilität*.

96. Not including heavy industrialists with older titles of nobility.

97. It is possible that some of these people belong to the commercial middle class. (Artisans belong to a different category.) However, this term was used, especially in the Hanseatic cities, for the heads of the great commercial companies.

wealthy business elite. One reason for this lies in the informal educational requirements for these positions, coupled with the fact that the lower classes were at this time largely excluded from the institutions of higher learning.[98] The sons of businessmen also had access to connections that could help advance their careers. For example, Paul Mankiewitz, later director of the Deutsche Bank, is said to have enjoyed "a little bit of protection" when he started out at a relatively lowly position at the Deutsche Bank. His mother was distantly related to a banking family with which the securities director of the Deutsche Bank was on friendly terms. When Mankiewitz came into conflict with his supervisors, he was not dismissed, but was transferred to the stock exchange, where his upward path began.[99]

Other studies also seem to indicate that the self-recruitment rate was high, though (as in the present study) it is often unclear whether the fathers who were businessmen belonged more to the upper middle or to the lower middle classes. Among the Westphalian businessmen (Commercial Councillors) studied by Hansjoachim Henning, the rate of recruitment from the business class (including the lower middle class) was seventy-two percent from 1880 to 1889 and eighty percent from 1890 to 1909. During these two periods four percent and two percent, respectively, of the investigated persons came from artisans' families.[100] According to Kaudelka-Hanisch eighty-nine percent of the fathers of Commercial Councillors in Westphalia and Dusseldorf were businessmen.[101] Out of 133 businessmen ennobled during the imperial period, 114 were the sons of businessmen.[102] Kaelble's study on businessmen listed in the *Neue Deutsche Biographie* points more clearly to the industrial, artisanal, and commercial lower middle class as a springboard for business careers before 1914.[103] Kaelble points out that what made this class so competitive was its technical training and experience abroad.[104] However, the recruitment of top corporate managers in 1907 was much more exclusive.[105]

---

98. See Kocka, "Bildung," pp. 297–314, esp. pp 311–13.

99. See Pinner, *Deutsche Wirtschaftsführer*, pp. 208–9.

100 See Henning, "Soziale Verflechtung." (Data on p. 5.)

101. See Kaudelka-Hanisch, "Preußische Kommerzienrate," pp. 175–76.

102. See Stein, *Der preußische Geldadel*, vol. 2, pp. 424–25.

103. Twenty percent of the group under study originated in this class. Kaeble's study includes 297 businessmen who were active between 1871 and 1914. See Kaelble, "Long-Term Changes," p. 409, column 2.

104. Also, see Kaelble, "Sozialer Aufstieg," p. 53; Kocka, *Unternehmer*, pp. 47–50

105 See Kaelble, "Sozialstruktur," p 157

The recruitment pattern of German businessmen reflects a fair degree of social isolation. In the pre-industrial elite and the educated bourgeoisie, a reserved attitude toward industrial society was quite pronounced. A mere two percent of the wealthiest businessmen in the *Yearbook of Millionaires* were the sons of officers or landowners; two percent were born into families of the upper civil service and three percent in other segments of the professional bourgeoisie. Only a slightly higher percentage of the managers came from the educated bourgeoisie (nine percent, including government officials).[106] This is indicative of a lack of bourgeoisification of the German aristocracy and of a segmentation of the bourgeoisie itself. In Great Britain, the fathers of the heads of the 200 largest British companies were more frequently big landowners or professional men and less often small-time businessmen than their counterparts in Germany.[107] Rubinstein's data on the monied elite do not show the same pattern, however.[108] It is generally recognized that the social isolation of the propertied bourgeoisie in Germany tended to limit its influence in society as a whole.

Other studies on Germany confirm my findings with regard to the pre-industrial elite and the free professions, while pointing to stronger ties of kinship with the bureaucracy. A fair percentage of the fathers of the businessmen in the *Neue Deutsche Biographie* were university-educated and non-university-educated government officials (nine percent and seven percent respectively).[109] In his later study on top corporate industrialists, Kaelble found that one-sixth were sons of civil servants.[110] Horst Handke arrives at an even higher figure for the chairmen of the boards of the seventy-three largest enterprises in 1897/98.[111] Here we find a distinguishing mark between very wealthy businessmen and top corporate management.

Overall, only eight percent of the businessmen in my study are known to have originated in the lower middle class, mainly from

106. Other studies show greater differences in the recruitment of managers and owners, especially as regards government officials, professional people, and academics See Kocka, "Bildung," pp. 311–13.

107. Perkin, "Recruitment," table 5, printed in Kaelble, *Historische Mobilitätsforschung*, p. 131.

108. See Rubinstein, *Men of Property*, pp. 182 and 189; and "Modern Britain," pp. 65–67. If my data are compared with those of Rubinstein, there are hardly any differences that cannot be explained by differences in the classification of professions. See also Cassis, "Wirtschaftselite," p 20.

109. See Kaelble, "Long-Term Changes," p. 409.

110. See Kaelble, "Sozialstruktur," p. 157.

111 See Handke, "Soziale Annaherung," p 15 and Appendix According to his data, one-fifth of the chairmen were sons of civil servants.

families with shops or other enterprises of their own, or with jobs in private industry. However, as has already been noted, the social class of nearly forty percent of the fathers (who were businessmen) cannot be determined. Only one case came to light in which one of the richest businessmen in the *Yearbook of Millionaires* probably rose from the lower class. Otto Gerstenberg, director of the Viktoria Insurance Corporation, was the son of a shoemaker. It is not known how he financed his university studies in mathematics. A second self-made man, not one of the 502 richest but undoubtedly a multimillionaire, was Heinrich Ehrhardt, the founder of Rheinmetall and son of an impoverished woodsman who made cans on the side. In his autobiography, Ehrhardt propagated a German version of the dishwasher-to-millionaire ideology, based on his own career.[112]

Self-recruitment was most frequent among the younger cohorts. The explanation lies in the age factor. The younger the businessman, the shorter was the length of time between his embarkation on a business career and publication in the *Yearbook of Millionaires*. Anyone who was not an heir needed a longer time to amass great wealth in the economy.

There were surprisingly few differences in recruitment between different industries and sectors of the economy. Almost all the businessmen in the textile, clothing, and leather industries were the sons of businessmen. Hans-Jürgen Teuteberg and Gerhard Adelmann obtained similar results.[113] In my study, recruitment from the middle class was most frequent among the heavy industrialists (with fifteen percent). Toni Pierenkemper's data on the social origins of Westphalian and Upper Silesian heavy industrialists are hardly comparable because of different categorization, but it is interesting to note that a significant percentage of the fathers of heavy industrialists in both regions were government officials, military officers, farmers, innkeepers, clergymen, and professionals.[114]

A surprising result of the present study is that the businessmen

112 "May this little book point out the way to many a young man and spur him on to struggle ahead even if he has no means at his disposal and the path ahead is steep and stony. Had I come into the world as the son of well-to-do parents, it is quite possible that I would not have gone as far as I did." Ehrhardt, *Kreuz- und Querfahrten*, pp 57–58. The results of the present study refute the myth of equal opportunity.

113. See Adelmann, "Führende Unternehmer," pp. 344–46, Teuteberg, *Westfälische Textilunternehmer*, p 26.

114. See Pierenkemper, "Entrepreneurs," p. 73. According to this study, seventeen of the forty-six heavy industrialists of Upper Silesia and fifty-nine of the 138 Westphalian heavy industrialists had fathers in these professions

in the growth industries varied so little from the heavy industrialists in their social origins. In general, the chances of advancement in these newer industries are regarded as having been greater. But in the present study, these industries were represented by several businessmen of the second or third generation.[115] This shows clearly that at this stage of industrialization great wealth was very rarely accumulated in one generation. This was true not only of all industries and sectors, but also for all regions and ethnic groups, and for both ennobled and bourgeois businessmen.

Education and Training

Data on education and training are generally hard to come by, and in the present study were available only for 194 wealthy businessmen and 197 wealthy businessmen's sons. The educational level seems to have been very high, though it is possible that the businessmen for whom we have no information were less well educated. Only a tiny minority of the businessmen and their sons left secondary school before graduation. The *Gymnasium*, which qualified a student for entry to a university, was the most important type of school. Banker's son Werner Weisbach writes: "I could not have done otherwise than to spend my secondary school years at a humanistic *Gymnasium*, because it was almost a foregone conclusion that that kind of school should be selected for any mentally normal boy from a prominent bourgeois family. A humanistic education was considered an advantage and worth the effort for anyone who could afford it."[116]

These findings contradict Fritz K. Ringer's thesis that a compartmentalization of the German educational system took place in the nineteenth century. Whereas the *Gymnasium* (emphasizing classical languages) prepared the student for academic professions and a career in government service, the *Oberrealschule* (emphasizing modern languages and mathematics) educated the student primarily for career in the economy; the *Realgymnasium* occupied a position halfway between. According to Ringer's data, from 1875 to 1899 forty percent of businessmen's sons attended the *Oberrealschule*, just over one-third the *Realgymnasium* and only one-quar-

115. For example, the Wurttemberg chemical industrialist Jobst, the General Director of Adlerwerke Heinrich Kleyer, the Hanover machinery manufacturer Berthold Korting (whose father was a gas works director), and the chemical industrialist Carl Leverkus

116. Weisbach, *Und alles,* p. 48

ter the *Gymnasium*.[117] However, Peter Lundgreen asserts that the numbers of students who attended the *Realgymnasium* and the *Oberrealschule* were far smaller, "that the overwhelming majority of the sons of men in *all* professional groups chose the *Gymnasium*."[118] One example: of all the sons of the upper middle class (both propertied and the educated bourgeoisie) who at the turn of the century attended a secondary school in the city of Minden, ninety percent chose the *Gymnasium*.[119] Of the ninety-one heavy industrialists in Pierenkemper's study who graduated from a secondary school, sixty-four attended a *Gymnasium*, twenty-three a *Realgymnasium*, and four an *Oberrealschule*.[120] According to the results of another research project, on the other hand, only thirteen percent of the businessmen attended a *Gymnasium*, but thirty-five percent attended a *Realgymnasium*, and thirty-one percent an *Oberrealschule*; eighteen percent received private instruction.[121] Trade schools and commercial schools played a larger role among the businessmen studied by Pierenkemper and Stahl than they did among the businessmen in the *Yearbook of Millionaires*, one-tenth of whom attended such an institution.[122] (The percentage dropped among the sons to three percent.)

One hundred and seven of the wealthiest businessmen attended a university, of whom fifty-six graduated.[123] It must be pointed out that doctoral degrees are probably overrepresented because in Germany the title of doctor is an integral part of the name.[124] However, even if none of the 290 businessmen on whom no information on education is available studied at a university the percentage of university students would still be twenty-two percent. (By comparison, twenty percent of the British millionaires and half-millionaires in Rubinstein's study, who died between 1900 and 1909, completed university studies.[125]) Twenty-seven (fourteen percent

117 See Ringer, "Bildung," pp 5–35, esp. pp. 16–18. Also, see Ringer, *Education*, pp. 301–10.

118 In Prussia, around 71,200 students attended the *Gymnasium* between 1875 and 1899, 12,600 attended the *Realgymnasium*, and 1,200 the *Oberrealschule* See Lundgreen, "Bildung," pp. 262–75, esp. pp. 268–69.

119 See Kraul, *Das deutsche Gymnasium*, p. 118. Also, see Lundgreen, Kraul, and Ditt, *Bildungschancen*, esp. pp. 77–78

120. See Pierenkemper, *Die westfälischen Schwerindustriellen*, p 51.

121 Kauldelka-Hanisch, "Preußische Kommerzienrate," p. 203. The data apply to fifty-five Westphalian and Dusseldorf Commercial Councillors from 1810 to 1918.

122. See Pierenkemper, *Die westfälischen Schwerindustriellen*, p 51; Stahl, *Elitenkreislauf*, pp. 229, 235.

123. Only in a few cases is the major known.

124. Honorary doctor degrees are of course not counted here.

125. See Rubinstein, *Men of Property*, pp. 254–55, 267–68.

of all businessmen on whom we have information) attended a technical university. Information on education and training is available on only thirty managers, twenty of whom studied at a university, thirteen receiving degrees (law degrees predominated). The emphasis on higher education increased significantly in the generation of the sons of the wealthiest businessmen. No fewer than 163 out of 197 sons (eighty-three percent) attended a university; thirty (fifteen percent of the total) attended a technical university. My findings are confirmed by Kaelble and Spode's study on top industrialists.[126]

Carl Friedrich von Siemens (born 1872) is somewhat unusual in that, having failed the final secondary school examination, he did not want to repeat it because he would not need a degree for his practical duties at the Siemens concern. However, Siemens advised his friend Julius Bötzow Jr. (born 1875), son of the wealthy brewery owner Julius Bötzow, to study chemistry. If he were to join his father's firm without a university education, he would have to concentrate on the merchandising side of the business and ". . . kill time sitting next to a capable head clerk." The prestige of the doctor title was another important argument Siemens used: "for the outside world you get your doctor's degree in chemistry and then you will be regarded everywhere as an educated and cultured man, even if you should later – though we would hope not – not take your work too seriously."[127] Georg Tietz, son of a department store owner, was strongly professionally oriented: "At the university my idea was to study, not just in order to pass an examination but in order to acquire as much knowledge as possible for my eventual profession."[128] However, in other cases, a college education turned the businessmen's sons away from a career in business, as will be discussed in a later chapter.

The apprenticeship had traditionally been part of preparation for a career in business. Two-thirds of the businessmen in my study

126. See Kaelble, "Sozialstruktur," pp 169 and 172 Two-thirds of the top industrialists in Kaelble's study and ninety-two percent of their sons attended a university However, information was only available on ninety-two businessmen and forty-six sons. A smaller percentage of less exclusive business groups received university training. See Kaudelka-Hanisch, "Preußische Kommerzienrate," p. 207; Pierenkemper, *Die westfälischen Schwerindustriellen*, p. 59, Stahl, *Elitenkreislauf*, pp. 229, 235. According to Konrad Jarausch the percentage of sons of the wealthy bourgeoisie (including the independently wealthy and bourgeois landowners) attending four German universities (Bonn, Berlin, Leipzig, Tubingen) rose from twenty-three percent in the 1860s to thirty-eight percent in the 1890s, then fell back to thirty-six percent in the 1910s See Jarausch, *Students*, pp. 124, 118–20.

127. G. Siemens, *Carl Friedrich von Siemens*, p 34; see pp 20–25, 33.

128. Tietz, *Hermann Tietz*, p 84.

underwent an apprenticeship or some other form of practical training. The one-third without practical training were primarily wealthy heirs who studied at universities and were shown the ropes once they joined the family company, probably after having been groomed for the entrepreneurial role for years. Only twenty-eight percent of the sons of businessmen in this study received practical training, whether a formal apprenticeship or not. (This figure includes sons who went into other fields.)

By contrast, fifty-five percent of the business owners in Stahl's study who were born in the nineteenth century, and fifteen percent of the managers born in the eighteenth and nineteenth centuries completed apprenticeships.[129] Practical training could be documented for 139 Westphalian heavy industrialists. In 108 cases, however, Pierenkemper found no information on such training.[130] Kaelble's figures on apprenticeships are much lower: thirty-nine percent for the top industrialists and a mere nine percent for their sons.[131] Kaelble found evidence of the state bureaucracy serving as a model in the fact that one-fifth of the major industrialists were trainees for the higher civil service (*Referendar*) and one-fifth started their careers as civil servants.[132] In my own study, a mere four percent of the fathers and four percent of the sons passed a civil service examination (*Staatsexamen*) after having completed a university degree and a trainee period (*Referendariat*).

Education had become a factor that tended to promote unity rather than segmentation in the bourgeoisie. In attending the *Gymnasium* and the university, men of elite business families were emulating a model of "*Bildung*" originally established by the *Bildungsbürgertum*. In these institutions of secondary and higher learning, sons (seldom daughters) of upper-middle-class business families were thrown together with sons of the educated upper middle class. In addition, there were growing parallels in the career patterns of the propertied and educated segments of the German bourgeoisie: an increasing number of years devoted to education, bringing with it an ever-lengthening period of career moratorium, and the postponement of marriage and independence. This would tend to create similar psycho-social conditions, values, and forms

129. See Stahl, *Eltenkreislauf*, pp. 229, 235. These figures do not include those who both attended the university and did an apprenticeship.

130. See Pierenkemper, *Die westfälischen Schwerindustriellen*, p. 58. Here I am omitting a professional officer that Pierenkemper included

131. See Kaelble, "Sozialstruktur," pp. 169 and 172.

132. Ibid., p. 146

of behavior. The sons of the wealthy bourgeoisie were, on the other hand, better off in that they were not subjected to the long period of unpaid or underpaid training typical of many professions (such as the civil service). On the whole, though, trends in education and training tended to contribute to the cohesion of the bourgeoisie.[133]

Conclusion

Though the primary intention of this chapter is to give background information on which the analysis of the next chapters is based, findings were also presented that are relevant to the major themes of this study. Though a high concentration of new titles of nobility could be expected in the wealth elite, it was somewhat surprising to find that eighteen percent of the wealthiest businessmen listed in the *Yearbook of Millionaires* were raised to the nobility after 1870. It could be argued that this created a split between two groups within the wealthy business elite – between those who would go to all lengths to procure a title of nobility, and those who proudly turned a cold shoulder to this symbol of aristocratization. However, upon closer inspection, we see that the motives – and the fronts – were not this clear. Only in the Mendelssohn family do we find a quarrel over this issue. It was particularly interesting to see that in Hamburg, the title of baron had become a prized status symbol among leading banking families who continued to form part of the backbone of the Hamburg business community and the socially and politically dominant patrician ruling class. This is perhaps a kind of secondary aristocratization that, while bespeaking a willingness to become the bedfellows of the aristocracy, is primarily indicative of a will to be socially accepted in the upper echelons of society, and not necessarily of a desire to flee from the business world. In the case of Hamburg, accepting a Prussian title of nobility was perhaps also a way of demonstrating loyalty to the Prussian-dominated empire.

Other honors were distinctly more popular, particularly state decorations and the title of Commercial Councillor. These reflected not so much aristocratization as loyalty to the state. The state had here an instrument at its disposal that could be used to disci-

133. See Haupt, "Männliche und weibliche"; Taylor, "Transition," pp 635–58

pline the bourgeoisie, but it was only partially able to make use of it, since the state also needed a way of rewarding public service and (in the case of Bavaria) of sugarcoating the bitter pill of social legislation. More importantly, it increasingly became possible to purchase titles and decorations. This is one of many examples of how crass capitalist values increasingly undermined the old order.

The wealthy business elite also had ties with other segments of the bourgeoisie, evidenced by the popularity of honors granted by universities in this group and – more importantly – by growing similarities in the education and career patterns of sons of the wealthy propertied bourgeoisie and of the academic and professional bourgeoisie. On the other hand, the patterns of the business elite's recruitment revealed strong tendencies toward social isolation: almost nine out of ten of the 502 businessmen were the sons of businessmen.

With regard to aristocratization, recruitment, and education, we find a remarkable lack of regional variations. Particularly the Hamburg example seems to indicate that a convergence was taking place. Even more remarkable are the similarities between Jews and Protestants within the wealth elite. Jews were not ennobled more frequently, were neither more nor less likely to come from business families, and they put as much (or more) emphasis on a humanistic secondary education and university studies as did non-Jews.

The new breed of top corporate managers and "entrepreneurs" (managers with a controlling interest in their company), making up nineteen percent of the wealthiest businessmen in the *Yearbook of Millionaires*, were a less modern group than might be expected. They were somewhat more likely to be ennobled than the supposedly more traditional owners of family enterprises. This is even true of the top managers in the newer growth industries – chemicals, electricity, and machinery. They were also almost as likely to come from a business background as owners, due to the educational requirements and professional connections needed to climb to the top of the corporate structure.

Chapter 2

Marriage

Courtship and Partner Selection

The choice of a marriage partner constituted a decision of great significance for the families of the economic elite. The plot of Theodor Fontane's critical period piece *Frau Jenny Treibel* revolves around this theme. Frau Jenny Treibel, wife of a successful industrialist, Commercial Councillor Treibel, indulges in romantic reveries and sings of love to a piano accompaniment:

What care I for gold? I love roses. . . .
Give, take, take, give,
And the wind plays around your hair.
Ah, only that, only that is living,
When heart beats to heart.[1]

Her son Leopold tries to live according to this philosophy by "falling in love" (albeit only half-heartedly) with Corinna, a professor's daughter. They became engaged without asking permission of either set of parents. But he is quickly brought back to reality by his mother: "In my house there is no engagement and no Corinna. . . . If I can give you a piece of advice, be wise and don't abandon the basic principles which sustain life and without which there is no genuine happiness, for the sake of a dangerous person and a whim."[2] The story has an ironic "happy ending." Leopold becomes engaged to a businessman's daughter selected by his mother, and Corinna becomes engaged to a young academic.

How prevalent in fact was this marriage of convenience described by Fontane in the propertied German bourgeoisie? Most family historians see the nineteenth century as an era of transition, in which most middle-class marriages were neither based entirely

1. Fontane, *Frau Jenny Treibel*, p. 187.
2 Ibid., p. 143.

on material considerations nor entirely on emotions.[3] To a growing extent, marriages fell somewhere between "arranged marriages" and "love matches." According to Marion Kaplan, partner selection took place more and more through "contrived coincidences" in the years before the First World War, especially in the urban middle class. Characteristic of this type of courtship was the "accidental" encounter, brought about after the parents had conducted their inquiries and negotiations. The future bride and groom knew nothing of the parents' plans, or at least acted as if they knew nothing. The negotiations were brought to a conclusion only if the couple were in agreement. If love did play any role in this, it was only after the engagement.

The next step consisted of *informal* "contrived coincidences" in which future marriage partners became acquainted in circles sought out by their parents, for example, on vacation, especially at spas, at weddings, and within the circles of friends and acquaintances of the parents. According to Kaplan, love marriages were a great rarity before the First World War. By Kaplan's definition, a love marriage was one in which the man and woman became acquainted in a circle selected by themselves and spontaneously (without parental approval) decided to marry. Common interests and convictions stood in the foreground, although a dowry was also usually paid.[4] Moreover, the parents still had a veto right.

There is a fair amount of disagreement concerning the extent to which arranged marriages had died out by the end of the nineteenth century. This is not an unimportant question, for it is intimately related to the question of how strong patriarchal structures were in this period. According to Jürgen Kocka, the marriage of convenience was bound up with the very important economic functions of the business family in early industrialization. Once other institutions took over many of these roles, it was no longer necessary for the parents to select a marriage partner, and businessmen's children – especially the sons – won greater freedom in the selection of a spouse.[5]

3. See Gay, *Bourgeois Experience*, esp vol 2, pp. 3ff., 98–99, 103, 106–7; Kaplan, "For Love," pp. 263–300; Kaplan, *Making*, pp. 85–116; Rosenbaum, *Formen*, esp. pp 332–39; Schenk, *Freie Liebe*, p 145, see esp. pp. 84–90, 145–47.

Peter Borscheid is atypical in that he only distinguishes between the marriage of convenience and the love marriage, taking as his point of departure the ideal of love as formulated by German Romanticism Not surprisingly, he comes to the (mistaken) conclusion that in nineteenth-century Germany there were only marriages of convenience. See Borscheid, "Geld," pp. 112–34

4. On the dowry, see Goody, "Bridewealth," pp. 17–21; Kaplan, *Marriage Bargain*.

5 See Kocka, "Familie," esp pp. 126–28, 134.

In his highly significant two-volume history of love and sexuality in the late nineteenth and early twentieth century, Peter Gay shows that love and sexuality were strong forces among the Victorian bourgeoisie, forces that frequently played a prominent role in the search for a mate and in married life.[6] Gay does not deny that the arranged marriage still predominated in some circles,[7] but he describes the late nineteenth century as a transitional period in which the old patriarchal structures were beginning to totter. Werner E. Mosse takes the rather extreme view that by the middle of the nineteenth century, arranged marriages no longer took place within higher Jewish society.[8] This flies in the face of the extensive primary research conducted by Marion Kaplan, which indicates that among the wealthy Jews of this period the "arranged marriage" was still quite common. The main motivation was the maintenance and augmentation of the family fortune, and the size of a woman's dowry was often a decisive factor.[9]

Marriage preliminaries constituted a very sensitive subject in the Wilhelmine period, especially since "dowry chasing" was often represented in the press as a preeminently Jewish behavior pattern.[10] My archival research brought to light no marriage contracts or other concrete documents related to marriage preliminaries among the families of the rich businessmen of the Wilhelmine period, so that here I had to rely strongly on the evidence contained in autobiographies and biographies and in the files on people considered for a title or decoration. For about twenty-five families of the Wilhelmine period (half of them Jewish), the details concerning spouse selection are known for at least one family member.

6. See Gay, *Bourgeois Experience*, 2 vols.
7. "The uppermost or most tradition-bound within the bourgeoisie – old commercial clans, rich and anxious parvenus, patrician Catholics, orthodox Jews – were more likely than their less proud or prosperous fellow-bourgeois to treat marriage negotiations as affairs of state rather than as affairs of the heart." Ibid., vol. 2, p. 100; see pp. 5–43.
8. See Mosse, *German-Jewish*, pp. 108–10.
9. See Kaplan, "For Love." She writes, "marriages were contracts between families: material factors were of primary importance. This varies according to class, with the upper strata, where marriages involved substantial property transfers, exerting the greatest control over love and courtship behavior" (p. 264).
Mosse only looks at a few cases, and does not analyze the extensive material with which Kaplan documents the survival of the arranged marriage. He criticizes Kaplan's typology, noting that elements of arranged marriages, "contrived coincidences," and love marriages can be found in the preliminaries of many marriages. This demonstrates a misunderstanding of Kaplan's typology, in which all three courtship types contain elements of compulsion, free choice, material considerations, and affection. He asserts that the motivation of women in the selection of a mate especially can no longer be reconstructed, ignoring the women's autobiographies and other sources extensively used by Kaplan
10. See Kaplan, "For Love," pp. 280–91.

A particularly fascinating source is the autobiography of Paul Wallich. He was born in 1882, the son of a very prominent Jewish banker, Hermann Wallich, who was co-founder of the Deutsche Bank, the largest joint stock company of the empire, which he headed until the mid-1890s. Paul Wallich, who was himself a banker (in the Berliner Handels-Gesellschaft) left behind memoirs that are remarkably self-critical and unconventional. His wife Hildegard (née Rehrmann) also authored an autobiography, which on many points supplements her husband's writings.[11]

Paul Wallich, like the overwhelming majority of men of his class, enjoyed many years of bachelorhood. (On the average, the businessmen in my study first married at the age of 29.)[12] He confirms the widespread impression that in bourgeois circles the young unmarried man enjoyed a large measure of sexual freedom, but only with a "certain sort" of woman, whom the young man under no circumstances could marry.[13] Not only prostitutes but also actresses, female singers and "jugglers," and women of the lower classes fit into the category of women considered available. To collect sexual experiences with such women was not considered immoral. In Paul Wallich's bachelor days, for example, his father gave him the money for a trip to Tyrol with a waitress.[14]

On the other hand, it was clear to the young man, then twenty years old, that women from bourgeois circles were untouchable. "If I was not dealing with professionals or young girls who were blinded by the glitter of my paltry gold, I was so shy that, for example, I did not dare to kiss a pretty milkmaid with whom I spent two hours churning butter alone in the dairy cellar. And the girl waited for it as a believer waits for the amen at church. But that is what rearing as a gentlemen does: it makes one shy and

11. P. Wallich, "Lehr- und Wanderjahre," pp. 159–426. It is unclear when these memoirs were written. They were first published (unabridged) in 1978 H. Wallich, *Erinnerungen*.

12. The exact figure is 29.4 years of age. Adelheid von Nell arrives at very similar figures for businessmen and wholesale merchants in Lower Saxony. From 1825 to 1874 the average age of marriage for this group was 31.5; from 1875 to 1899 it was 28.5; and from 1900 to 1914 it was 29.6. For senior government officials, professional men and army officers, however, it was thirty-three years during the period 1875 to 1899. See Nell, "Die Entwicklung," pp. 69, 75. The businessmen in my own study all married after 1840 (most after 1870).

In the period between 1875 and 1910 the median age for first marriages was twenty-eight for men. See Knodel, *Decline*, p. 70.

13. On the sexual freedom of male students, see Jarausch, "Students, Sex," pp. 285–303. On the bourgeois double standard, see for example Robertson, *Experience*, pp. 93–131. Further example in Liebermann von Wahlendorf, *Erinnerung*, pp. 51, 54.

14. See P. Wallich, "Lehr- und Wanderjahre," pp. 183–84, 205; however, Wallich claims to have had only "modest success" on this occasion. At this time he was about twenty years old.

degenerate."[15] As was the custom in certain bourgeois circles, Wallich kept a mistress. In the Hamburg Sport Club – "the rendezvous of the young, fast set" – some of the sons of the very rich businessmen made appearances with their "elegant mistresses." Wallich obviously never considered marrying such a woman. He wrote about his relationship with an actress: "I could love her with all my heart, but I could not even think of making her my wife."[16]

However, Wallich never lost sight of the goal of marriage. The significance of this objective in his life was in part a consequence of his social ambitions. He wrote: "The main goal of my life at that time was to raise the social status of my family. There were only three means of accomplishing this, and if at all possible all three should be employed": namely, joining a *Korps* (fraternity), becoming a reserve officer, and marrying a woman of "good family."[17] Herman Wallich had had his children baptized and it was his wish that they should marry non-Jews in order to become fully assimilated.[18] But the bourgeois marriage ideal with its emphasis on personal feelings also had a hold on Paul Wallich. He wrote: "I wanted to get married. The unrest of life as a wanderer and a bachelor, the meager successes and the numerous though not deep disappointments I had experienced as a man of the world, and finally the fanciful belief that there was such a thing as happiness and that it could be found in marriage – all these things lured me on." He was searching for an understanding person with whom he could talk, and at the same time "sensual acceptance" and "tenderness."[19]

Wallich spent long years searching for a wife who incorporated the material and emotional characteristics that were important to him. During his period of training in Hamburg in 1905/1906 he became acquainted with Julius von Rath, who came from a very wealthy family of sugar industrialists. Wallich fell in love with Julius' sister. "And this splendid friend forgot his prejudices as a Cologne patrician to such an extent that he actually sought his sister's hand for me." But his mother sharply rejected such a marriage. "She probably replied to her son's proposal, 'You have to draw the line somewhere.' "[20] Thus, as a baptized Jew, Wallich was not considered an acceptable match in these circles.

15. Ibid., p. 185.
16. Ibid., p 340; see pp. 224, 232–33.
17. Ibid., pp. 167–68.
18. See H. Wallich, *Erinnerungen*, p 110
19. P. Wallich, "Lehr- und Wanderjahre," pp 338–39
20 Ibid., p 221.

During his period as an unpaid trainee in Berlin in 1906, he had a number of "flirts" that for various reasons came to nothing, the first one because the girl's father died without leaving a fortune. He became acquainted with a number of wealthy businessmen's daughters. His remarks about the positive characteristics of these women, which caused him at least briefly to consider marrying them, are somewhat vague and contradictory. Among these were common interests (certain books, natural sciences, horseback riding, music, etc.), good judgment in business matters, appearance, an attractive personality and "good character" (sometimes "good-naturedness" or "a faithful heart," or sometimes "high-spiritedness").[21]

More unequivocal were the reasons for not marrying. One was ". . . without a figure or a face, not even intelligent, and as I said before, without social skill." He wrote concerning the Jewish banker's daughter Eva Steinthal: ". . . it was the hope of both sets of parents to see a lasting relationship develop. The fact that I did not marry this fine, honorable girl, who loved me and whose affluence attracted me, was due in part to her race, but most of all because of her appearance, which did not attract me at all."[22] Difference in class was a major factor in the break-up of a relationship with the daughter of a bankrupt businessman who had herself become a successful businesswoman. He wrote: "But quite aside from the financial worries one would bring upon oneself in acquiring a bankrupt but still enterprising father-in-law, there was something petty bourgeois, second class about Ilse Wendringer, the wrong kind of snobbishness, which was especially aggravated by the fall in social status and therefore produced an effect that was all the more annoying."[23]

An arranged meeting with the daughter of a Bremen millionaire friend of his father's turned out to be pointless since he found ". . . no kind of common meeting-ground . . . heaven and earth, art, and society, and anything else that occurred to me, elicited from her only a well-bred word of agreement or at most a politely delicate exclamation of astonishment."[24] He liked the daughter of the rich merchant family Staudt, although she was almost exclusively interested in equestrian sports. In this case personality and appearance were probably important factors. However, the woman chose another suitor.

21. See Ibid., pp. 243, 345–50.
22. Ibid., pp. 243, 346
23. Ibid., p. 348
24. Ibid., p. 349.

After this long series of disappointments Wallich went to a matrimonial agency. When he was asked how much dowry he required, "I said that this factor was immaterial to me, but that I would give preference, other things being equal, to the more well-to-do." The agency was unable to find a woman who would have been the slightest bit interesting to him. Through a brief appointment at the home of a big landowner he tried in vain to become acquainted with the daughter of a Junker.[25]

He fell in love with the actress and author Marion Brennan: "Never before had a woman exercised such powerful magic on me with such physical and at the same time psychological effect." For three years he played with the idea of marrying her. The fact that she was divorced, the fear that as an Englishwoman she might not be able to be happy in Germany, even the fact that his parents would not have approved of the marriage – none of these considerations would have stood in the way of a marriage. In the final analysis, Wallich did not marry her because he would never have been able to be sure that before him she had slept only with her husband.[26]

Wallich is astonishingly silent as to how his marriage to Hildegard Rehrmann came about, so that here we have to rely on her autobiography. Hildegard Rehrmann, the daughter of a headmaster at a cadet academy, was an unusually cultivated woman. She studied piano at a conservatory for a time, attended lectures on literature and music at the Sorbonne during a stay in Paris, attended a language seminar where she passed the government examination, and was an exchange student in France and England. At the home of a schoolmate, the daughter of a Protestant minister, she became acquainted with Paul Wallich, who is said to have decided at this very first meeting to marry her. She wrote: "We talked about everything imaginable – he had also been in Paris and asked if I knew Romain Rolland, who had been my instructor at the Sorbonne and for whom I had such great admiration, so I told him about that. We had a delightful conversation. He had a good sense of humor in his own quiet way – that especially appealed to me." At a second meeting at the home of their common acquaintance he offered to lend her one of Rolland's works, consisting of several volumes. He sent each volume individually and enclosed a letter with it.[27]

25. See Ibid., pp. 360–61; quotation on p. 355.
26. See Ibid., pp. 358–59; quotation on p. 358.
27. See H. Wallich, *Erinnerungen*, pp. 75, 81, 104–7; quotation on p. 107.

Finally, one day when they were out walking he asked her to become his wife. She asked her brother's advice and introduced him .to Paul Wallich. The brother was ". . . quite impressed and charmed by him." Soon afterward, they became engaged and bought engagement and wedding rings on the same day. Rehrmann bought Wallich's wedding ring with money she herself had earned. They went walking together and Wallich telephoned his parents from a restaurant to tell them he had become engaged. It was only after the engagement that each of them became acquainted with the future parents-in-law. Hildegard Wallich writes: "It was a new world that I now entered."[28] Her father arranged for a luxurious trousseau ("We did not have such elegant underclothing in our house") with savings out of his ". . . monthly payments into his military savings account." It is unlikely that Rehrmann brought a dowry worth mentioning into the marriage. The opinion of her family with regard to Hildegard Rehrmann's sexual innocence is made clear by a minor incident. The famous singer Cläre Waldorf appeared at the engagement party. Hildegard was compelled to leave the celebration early because in the opinion of the parents ". . . these verses are mostly unsuitable for the ears of young girls or even brides-to-be."[29]

The marriage of Paul and Hildegard Wallich fits perfectly into Marion Kaplan's definition of a love marriage. However, the story of Paul Wallich's amorous adventures and search for a wife also shows clearly that among the Wilhelmine higher bourgeoisie, love, and above all, a love marriage, were not to be equated with pure, unadulterated feeling. In the first place, a distinction was made between women that one married and women that one did not. Wallich's comments on the affair with the actress should be recalled: "I could love her with all my heart, but I could not even think of marrying her." Wallich's suspicions that his "great love," Marion Brennan, was not a woman whose sexual morality conformed to the prevailing bourgeois norms caused him to leave her. Only a few businessmen of the Wilhelmine period married former mistresses or women from social groups that were not considered respectable (that is, not in conformity with the bourgeois sexual morality, but more important-ly, of lower social and economic status). In addition to this first rule, in the case of Paul Wallich there was a second: his bride-to-be could not be Jewish. His father had already stipulated this.

28 Ibid., p. 109; see pp. 107–9.
29 Ibid , pp. 115, 113.

Framed by bourgeois morality and Jewish aspirations for assimilation, Paul Wallich's search for a wife took place within an informal type of marriage market in which many businessmen's sons and daughters participated. Wallich was looking for an optimal package of characteristics[30] that contained within it all the contradictions of the bourgeois marriage. On the one hand, Wallich wanted to raise the social status of his family through marriage with a woman of "good family." The significance of the dowry was minimal, however, since sufficient capital was already available. After a businessman's family had attained economic power and wealth, it could turn to the consolidation of its social position. These efforts were especially important in the case of the socially less esteemed Jewish businessmen.

Wallich was also looking for a woman who would make a good banker's wife, a woman who could raise a future generation of businessmen, run a great household, cultivate a network of social contacts, and do charity work, a woman who had social skills, was patrician in bearing and appearance, and perhaps had some understanding of business affairs. In addition, Wallich's bride-to-be also had to possess qualities that conformed to his private needs and interests. In particular he attached great value to education and the ability to carry on a cultivated conversation. He rejected one good match because he could not converse with the woman. The conversation about Romain Rolland shows that Hildegard Rehrmann's education was an important factor in his decision to marry her. Their marriage was unusually "modern," typical perhaps only for the culturally inclined younger Jewish businessmen of Berlin. In general, however, very high and very contradictory demands – though mostly not of an intellectual nature – were placed on the wives of this elite. Like other wealthy young businessmen, Paul Wallich came to realize that older customs – "arranged marriages" and "contrived coincidences" – were increasingly irrelevant as the importance of the dowry declined (due to the rise of corporate capitalism or, especially here, due to the great wealth of the prospective bridegroom's family) and the personal characteristics of a wife became more important. It should be noted that the woman was often relegated to a passive role, in part because she was a good deal younger than her suitor. The wealthi-

30. Erich Fromm criticizes the twentieth-century conception of love, equating it with a search for an optimal package of characteristics under market conditions. See Fromm, *Art*, pp. 17–18 Also, see Bourdieu, *La distinction*

est businessmen in the *Yearbook of Millionaires* married women who on the average were 7.3 years younger, i.e., 22.3 years of age.[31]

A series of cases for which the term "love match" seems to fit could be found in the biographical and autobiographical literature.[32] For example, Robert von Mendelssohn met his wife, the Italian singer and pianist Giulietta Gordigniani at a reception of the actress Eleonora Duse.[33] His choice of a wife was related to the musical interests of his family. A second case: When Professor Kuhlbaum asked Georg von Siemens, director of the Deutsche Bank, for the hand of his daughter in 1898 and announced that the daughter also wanted to marry him, Siemens replied: "Very unpleasant! Very unpleasant! But I can't say anything against it."[34] Even if this were nothing more than an outburst of fatherly jealousy, this incident shows that Siemens had not brought the couple together, either directly or indirectly. There were also some initial misgivings when Ellen Warburg, a Hamburg banker's daughter (born 1877), wanted to marry a young government official. Her daughter commented later: "They (the parents) were perhaps thinking of a genuine Hamburg businessman."[35]

Marriages with women of the lower classes can be even more unequivocally classed as love marriages. Such marriages might come about when a young man fell in love with a mistress. In such a case he could find himself in conflict with his parents. When Carl Friedrich von Siemens (born 1872) was in his mid-twenties he married an actress in London. His mother wanted to break off all relations with him. His brother, Wilhelm von Siemens, regarded the situation as dangerous because he suspected that the woman was a fortune hunter. Under the terms of their father's will (Werner von Siemens), Carl Friedrich was to become an equal partner in the firm at age twenty-eight. Wilhelm arranged for an

31. This was an unusually early marriage age for women. Nell calculated an average age of 24.9 for marriages to businessmen that took place between 1875 and 1899 and 24.2 for those that took place between 1900 and 1914. These figures are only for Lower Saxony See Nell, "Entwicklung," p 75. From 1900 to 1914, Lower Saxon government officials, military officers, and members of the free professions married women who were on the average 26.8 years old. The median age of marriage for the female population of the empire during the period from 1875 to 1910 was about 25.5 years See Knodel, *Decline*, p. 70.

32 Whether the term "love marriage" should be used in each of these cases depends on how one defines love. If one takes the contemporary conceptions as a starting point, then they were indeed in most cases "love marriages."

33. See Kupferberg, *Mendelssohns*, p. 245.

34 Helfferich, *Georg von Siemens*, vol. 3, p. 256.

35. Wenzel-Burchard, *Granny*, p. 22; see pp. 20–23.

investigation of the woman and persuaded his brother to leave her. The marriage was dissolved by means of a court annulment.[36] In four other cases, however, the young businessman did *not* abandon a wife who did not come from the bourgeoisie. For example, the very successful Lübeck wholesale merchant Emil Possehl (1850–1919) married an actress who was not accepted by his relatives, yet they remained together until his death.[37] The writer Carl Sternheim was born in 1879 in Hanover as a premarital child of the daughter of a master tailor and the Jewish banker Jacob (called Carl) Sternheim. Their marriage did not break up.[38]

The Berlin construction magnate Georg Haberland "escaped the danger" of a forced marriage to a woman of the lower classes during a stay abroad in the 1880s. He describes the perils of the situation of a naive young man abroad in his autobiography: "The innkeeper's daughter reacts warmly to the young lodger, goes walking with him, even goes on a weekend outing with him. But if he forgets himself and presses a kiss on her lips, that signifies an engagement." A French girl of the lower classes was identified with a sensuality that could morally ruin a solid German merchant's son. "The 'ménage à deux' has meant the downfall of many a young German. In Paris some of my Bradford classmates have fallen completely under the influence of a mentally and spiritually inferior woman. They have become enervated and listless and have destroyed their future."[39] In a way typical of his day, Haberland associated the destructive power of a sexuality not tamed by the bourgeois institution of marriage with the lower classes and with foreigners. Interestingly enough, in his second marriage Haberland wedded his secretary, a fact that he did not conceal in his autobiography.[40]

During the First World War Hans Adt, a Lorraine industrialist, married a woman whose father, a pharmacist, had died and whose stepfather was a day laborer (the engagement took place secretly in 1912). In his autobiography Adt devotes seven pages to the childhood and youth of his wife. He reveals his pride in this woman who had overcome many difficulties in order to obtain a position as the "right hand" of a married couple on a nobleman's estate,

36. See G. Siemens, *Carl Friedrich von Siemens*, pp. 27–29. The investigations revealed that the woman had lied about her previous life.
37. See Niendorf, *Geschichte*, p. 129
38. See Emrich and Linke, "Lebenschronik," esp. p. 1097.
39. Haberland, *Aus meinem Leben*, pp. 37, 39.
40. See ibid., p. 200.

and then finally to marry Adt. In any event Adt was quite conscious of his own role in this Cinderella story: "Through her marriage to me, Annie, the little dairy-maid from Sion, had become the wife of an industrialist. She had become the wife of a man who was to take over the factory in Forbach, and since the wealth of the Adt family still consisted of extensive lands, etc., Annie had become a rich woman."[41] It is interesting that in this case the old "rags-to-riches" story centers on a woman. Fritz Stern handles this theme quite differently in *Gold and Iron*, leaving the reader with the impression that marriages, such as those of Gerson Bleichröder's sons, with women of the working class were signs that a family was in trouble, in danger of a ". . . rapid decline into decadence, debauchery and sloth."[42] From the above examples it becomes clear that a non-bourgeois marriage was no more indicative of moral decay or the decline of the entrepreneurial spirit than was a bourgeois marriage.

It has often been assumed that marriage connections between business families were not love matches. This was not always the case. Willy Liebermann von Wahlendorf, of the Jewish textile-industrial Liebermann family, fell in love at age twenty with a twenty-five-year-old woman of the Herz family, who were wealthy Jewish businessmen. His father forbade him to marry her, not because he was too young, but because of the difference in age.[43]

The very successful and socially respected co-owner of the Berliner Handelsgesellschaft, Carl Fürstenberg, had an extramarital love affair with Aniela Treitel, née Natanson, who came from a Polish-Jewish banker's family. Aniela Treitel was a highly cultivated woman who frequented the intellectual salons of the capital and – what was most unusual for her time – exercised the right of sexual freedom. The following was reported in the police files: "In the 1880s Mrs. Fürstenberg, who was then married to Mr. Treitel, a man of independent means, was a beauty who had many admirers, among whom were personages of the hereditary and monied aristocracies, such as Prince von Ratibor, Herbert von Bismarck and the like. Her present husband, Mr. Fürstenberg, was a close friend

41. Adt, *Aus meinem Leben*, p. 161; see pp. 151–59.

42 James von Bleichröder's first marriage was to the daughter of a prominent businessman, Adolf Alexander, but his second marriage was to the daughter of a horse dealer. He tried to conceal her origin through a sham adoption and a sham marriage. She later left Bleichroder for a South American diplomat. James's brother Hans married the daughter of a launderer after he had fathered her two illegitimate children. See Stern, *Gold and Iron*, esp. pp. 485–92, 543, 546.

43. See Liebermann von Wahlendorf, *Erinnerung*, p. 42.

of Treitel and as such was a frequent guest in their home. . . . It is said that at that time Fürstenberg was the favorite suitor, but it is not known whether the marriage was dissolved for this reason." Fürstenberg married Aniela, who became a queen of Berlin high society.[44]

Each of these two people personified what the other was looking for in a mate. Fürstenberg wrote: "When I met my future wife for the first time, she captured my full attention, She was intelligent, distinguished and dazzlingly beautiful. . . . I myself was considered by many to be the financial genius of the rising generation to which the future then seemed to offer infinite possibilities. So we encountered one another as two people who could attract one another's entire attention and arouse no small amount of admiration in one another." Aniela was not only a cultivated woman who could move about easily in society but was also a woman who could discuss business affairs with her husband.[45] This banker had found his way to a woman of the haute bourgeoisie because a woman from this milieu was the most likely to possess the qualities that he admired in a woman, which were in large part molded by his social class. Aniela's lifestyle in earlier years admittedly did not conform to standards of bourgeois morality, but this came to be forgotten, and at the turn of the century her home was a center of Berlin social life.[46] Wealth and economic power enabled this couple to disregard bourgeois conventions with regard to sexual morality.

This was not an isolated case. Shortly after the turn of the century Katharina von Kardorff-Oheimb, née Endert, a businessman's daughter, married her second husband, Ernst Albert, who had been her lover during her first marriage. When she was eighty years old she told Ilse Reicke how she had met Albert at the home of the banker Trinkaus, whose trainee Albert was, and how she seduced him: "I was Ernst's first love. He was completely innocent and knew nothing about women and the ways of love when he met me." Material motives were also a factor for her: "Along with my passionate love for Ernst, it had from the beginning been a most pleasant thought for me that in the future I would be a very rich

44 "Kommissariat für Militair- und Gnadensachen p.p. an Polizeiprasident Berlin," 2.3.1906, StA Potsdam, Pr.Br Rep 30 Berlin C Tit. 94 Nr. 9929.

45. See C. Furstenberg, *Lebensgeschichte*, p 231, quotation on p. 229.

46. "Kommissariat fur Militair- und Gnadensachen p.p. an Polizeiprasident Berlin," 2 3.1906, StA Potsdam, Pr.Br.Rep. 30 Berlin C Tit. 94 Nr 9929 Carl Furstenberg failed to mention these details in his autobiography. See C. Fürstenberg, *Lebensgeschichte*, esp. pp. 216–20, 229–31, 241.

woman." As in the case of Aniela Fürstenberg, the wealth and power of the man allowed her to sidestep bourgeois morality: "Since I now had the protection of a beloved man, all those people who had left me, a divorced woman, defenseless and alone, came crowding around me, could not show enough friendship, which I no longer needed."[47]

Marriage to a relative could likewise be a love match. The marriage between Margarete Sachs, whose father had founded the Bismarkhütte (mining company), and her cousin cannot be classified as either an arranged or planned marriage. They became engaged secretly and were forced to wait three years to get married, until he established himself professionally.[48]

The "love marriage" of Felix Warburg calls for a bit more skepticism, however. In 1894 Warburg, the son of the banker Moritz Warburg, decided immediately to get married when he met Frieda Schiff, the daughter of a German Jew who had emigrated to the United States and had become a multimillionaire as a banker in the firm of Kuhn, Loeb & Co. Fritz was ready to go to the United States. Both fathers were against it. Moritz Warburg wanted to make Felix his successor. Jacob Schiff, according to biographer Jacques Attali, considered the Warburgs to be "much too modest a match." Frieda Schiff and Felix Warburg had to wait a year to get married, a year during which they were not allowed to see one another. Finally, both sets of parents gave in. After the wedding, Felix joined the firm Kuhn, Loeb & Co. At the wedding his brother Paul fell in love with Nina Loeb, a relative of the bride. They in turn were allowed to marry, and Paul Warburg also joined the firm Kuhn, Loeb & Co.[49] Alfred Vagts comments on this connection as follows: "In the first half of the nineteenth century and beyond, it was almost a rule that family connections formed the basis for business relationships among German businesses overseas, especially those in America. Such relationships were strongest and longest-lasting among the private banks – and therefore among the Jewish banks which proved to have greater longevity in the face of the all-

47 Kardorff-Oheimb, *Politik*, pp. 54, 50–51. In any event the four children from her first marriage were taken away from her

Extramarital relationships that were not later legalized by marriage usually resulted in a scandal if they became known Examples in C. Fürstenberg, *Lebensgeschichte*, p. 45; report in. *Die Wahrheit*, Nr. 3 (18.1.1908), StA Potsdam, Pr.Br.Rep. 30 (Berlin C Tit. 94 Nr. 8968 [in dossier on Georg Buxenstein]); Report of the German consul general, Geneva, 1916, StA Potsdam, Pr.Br.Rep. 30 (Berlin C Tit. 94 Nr. 10265 [in dossier on Albert Freundenberg]).

48 See Grünfeld, *Alte unnennbare Tage*, p. 28

49. See Attali, *Siegmund G. Warburg*, pp. 67–68.

absorbing growth of the stock companies."[50] Although it cannot
be proved, material considerations were probably a major factor in
the Warburg brothers' choice of mates. However, it should be
emphasized that in the case of the elder brother no arranged marriage was involved from the point of view of either the bride or the
groom. We are probably dealing here with marriages, at least partially motivated by material factors, which came about without any
parental intervention. In any event, there was one love marriage in
this family. Aby M. Warburg, a brother of Felix and Paul, was the
first Warburg who married a non-Jew, over the opposition of his
father and brothers.[51]

There is abundant evidence of "contrived coincidences" and
"planned marriages" among the Wilhelmine economic elite. The
engagement of Max Warburg (brother of Felix, Paul and Aby M.)
in 1898 is a typical example: "It was an eventful year for many of
my friends as well as for myself. Engagements of brothers and sisters, of male and female cousins came one after another. . . . My
wife was one of the best friends of my sister Olga. We met often,
and at parties we were always seated next to one another."[52] After
the termination of his first marriage, Carl Friedrich von Siemens in
1898 married Tutty Bötzow, daughter of Julius Bötzow, the very
wealthy owner of a brewery and a landed estate. Siemens, who was
an enthusiastic sportsman, first met Tutty Bötzow on the tennis
court. "Her age group already formed the transition from the anx-
iously protected daughter . . . to a freer pattern of living. This
manifested itself in an inclination toward sports activities among
young girls that were not obligated to take up a profession."[53]
Hugo Stinnes, the heavy industrialist, became acquainted with his
wife Cläre, née Wagenknecht, the daughter of a wealthy merchant,
in his parents' home. His mother had invited her in the hope that
she would marry the oldest son, Heinrich. Instead she married
Hugo (in 1895).[54] The banker Werner Pfeiffer, who married the
great-granddaughter of Wilhelm Ahlmann, founder of a private
bank in Kiel, commented as follows on the marriage patterns of the
families of Wilhelm and Ludwig Ahlmann (Ludwig, son of
Wilhelm, became co-owner of the bank in 1889): "Neither
Wilhelm nor Ludwig Ahlmann influenced their children's choice of

50. Vagts, "M.M. Warburg," p. 291.
51. See Attali, *Siegmund G. Warburg*, p. 71.
52. Warburg, *Aus meinen Aufzeichnungen*, p. 17.
53. Siemens, *Carl Friedrich von Siemens*, p. 30.
54. See Klass, *Hugo Stinnes*, p. 70.

mates. There was ample opportunity at the numerous social gatherings of the better society for the young people to become acquainted, and a 'marriage strategy' never played a role."[55]

There is also evidence that the arranged marriage had not yet died out in this class. Erika Brandes, in a methodologically innovative genealogical study, documents a high degree of inbreeding among the patrician families of Bremen up to the First World War. This inbreeding was brought about primarily through arranged marriages. New heads of companies were recruited and business connections were maintained through marriage alliances. This strategy helped to preserve the patrician class: "'Competing adjacent classes' were not only socially excluded, but they and upward-striving competitors were regarded as upstarts, were combated in order to secure and strengthen the power position of the patricians."[56] Within the framework of the present study it was not possible to determine what significance closed marriage circles had in other cities.[57] But there are many indications that they were primarily typical of cities in which an entrenched patrician class was still in power, thus primarily typical of the Hanseatic cities. There were also closed marriage circles within the German-Jewish elite.[58] The frequency of marriages between relatives in a number of families of the economic elite – often Jewish – leads one to presume that they may have been arranged. There are examples of this in the Rothschild and Mendelssohn families.[59] Indirect evidence that arranged marriages were more prevalent in Jewish business families comes from the *Yearbook of Millionaires* study: the man was over ten years older than his wife in thirty-five percent of the Jewish marriages, but only in eighteen percent of the non-Jewish marriages. Large differentials in marriage ages are generally thought to be typical of arranged marriages.

Circumstantial evidence points to a number of arranged marriages in autobiographies and biographies. Mary Sloman, née Albers-Schönberg, the daughter of a Hamburg merchant, met her

55. This comment relates, among other things, to the selection of a marriage partner by Werner Pfeiffer's in-laws. Letter from Werner Pfeiffer to the author, dated 30 May 1987.

56 Brandes, "Der Bremer Überseekaufmann," p. 47, see pp. 25–52

57. The criterion for inclusion in the present study was wealth, not social exclusivity. In addition, individual persons were researched, not families. In order to identify closed marriage circles, it would be necessary to investigate the marriage behavior on a city-by-city basis of the "best families."

58. See Euler, "Bankherren," p. 135; Mosse, *German-Jewish*, p. 94.

59 See Gilbert, introduction to *Bankiers*, p. XXXIV Further example in Reissner, "Histories," p. 239.

future husband at her first ball. A short passage in her autobiography strongly suggests that her parents had decided that she should get married. Here, she recalled how often, after a party at her home, she had lain in bed and mused, "I wonder if I will soon become engaged. I hope not. I want to paint and not get married."[60] It is also obvious that many marriage connections brought with them economic advantages. When heavy industrialist Karl Röchling married Alwine Vopelius in 1857, he received shares in a coal mine. Through the marriage of his nephew Fritz Röchling to Maria Vopelius in 1887, the Röchlings gained decisive influence within the firm.[61] The daughter of Heinrich Ehrhardt, the founder of Rheinmetall, married a steel specialist named Heye. Ehrhardt founded a steel factory with his son-in-law in order to become independent of unreliable suppliers.[62] Arthur von Gwinner, director of the Deutsche Bank and the son of a government official, acquired his wealth through his marriage to Anna Speyer of the very rich banking family Speyer-Ellison.[63]

In the Krupp family, the choice of a mate became an affair of state. The emperor himself appears to have decided that the heiress Bertha Krupp should marry the diplomat Gustav von Bohlen und Halbach.[64] Why was he chosen? First of all, his career fulfilled societal expectations in almost every regard. Gert von Klass writes: "Everything was in precisely the right place, in conformity with contemporary ideals: He had passed the middle school examination at age eighteen, then military service as a one-year volunteer in the Second Baden Dragoon Regiment in Bruchsal, then law studies in Lausanne, Strasbourg, and Heidelberg, then at the appointed time Doctor of Law and reserve lieutenant, and then entry-level admission into the upper echelons of the professional civil service."[65] His career as a diplomat was a good preparation for his responsibilities as head of the Krupp Corporation, since he was expected to be more a public representative of the corporation than a manager.[66] It was also advantageous that he was known as a man who was scarcely interested in politics and who bowed to state

60. Sloman, *Erinnerungen*, p. 85, see pp. 82–85.
61. See Nutzinger, *Karl Röchling*, p. 55.
62. See Ehrhardt, *Hammerschlage*, pp. 60–61 The marriage took place in the Wilhelmine period.
63 Gwinner omits this fact in his autobiography, see *Lebenserinnerungen*, p. 14.
64 See Manchester, *Arms*, p. 248, Schwering, *Berlin Court*, pp 212–13.
65. Klass, *Die drei Ringe*, pp 311–12.
66 See Berdrow, *Alfred Krupp*, pp. 217–18.

authority when called upon to do so.[67] Through this marriage the symbiosis between the state and the Krupp Corporation thrived.[68]

Thus, for the economic elite the Wilhelmine era was a transitional period in which patriarchal structures were able to survive here and there, but were in a general state of dissolution. The arranged marriage and the closed marriage circle survived primarily among Jews who wanted to hold onto their religious identity and within the traditional patrician elite (especially of the Hanseatic cities). Spouse selection was generally based on a complex interplay of emotional and practical factors. In many cases young businessmen and businessmen's daughters were probably genuinely "in love," but they were generally responding emotionally to those characteristics that were highly valued in their social stratum. Ideas concerning what was attractive in a woman were formed to a certain extent by the demands placed on the wife in this class. Thus the young businessman sought a wife who could make an appearance in society, self-assured and familiar with the ways of the world, who had a command of the forms of representation, and who could manage a large household. Since she would also be responsible for raising a future generation of businessmen, it was a distinct advantage if she herself had received a bourgeois education.

However, the personal qualities of the woman could only play a larger role in the selection of a mate once the significance of the dowry had diminished. A development in this direction became evident among businessmen of the successor generation such as Paul Wallich, Georg Tietz, and Hans Adt. Parents were in the best position to arrange a marriage with a dowry, but the young businessman himself was in the best position to evaluate the characteristics and capabilities of a potential wife. No doubt this often occurred without conscious deliberation. Even in cases where practical questions such as the size of the dowry, business connections, or the recruitment of a businessman were a major factor, many children of businessmen (like Felix Warburg) sought out the marriage partners themselves. Thus, it came to be increasingly recognized that the younger generation, when given a fair degree of freedom in this regard, usually selected a suitable mate. Businessmen's sons doubtless enjoyed greater freedom than businessmen's daughters. Marion Kaplan's findings probably differ

67. See Manchester, *Arms*, p. 250; Engelmann, *Krupp*, p. 349.

68. "The marriage of Bertha Krupp to Bohlen und Halbach became a symbol of the liaison between government and industry in Wilhelmine Germany." Boelcke, *Krupp*, p. 175.

somewhat from my own – stressing the arranged marriage more – because hers are based more heavily on the testimony of women.[69]

Patterns of Intermarriage

Not every Wilhelmine businessman was pleased if his daughter decided to marry an aristocratic officer, as the lament of Emil Schulz, a manufacturer of gas and water systems in Berlin, attests: "And . . . a noble lieutenant, at that! If he were only a school teacher or a government employee! It would suit me best if he were a construction man. I, the toilet maker (should have) a noble son-in-law, a lieutenant!"[70] Such confrontations of disparate social values were probably not uncommon, judging from quantitative data on intermarriage between the wealthiest businessmen and other social groups. Table 2 summarizes data on profession of the businessmen's fathers-in-law, sons-in-law, and the fathers-in-law of the businessmen's sons which are to be used here as indicators of social class.

In this elite, we find strong tendencies towards social endogamy (i.e., intermarriage with families of the same social group). The majority (about two-thirds) of the wealthiest businessmen in the *Yearbook of Millionaires* on whom we have information were married to the daughters of businessmen (including twenty-nine percent whose fathers-in-law were known to be big businessmen, and thirty-nine percent whose fathers-in-law could have been big businessmen or medium-scale businessmen). Almost half of their sons, but just over one-third of their daughters, married into business families (class not determinable). On the other hand, intermarriage with the traditional ruling class was somewhat more prevalent among the daughters of businessmen (one-third of all cases with information) than among the sons (one-quarter), and was more prevalent among the sons than among the businessmen themselves (one-tenth).

How can these differences be explained? The companies and corporations of many of the businessmen in this study – even those who were themselves sons of businessmen – were in the growth phase when these individuals married. They often wedded busi-

---

69 Another possible explanation is the divergent behavior of unconverted Jews. It is also possible that her theories are more applicable to the educated bourgeoisie and to the smaller towns.

70 Haberland, *Aus meinem Leben*, p 80. Haberland was a friend of Schulz's

Table 2. Intermarriage in the Wealthy Business Elite[a] (in %)

OCCUPATIONAL GROUP	RELATIONSHIP TO BUSINESSMEN		
	FATHER-IN-LAW	SON'S FATHER-IN-LAW	SON-IN-LAW
Pre-industrial elite (without civil servants)	8.9	23.9	32.0
Upper civil servants	3.5	7.7	9.6
Professionals, academics[b]	8.6	10.8	10.7
Big businessmen	29.4	18.8	16.6
Businessmen: status unknown	38.5	30.3	19.6
Lower middle class	6.8	6.5	9.4
Lower class/Lower or lower middle class	0.9	—	—
Other[c]	3.3	2.2	2.1
Total (in %)	99.9	100.2	100.0
Total (absolute)	312	234	428

[a] Excluding eighteen businessmen who belonged to the aristocracy or whose families had been integrated into the aristocracy. Only cases with information. Second and third marriages included. Data on fathers-in-law were available for 282 businessmen; data on sons' fathers-in-law were available for 130 businessmen; data on sons-in-law were available for 213 businessmen.

[b] Universities, college preparatory schools, and school administration.

[c] Rentiers; upper class, profession unknown.

nessmen's daughters out of a desire to supplement their company's capital with a large dowry, to improve business connections, to take over the direction of a new company, or even to become a businessman in the first place. The economic position of the family was usually firmly established by the time the sons and daughters married. The family could now turn its attention to the consolidation of its social position. Max von Schinkel, who was born in 1849, had no entrée to Hamburg high society, though he was the son of a wealthy merchant and was himself a successful Hamburg banker. He was not socially accepted by the patricians of the city until he married a woman in those circles. He was thoroughly aristocratized in his way of thinking, and his children married almost exclusively into aristocratic circles.[71]

71. See Rohrmann, *Max von Schinckel*, pp. 79, 186, 285–89.

The marriage of the daughter of the banker Eugen Gutmann to an army officer in 1898 obviously was for the purpose of raising the prestige of the family. The following was reported in a newspaper article covering this event: "The sincerity of the good wishes with which the Court of Baden hails this union of hearts is demonstrated by the fact that the Grand Duke of Baden some days ago sent a basket of flowers to the lovely bride and by the fact that Prince Max von Baden, Lieutenant in the Garde-Cuirassier-Regiment, will accompany Fräulein Gutmann to the altar on 1 May as the bride's escort."[72]

The purpose of such unions could also be, in some cases, the establishment of relationships with the power elite. Such a strategy was followed, for example, by the Mendelssohn family, one of the most prominent ethnically Jewish banking families of the imperial period, which established marriage connections with officialdom. Felix Gilbert, a descendent of the family, writes, ". . . marriages to government officials and army officers were above all the means by which connections were established with the leadership of the official hierarchy. The male members of the family much more rarely enter such professions, and that is especially true of those members of the family who carry the Mendelssohn name."[73] However, the daughter of a businessman could also arrive at the decision to marry an aristocrat quite independently, even against the wishes of her parents, as the example of Emil Schulz above illustrates.

Why did more daughters than sons marry into the nobility? If the son was a businessman – which often was the case – his professional life brought him into less frequent contact with the aristocracy. From the point of view of the nobility, the marriage of a son to a businessman's daughter was a more attractive proposition than the marriage of a daughter to a businessman, since a daughter normally became a part of her husband's world. The daughter of a landowner or army officer who married a businessman did not necessarily move into a house next to the factory, but she did become a businessman's wife and usually lost her title of nobility. In addition, when a big landowner entered a marriage in which a dowry was involved, capital flowed into agriculture. Conversely, a businessman married to the daughter of a big landowner normally did not invest a sizable proportion of his wealth in land.

---

72 Newspaper clipping from *Staatsbürgerliche Zeitung*, 23 March, 1898, StA Potsdam, Pr.Br.Rep 30 Berlin C Tit. 94 Nr. 10239.

73. Gilbert, *Bankiers*, p XXXIV.

Marriage alliances with the educated bourgeoisie (including government officials) were not quite as frequent as those with the pre-industrial elite. Nuptial ties with the lower middle class were even more tenuous. However, it will be recalled that the social status of the merchants is not determinable and also that among the cases on which we have no information, the lower middle class may be overrepresented.

Was the daughter of a businessman more likely to marry a businessman if she did not have a brother who was willing and able to go into the father's business?[74] In families in which there was no son at all, the daughters married businessmen only slightly more frequently: thirty-nine percent of the sons-in-law were businessmen, as opposed to thirty-six percent over all. However, if there were sons in the family, but these did not become businessmen, the daughters married businessmen *less frequently* (in twenty-two percent of the cases). This rather surprising finding shows that sons-in-law were not generally used to replace sons unwilling or unable to go into business. Rather, families tended to follow a bourgeois or an aristocratic model. Thus, young businessmen often had a businessman for a brother-in-law.

What effect did the birth rank of brothers and sisters have upon their choice of partners? According to Hedwig Wachenheim, a banker's daughter born in 1891, the marriage of the eldest daughter was given the first priority in families of the upper bourgeoisie.[75] Yet my data show that the husband of the eldest daughter came from the same social circles as those of the younger daughters. Businessmen were the husbands of thirty-six percent of the eldest daughters, thirty-eight percent of the second-born, thirty-three percent of the third-born, and thirty-five percent of the fourth-born. Other differences in the professional distribution are virtually insignificant. It may be that these data mask certain subtle differences of status. The least we can say is that there does not seem to have been a typical marriage strategy that involved finding a husband of a particular professional group (say, a businessman) for the eldest daughter, and husbands of another professional group for younger daughters. This would seem to indicate (though this is not certain) that arranged marriages were no longer the norm.

According to a cohort analysis, businessmen born between 1860

74 A son-in-law who did not go into business until after his marriage was counted as a businessman.
75 See Wachenheim, *Vom Großburgertum*, p. 6.

and 1869 and their children were more likely to intermarry with
the traditional ruling class than were businessmen of the older generations. Aristocratization also increased to some extent as wealth
increased. One explanation might be that the less wealthy businessmen had a greater need for capital and better business connections,
whereas the wealthiest businessmen were in the best position to
bestow a large dowry on an aristocratic son-in-law. Furthermore,
the wealthier businessmen could better afford an aristocratic
lifestyle – the purchase of an estate, for example – that would make
their sons and daughters acceptable marriage partners.

There were hardly any ethnic differences in the pattern of marriage alliances. (See table 3.) Aristocrats were slightly underrepresented among the sons-in-law of Jewish businessmen, but were
slightly overrepresented among the fathers-in-law of the Jewish
businessmen's sons. This finding is surprising, since Jews were
overrepresented among the relatively strongly aristocratized group
of wealthiest businessmen.[76] Some might argue that concerted
Jewish efforts to find an aristocratic spouse were canceled out by
anti-Semitism. However, it should not be forgotten that the nobility was greatly interested in marriage connections with the Jewish
monied elite. Willy Liebermann von Wahlendorf at least claims
that he could easily have found a noble wife at the balls in Baden-
Baden.[77] In Berlin, army officers attended the balls and parties of
wealthy Jews in order to meet wealthy women.[78] It was thought
necessary to prohibit officers from seeking wives through marriage
brokers.[79] The family of the heavy industrialist Fritz von
Friedländer-Fuld was not completely accepted into Berlin society
until the daughter came of age. Many non-Jewish parents hoped
that their son would win the hand of this future heiress, who
would not only bring a large dowry into her marriage, but also as
an only child would also inherit a large fortune.[80]

For Jews who did not want to convert, endogamy was essential
to the preservation of Jewish identity. Werner Mosse holds the
opinion that even wealthy baptized Jews preferred to marry Jews.
"Mixed marriages created a variety of psychological and social

76. It is highly unlikely that this is the result of a skewed distribution of Jewish businessmen
in other categories. The cohort distribution and percentages of untitled and newly ennobled
persons were essentially the same as with non-Jews.
77. See Liebermann von Wahlendorf, *Erinnerung*, p. 116
78. See Huret, *En Allemagne. Berlin*, p. 347.
79. See Zobeltitz, *Chronik*, vol. 1, p 74.
80. See Schwering, *Berlin Court*, p. 217.

Table 3. Intermarriage by Religion[a] (in %)

a. Jewish businessmen

	RELATIONSHIP TO BUSINESSMEN		
OCCUPATIONAL GROUP	FATHER-IN-LAW	SON'S FATHER-IN-LAW	SON-IN-LAW
Pre-industrial elite (without civil servants)	5.9	24.2	26.7
Upper civil servants	2.0	3.0	5.8
Professionals, academics[b]	9.8	12.1	9.3
Big businessmen	43.1	39.4	23.3
Businessmen: status unknown	31.4	15.2	19.8
Lower middle class	7.8	3.0	12.8
Other[c]	—	3.0	2.4
Total (in %)	100.0	99.9	100.1
Total (absolute)	51	33	86

b. Protestant and Catholic businessmen

Pre-industrial elite (without civil servants)	9.8	23.9	33.1
Upper civil servants	4.5	8.5	10.7
Professionals, academics[b]	9.0	10.4	11.2
Big businessmen	28.2	15.4	14.5
Businessmen: status unknown	42.0	32.8	20.1
Lower middle class	6.5	7.0	8.6
Other[c]	—	2.0	1.8
Total (in %)	100.0	100.0	100.0
Total (absolute)	245	201	338

[a] Differentiation of data in table 2. Without cases in which religion or ethnic identity is unknown.

[b] Universities, college preparatory schools, and school administration.

[c] Rentiers; upper class, profession unknown.

84

problems resulting from disparities in cultural attitudes and interests, in social origin and life styles."[81] Fritz von Friedländer-Fuld, according to family friend Carl Fürstenberg, very much wanted to marry a Jewish woman.[82] In addition, many Jews did not think highly of marriage connections with the nobility, because they feared that a noble man or woman would have little respect and love for their children. These fears were by no means unfounded. For example, shortly after the 1887 wedding of Gerson Bleichröder's daughter Else to Baron Bernhard von Uechtritz, the marriage broke up. Uechtritz kept the dowry, amounting to 2.5 million marks.[83] Friedländer-Fuld did not allow his daughter to marry a German aristocrat but sent her on a trip to England. As was to be expected, she fell in love with an English nobleman whom she later married.[84] Thus, the thesis that in Wilhelmine Germany Jews overcompensated for feelings of inferiority through aristocratization does not hold true insofar as marriage is concerned, not only because of the exclusivity and anti-Semitism of the nobility, but also because of a healthy reticence on the part of the Jewish economic elite and their social cohesiveness.

One of the most striking findings is that the newly ennobled businessmen – constituting eighteen percent of the businessmen of this study, but a very tiny percentage of all the big businessmen in the German Empire – behaved with regard to aristocratization in a manner that diverged from that of the rest of the group. (See table 4.) Whereas the degree of assimilation of bourgeois businessmen's families with the pre-industrial elite can be described as moderate, the aristocratization of the newly ennobled families was extensive, though not overwhelming. Ennoblement thus constituted an important decision in the history of a businessman's family, opening the way towards further aristocratization. This process was confined to a small, though highly visible, group of businessmen.

Procreation

In data on the 502 wealthiest Wilhelmine businessmen, we find clear signs of conscious attempts to limit the number of children.

---

81. Mosse, *German-Jewish*, p. 93

82. See H. Furstenberg, *Erinnerungen*, p 128

83 See Stern, *Gold and Iron*, p. 492

84 See Buchanan, *Ambassador's Daughter*, p 46; Schwering, *Berlin Court*, p 218 She later left him, according to her mother-in-law, because she discovered that she was too much of a German to be able to spend the rest of her life in England

Table 4. Intermarriage by Titles of Nobility[a] (in %)

a. Businessmen without a title of nobility

	RELATIONSHIP TO BUSINESSMEN		
OCCUPATIONAL GROUP	FATHER-IN-LAW	SON'S FATHER-IN-LAW	SON-IN-LAW
Pre-industrial elite (without civil servants)	3.3	11.3	22.9
Upper civil servants	4.3	8.5	10.6
Professionals, academics[b]	10.5	12.7	13.0
Big businessmen	27.6	21.8	18.3
Businessmen: status unknown	45.2	37.3	24.3
Lower middle class	9.0	5.6	9.0
Other[c]	—	2.8	2.0
Total (in %)	99.9	100.0	100.1
Total (absolute)	210	142	301

b. Businessmen with a title of nobility granted after 1870

Pre-industrial elite (without civil servants)	19.4	42.3	49.5
Upper civil servants	2.8	2.8	8.1
Professionals, academics[b]	6.9	8.5	6.3
Big businessmen	40.3	15.5	12.6
Businessmen: status unknown	27.8	21.1	9.9
Lower middle class	2.8	9.9	11.7
Other[c]	—	—	1.8
Total (in %)	100.0	100.1	99.9
Total (absolute)	72	71	111

[a] Differentiation of data in table 2. Without cases in which religion or ethnic identity is unknown

[b] Universities, college preparatory schools, and school administration

[c] Rentiers, upper class, profession unknown.

86

On the average, the businessmen in my study fathered 3.7 children, of which 3.5 were the issue of the first marriage.[85] Only eleven percent had seven to twelve children. Large families (with six or more children) became increasingly uncommon from one cohort to another, falling from twenty-three percent of the families of businessmen born in the 1840s, to sixteen percent of those born in the 1850s, to eleven percent of those born in the 1860s. Family planning evidently played a role (though it is difficult to explain the rise in the number of childless marriages). Heidi Rosenbaum ascribes the decrease in the number of children in businessmen's families to "the decreasing utilization of the family for business purposes at the end of the century."[86]

In the Wilhelmine monied elite, Jews had smaller families than non-Jews. In the literature on this subject, low marital fertility among Jews in imperial Germany is usually attributed to the fact that they belonged largely to the middle class and lived in cities.[87] However, my data show differences in fertility between Jews and non-Jews within the *same* social stratum. Most likely this was a response to the lack of alternate professions open to sons, as well as to the scarcity of appropriate marriage partners (i.e., those who were both wealthy and, in the case of practicing Jews, Jewish) for daughters and limited financial resources available for dowries. Thus, this seems to have been part of a broader strategy aimed at maintaining social status and ethnic identity in the next generation.

Schulamit Volkov sees low fertility rates in the German-Jewish upper middle class as a reaction to the wave of anti-Semitism of the Bismarck era. She sees this not as an indication of a continuation of peculiarly Jewish behavior – in the early nineteenth century the marital fertility of Jews was higher than that of non-Jews – but as the development of new ethnic characteristics that made Jews more modern than non-Jews. According to Volkov, this strategy developed in the face of discrimination made Jews the forerunners as far as the limitation of family size and education of children are con-

85. For comparative figures, see Nell, *Entwicklung*, pp. 58, 115. See also the figures for Breslau house owners in Knodel, *Decline*, p. 128 and for independents in industry (a category that also includes artisans, small-time manufacturers, and tradesmen) in Castell, "Forschungsergebnisse," p. 167. On the decline of marital fertility and on contraception in the English bourgeoisie, see Banks, *Prosperity* and *Victorian Values*, pp. 97–116.

86. See Rosenbaum, *Formen*, p. 354.

87. See Richarz, *Jüdisches Leben*, vol. 2, pp. 13–14. The low birth rate was also related to the age structure in the Jewish population. Because of large-scale emigration, a smaller percentage of Jews were in the marriageable or fertile age groups than in the population at large. See also Prinz, *Juden*, pp. 160–61.

cerned. Paradoxically, the modernity of Jewish "intimate culture" made Jews "different," and thus actually prevented the acceptance of Jews.[88]

In the group under study here, lower fertility rates were achieved at least in part through late marriage. Only three percent of the non-Jewish businessmen, but nine percent of the Jewish business-men in my study, married between the ages of forty and forty-nine. Their brides were also somewhat older. Moreover, an unusually high percentage never married: seventeen percent of the 115 Jewish businessmen remained single at least to the age of forty, as opposed to seven percent of the 270 Protestant businessmen and three percent of the thirty-six Catholic businessmen.[89] The expla-nation appears to lie in the difficulties wealthy Jewish men had in finding an appropriate wife, as well as the anti-fertility strategy of this group. It is striking that discrimination and minority status had such a marked impact on the behavior of the members of this very privileged elite. Volkov to the contrary, this behavior was decidedly un-modern in an important respect: it involved a high degree of gratification postponement or gratification denial.

Conclusion

As far as courtship and spouse selection are concerned, patriarchal structures were on the decline in wealthy business families of the pre-war era. Arranged marriages and more indirect forms of parental intervention were gradually being supplanted by a more individualistic model. This came about because of the declining importance of the dowry and the increasing complexity of the woman's role in the business family. Who but the businessman himself could best select a woman who could fulfill this role? What was termed "love," or at least the sort of love that could lead to

88. See Volkov, "Jüdische Assimilation," pp 332–47

89. Including only cases on which information was available (In nineteen cases the marital status was unknown.) This figure does not include heavy industrialists with older titles of nobili-ty. Forty years was used as a cut-off because in many of the contemporary primary sources, we often only learn about the businessman's life until about this age.

In 1910, eight percent of the entire male population in the 50- to 54-year-old age group was single. This figure was calculated by John E. Knodel on the basis of employment statistics. The percentage of unmarried people in the cities was somewhat higher. An exact figure for the cities is not given. See Knodel, *Decline*, pp. 70, 96. The nuptiality rate for Jews in the population at large was also lower than that for non-Jews. See Schmelz, "Die demographische Entwicklung"; Volkov, "Jüdische Assimilation," p. 341.

marriage, was strongly colored by an attraction to characteristics held in high esteem by one's social class. Thus, the emergence of the "love marriage" did not undermine either the economic role or the social status of the business family.

Patriarchal structures were not yet dead, however. What was a "love marriage" from the man's perspective could be an arranged marriage from the woman's perspective. Moreover, in this class, only men were allowed to engage in premarital sexual relations, though there were individual cases of wealthy women who claimed sexual freedom for themselves in certain phases of their lives.

What social classes did wealthy business families intermarry with? In this elite, endogamy was stronger among the businessmen than among their offspring. Conversely, intermarriage with the aristocracy was commoner among the children, particularly the daughters. From this one might conclude that while the males ensured the continuing role of the family in business (as will be seen in a later chapter), the female lines secured ties with the pre-industrial elite. Though this certainly did happen in some families, it is important to remember that daughters were more likely to marry businessmen if their brothers went into business. Conversely, in families in which the sons turned their backs on the business world, daughters seldom married businessmen. This means that each wealthy business family tended to orient itself either to a bourgeois or an aristocratic model. The latter was largely confined to newly ennobled families, a tiny elite-within-an-elite. Clearly a fusion of capitalist and agrarian elites did not take place, and most of the monied business elite retained a bourgeois pattern of intermarriage.

Was this just the result of the nobility's social exclusivity? There is a fair amount of evidence to the contrary. As we have seen in the last chapter, the ennobled business elite was at least in part a self-selected group. Seeking or accepting a title of nobility was evidently in many cases part of a larger agenda that a family had set for itself. Most families were not attracted by this social model. Moreover, it is certainly clear that Jewish heiresses were very much in demand among officers and other noblemen who were not economically well-off. Presumably, this would be even more the case for the daughters of very wealthy Protestant and Catholic businessmen.

Ethnicity had a definite impact on behavior. Though the Jewish business families in this study showed no greater tendency towards aristocratization than the non-Jewish, distinctly Jewish patterns were found in courtship, marriage, and procreation. The arranged marriage seems to have been more prevalent among Jews because endogamy was necessary for those who wanted to preserve their ethnic or religious identity, while the pool of prospective Jewish partners was small. Jewish businessmen remained single more often or married later than their non-Jewish counterparts, apparently in response to the lack of suitable Jewish partners, but also as part of an unconscious attempt to keep the fertility rate down. This pattern of gratification postponement or gratification denial (also to be found in arranged marriages) may be seen as a strategy aimed at maintaining ethnic identity and social status in the face of anti-Semitism, which limited the marriage and career opportunities open to Jewish men and women, even those born into the elite. In this case, discrimination tended not to promote "modern" behavior, but to preserve patriarchal structures. On the other hand, the Jewish promotion of education (also a response to anti-Semitism) had the opposite effect. Moreover, the wealthiest Jewish business families seem to have felt that they could very well afford "modern" behavior, ranging from Carl Fürstenberg's unconventional love marriage, which grew out of an illicit relationship, to Paul Wallich's choice of a wife who shared many of his intellectual interests. While the meaning of the differences in behavior between Jews and non-Jews is ambiguous, it is clear that they did exist.

Chapter 3

Family Life and Power Relations within the Family

The Men of the Family: Fathering and the Socialization of Sons

How did the rearing of boys in this class help them to become men, specifically businessmen? What part did the father play in the transmission of professional, class, and gender roles? Was he an unchallengeable authoritarian figure? The image of the authoritarian German father has been with us for a long time, but little empirical research has been done on this subject. In a recent study on the mentality of the "Wilhelminians" (the generation born between 1853 and 1865), Martin Doerry suggests that authoritarian family structures (and the inability of the "Wilhelmians" to rebel against them) were part of the foundation of the authoritarian political system of Wilhelmine Germany. Ingebord Weber-Kellermann has gone so far as to link the authoritarian German family with the rise of National Socialism.[1]

The authoritarian father implicitly plays an important role in debates concerning the nature of (male) adolescence in turn-of-the-century Germany. Across Europe, adolescence had come into existence earlier, but only in the late nineteenth century did it take on the more modern form of a prolonged stage of dependence and crisis, particularly for young men.[2] Boys needed help in coping

1. See Doerry, *Übergangsmenschen*, esp. pp. 99–100, 176–78, 187–89. He believes that among those born after 1865 there was a change in mentality brought about, not by changes in the family, but by larger political developments (apparently meaning German unification). This change of mentality found expression in a greater capacity for self-criticism and in a decline of militarism, imperialism, and nationalism, leading to "the crisis of the Second German Empire" and the transition to modernity. See Weber-Kellermann, "German Family."

2. Since the eighteenth century, adolescence has for a wider range of classes become a stage of self-discovery that has led to the development of an "inner-directed personality." There is some evidence, however, that youth, as a phase of life, existed much earlier. See Mitterauer, *Sozialgeschichte*, pp. 22–25. See in addition Hermann, "Jugend," pp. 133–5. Development psychologist Erik Erikson regards the crisis of adolescence as a universal phenomenon. He considers it a necessary phase of life that is linked to physical sexual maturation. The thesis of the universality of the adolescence crisis has been refuted in historical studies. See Mitterauer, *Sozialgeschichte*, pp. 19–20.

with the psychic and social consequences of this long phase of dependency (brought about by growing training and educational requirements). John R. Gillis believes that the institutional setting was far superior in Britain, where young men attended "public schools," than in Germany, where they spent their teenage years in the (authoritarian) family.[3] Tom Taylor has challenged the notion that, in Germany, middle-class families were authoritarian and middle-class teenage boys more repressed and alienated than in other industrialized European countries. He presents evidence that German youth was sexually active and that student and youth suicide was neither very prevalent in Germany nor atypical for industrialized European societies. He also argues that the major cause of conflict between fathers and sons was not the authoritarianism of the father, but the fact that middle-class males were forced to devote many more years to education and training than, say, in the United States. As a result, in Germany young men were forced to live at home longer and postpone marriage and the attainment of independence.[4]

In terms of inner dynamics, did the wealthy business family fit the mold of the middle-class family, or did it reorganize itself in response to the enormous tasks, as well as privileges, of this elite? Were relations between parents and children characterized by the emotional intensity described by Shorter and by the preoccupation with children's education and discipline described by Ariès?[5] This section is devoted to the rearing of boys, especially by their fathers. The story will be taken up again in chapter 4, where we turn to adolescent rebellion and its impact on the professional lives of businessmen's sons. The second half of the present chapter is devoted to the role of girls and women in the wealthy business family.

It must be cautioned that the value of memoirs as a source of information on childhood and youth is limited. The tendency to romanticize this period of life is notoriously great. In addition, the powers of recollection of many human beings are not sufficiently great to reconstruct childhood experiences accurately thirty or fifty years later. Such sources need to be interpreted with great care. The typical businessman's son provides little information on his socialization as a future businessman. The businessman himself and his wife almost never give details in their autobiographies about

3. See Gillis, *Youth*, esp pp. 95–132.
4. See Taylor, "Images"; Taylor, "Transition," pp 635–58, Taylor, "Crisis."
5 See Introduction See also Ariès, *L'Enfant*, Shorter, *Making*; also Schutze, "Mutterliebe."

their ideas on child rearing. Probably this was regarded as too mundane a subject to merit a place in an autobiography. It is also possible that little thought was given to the raising of children, despite the Enlightenment and Freud. Such material as exists will be presented here.

The birth of the first son was regarded as a joyful and significant event in a wealthy business family, since great importance was attached to male succession. In the final analysis many businessmen considered the main purpose of their labors to be the building of a family enterprise that would be passed on from generation to generation. A union official is said to have asked Hugo Stinnes, "Tell me, Herr Stinnes, for what do you work so hard and torment yourself so much?" To which Stinnes replied, "For my children."[6] August Thyssen wanted to establish a dynasty.[7] F.A. Krupp mentions in his will that his wife had failed to bear him a son. When Gustav Krupp von Bohlen und Halbach's first son Alfred was born, the father sent an announcement to the firm's board of directors that contained the wish: ". . . may he grow up in the Krupp works and through practical work prepare himself for the assumption of the responsible duties whose magnitude I recognize with each passing day."[8]

Hans Adt writes of his own birth in 1888: "Since my father was the only son of my grandfather Johann Baptist Adt, as his brother Otto had died a few years previously, there was great joy over the fact that the very first child was a son who would carry on the name. As was then the custom, the first son was given the Christian names of all living ancestors."[9] The Leipzig publisher Alfred Ackermann and his wife were married for fifteen years and had three daughters before a son was born to them in 1900. The wife wrote, "The joy and surprise was great for all of us and especially for my elderly father-in-law when, on 5 June 1900 in the Ackermann home on Bismarck Street, the long-yearned-for heir and bearer of the name was born."[10]

Most businessmen's sons were initiated into the business activities of their fathers at home, not in any planned or organized way, but rather simply because the father brought his preoccupations and sometimes even his work home. For example, Hans

6 Brinckmeyer, *Hugo Stinnes*, p. 11.
7. See Treue, *Die Feuer*, Arnst, *August Thyssen*.
8. Klass, *Die drei Ringe*, p 325. On F.A Krupp, see Boelcke, *Krupp*, p 173.
9. Adt, *Aus meinem Leben*, pp. 130–31
10 Quoted in Schulze, *Geschichte*, p 121.

Fürstenberg (born 1890) wrote: "If I ask myself when my professional life actually began, I am almost inclined to answer: in early childhood, because I spent it, as I have already reported, in a family home to which the father often brought business friends. Besides, he discussed business matters with our wise mother almost every day in the presence of the children . . . From the time when I was barely ten years old I gradually got to hear more and more about the affairs of my father's bank, the *Berliner Handels-Gesellschaft*, though I, of course did not retain much more of what I picked up than just the names."[11] Edmund Stinnes (born 1896), the son of Hugo Stinnes, told the journalist Andreas Kohlschütter that in the dinner table conversations in his home, almost nothing but business was discussed. Edmund Stinnes developed a critical attitude toward this: "My father's business interests crowded out every other topic of conversation. And he had it all at his fingertips; he knew everything by heart: numbers, dates, details. He always gave us children business reports and files to read in bed instead of picture books or fairy tales."[12]

Since the businessman's place of residence and his place of work were almost always separate from one another by the Wilhelmine period, the businessman's son did not come regularly to his father's workplace. For example, when the family of the owner of the Tietz department store rose socially, little Georg Tietz (born 1889) was no longer allowed to visit the store daily because this was not deemed proper. Not until he was older did he again come into contact with the business world of his father. He wrote: "It was a piece of good luck for me that I gained insight into business management, the establishment of new enterprises, the purchase of real estate, construction, and many other things, almost as if it were a game."[13]

Many businessmen were afraid that their wealth would weaken the entrepreneurial spirit in their sons. Wilhelm Merton wrote, "When wealth increases in a flourishing commercial enterprise, the magnitude of the responsibilities of the head of the company increase proportionately. But the younger generation forms the concept in childhood and youth that if the wealth is there, it will of course always increase. This must have a harmful effect that detracts from their vital energy."[14] As a reaction to this danger

11 H. Furstenberg, *Erinnerungen*, pp 15–16.
12. Kohlschütter, *Ein Genie*, p. 44; see p. 43
13. Tietz, *Hermann Tietz*, p 74; see pp. 50–51, 64
14 Achinger, *Wilhelm Merton*, p. 244 Quotation not footnoted.

94

many parents tried to teach their children the "value of money." Although he spent large sums for other things, the Berlin private banker Valentin Weisbach watched over the small expenditures of his son in order to prevent "extravagance." At the same time he advised the son to dress well because it was important to make a good impression. A second example is that of Carl and Aniela Fürstenberg. While they spent their evenings at elegant soirées, their children sat at home eating "plain food."[15] Daughters received similar treatment. F.A. Krupp's wife Marga raised her daughters Bertha and Barbara in almost Spartan simplicity. Countess Brockdorf wrote in her diary after a meeting with that family: "It was almost touching what pains Frau Krupp took to dress and raise her two daughters, charming little girls, as simply and modestly as possible – certainly no small task in this environment."[16]

Marga Berck, née Melchers, the daughter of the very wealthy Bremen wholesale merchant Carl Theodor Melchers, relates in her autobiography: "Bertha [her sister] and I were raised quite simply. Our clothing was handmade, while the other children were dressed in the most enchanting clothing from Lessmann. We had been so convinced of our poverty up to that time that we accepted our lot modestly and with resignation." The children were required to use the service entrance in order to spare the runners on the stairways.[17] Another member of the family, Gustav Adolf Melchers (born 1869), received one mark per week as pocket money when he was seventeen years old, but he had to keep a record on how he spent it. However, his mother and grandfather secretly gave him a bit more.[18] The contrast in this family between private parsimony and public show of wealth could hardly have been greater.[19]

However, not every family followed this strategy. Edmund Stinnes writes: "It is common knowledge that the opinions of rich parents vary considerably with regard to handing out pocket money. Some want to give their children a minimum so that they will learn to appreciate the value of money. Others believe that their children should have access to a great deal of money as early

15. See Weisbach, *Und alles*, p. 117; H. Fürstenberg, *Erinnerungen*, p. 8.

16. Quoted in Klass, *Die drei Ringe*, p. 301. On Gustav Krupp von Bohlen und Halbach, see pp. 322–24. Further examples in Klass, "Bertha Krupp," p. 3; Manchester, *Arms*, p. 226.

17. Berck, *Aus meiner Kinderzeit*, p. 12. She is referring here to the 1880s. Fritz Andreae is also said to have concealed from his daughter, Ursula Mangoldt, the fact that her family was rich. See Mangoldt, *Auf der Schwelle*, p. 58.

18. See Melchers, *Erinnerungen*, p. 97.

19. See ibid., p. 76.

Carl Fürstenberg with his son Hans, about 1900

as possible so that they will learn from their financial mistakes while they are still young. My father belonged to the first group."[20] Moritz Warburg, a Hamburg banker, gave his sons as much pocket money as they wanted.[21]

What other values did the parents try to teach their children? Hedwig Wachenheim (born 1891), the daughter of a Mannheim banker, points out in her autobiography that in the upper middle class, parents sent their children to church without attending themselves. In the economic elite, the parents did not rely on schools and universities to make cultivated human beings out of their children, but tried themselves to pass on their appreciation of culture. And of course the parents introduced their children into society. Carl Friedrich Siemens (born 1872), who later became head of the Siemens concern, spent the winter of 1894/95 with his mother in Munich: "The rich cultural treasures of the city, its theaters and concert halls, but above all its stimulating social life, represented excellent cultural values for her son, and she intended to participate in their transmittal."[22] Heinrich Wiegand (born 1855) read aloud to his children from history books in the evening and discussed works of art with them. Gerta Warburg showed art books to her grandchildren (ages five to eleven), teaching them to identify works of art and the names of the painters, and testing them on their knowledge from time to time.[23] Parents were also concerned about their children's physical fitness, especially their posture. For example, a gymnastics teacher was hired by the Warburgs in order to improve the posture of their children.[24]

Many autobiographies convey the impression that the children of this class were pushed, protected, and controlled to a high degree. The following passage, which related to Hans Adt in his thirteenth year, clearly shows what a protective environment he grew up in: "I remember clearly that we were all compelled to go to confession. Since I had been so strictly controlled at home by my parents, it was difficult for me to think of some sort of sin that I might have committed. After thinking it over I actually came up with some sins, namely, that I had once misbehaved toward my

20. Kohlschutter, *Ein Genie*, p 37

21. See Warburg, *Aus meinen Aufzeichnungen*, p. 12; Wenzel-Burchard, *Granny*, p 42

22 G Siemens, *Carl Friedrich von Siemens*, p. 26. On Wachenheim, see Wachenheim, *Vom Großburgertum*, p 11.

23. On Wiegand, see Petzet, *Heinrich Wiegand*, p 293. On Warburg, see Wenzel-Burchard, *Granny*, p. 27.

24. See Wenzel-Burchard, *Granny*, pp 43–44

mother and that I had use a naughty word. I was happy that I did have something that I could confess."[25]

In these families the father was usually absent because of his work. When Georg Tietz was little, his father Oscar left the house at seven, came home at noon for lunch, which lasted half an hour, then went back to work, came to supper at seven, went back to work after half an hour, and finally came home for the day after the child was asleep. Oscar Tietz never took a vacation. In summer he sent his wife and children to Tölz or Lake Tegern, where he could visit them on Sundays.[26] Hans Fürstenberg writes: "Let it be clear that except for vacations, about the only time I could see my father was on Sundays and holidays and for a few moments in the early evening. Since the Berlin 'season' lasted about eight months and literally every evening my parents either were invited out to dinner or entertained guests themselves, my encounters with my father were almost completely limited to the time when he was getting dressed. When I was especially high in his favor, I was allowed to go into the bathroom with him beforehand. . . ."[27] Gustav Krupp von Bohlen und Halbach is said to have spent only an hour a week with his eight children (born from 1907 on). A biographer of Heinrich Ehrhardt says that he also had little time for his family. He only went walking in the woods with his wife and children (born from the late-1860s on) sometimes in summer when he was staying in Thuringia. Mine director Gustav Knepper could not have had much time for his children (born from 1898 on): during the years 1905 to 1915 he took no vacations and went hunting on weekends. Munich banker Wilhelm von Finck had little time for his family according to his biographer Bernhard Hoffmann, who otherwise found much to praise in Finck. When he was in Munich he worked eleven hours a day. Once a year he took three weeks of vacation.[28] Baron Walther von Selve (born 1876) writes about his father Gustav Selve, owner of a brass rolling-mill: "He was little concerned about the raising of the children. He spent the time he was not working in intense social activity. . . ."[29] The men of the business world also took extended business trips that kept them

25 Adt, *Aus meinem Leben*, p 135.

26 See Tietz, *Hermann Tietz*, pp 37, 49

27 H Furstenberg, *Erinnerungen* , pp. 6–7.

28 On Krupp, see Manchester, *Arms*, p. 252. On Ehrhardt, see Wilden, "Heinrich Ehrhardt," p. 185. On Knepper, see Bacmeister, *Gustav Knepper*, p. 86 On Finck, see Hoffmann, *Wilhelm von Finck*, pp. 183–84

29. Selve, *Treue um Treue*, p. 82.

away from home. There are very few examples of businessmen who regularly spent time with their children. Frankfurt banker Wilhelm Daniel Weismann, who did not marry until he was forty-five, can be regarded as one such exception.[30]

The habitual absence of the father had varying effects on the son. Carl Fürstenberg succeeded in developing a positive emotional relationship with his son Hans, who writes: "My father made up for a lot of this in long weekend outings and long hikes in the Grunewald. He liked to be with me, wanted to teach me about things, liked to talk to me." Carl Fürstenberg was at the same time a towering figure of authority in his son's life. Hans Fürstenberg wrote about his apprenticeship in the *Berliner Handelsgesellschaft*: "I am indebted to my father for the fact that I work hard. On the other hand, I was sometimes afraid of asking too many stupid questions. I can imagine that the same thing has happened, and is still happening, to some of the sons of prominent fathers, and hence I would like to advise the fathers of gifted sons to send them off for training somewhere else, rather than in their own business."[31]

On the other hand, Werner Weisbach (born 1873) wrote that his father Valentin, a Berlin private banker, was always "a complete stranger" to him. The reason, however, seems to lie more in the father's authoritarianism than in his neglect. The passages in Weisbach's memoirs about him constitute an almost classic description of the authoritarian father:

> Every day he appeared in the children's room for only a few moments, and at such times he usually made a harried and ill-humored impression. He had no ability whatever to understand the spirit of a child. He used the few moments we were together, crammed into his strenuous business day, to remonstrate, to reproach, and if some irregularity had taken place, to administer a spanking. Along with all the respect I felt for him, he appeared to me as a sort of punitive deity; my only feelings toward him were of anxiety, and I awaited his coming with fear and trembling. The only thing he accomplished through his behavior was to frighten and intimidate. . . .The constant nagging about the smallest and pettiest matters helped to depress my spirits. Whether one ate at the hotel dining room and put too much of one dish on one's plate, whether one did not sit straight enough in one's chair, whether one showed too little respect in greeting an older person, – those and similar actions led to sharp reprimands. Even when I left school and went to the university, yes, as long as he lived my father felt duty-bound to intervene in my

30. See Klotzer, "Wilhelm Daniel Weismann," p. 254. His children were born after 1893.
31. H. Fürstenberg, *Erinnerungen*, pp. 8, 20.

personal affairs and to make decisions, even when he had no insight into the matter at hand. His deepest desire was to be my constant adviser and mentor in all things. Nothing was supposed to happen without his knowledge and consent. He had worked out a system of ethics and teaching that he liked to elaborate for me while taking walks and the essentials of which he worked into his letters when I was away. . . . The intention behind his method of child rearing was not so much that I should develop and mature, but rather that he should rework me and prepare me for a relationship to the outside world that suited him. No thought whatsoever was given to my spiritual nature and potential.[32]

The relationship between Emil and Walther Rathenau, as analyzed by Hans Dieter Hellige, also has certain authoritarian aspects.[33] Having once failed in business, Emil Rathenau was obsessed with rebuilding his company, much to the detriment of his family. As a child, Walther Rathenau clearly felt a great deal of resentment towards his overbearing, emotionally distant father. Later Walther Rathenau embraced art and culture as a reaction to what he saw as his father's crass materialism. Walther's sister Edith (born 1883), whose married name was Andreae, also suffered under the lovelessness of this home. Her daughter wrote: "My mother was very unhappy at home because she, who had a great need for affection, found no response to her romantic desires, no fulfillment of her dreams. Actually she received kindness and warmth only from our servant girl Bertha."[34]

Gustav Krupp von Bohlen und Halbach has been portrayed as an authoritarian father: "The authority of the master of the house, husband and father is never in any doubt, and automatic respect causes the children to consider carefully with what kinds of requests they can approach their fathers. He is an inexorable disciplinarian who is not perceived as such only because his own self-discipline serves as a model."[35] Paul Ernst writes about August Thyssen: "His heart was as hard as his steel; anyone who got in his way found that out, and so did the members of his own family. He did not in any way respond to expressions of feeling or to ethical considerations in any of his dealings. Economic advantage was his only guiding principle, and its ruthless pursuit constituted the great unifying feature of his entire activity."[36] Edmund Stinnes

32. Weisbach, *Und alles*, pp. 21, 117–18
33. Hellige, "Rathenau," p. 30.
34. Mangoldt, *Auf der Schwelle*, p. 21
35. Klass, *Die drei Ringe*, pp. 325–26 A problematic aspect of this biography is the fact that it includes no footnotes and no identification of sources.
36. Arnst, *August Thyssen*, p. 71. His children were born in the 1870s

characterizes his relationship to his father in the following terms: "I had difficulties with my parents and especially with my father. He was an overwhelming man, a powerful man, and not only in Germany. But in his own way he had a loving attachment to his three eldest children."[37] Corporal punishment is mentioned in only two cases. One appears in Werner Weisbach's autobiography. In the other case it was not the father but the tutor that was involved.[38] Silence on this taboo subject does not, however, mean that children were no longer beaten or whipped in this social class. Moreover, the authoritarian structures at home were reinforced by those at school.[39]

However, numerous examples of more liberal child rearing methods can also be found. Carl Duisberg, the general director of the Bayer corporation, wrote in a letter: "Our young ruffians get wilder and sassier every day, but that does not disturb me, because it is easier to tame than to bring to life." Duisberg reportedly encouraged the "human individuality" of his children (who were born from 1889 on). When one of his sons had problems at school, he is said to have reacted with understanding.[40] Wilhelm Merton also appears to have been a patient, liberal father. A letter from his 14-year-old son Adolf written in 1901 attests to a warm, relatively open relationship between them. In a congratulatory letter from Adolf to his father, the tone is unconstrained and jocular: "Today at lunch at the Ladenbergs' I ate with the boys, while uncle and aunt ate earlier with mother and Walter. My behavior was lively, if not to say boisterous. Then I went to the drawing class at school, but I cut the second hour of it because I had a bad case of stage fright." At the end of the letter, he congratulated his father on the receipt of the *Wilhelmsorden* (an imperial decoration) followed by the words of a little ditty vaguely similar to "For he's a jolly good fellow. . . ." The tone of another passage reflects a deep admiration for the father.[41] The letters of Georg von Siemens to his daughter contain affectionate passages, and also light-hearted ones such as the following: "I want to add only a few words to your mother's letter to tell you that one does not need to be very sick in order to feel a strong aversion to business trips and social

37. Kohlschutter, *Ein Genie*, p 9.

38 See Selve, *Treue*, p. 86.

39. See Hellige, "Rathenau," p. 31; Tietz, *Hermann Tietz*, pp. 38–39, 52, 57; Weisbach, *Und alles*, p 53.

40 See Flechtner, *Carl Duisberg*, pp. 171–72; quotation on p 171

41 Achinger, *Wilhelm Merton*, pp. 231–32; see p. 225. Also see letter from Walter Merton, pp. 233–35.

amusements. A little coughing and sniffling alone suffice to bring about such an aversion; they are injurious to one's mood but not to one's health. Incidentally, if Herr Cassel, whose letters I for some time have not answered, considers me to be sick and therefore excuses me, do not contradict him. I have recently committed so many sins of omission that I can cheerfully accept the sympathy of my fellow men as a reinforcement for my apologies."[42]

Willy Liebermann von Wahlendorf writes about his father:

> Our father was a proud, distinguished, infinitely kind, tender-hearted man, and a good Jew. His three sons were his great worry and his great joy. His image – I knew my mother too slightly – has always been in my mind's eye, encouraging or consoling, through all the happy days, and even more frequent days of suffering – of my most eventful life. And just as I am sure that he in his infinite kindness would have forgiven me for the many stupidities I have committed – I have never done real harm to any human being – I have always up to this very day accounted to him in spirit for all my actions that I could assume he would not have approved.[43]

Edmund Stinnes describes his father as being tyrannical and unjust, but in the final analysis the positive predominates: "We had a good relationship until my father's will was read.[44] I would say that in general, the more one can admire a person, the more difficulties one has with that person. That is not a contradiction. What especially impressed me about my father was his greatness of spirit in a completely chaotic time."[45] This businessman's son overcame his feelings of fear and hatred toward the towering figure of his father in the knowledge that he would become, or had become, just as strong. There is a decided consciousness of his own strength in the sentence "the more one can admire a person, the more difficulties one has with that person." In sum, though the stereotypical authoritarian German father was still alive and well in this class, we also find many examples of loving fathers. It cannot be said with certainty whether this is the result of the decline of patriarchal structures. Patriarchal structures did not necessarily preclude emotionally satisfying relationships, particularly between fathers and sons. However, the most important point is that the authoritarian

---

42. Letter dated 12 January, 1892. Quoted in Helfferich, *Georg von Siemens*, vol. 3, p. 336; also, see pp. 245, 254–56.

43. Liebermann von Wahlendorf, *Erinnerung*, p. 99.

44. In it partiality was shown to a younger brother.

45. This refers to the period after the First World War. Kohlschütter, *Ein Genie*, p. 14; see pp. 9, 12.

father was by no means the norm in this class. In the next chapter, we will look at how the sons responded to these fathers, authoritarian and liberal.

How were wealthy business families able to motivate the sons to become businessmen if the fathers spent so little time with their sons? What kind of role model was the (largely) absent father? The son often saw the father when the latter was busy – discussing business affairs with the family or business associates, reading reports, or working in his office (when the son visited him there). The psychological implications of this tendency to reduce the father-son relationship to an introduction into professional life are interesting. Essentially, the idea was conveyed to the son that his father's love could be won only through professional successes comparable to those of his father. The father was a rather mysterious figure whom the son admired and longed to emulate. However, this must have seemed like quite a difficult task to a child or teenager. This was a psychological burden for many businessmen's sons, but in the final analysis it usually spurred them on to great achievements, as will be seen in chapter 4.

How middle class was the elite business family? The very wealthy businessman probably had less time for his children than was otherwise usual in the middle class. However, the wealthy business family shared other characteristics with other upper-middle-class families. Children of wealthy parents were generally closely supervised and insulated from the dangers of the outside world. Many parents of this class were very much concerned that their children not be corrupted by their wealth. They saw a Spartan upbringing as a way of teaching children that money could not be taken for granted. This meant that children of the wealthy propertied bourgeoisie had a great deal in common with children of the educated bourgeoisie. However, the growing tendency in some families to give children large allowances may have undermined this common ground. Many parents seem to have tried to introduce their children to high culture. Religion, on the other hand, does not seem to have played a very great role in this class.

The Role of the Businessman's Wife

The role of the wife in the bourgeois family of the nineteenth century has in recent years become the subject of a debate that has been shaped by larger debates within feminism. A number of historians are of the opinion that the polarization of gender roles in the nineteenth century[46] entailed a significant curtailment of the women's potential for development that was not in any way compensated. An important study by Ursi Blosser and Franziska Gerster about women in the upper bourgeoisie of Switzerland around 1900 emphasizes that "polite society" prescribed for women a role that required a high degree of suppression.[47] The "process of civilization"[48] put especially narrow limits on women, who were restrained not only by corsets and the rules of propriety, but also by socializing forces that suppressed sexuality and forcefully imposed passivity and obedience. Any woman who did not abide by the prevailing norms was threatened by exclusion from high society. Sibylle Meyer brings in another aspect in a study on Wilhelmine Germany, presenting bourgeois social life as a long succession of tedious, tiring, empty ceremonies that for women meant endless housework.[49]

The older literature sees the role of women in the upper bourgeoisie as subordinated to class interests. According to Thorstein Veblen, the "conspicuous leisure" of the middle-class wife had special significance as a status symbol. Wealth was also put on display through consumption and lavish entertaining, for which the wife was primarily responsible.[50] Dieter and Karin Claessens, on the other hand, see the role of the wife in the context of a strategy of self-legitimation, employed by capitalists to conceal the injustice of their position of dominance and to relieve their own feelings of guilt. The wife personified non-material traditional values, which reflected favorably on the capitalist, showing that he too valued things other than success. But the businessman's wife also demonstrated capitalist virtues, such as industriousness and thoroughness.[51]

Leonore Davidoff shows that the "ladies" of English society, while promoting the interests of their class, at the same time exercised real power.[52] Society functioned like an extended family that

46. See Allen, *Feminism*; Gerhard, *Verhältnisse*, p 65; Hausen, "Polarisierung", Pope, "Angels," pp 296–324, esp. pp. 298–304; Rosenbaum, *Formen*, esp pp. 373–78.
47. See Blosser and Gerster, *Töchter*. Also, see Kößler, *Mädchenkindheiten*; Eicke, "Teenager."
48. Elias, *Über den Prozeß*
49. See Meyer, *Das Theater.*
50. See Veblen, *Theory.*
51. See Claessens and Claessens, *Kapitalismus*, pp. 159–74.
52. See Davidoff, *Best Circles.* See also Davidoff and Hall, *Family Fortunes*, esp. pp. 279–87.

accepted and assimilated newcomers on a limited basis. Women were in charge of the rituals of acceptance and the rules of propriety that prevented new wealth from supplanting the old. Wives – primarily the matrons – decided who belonged to the "best circles" and who did not. The power of the wives reached its zenith in the period (about the middle of the nineteenth century) when political decisions were arrived at in private circles.

Bonnie G. Smith demonstrates that the wives of the northern French wealthy bourgeoisie wielded real power and participated in the shaping of their gender roles.[53] During the nineteenth century, as middle-class women stopped taking an active part in business, female values were re-defined. Reproductive and social functions gave the wife the feeling of power. For women, conspicuous consumption and the rules of society meant something different from what it did for men, in particular a glorification of the woman's role as wife and mother. Thus, far from being forced to conform to rules of etiquette and participate in rituals that only served their husbands' interests, bourgeois women helped mold rules that reflected female values, using domestic and social activities to put their own reproductive power on display.[54] Ideologically, the women of the bourgeoisie felt most attracted to the religious concept of the world in which the family and not the independent individual was the smallest element of human society. While the mentality of the northern French bourgeois men was strongly influenced by the rationalism of the Enlightenment, the women retreated into traditionalism. Thus came into being a destructive polarization of the roles of the sexes, along with a dangerous political trend.[55] Nonetheless, gender roles were generally not antagonistic. Especially the social efforts of the wives, while primarily "representing themselves," also furthered the interests of their husbands. Only in the realm of welfare work did the wives seek to impose their philosophy of life on the entire society, over the objections of men.

Other historians have drawn an unequivocally positive picture of the changes in gender roles in the nineteenth century, pointing to women's growing authority in the family as mothers,[56] women's

53 Smith, *Ladies*.
54. Smith points out contradictions in the way women saw themselves. "Femininity" meant for them both power and weakness (in particular, dependence on men).
55. "Science, rationality, and the values of liberal society passed her by as she maintained a reactionary posture Corporate politics appealed to her because they emphasized the hierarchic, tribal, blood-cult, anti-individualistic quality of the home." Smith, *Ladies*, p. 215
56 Schutze, "Mutterliebe," pp 118–33.

involvement in the spread of new technologies,[57] financial power, and participation in male relatives' professional activities.[58]

This study can make only a very modest contribution to this debate. The biographical and autobiographical literature utilized for this study provides a one-sided view, and does not do justice to the private "feminine" sphere. Areas such as sexuality and etiquette are hardly touched upon. This literature does contain interesting material on gender roles and power relationships, though the wife appears primarily in her social roles.

Representational duties undoubtedly held an important place in the life of the wife in the economic elite. Urban social life in the business elite was typified by frequent social gatherings, as will be discussed in chapter 6. Some of the wives were required either to entertain guests or to attend a social function outside the home every evening. The ladies of high society normally "received" on a particular day of the week.[59] In addition, a great deal of time was needed to take care of the correspondence required by etiquette. During her honeymoon in Rapallo, Hildegard Wallich, née Rehrmann, felt obliged to write thank-you letters for wedding presents – "not an especially pleasant diversion for a honeymoon trip."[60] Even if it did not conform to their personal inclinations, the wives took pains to fulfill their social obligations.[61]

This was an especially onerous burden for women whose husbands did not do their share. Mary Amelie Sloman, for example, wrote the following lines concerning her mother-in-law Criska Loesener, née Sloman (1841–1933), who lived in the home of her father, the Hamburg shipping magnate Robert Sloman; "I admired my mother-in-law Loesener who served as hostess in the home of her father. I know that she suffered from the fact that her husband had no liking for this social circle. He spoke no English and with-

---

57. See Branca, *Silent Sisterhood*. Also, see Branca, *Women*. Branca believes that women of the upper class were not compelled to adopt innovations such as the sewing machine because of their wealth, and thus remained more traditional in their patterns of behavior. For a critical appraisal of Branca's work, see Lewis, *Women*, esp. pp. 81–86 and 112–18.

58. See Peterson, *Family*. Petersen argues—most unconvincingly—that middle-class women in Victorian England were financially largely independent and that there was no real polarization of gender roles.

59. See, for example, Wenzel-Burchard, *Granny*, p. 16.

60. H. Wallich, *Erinnerungen*, p. 121. A similar example in von der Heydt, *Unser Haus*, p. 44

61. Albert Ballin's wife, who was not from a wealthy family, is a good example here. See Cecil, *Albert Ballin*, p. 29. For a further example, see Niendorf, *Geschichte*, p. 129. Wilhelm Merton's wife sometimes found it annoying to have to go somewhere in her husband's place. See Achinger, *Wilhelm Merton*, pp. 226–33.

drew to his room early in the evening. But she could not follow him because she had to entertain the guests."[62] Fritz Krupp in the last years of his life refused more and more to play host, thrusting this obligation upon his wife.[63] Several passages in the memoirs of Carl Fürstenberg show that he was very grateful to his wife for the enthusiasm and remarkable social skill with which she represented his bank.[64]

Closely related to the wife's representational duties was her responsibility for conspicuous consumption and for managing the household. Edith Andreae, née Rathenau, the wife of the banker Fritz Andreae, designed their first villa in Grunewald (a residential suburb of Berlin) and a country home on Lake Starnberg, decorating both houses to her own taste. Aniela Fürstenberg independently carried out the furnishing and decorating of the family villa in Grunewald.[65] In the more "modern" marriages, at least, the wife had considerable freedom with regard to other purchases. Hildegard Wallich writes: "He [her husband] would have bought anything I thought was pretty, and I soon learned that I had to be careful about admiring nice things, otherwise he bought them immediately, regardless whether we needed them or not."[66] Katharina von Kardorff-Oheimb (born 1880), whose first marriage was to the Berlin industrialist Felix Daelen, expressed herself similarly in her autobiography: "Felix and I loved one another. Both of us were high-spirited and happy, but I wasted much too much money. So I was happily married and was spoiled to an incredible degree by my husband."[67]

Considerable managerial skills were needed to run the large businessman's household. Gustav Krupp von Bohlen und Halbach turned over the management of the household almost completely to his wife Bertha. She drew up regulations for seventeen manservants

62. Sloman, *Erinnerungen*, p. 93.

63 See Berdrow, *Alfred Krupp*, pp. 208–10; Meisbach, *Friedrich Alfred Krupp*, pp 15–16

64. "Aniela successfully endeavored to give social activities in our own home a special flair. I have never been by nature a sociable person though I did have an extensive circle of friends and acquaintances in the 1870s and 1880s. It is only thanks to my ties to a beautiful, socially adept wife, who was exceptionally skilled in household matters, that my home was for twenty years one of the most sociable in Berlin." C. Fürstenberg, *Lebensgeschichte*, pp. 397–98. Admittedly, though, it is difficult here to distinguish between Carl Fürstenberg's feelings and those of his son Hans, who was the ghostwriter of this memoir.

65. Mangoldt, *Auf der Schwelle*, p. 56, C. Fürstenberg, *Lebensgeschichte*, p 331

66. H. Wallich, *Erinnerungen*, p. 121.

67. Kardorff-Oheimb, *Politik*, p. 43. However, the husband had a veto regarding his wife's appearance. For example, Wilhelm Merton once forbade his wife in Paris to wear a certain hat, because to him it seemed too unconventional. See Achinger, *Wilhelm Merton*, p. 246.

**Aniela Fürstenberg, reproduction of a painting by
L. Horovitz.**

and twenty-four maids and is said to have supervised them strictly in order to prevent love affairs and theft. When Gustav wanted to criticize the service personnel, he spoke to his wife who passed along the reprimand. In other households there was a smaller though still respectable number of domestic employees to oversee.[68]

The purchases for a large household also required organizational know-how.[69] Carl Fürstenberg expressed admiration for his wife in this regard: "The management of such a household needs to be organized. I, who always took things for granted, was astonished later on to find voluminous notebooks in which great numbers of memoranda, visiting cards, and addresses were collected. They showed me for the first time how comprehensive the management of a household can be without the husband having the slightest inkling."[70] In many families the housewife kept book on receipts and expenditures.[71] Gertrud Wenzel-Burchard tells this story about her grandmother, Gerta Warburg, née Rindkopf: ". . . she entered all the expenditures of her large household in a notebook with many columns which grandfather audited from time to time. If there was a discrepancy between the expenditures and the remaining household money, Granny cheated with a flourish and wrote down: sundries, 100 marks (for which at the beginning of this century one could have bought out an entire shop full of needles, yarn, buttons and rubber bands)."[72] The first conclusion one might draw from this passage is that this bookkeeping was not conducted too seriously (perhaps arithmetic was considered "unfeminine"). The second might be that the husband did not hold his wife too strictly to account for her expenditures.

Women of this class did not have to do any housework themselves.[73] However, their husbands sometimes expected little services that had more of a symbolic significance. These little "tokens of love" tell us a great deal about the true power relationships in these marriages, as the following anecdote from Hildegard Wallich's autobiography illustrates. (This relates to a stay in Genoa during their honeymoon.)

68. Klass, "Bertha Krupp," p 7, Muhlen, *Die Krupps*, p 84.
69. See C. Furstenberg, *Lebensgeschichte*, p. 505.
70. Ibid , pp 505–506.
71. See ibid , p 505; Achinger, *Richard Merton*, pp. 22–23; Duisberg, *Nur ein Sohn*, p. 20.
72. Wenzel-Burchard, *Granny*, p 25
73. Despite the presence of servants in many middle-class homes, it was unusual – the privilege of the wealthy – for the wife to be freed from housework See Kaplan, *Making*, pp 25–41, and Meyer, *Das Theater*

We stayed there a few days longer than we had actually intended, and this was the reason: My father had accustomed me to the idea that on a trip everyone was supposed to pack his own belongings – everyone also carried his own suitcase, and in that way we did not need a porter. That was not necessary for Paul and me, but I thought that Paul would at least pack his own things. But he had never done so, except probably for his school bag, and he did not want to do so in the future. Wives always do that, he assured me. I did not agree and so the suitcases remained unpacked – his, at least. We did not quarrel about it at all – on the contrary, he was extremely charming and attentive, as ever – but he did not pack. He even offered to have the bell-boy pack his suitcase, or the chambermaid, but I did not want that. So we stayed on in Genoa where we had already seen everything and would have liked to travel on. It gradually became clear to me that this was a sort of test of strength against which I could do nothing except give in and always pack all the suitcases. So I have done that all my life and have never tried to dissuade him from his point of view. Besides, I did not mind packing suitcases, as he did, and so it was no sacrifice."[74]

This incident shows that even in what was obviously a "love marriage," the woman was at the man's beck and call.

The wives of the economic elite, occupied with so many other duties, increasingly left the raising of their children to others.[75] Hedwig Wachenheim (born 1891), the daughter of a Mannheim banker, was of the opinion that women of her grandmother's generation had raised their own children, but that this was no longer the case in her mother's generation.[76] Georg Tietz (born 1889), the eldest son of Oscar Tietz, was raised by his mother, but his younger siblings were left to nursemaids and governesses. This presumably is related to the social rise of that family in the 1890s.[77] The memoir literature seems to indicate that such an upbringing was usually fully accepted by the children, who were happy to have grown up in homes that were more open to the outside world than was otherwise the case in the German middle class. Hedwig Fischer, the wife of publisher Samuel Fischer, had little time for her children because she was so caught up with the literary circles that congregated in the Fischer home. (Her husband also had little

74. H. Wallich, *Erinnerungen*, p. 122. A further example in P. Wallich, "Lehr- und Wanderjahre," pp. 231–32.

75. Here the economic elite was unusual. In general, great stress was placed on the woman's role as mother in the German middle class. See Kaplan, *Making*, pp. 41–63; Schütze, "Mutterliebe." However, Davidoff found that the role of mother was of less significance in the "best circles" in England. See Davidoff, *Best Circles*.

76. Wachenheim, *Vom Großbürgertum*, p. 8.

77. See Tietz, *Hermann Tietz*, p 38

time for the family.) Nonetheless, her daughter expressed great admiration and affection for her in her memoirs.[78] Aniela Fürstenberg was clearly delighted when her children were old enough that she could again participate fully in social activities,[79] and yet she had a very close relationship with her son Hans.[80] Maria Lanckoronska, née Wertheimber (born 1896), the daughter of the Frankfurt banker Ernst Wertheimber, was cared for as an infant by a German wet-nurse and an English nursemaid. Later a governess was hired for her. However, her mother took care of her when she was sick, "and even today I recall her loving care in my childhood and youth."[81] However, the sons of Hugo Stinnes were raised by governesses, and Hugo Stinnes Jr. had a close emotional attachment to the governess who took care of him when he was sick.[82] Edith Andreae, née Rathenau, was neglected by her parents and was left completely to the care of family servants. However, the lack of warmth in her parents' home was probably an exception.[83]

Werner Mosse argues that the relationship between father and son was in general closer than that between mother and son because the mothers in this class of society neglected their children in order to pursue their social ambitions.[84] The sources contradict this assertion. For example, Mosse maintains that Georg Tietz and Hans Fürstenberg harbored resentment against their mothers. The passage in Fürstenberg's autobiography from which Mosse draws this conclusion does not support his thesis: "I was a trainee working at the dividend coupon counter and when I entered the elegant paradise of my mother, where frequently lively socializing was in progress and where I personally had a two-room apartment decorated in antique style at my disposal, this was a change of climate that not every hard-working trainee could have experienced without being damaged by it. Then the next morning it was back down to the dividend coupons."[85] The same ironic tone can be found in passages relating to Fürstenberg's father.[86] He describes his

78. See Fischer, *Sie schrieben*, p. 41
79. See C. Fürstenberg, *Lebensgeschichte*, p. 315.
80. See both ibid. (ghostwritten by Hans Fürstenberg) and H. Furstenberg, *Lebensgeschichte*.
81. See Lanckoronska, *Li(e)ber Beda*, pp. 9, 15, 17–18.
82. See Kohlschütter, *Ein Genie*, p. 54. Eduard Stinnes actually claims that his mother lost the affection of his father because she was too much of a housewife and not enough of a *grand dame* (p. 48) However, his statements regarding his mother are colored by a vitriolic quarrel over inheritance and are therefore very unreliable.
83 See Mangoldt, *Auf der Schwelle*, pp. 20–21
84. See Mosse, *German-Jewish*, pp. 114–16.
85. H. Fürstenberg, *Erinnerungen*, p. 21.
86. For example, when he comments on the absence of his father. See above. Also, see ibid., p. 7.

"mama" as "smart" and "a good listener."[87] Carl Fürstenberg's "autobiography," which was actually written by Hans, is full of praise, love, and admiration for Aniela Fürstenberg.[88] He describes his childhood as "healthy, happy and full of sunshine."[89] References to serious conflicts with the mother can likewise not be found in the Tietz autobiography.[90] A contrary example would be that of Richard Merton, who had a close relationship with his father, Wilhelm Merton. Achinger points out that the mother was almost never mentioned in the letters of the sons. She never tried to make a grand appearance in society, and in the family was kidded about her "home-spun characteristics." Her son apparently could not identify with her precisely because she played the role of the traditional housewife.[91] Moreover, Mosse completely misinterprets the nature of women's participation in high society, seeing it as a weakness of character rather than what it really was – a way of advancing her husband's and her family's interests. (This is one of the main themes of chapter 6.)

The bourgeoisie tended to view women's social welfare activities as an extension of their role as mothers. The businessman's wife was supposed to concern herself in motherly fashion with the welfare of the employees and workers of the firm. These personal contacts could lead to active involvement in company social policy. The wife of Emil Possehl, a wholesale merchant of Lübeck, is reported to have exerted her influence in behalf of the apprentices.[92] Margarete Krupp and her daughters Bertha and Barbara were among the first to visit workers' homes. Margarete later worked through charitable foundations.[93] Ida von Stumm-Halberg, née Böcking (born 1839), the wife of Baron Carl Ferdinand von Stumm-Halberg, participated in the direction of her husband's firm's welfare activities.[94] Two of the wives of the Röchling family of heavy industrialists founded a sewing school for the daughters of the miners.[95] The wives of Carl Poensgen, Gustav Selve, and Carl Duisberg[96] were also active in social welfare organi-

87. See ibid., p. 7
88. See C Furstenberg, *Lebensgeschichte*, passim.
89 See H. Furstenberg, *Erinnerungen*, p. 1.
90 See Tietz, *Hermann Tietz*.
91 See Achinger, *Richard Merton*, pp. 22–23
92 Niendorf, *Geschichte*, p 129.
93. See Klass, *Die drei Ringe*, pp 301–2; Manchester, *Arms*, pp 243–44.
94 See Hellwig, *Stumm-Halberg*, p 304
95. See Nutzinger, *Karl Rochling*, p 117.
96 The women involved here were Clara Poensgen, née Albers, Maria Selve, née Fischer, and Johanna Duisberg, née Seebohm.

zations within the firms their husbands directed.[97] Participation in charity organizations outside their husbands' firms was less frequent for women of this social stratum.[98] It would appear that the social welfare activity of the wives of wealthy businessmen furthered the interests of their husbands and by no means placed them in alliance with the opponents of their husbands. The sources used say little about the social dimension of charity work, and it therefore was not possible to determine to what extent the welfare organizations in Wilhelmine Germany were exclusive clubs that advanced (as in England[99]) the social ambitions of the wives of the wealthy bourgeoisie.

In the Wilhelmine economic elite, few wives engaged in business activities. The most significant businesswoman was probably Sophie Henschel, née Caesar (born 1841).[100] Her husband Oscar Henschel, owner of the largest locomotive factory in the German Empire, essentially made her a business partner. In his will he stipulated that after his death she should take over the direction of the firm and should have independent control of his estate. The factory was put in her name. In anticipation of the likelihood that she would survive him, he prepared her to succeed him as head of the firm. In her memoirs, Sophie Henschel wrote: "Also in business matters Oscar shared his interests, his worries and his aspirations with me because he believed that I would make sure that the work would continue in accordance with his ideas."[101] When he died in 1894, she took over the direction of the enterprise. Business historian Wilhelm Treue evaluates her achievements as follows: "In 1894 she was able, from one day to the next, not only to take over sole responsibility as a big businesswoman but also to direct the activities of the enterprise in an outstanding manner."[102] She directed the firm alone until 1900 when her son became a partner. In that year Sophie suffered a stroke, but during her illness her son, who was almost thirty years old, did not act in her place. The top executives of the firm took care of day-to-day decisions and conferred with her at her sickbed. During this time she decided against plans that her son had drawn up.

97. See Hatzfeld, "Ernst Poensgen," p 207; Selve, *Treue*, p 83, Duisberg, *Nur ein Sohn*, p. 21

98 Examples in Achinger, *Richard Merton*, p 22, Kardorff-Oheimb, *Politik*, p. 51.

99. See Davidoff, *Best Circles*, p. 56.

100. See Treue, "Henschel & Sohn."

101 Quotation out of unpublished memoirs in ibid., p. 9.

102. Ibid., p 7.

Her son did not become sole owner until 1912. Treue's overall evaluation is very positive: "Her entrepreneurial achievements actually surpassed those of Bertha Krupp and even those of several men who are not only listed ahead of her in Martin's list of millionaires but are also ranked ahead of her in the economic history writings of the present day."[103]

There are further isolated examples. Prince Guido Henckel von Donnersmarck was able to greatly expand his industrial enterprises[104] thanks to the entrepreneurial talents of his wife, Blanche de Païva.[105] The prince said of his wife, "My proudest accomplishment in life was to have found and understood this great spirit and to have bound her to myself."[106] After the death of her husband, Gustav Selve, Maria Selve participated in the direction of his brass rolling-mill.[107] Fritz Krupp stipulated in his will that after his death the Krupp firm should be converted into a joint stock company. He bequeathed almost all of the stock to his daughter Bertha. His widow Margarete was named trustee. Margarete wrote in her memoirs: "Since my husband adhered to the principle that business affairs were only a man's concern, I was little prepared for the task that fell upon me after his death."[108] When Bertha married, she attained majority and her husband took over the direction of the firm, but behind the scenes she was able to influence his decisions.[109]

Wives more often had an advisory function. Hedwig Fischer influenced her husband's decisions regarding what books would be published.[110] In 1899 Elise von Siemens, née Görz, dissuaded her husband, Georg von Siemens, from leaving the Deutsche Bank.[111] Aniela Fürstenberg appears to have understood a great deal about her husband's business. Carl Fürstenberg wrote: "In later years I never made an important business decision without having discussed it in detail with my wife. The reader will understand what a

103 Ibid., pp. 21–22.
104. See Fuchs, "Donnersmarck," pp 76–91, esp. 78–81 Also, see C. Furstenberg, *Lebensgeschichte*, p. 87
105 The widowed Marquise de Paiva was the daughter of the cloth manufacturer Martin Lachmann.
106 Quoted in Czaja, *Der industrielle Aufstieg*, p. 65, quoted in Fuchs, "Donnersmarck," p . 81. Donnersmarck married the widowed Marquise de Paiva, née Lackmann, who was eleven years his senior, in 1871 because he recognized her talents as a businesswoman.
107 See Selve, *Treue*, p. 83.
108. Quoted in Berdrow, *Alfred Krupp*, p. 212. See Manchester, *Arms*, pp. 241–43; Muhlen, *Die Krupps*, pp 74–75
109 See Muhlen, *Die Krupps*, p 84
110. See Fischer, *Sie schrieben*, p. 40.
111 See Helfferich, *Georg von Siemens*, vol 3, p. 238.

relief that must have been for a man who was almost always weighed down with heavy responsibilities."[112]

On the other hand it was almost impossible for a woman of this class to follow her own profession or appear as an independent person in public. It was more acceptable for a wife to pursue painting as a career. Philippine Wolff-Arndt, a recognized painter, married Anton Heinrich Wolff, a Leipzig wholesale merchant, in 1880.[113] Mary Sloman, née Albers-Schönberg, who married into a Hamburg merchant family, painted, though she probably did not sell her pictures or exhibit them publicly. Nonetheless, Sloman found quite a contrast between her own life and that of her mother: "There has hardly been a more harmonious marriage than that of my parents. My father did everything for his Amelie. She was of a timid and dependent nature, a woman of the old school according to which women were a luxury item that belonged in the home and not in public. My mother never went to the post office, never bought a railroad ticket. . . . She was entirely at home in her role as wife, mother, grandmother and housewife. Her kingdom was her family and her circle of friends."[114] Her daughter was not content to be relegated to such passivity, though she had to adapt herself outwardly to the expectations of her environment. "Whenever genius inspired me, there was certain to be a knock at the door. Our servant Gustav appeared with the words: 'Herr Sloman asks whether the gracious lady would find pleasure in going out for a ride with Herr Sloman.' Of course I had to find pleasure though inwardly I was raging."[115] Clara Poensgen dared to step forward even further. She was interested in women's issues, and around the turn of the century she on several occasions held women's conferences in her home. As the mother of ten children she knew something about the training of merchants, and this led her to become a member of the administrative committee for business schools of the Düsseldorf Chamber of Commerce in 1903.[116] Unfortunately, other such cases could not be found in the literature.

Was a woman's role in this social stratum simply a function of her husband's interests? To what extent was a woman's career determined by her class?[117] Insofar as she, with the help of servants,

112. C. Fürstenberg, *Lebensgeschichte*, p. 231.
113. See Wolff-Arndt, *Wir Frauen*.
114. Sloman, *Erinnerungen*, pp. 40–41.
115. Ibid., p. 91.
116. Hatzfeld, "Ernst Poensgen," pp. 207–8.
117. For the debate on whether women's careers were determined mainly by class or mainly by gender, see Haupt, "Männliche und weibliche."

relieved her husband of any responsibility for the raising of children and the management of the household, she enabled him to devote himself entirely to his profession. Through her representational activity within their social group and through her activities in connection with the social policies of her husband's firm, she furthered his professional goals. Naturally, a woman understood her position in the family in terms of her own role. As Bonnie Smith has shown, women's representational activities and charitable endeavors bore the strong imprint of feminine values. However, it seems that within the Wilhelmine economic elite the reproductive and social aspects of life were subordinated to the productive (that is, to the business activity of the husband). The feminine value system did not create the gender tension that existed in the northern French wealthy bourgeoisie in the realms of religious beliefs, political philosophy, and social policy. One explanation is that for the Protestant German bourgeoisie, there was no equivalent to the convent education for women so common in France. In addition, the Enlightenment and the French Revolution had left an indelible imprint on Frenchmen, while German middle-class men had become much more conservative and backward-looking since 1871.

To what extent were women of the business elite able to move beyond the narrow confines of their "separate sphere"? Wealthy businessmen's wives were not able to lead independent lives, and yet the duties that were thrust upon them involved a fair degree of responsibility and autonomy. They played a central role in the organization and regulation of "society," which constituted a semi-public space in which political and economic power-brokering took place, as will be demonstrated in chapter 6. In social life wealthy businessmen's wives helped write the rules of the game, deciding who should mix socially and who should be excluded. They had some influence over business decisions. These semi-public roles (which allowed women to perform functions that went beyond those of the private sphere without giving them full access to public spaces) necessitated at least the partial emancipation of women from reproductive functions, in particular from the duty of constantly looking after their children. Their privileged social position allowed them to escape at least to a certain extent from the restricted feminine role that one encountered in most of the middle class.

This had a major impact on family life. Women did not compensate for the fathers' lack of time for their children. As a result, in this class the family tended to be more open to the outside world and less emotionally intimate than otherwise in the German middle class.[118]

Did the businessmen's wives have companionate marriages (i.e., marriages characterized by companionship and shared experiences)? To a large extent, yes. Typically, the husband was no more than ten years older than his wife,[119] though marriages in which the wife was older were a great rarity. Reading through the memoirs, one gets the sense that the husbands and wives of this class liked to see themselves as a team, working toward common goals. The wealthy businessman was a towering figure, a source of wealth and power. But in his wife he could also find a person who commanded respect, a woman who was not primarily a housewife, but rather the administrator of a household and a prominent woman in society. Such a woman could be consulted about business matters. Carl Fürstenberg and others expressed the admiration they felt for their wives in their memoirs. There is evidence that these women were generally allowed to exert authority in the domestic sphere without undue interference. (They made decisions regarding the servants; their bookkeeping was not constantly supervised.) Nonetheless, a husband could forbid his wife to wear a hat, or force her to pack his suitcase, and could assume that she would drop everything to go out for a ride with him. In the final analysis, the wife was subject to the authority of her husband – or at least he needed to have the illusion that this was the case. She was a companion, though by no means on the basis of full equality.

Girlhood in the Wealthy Business Family

> My dear mama gave me the prettiest dolls and did everything she could to develop my precious femininity and to induce me to play with dolls.[120]

These words, written by Mary Sloman, exemplify the traditional aspects of growing up as a girl in the wealthy bourgeoisie. Sloman goes on to tell us in her memoirs that her mother thought that school had a negative effect on her daughter's health, and that she

---

118. On the Jewish middle class, see Kaplan, *Making*, chapter 4.

119. In seventy-six percent of the cases in my study, the businessmen were one to ten years older than their wives

120. Sloman, *Erinnerungen*, p. 53.

was forced to drop out of school for a year. Throughout her childhood, she was excessively protected: "While all the other children
were allowed to walk home from school, meet boys, or stop at a
little shop on the *Hofweg*, my Fräulein Krukenberg stood like a
sentry at the door of the schoolhouse. She accompanied me to
school every morning to make sure I got there safely and to carry
my satchel. My mother was afraid I would become deformed if the
weight of the satchel pulled down on my arm!"[121] Maria
Lanckoronska, née Wertheimber, had somewhat fonder childhood
memories: ". . . in those days, a girl of the upper middle class led a
rather carefree day-to-day existence, was fed well and luxuriously,
attached considerable importance to a well-groomed appearance,
spent her time at parties, games, dances, concerts or the theater,
and dabbled in music or painting."[122] Daughters were also taught
good manners and comportment.[123]

In many families the girls attended finishing schools where they
received training designed to prepare them for the conventional
female role. Whereas the sons of the bourgeoisie received instruction in school that was strongly oriented towards the professional
world, rational thought was hardly promoted in girls' schools. The
instruction was designed rather to promote emotionality and
domesticity.[124] In addition, girls received private lessons in sewing,
cooking, drawing, music, and foreign languages.[125] Some sent
their daughters abroad to school or on *Bildungsreisen* – travels
intended to broaden one's horizons.[126] Especially popular were
Swiss boarding schools that, like the German girls' schools, prepared young women for activities in the domestic and social
spheres.[127] Women were denied an education that would have prepared them for an independent existence, not only with respect to
the curriculum, but also with respect to the institutional framework, which contributed to the one-sidedness of female socialization. At the small schools for girls, a very personal atmosphere prevailed that was reminiscent of life in the family, and so the young
women did not learn how to deal with impersonal relationships.[128]

121 Ibid., p. 59; see pp. 56–57.
122. Lanckoronska, *Li(e)ber*, pp. 18–19
123. See, for example, Wenzel-Burchard, *Granny*, p. 20.
124. Hausen, "Polarisierung," pp. 388–89; Robertson, *Experience*, pp. 206–7; Manchester, *Arms*, p. 241; Jacobi-Dittrich, "Growing Up," pp. 210–13.
125 See Wenzel-Burchard, *Granny*, p. 20; Sloman, *Erinnerungen*, pp. 74–76.
126. See Schulze, *Geschichte*, pp. 122–24; Helfferich, *Georg von Siemens*, vol. 3, p. 254.
127 See Blosser/Gerster, *Tochter*, pp., 191–201
128. See Davidoff, *Best Circles*, pp. 92–93.

Only in a few families did the girls receive a scholarly or professionally oriented education. Around the turn of the century, new educational opportunities started opening up for middle-class women. From 1892 on, women were allowed to take the *Abitur* – the examination for graduation from the *Gymnasium* – in Baden. Berlin followed suit in 1896. From 1899 on women could register as regular students in the universities in Baden, although the doors of the Prussian universities were not opened until 1908. At the beginning of the winter semester of 1908/1909, 1,132 female students were enrolled in German universities. An unusually high percentage of German women who attended the *Gymnasium* or university in this period were Jewish.[129]

Hildegard Wallich describes the situation in the upper bourgeoisie as follows: ". . . at that time the daughters from good families seldom prepared themselves for a profession – it was not 'in keeping with one's class.' If they did, they were regarded as 'blue stockings' that were seldom popular with men and therefore often did not marry. But women's emancipation was beginning to make headway. We lived in a transitional period, and it was not always easy."[130] Robert Bosch's two daughters attended a university.[131] Carl Fürstenberg's daughter Aniela was one of the first women to graduate from a *Gymnasium* in Germany, later attending lectures at the University of Berlin.[132] Maria Lanckoronska, née Wertheimber, wanted to go to college but her father did not allow it, pointing out that later she was going to get married. When she asked to be allowed to do an apprenticeship in his bank in 1914, he agreed, but her brother quickly rose to an executive position while she remained a bookkeeper.[133] Hildegard Schreiner, née Bienert (born in 1890), daughter of the Saxon mill owner and multimillionaire Theodor Bienert, and Betty Warburg (born 1881), daughter of the banker Albert Warburg, became physicians.[134]

In some families, at least, the daughters were raised to be self-confident, self-reliant human beings, whether or not they received

---

129. See Haupt, "Männliche und weibliche," pp. 148–51; Huerkamp, "Frauen," in *Bürgerliche Berufe*, pp. 205 (on the opening of universities), 207–8 (on Jewish women); Robertson, *Experience*, p. 400. On Jewish women, see Kaplan, *Making*, p. 138
130. H. Wallich, *Erinnerungen*, p. 69.
131. See Heuss, *Robert Bosch*, p. 263.
132. C. Fürstenberg, *Lebensgeschichte*, p. 444.
133 See Lanckoronska, *Li(e)ber*, pp. 19–22.
134 Source· *Yearbook of Millionaires* study.

a higher education. While two daughters reported that they were neglected by their parents because they were girls,[135] most women felt that their parents had appreciated them and had helped them to develop their abilities. The Duisburg tobacco manufacturer Arnold Böninger wrote about a daughter who had died at nine years of age, "I think I can safely say that our child was endowed by nature with marvelous mental gifts such as few human beings possess."[136] When Wilhelm Merton traveled to his vacation home in Tremezzo in October 1901, he took his five-year-old daughter with him, while his wife and the other children, who were of school age or older, remained in Frankfurt.[137] Friedrich A. Krupp is said to have enjoyed spending his leisure hours with his daughters Bertha and Barbara and to have introduced them to his scientific hobbies.[138]

Georg von Siemens had a close emotional relationship with each of his six daughters. In 1883 he wrote to his mother about the birth of his fourth daughter: "I think Elise [his wife] wanted a boy. I must admit that I personally attach no importance to the matter, and I think Elise will very quickly get over this little disappointment; the family is so numerous that there is little prospect that our name will die out in the near future."[139] Siemens was griefstricken when his youngest daughter died in 1889.

He tried – within the limits of conventionality – to raise his other daughters to independence. In 1891 he allowed his sixteen-year-old daughter to travel alone from England back to Germany. In a letter to his wife he wrote: "I have no reservations about allowing Lili to travel alone from London. One must accustom children to looking out for themselves. There are much greater dangers in letting them become too soft and helpless than those posed by the world around us."[140] He tried to instill a critical faculty in his daughters by sometimes saying something that was untrue, in the expectation that they would contradict him. His daughter Marie constantly asked him questions about current political developments, which he answered in great detail in a number of letters. He also told his daughters about his own political activity as a Reichstag delegate. He took them with him on var-

135. See Fischer, *Sie schrieben*, p 50; Mangoldt, *Auf der Schwelle*, pp. 20–21.
136 Ring, *Geschichte*, p. 281.
137. See Achinger, *Wilhelm Merton*, pp. 228–29
138. See Berdrow, *Alfred Krupp*, p. 210.
139 Helfferich, *Georg von Siemens*, vol. 3, p. 319
140. Ibid., p. 254; see p. 253

ious trips abroad. His liberal attitude towards child-rearing is evident in the fact that in 1892 he read Fielding's *Tom Jones* on the recommendation of his seventeen-year-old daughter. He attached importance to the "education of the heart," by which he meant particularly the development of social consciousness. He provided his daughter Marie with professional training. The management of the household was turned over to her, for which she received a small salary. She became acquainted with double-entry bookkeeping and business management, and she worked for him as secretary in connection with the management of his private fortune. On reaching adulthood each daughter received a certain amount of capital to use at her discretion, with which she was to cover her running expenses.[141] Siemens certainly did not intend for his daughters to lead an independent existence. In fact, all five daughters who lived to adulthood married. However, Siemens obviously believed that in the upper middle class, the role of women required a large degree of self-reliance.

In the literature on the bourgeois family, it is often assumed that the daughter was not loved as a unique individual but only to the extent that she conformed to a prescribed role and to the accepted rules of conduct.[142] However, in some families of the Wilhelmine business elite, the conditions under which the girls were raised were quite favorable to the development of their personalities. Within certain limits these girls had their own interests and a will of their own. For example, Ilse Wallich (born 1879), daughter of Hermann Wallich, was described as follows by her sister-in-law: "She was extraordinarily smart and had many interests; she painted well and took lessons from the well-known Professor Orlik. She was an entertaining conversationalist, absolutely honest, and always spoke her opinion which, however, offended many people."[143] Paul Wallich describes a number of other businessmen's daughters who possessed a certain degree of independence. One was the banker's daughter Etta Rosenthal: ". . . not pretty, but a smart girl who, like her musical sister, preferred to study outside Berlin, who let her elderly and frequently ill parents suffer in loneliness. When she came home on vacation, we sometimes discussed whether a young lady's first duty was to herself or to her parents, and to me it was rather remarkable to hear this decent girl, completely inexperi-

141 See ibid , pp 254–56, 335, 339–40.
142. Blosser/Gerster, *Töchter*, pp. 217–18
143. H. Wallich, *Erinnerungen*, p. 114.

enced in business affairs, make critical remarks about her father's business activities which corresponded fully to the judgment of experts in this field."[144] Hugo Landau described his daughter Lizzie (born 1884) as ". . . very lively in temperament, exceptionally well-bred, musically gifted and, in spite of her sharp tongue, at heart a good guy (*Kerl*). She composed."[145]

It would be difficult to argue that the examples cited here are representative. Georg von Siemens was certainly not a typical father of this class, because most of the fathers had hardly any time for their children, sons or daughters. Autobiographies, biographies, and letters provide little insight into the oppressiveness of societal norms. In the memoir literature, the positive aspects of women's upbringing are undoubtedly placed at center stage, negative aspects glossed over. However, it is significant that there were emancipatory tendencies in at least some of these families. It should be recognized that at least some parents regarded their daughters as intelligent, worthwhile individuals, and that in some families the girls were given support, encouragement, and a good education, though probably not as much as the boys.

Conclusion

In its family life, the Wilhelmine monied elite shared many characteristics with the middle class, from which it had emerged, but there were differences as well. From birth, children of both genders were showered with concern and attention. They were constantly supervised, disciplined and protected, and were forced to conform with the norms and values of their class. In many families, children were subjected to a surprising degree of material deprivation so that they would learn "the value of money," and therefore be motivated to work. Our sources hardly mention another element of the bourgeois childhood, namely sexual repression. Formal education was generally left to the schools, whereby boys received a preparation for professional life, while girls' training focused on domestic tasks and the acquisition of bourgeois refinement. This was typical for the entire middle and upper middle classes. However, the father's "shop talk" and the presence of busi-

144 P Wallich, *Lehr- und Wanderjahre*, p. 345
145 Ibid , p. 346.

ness associates in the home contributed to an atmosphere quite different from that in the educated bourgeoisie. This was somewhat attenuated by exposure to cultural values and to anti-materialism (implicit in the spartan upbringing to which many children were subjected). The wealthy business family differed most from the middle class family in that parents had less time for their offspring. In most families, the father was usually absent, while the mother was very much caught up in social obligations, charity work, and the like. As a result, these families were not as closed to the outside world and emotionally intimate as most middle-class families. If this caused resentment, it was seldom expressed in print.

Subtle shifts in emotional dynamics and authority structures were taking place in these families, undermining traditional, patriarchal family structures. In this transitional era, we find both authoritarian fathers who tried to force rigid notions of morality and duty and fixed behavior patterns on their children, and a number of fathers who showed a great deal of interest in encouraging the development of their children in all their individuality. This extended to girls, as well. Earlier in the century, girls were prepared in school and in the family for a role of absolute conventionality, passivity, and domesticity. By 1900, however, girls in wealthy business families – as in the upper middle class as a whole – were being given new freedoms and better schooling, though seldom first-rate professional training. Young women could develop their talents and personality to a greater extent than in earlier generations. Some, such as Mary Sloman, were quite aware of the differences between themselves and their mothers.

The progressiveness of the wealthy business elite in the rearing of girls (relative, for example, to the broader middle class[146]) can in part be traced to the role of women in this elite. In order to successfully perform duties that were expected of her, such as the cultivation of friendships and social connections, the organization and management of a large household, and charitable activities, the rich businessman's wife had to possess self-assurance and a good education. Though the wife's sphere of activity was defined by her husband's

146. It is difficult to make comparisons as far as the atmosphere in the family is concerned There is no reason to believe that women were treated more liberally in the educated bourgeoisie than in the business elite However, we do have data on the women who studied at German universities. In 1911/12, thirty-nine percent were the daughters of officers or of university-educated professionals or academics; fourteen percent were the daughters of businessmen, and seventeen percent the daughters of middle- or low-grade civil servants or elementary school teachers.

interests, she was largely liberated from repetitive work and began to move beyond the traditional reproductive sphere into semi-public spaces. These were companionate marriages, though ultimately these women had to defer to their husband's authority. Thus, wealthy businessmen's wives enjoyed greater opportunities for personal fulfillment than was generally the case in the middle class.

Chapter 4

Family Solidarity, Youthful Rebellion, and the Sons' Choice of Profession

B orn into great wealth, a position of power and prestige awaiting him, the wealthy businessman's son seemed destined to claim the throne of a mighty empire. In the early nineteenth century, family solidarity made it unthinkable for him to do otherwise. But such traditions had begun to crumble by the fin-de-siècle, which in Central Europe was an era of both of great promise and of troubling developments. As bourgeois ascendancy reached its peak, anti-bourgeois sentiment flourished. Cultural brilliance coincided with cultural despair. Jews achieved a dominant position in high finance and high culture, but were hounded by an ugly anti-Semitic press and haunted by self-doubt. This was also the classic age of father-son conflicts, in which Freud formulated his theory of the oedipal complex. Did the bourgeoisie become enervated, did the siren calls of the military, philosophy, or art history lure businessmen's sons away from prosaic money-making? The Buddenbrooks[1] to the contrary, the German plutocracy proved to be remarkably resilient, flexible, and energetic. Though great wealth afforded young men unique opportunities for dalliance, indecision, and rebellion, in the end class mentality triumphed and the overwhelming majority claimed its patrimony. As in the bourgeoisie at large, adolescence became a time of self-discovery and rebellion, a stage of life in which the son (but usually not the daughter) could cultivate a sense of idealism and revel in a feeling of freedom to choose a life different from his father's, though he

---

1. Mann, *Buddenbrooks* Thomas Mann's novel concerns the decline of a Lubeck merchant family. See Percy Ernst Schramm's comments in Schramm, *Neun Generationen*, vol. 2, p. 408.

seldom ultimately did so. This was no mere narcissistic game. For many sons of very successful men, the family's expectations were a great psychic burden that apparently became bearable only if the son was able to establish a feeling of autonomy and a strong sense of his own identity.

Anti-Semitism created special strains, and young Jewish men were under particular pressure to deny their class and ethnic identity. Hans Dieter Hellige believes that "Jewish self-hatred" was common, and that it often found its tragic expression in youthful rebellion. In order to escape identification with the Jewish community, the Jewish businessman's son, raised in an authoritarian environment, rebelled against his father whom he previously had regarded as menacingly powerful but whose authority was weakened by anti-Semitism. Hellige points to many examples of Jewish businessmen's sons (and some non-Jewish businessmen's sons) in Germany and Austria who turned their backs on capitalist pursuits, becoming intellectuals who espoused the kinds of anti-capitalistic and anti-Semitic views found in the pre-industrial elite. They entered into an "alliance with the social adversaries of [their] father[s]" that brought no liberation, but rather the opposite.[2] Hellige is mistaken in his assumption that authoritarian fathers were the norm in the German-Jewish business class, and he makes false generalizations based on the cases of a small number of individuals. Since he only studied men who turned their backs on the business world, he did not realize that in most business families the generational conflict was ultimately resolved, and that the sons "returned to the fold."

While Werner Mosse discounts the importance of the generational conflict in wealthy Jewish business families, he is of the opinion that anti-Semitism led to a deformation of personality, especially in the younger generation: "Whilst Gentile capitalists would disdain them socially as Jews, fellow Jews would object to them as wealthy capitalists and 'fat cats.' Within their own group, whilst there was often a sense of solidarity, there were also bitter rivalries and quarrels. The correspondence of a Fürstenberg, a Ballin, a Walther Rathenau with Maximilian Harden suggests a good deal of loneliness, dissatisfaction, indeed unhappiness, in outwardly suc-

---

2. See Hellige, "Generationskonflikt." Hellige points out that rebellion could take on other forms as well, depending on the circumstances. In the years before the First World War a "defeudalization" took place as a result of the brusque rejection experienced by Jews seeking the acceptance of the pre-industrial elite and as a result of the successes of industry and the weakening of agriculture. Free conservatism, liberalism, and socialism appealed more to this generation that was not so strongly turned against the values of its fathers.

cessful men." He sees melancholy, covered over by "a thick skin" or irony, as a very Jewish characteristic, along with a distinctive kind of intellectuality.[3] Focusing exclusively on Jewish business families, Mosse is not in a particularly good position to discuss differences between Jews and non-Jews, and in fact he tends to exaggerate ethnic characteristics.

The first three sections of this chapter deal with these issues: the attraction of professions outside of business, anti-capitalism, Jewish self-hate, the psychological burdens of being the successor to a very successful businessman, rebellion against the father, the rise of adolescence as a distinct phase of life (lasting in this class and period into the twenties), and the tensions between growing individualism and traditional family solidarity. This chapter also looks at aristocratization and relations with other classes (as revealed by the son's choice of a profession). In the final sections, we turn to the question of what happened when more than one son wanted to join the family firm. Family solidarity required the equitable division of inheritance, which meant the fragmentation of family property. This endangered the profitability or even the existence of the firm. Various strategies were open to the head of the family. He could buy additional businesses for the younger sons or convert the firm into a joint stock company. Or he could make all of the children joint owners, writing special provisions into his will that would make it difficult to withdraw capital from the business or to contest the authority of the son designated as head of the company or corporation. We will look at various cases of joint ownership in this generation of sons.

The Crisis of Adolescence and the Choice of a Profession

In the Wilhelmine business elite, parents generally reacted with surprising equanimity to their sons' late adolescent crises (often taking place in their twenties). They seemed to realize that, unlike in earlier eras, sons entering adulthood could not be forced into business against their will. At times, Wilhelm von Siemens put pressure on his son and on his brother, who was his junior by seventeen years, to join the family firm, but his general strategy was quite flexible. When it came time to select a profession for his son

3. Mosse, *German-Jewish*, esp. pp. 114–16, 158–59, 355; quotation on p. 353. See also Warburg, *Aus meinen Aufzeichnungen*, p. 99; Weisbach, *Und alles*, p. 386; Mangoldt, *Auf der Schwelle*, p. 29; Liebermann von Wahlendorf, *Erinnerung*, p. 126.

Werner, he wondered what kind of work his son was suited for: "I am still not sure whether Werner is suited for a career in industry. There is no connection between his inclinations and his studies in Dresden. His incompetent instructors are probably to blame. But he says he has no taste for practical and mathematical subjects, and that all those sorts of things are so mindlessly mechanical. Our children decidedly have no academic talent. Neither did we have any."[4] (Wilhelm von Siemens had failed the examination for graduation from the *Gymnasium*.[5]) Werner, who was more interested in music than in technical subjects, apparently took up a technical course of studies under pressure from his father.[6] Later he joined the Siemens firm. Wilhelm von Siemens thought that Carl Friedrich was the best qualified to become head of the firm, but the latter also failed the *Gymnasium* comprehensive examination in 1892. Wilhelm tried to persuade him to repeat the examination, but Carl Friedrich argued that academic diplomas would not be essential for his later career. Wilhelm apparently went along with him. Carl Friedrich was allowed to go with his brother on a business trip to the United States where he remained on vacation for several months. Later on he attended lectures at the *Technische Hochschule* (Technical University) in Berlin[7] and eventually became head of the firm.

Several wealthy businessmen's sons were treated with patience and understanding as they tried to decide on a profession: Hans Fürstenberg, the Warburgs, Max von Oppenheim, Carl Ludwig Duisberg, Johann Gottfried Schramm, and Carl Poensgen Jr.[8]

Closely related to this trend is the emergence of adolescence as a stage of life typified by leisure and an identity crisis.[9] In a letter to his brother-in-law Julius Bötzow Jr., Carl Friedrich admitted that before joining the firm, he "for a long time did nothing or at least seldom did anything at all."[10] In Heidelberg, Hermann von Siemens devoted himself more to fraternity life than to his stud-

4. SAA 4/Lr 563, letter dated 24 July 1908 from Wilhelm to Carl Friedrich von Siemens.
5. See Rotth, *Wilhelm von Siemens*, p. 15.
6. See Siemens, *Carl Friedrich von Siemens*, p. 68.
7. See ibid., pp. 20–31, 69. Before the First World War, one could attend the university without a certificate of graduation from the *Gymnasium*. However, one could not then take the academic examinations. With regard to Carl-Friedrich's marriage to an actress, the family did not react so liberally and forced him to divorce her.
8. See later sections of the present chapter.
9. On the origins of a chronologically standardized "normal career," see Kohli, "Die Institutionalisierung," pp. 1–29
10. Siemens, *Carl Friedrich von Siemens*, p. 33.

ies.[11] Ernst Poensgen (born 1871), the eldest son of the heavy industrialist Carl Poensgen, was a cycling enthusiast, much to the dismay of the adult world in Düsseldorf. His participation in a race nearly cost him his *Abitur*. "The principal of the *Gymnasium* . . . was forced to take action because of the indignation of his colleagues who considered sweaters as 'clown jackets' and knee pants as 'infantile bathing trunks.' Perhaps the only thing that saved the graduation certificate for Ernst was the fact that he was 'Crown Prince' Poensgen."[12]

One of the sons of Carl Fürstenberg, Carl Jr., who did not become a businessman, went through an identity crisis that came to a sudden end. "My son Carl grew up to be a highly gifted but impetuous young man, given to kicking over the traces. It was his own inclination that led him to study medicine, but as an enthusiastic fraternity member, dueling was more on his mind than the study of medicine. It was easy to get him involved in any crazy prank. Then he suddenly turned a corner. In a few months of strenuous work he caught up with all that he had neglected, and he passed his preliminary medical examination with remarkable success. For me it was a great pleasure to accept him back into the family circle in full recognition of his achievements.[13]

Eugen Langen, a machinery manufacturer in Cologne, pointed out to his son, who had just begun to work for the Deutz gasoline engine factory, that he must improve his work habits if he wanted some day to become director. As director he could dispose of his time as he liked. "*But until then on weekdays* (during work hours from eight a.m. to six p.m.), *anything* that is not work, such as hunting, horseback riding, driving around, etc. etc. is out . . . There are to be no swimming and no pleasure trips, only business trips from time to time. All of these amusements are frowned upon. In short, during the next few years you must step out with such enthusiasm and spiritedness that you will win the respect of your former acquaintances and your previous supervisors to such an extent that you will be able to sit down in your director's chair after having already established your right to it."[14]

Georg Tietz (born 1889) was much more serious-minded about

---

11. This is mentioned in a letter from Arnold to Wilhelm von Siemens. SAA 4/Lr 563, letter dated 19 March 1906.

12. Hatzfeld, *Ernst Poensgen*, p. 208.

13. C. Furstenberg, *Lebensgeschichte*, pp 107–108.

14 Economic Archive of Rhineland-Westphalia: Rheinisch-Westfälisches Wirtschaftsarchiv, 7-9-5, letter from Eugen to Gustav Langen dated August 12, 1889.

becoming a businessman, and when he was sent to Paris for six months after completing his studies, he suffered from "inactivity."[15] He got involved in business, but went through a restless phase in which he first considered staying in Paris and opening a department store there, and then during a training period in the United States thought of staying there and becoming an American citizen. During all this time he was, according to his own testimony, a "leftist." In the end he returned to Berlin to become his father's successor.

An authoritarian style of parenting was no longer the norm in the wealthy business elite, and was clearly not accepted in the younger generation of businessmen's sons. An overly rigid handling of the question of choice of profession led more often than not to open revolt or to the son's failure. Lack of flexibility on the part of Hugo Stinnes was probably a major factor in the failures of his sons. He deigned his second son, Hugo Jr., his successor, but this role was too heavy a burden for the boy to carry. Edmund Stinnes commented, "It is obviously not easy to be looked upon as the 'chosen one' as in the case of my brother Hugo. That was his handicap in life. Hugo was actually the victim of his father."[16] Edmund, the eldest son (born 1896), considered himself to be disadvantaged, and resentment and jealousy were much in evidence in his conversations with Andreas Kohlschütter. "My achievement was passed over with indifference," he complains at one point. The mother, as sole heiress of the fortune, wanted to treat all the children equally, but Hugo Jr. was not willing to work with his younger brothers on the basis of equality, and he left the firm under unfavorable conditions. For Edmund, the worst blow came when he learned that his brother Hugo was the main benefactor in his father's will. Edmund expresses dark satisfaction over the fact that in the end his three brothers went bankrupt.[17]

One of the most prominent cases of rebellion against an authoritarian father is to be found in the Thyssen family. August Thyssen dreamed of founding an industrial dynasty. Harmonious collaboration would have been especially desirable in this family since August Thyssen had made a contract in connection with his divorce that made him usufructuary of his fortune, which henceforth belonged to his children.[18] Thyssen's problems with his chil-

---

15. See Tietz, *Hermann Tietz*, pp. 97, 113, 133.
16. Kohlschütter, *Ein Genie*, pp. 12–13.
17. Ibid., pp. 12, 14, see pp. 59–61.
18. See Treue, *Die Feuer*, p. 166.

August Thyssen with his sisters Balbina Bicheroux (1846–1935), left, and Theresia Hoosemans (1860–1920), right, probably on Balbina Bicheroux's birthday, October 10, 1906.

dren stemmed in part from the fact that he had divorced their mother when they were little and separated them from her, and in part from his inability to develop an emotional relationship with them. Josef Winschuh writes: "Thyssen was a workaholic. He sacrificed his family, happiness and domestic life to the narrow goal of productivity."[19] Fritz Thyssen (born 1873), the most compliant son, eventually became head of the firm. He did, however, clash with his father over his choice of a wife.[20]

On the other hand, August Jr. (born 1874), Heinrich (born 1875), and Hedwig (born 1878), were on bad terms with their father. Superficially, their constant wrangling appeared to be about whether the family would continue in business or whether it would assimilate with the aristocracy: they tried to persuade their father to set up an entail in order to obtain the title of baron. Heinrich became a big landowner in Hungary, had himself adopted by his brother-in-law, a Hungarian count, and took the name Thyssen Bornemisza de Kaszon. (He was also an important collector of

19. Winschuh, "Der alte Thyssen," pp. 112–13. See Arnst, *August Thyssen*, pp. 71–73.

20. See letter to the editor from Dr. Mandel in *Der Roland von Berlin*, 8 December 1904, pp. 1–5; report in *Der Roland von Berlin*, 12 January 1905, pp. 41–45. Thyssen Archive. Thyssen does not cover the pre-war period in his memoirs (Thyssen, *I Paid Hitler*).

art.) However, the squabbling also had a more materialistic side: the children pressed for an increase in their regular allowances and even for advances on their inheritance.[21] The ultimate cause of this family feud was undoubtedly emotional.

The most violent conflicts were those between August Sr. and August Jr., who became a reserve officer in the aristocratic Bodyguard Squad of the Hussar Guard Regiment and a member of the exclusive Union Club.[22] He went through the pretense of an engagement to a woman of the "demimonde," probably in an attempt to force his father to obtain the title of baron. At that point the father reportedly tried to have his son committed to a mental institution.[23] August Sr. wrote to his son, "You have tried by all means fair or foul to get a firm foothold in the circles of nobility and at court; you have aspired to gain access to court circles and positions; in order to gain the favor of those people you have sacrificed millions, all your energies, your father and your family."[24] In 1902 he wrote to Carl Klönne: "My sons should be striving wholeheartedly with me and my brother to develop our ventures into really great and independent enterprises. Our future does not lie in Potsdam."[25] He very much wanted his company to continue to be a family enterprise, partly because he would have greater authority over family members.[26]

This is not a clear-cut case of aristocratization, however. August Jr.'s actions are contradictory. He founded his own firm but had to declare bankruptcy. Later he apparently became involved in shaky business deals as a result of which he went deeply into debt.[27] On 20 May 1910, August Jr. made the following proposal to his

21. See Arnst, *August Thyssen*, pp. 69, 74; Treue, *Die Feuer*, p. 162.

22. See Arnst, *August Thyssen*, p. 73.

23. August Sr. wrote to August Jr. in 1910: "I have never thought of putting you into an insane asylum, and besides I would have had no legal basis for doing so." Thyssen Archive: A/886, undated letter from August Sr. to August Jr., Anlage 12. An accusation to this effect had appeared in the press in 1904. August Jr. is reported to have sued his father for defamation. Thyssen Archive: report in *Der Roland von Berlin*, 24 November 1904, pp. 1–5; letter to the editor from Dr. Mandel in *Der Roland von Berlin*, 8 December 1904, pp. 1–5; report in *Der Roland von Berlin*, 2 March 1905, pp. 317–325; report in *Rheinisch-Westfälischen Zeitung*, 10 November 1906; report in *Berliner Morgenpost*, 20 January 1905.

24. Thyssen Archive: A/886, undated letter from August Sr. to August Jr., Anlage 12.

25. Quoted in Treue, *Die Feuer*, p. 164. The Hohenzollern had a palace in Potsdam, a city dominated by the old aristocratic elite.

26 See Winschuh, "Der alte Thyssen," p. 109.

27. This comes out in correspondence between August Jr. and August Sr. Thyssen Archive. A/886, letters from August Sr. to August Jr., 22 May 1910 and 30 May 1910. Further details on August's bankruptcy in 1911 in A/1788, Walther Däbritz, manuscript (rough draft of a company history).

father: "I am hereby posing the question to you whether you are willing to provide me with the necessary means and allow me to take over the management of the ore fields. I am once more giving you the opportunity to provide me with an employment that is suited to me and if possible in an area of activity separate from that of Herr Fritz Thyssen so that we may at last work peacefully next to one another. I am also prepared, in order to put an end to the perpetual family quarreling, to have myself naturalized here."[28] (He was visiting France and apparently wanted to head the French subsidiary.) August Sr. answered that his son should "renounce any claim to a position that you cannot and may not occupy" and stop initiating new ventures that in the end had to be liquidated.[29] August Sr. considered having his son placed under guardianship in order to "keep him out of the claws of his so-called friends."[30] In 1913 he actually initiated proceedings to have his son, August Jr., declared mentally incompetent.[31] At that time he wrote to his son: ". . . unfortunately you bear my name which you have sullied and dishonored wherever you have gone. I no longer dare to speak your name because I am afraid to discover more of your misdeeds. A man who does not fight with honorable weapons, who can only utter threats against his natural father, cannot possibly be my co-worker." At another point he even wrote, "You have never yet given me a happy moment in my life."[32] The estrangement between the two was almost complete. The question as to which of them was to blame does not concern us here.[33] It is particularly significant that the son tried to become active as a businessman and repeatedly requested a position similar to that of his brother, of whom he was obviously very jealous. Ultimately, this conflict was about emotional issues and power rather than about aristocratization.

The best example of the successful use of authoritarian methods to force a son to become his father's successor is that of Georg Haberland (born 1861), the son of the construction giant Salomon Haberland.[34] Forced to give up his dream of becoming a doctor and to undergo long years of training which he hated, in

28. Thyssen Archive: A/886.
29. Thyssen Archive: A/886, letter from August Sr. to August Jr., 30 May 1910.
30 Thyssen Archive A/886, letter from August Thyssen Sr., addressed to "Herrn Assessor," 30 May 1910
31. See Arnst, *August Thyssen*, p. 74.
32. Thyssen Archive: A/886, letter from August Sr. to August Jr., 17 June 1910.
33. See Treue, *Die Feuer*, pp. 164–65.
34. Haberland, *Aus meinem Leben*.

the end he expressed gratitude towards his father. This was quite atypical for the Wilhelmine monied elite.

These examples indicate that in this period a weakening of patriarchal structures and an increase in personal freedom took place in the families of the business elite. Far from encouraging sons to turn away from involvement in business, the growing liberality of the family made business appear to be a very attractive sphere of activity. On the other hand, to an ever-growing extent, rigid, authoritarian reactions by parents proved to be counterproductive, leading sons to rebel or to fail.

The Attractions of Art and Scholarship

Only the occasional son of a wealthy businessman found his profession in an artistic, scholarly, or other creative field. Of the sons of the wealthiest businessmen listed in the *Yearbook of Millionaires*, at most seven percent went into such fields.[35] However, many more businessmen's sons seriously considered such a profession at some point in their lives, particularly in adolescence. Youthful rebellion could take the form of turning against one's father and one's class, disdaining crass money-making for the "higher" things in life.

Attraction to the worlds of art and scholarship, youthful rebellion against an authoritarian father, and "Jewish self-hate" all come together in the case of Walther Rathenau (born 1867) in a way that Hans Dieter Hellige – wrongly – considers to be typical of the Wilhelmine propertied bourgeoisie. Walther Rathenau's rebellion against his authoritarian, workaholic father (Emil Rathenau, founder of AEG) expressed itself first in the dream of emigrating to America, then in an attempted suicide, and later in identification with his mother, who had strong cultural inclinations. "Down to the last detail Rathenau's youthful letters bear the traits of the 'critical German puberty' of the imperial period: open revolt, despairing withdrawal, cynical resignation to the point of self-surrender, adaptation to the world of the parents, and finally the assumption of the father's role."[36] As a Jew he suffered from feelings of inferiority at school, at the university, and in the military

35 If one lumps together university professors, heads of scholarly institutions, the higher free professionals, teachers, private scholars, and free professionals in the artistic and literary fields. See table 5, p. 146.

36. Hellige, "Rathenau," p. 31.

service. To combat his neuroses, he adopted the conservative, anti-capitalistic values that predominated in these institutions. His dream of remaining after the end of this military service as an officer in an exclusive guard-cuirassier regiment was not realizable because of his religion. He became a businessman but regarded himself as a philosopher. Nonetheless, as a businessman he was very ambitious: "Since he did not succeed in detaching himself from his father, the compulsion to demonstrate his superiority and also to force his father's recognition was overpowering."[37]

In spite of his enormous successes, Rathenau was a tortured human being who told his friends that as a member of a persecuted, hated minority, he sometimes wished that he had never been born. On the other hand, he was capable of writing (in 1897) that there was "in the midst of German life a distinct and strange race of men, splendidly and conspicuously dressed, of passionate and mercurial temperament. On the sandy soil of Brandenburg an Asiatic horde."[38] Once at a social function he made an anti-Semitic remark in the presence of a conservative Gentile.[39] Yet interestingly enough, he resisted conversion to the end, regarding it as an opportunistic, ignoble act. There are indications that this very conflicted man was barely capable of entering into close relationships, whether of a sexual nature or not.[40]

In intellectual circles, other Jewish businessmen's sons were to be found who rebelled against an authoritarian father. Hellige mentions four writers with anti-capitalistic and anti-Semitic leanings, Georg Hirschfeld (born 1873), Arthur Landsberger (born 1876), Ernst Lissauer (born 1882), and Carl Sternheim (born 1897), all of whom were sons of wealthy Jewish capitalists. The poets Rudolf Borchardt and Karl Wolfskehl, both of whom belonged to Stefan George's circle, were nationalistic and anti-capitalistic without being anti-Semitic. (Here, then, Jewish "self-hate" was not the driving force.) Like Borchardt, many of these intellectuals felt that they "had had no home and no family." Their ties

37. Ibid., p. 38.

38. Walther Rathenau, "Höre Israel," *Die Zukunft*, 6 March 1897 Quoted in Harttung, *Walther Rathenau*, p. 89. It is said that he later regretted having written the article. See also Kerr, *Walther Rathenau*, p. 111; Hellige, "Rathenau," pp. 30–35

39. See Kerr, *Walther Rathenau*, pp 42–43, 128; See also Kessler, *Walther Rathenau*, pp. 31–33.

40. Rathenau did not marry. No serous love affair has come to light. He is said to have loved Lili Deutsch, the wife of AEG director Felix Deutsch, without it ever having come to a relationship between the two. See Mangoldt, *Auf der Schwelle*, p. 27; Federn-Kohlhaas, *Walther Rathenau*, pp. 204–13; Berglar, *Walther Rathenau*, pp. 310–11; Eynern, *Walther Rathenau*, for example p. 59; Kessler, *Walther Rathenau*, p. 75.

with the propertied bourgeoisie were completely broken off.[41] In the case of Borchardt, the connection between the conflict between the generations and alienation from his class of origin is especially clear:

> In contemplating my father's deadly seriousness, which could have something menacingly uncommunicative about it as well as something silently grieving, I have never lost the impression that he did not feel he was in the right place, that he did not do his work whole-heartedly, that in his human and class relationships he missed the decisive, the truly satisfying element, that he put duty ahead of happiness, and that the income from his business, which was always quite adequate and sometimes more than ample, did not compensate for this spiritual maladjustment. And since I must now confess that during the greater part of my youth, which I am now portraying, I stood in opposition to him, in a most antagonistic conflict with him, and finally in bitter enmity, I am hardly exaggerating when I say that in my life I have not done anything or become anything for any reason other than his wanting me to do or become the opposite.[42]

The syndrome described by Hellige does not apply to most of the scholars and intellectuals who came from the upper strata of the Jewish propertied bourgeoisie, who were generally neither anti-Semitic nor anti-capitalistic.[43] Most went into an artistic or scholarly field out of personal inclination and not in order to do battle with their fathers. A good example is Aby Warburg (born 1866), from the Hamburg banking family, who fell in love with art history as a boy and went on to become a Renaissance specialist (with a particular interest in the role of Florentine bankers in the Renaissance), as well as the founder of the Warburg Library for Cultural Studies.[44] There is no hint of either rebellion against an authoritarian father or of anti-Semitism in the case of the Cologne banker's son Max von Oppenheim (born 1860), either. He became interested in archeology in his childhood: ". . . absolutely decisive for my life is the fact that I enthusiastically read and studied the *Arabian Nights* in the big four-volume Weil edition which I received as a Christmas present when I was still in the *Sekunda*

---

41. See Hellige, "Rathenau," pp. 51–55. On Sternheim and Brochardt, see Gay, *Freud*, pp. 146, 198 On Brochardt, see Kraft, *Rudolf Borchardt*, esp pp. 12–21 (quotation on p. 12). On Sternheim, see Emrich and Linke, "Lebenschronik," pp 1097–1108.

42. Rudolf Borchardt, "Aus meiner Schulzeit," *Die Einkehr*, section of *Munchener Neueste Nachrichten*, 1 March 1928. Quoted according to Kraft, *Rudolf Borchardt*, p. 14.

43. See Gay, *Freud*, pp. 127–28, 133.

44. See Warburg, *Aufzeichnungen*, p 6.

[roughly equivalent to the sixth grade]. More and more it reinforced my desire to go on research expeditions to the Islamic
Orient, an idea that never left me."[45] In the case of both Warburg
and Oppenheim, it was not teenage rebellion, but childhood
dreams that led to an unusual career choice.

A son of Samuel Fischer, who was born around the turn of the
century and died early, composed and wrote verses, having studied
at the Academy of Music. These cultural interests undoubtedly
originated in his parents' home, which was frequented by many of
the authors who published with the Fischer-Verlag.[46] Though
three of Wilhelm Merton's four sons were active in their father's
corporation, the *Metallgesellschaft* (a major producer of metal
products), the youngest, Adolf (born 1886), became an art historian. The topic of his doctoral dissertation was "Book Illumination
in St. Gallen from the Ninth to the Eleventh Century" – certainly
an innocuous theme.[47]

Admittedly, an important motivation in Werner Weisbach's decision not to become a banker was his deep antipathy toward his
authoritarian father, a banker. Under constant pressure to succeed,
he sought an escape in art history, an area in which his father,
Valentin Weisbach, was interested. The father was a collector of art
and a friend of the director of the Berlin Museum, Wilhelm Bode.
Thus, Werner Weisbach's decision was both an act of rebellion and
an act of homage. And there were no anti-capitalistic or anti-
Semitic elements in the son's scholarly activities.[48]

Although such cultural interests often had their origin in the
parents' home, the decision of the son not to go into business
often led to a protracted struggle. Max Oppenheim's father wanted
him to become his successor in the bank, and a long battle of wills
ensued. Father and son first agreed on a "compromise profession."
Max was to study law and take up the career of a government official. The father still hoped that the son would come into the banking business; the son still hoped that the father would finance his
scholarly expeditions. During his training period in the government service he was able to take a research expedition to the
Orient. In 1888 he passed the government examination and
worked a year in government service. In 1889 his father asked him
if he "really could not get any pleasure out of a career in govern-

45. Treue, "Max Freiherr von Oppenheim," p. 40.
46. See Fischer, *Sie schrieben*, pp. 17, 31.
47. See Achinger, *Wilhelm Merton*, p. 332.
48. See Weisbach, *Und alles*, esp. pp. 48–49, 109 and 121.

ment," if he was going to cling to his "tragic passion." Prominent scholars, who were friends of Max von Oppenheim, appealed to the father to financially support the expeditions, and eventually he gave in to his son's wishes.[49]

If the father relented, he was usually adamant in his insistence that one or more of his other sons go into the family business. In the case of the Warburgs, some sons were more willing than others. Aby's brother Max relates in his autobiography: "When I was twelve years old, Aby proposed that I should buy his birthright from him, not for a bowl of lentil soup, but for an obligation on my part always to pay for his book purchases."[50] Peter Gay remarks, "It is a bizarre and touching incident, but the point is that what Aby was ready to discard, Max was ready to accept."[51] This is not entirely accurate, however. Max relates in his autobiography that for a time he wanted to study chemistry. "It is almost impossible to describe how shocked my father was. . . . He repeatedly exhorted me and spoke to me about my duty so long that I finally gave in and allowed myself to be dissuaded from my intentions." From 1888 to 1890, Max again had to be talked out of becoming a career officer in the Bavarian army. Shortly afterwards he became a banking trainee in Paris, and at age thirty became the actual head of the firm. "During the three following years I worked continuously, beyond all reasonable limits, and finally I was at the end of my strength."[52] Brothers Felix and Paul married Americans and joined the banking firm Kuhn, Loeb & Co. in New York. Later they gave up their partnership in the Warburg bank. A fifth brother, Fritz, was supposed to become a lawyer, a profession much to his liking. But when Felix and Paul went to America, he entered the Hamburg firm, which thus acquired a very capable head.[53]

Carl Duisberg reluctantly assented, "with pain and regret," when his son Carl Ludwig (born 1889) decided to become an actor, because he regarded that profession as "unproductive." The second son, Walther, was forced to study chemistry,[54] but seems to have come to strongly identify with his profession. The third son, Curt, wrote, "My brother Walther . . . suffered long from the great

49. See Treue, "Max Freiherr von Oppenheim," pp 41–57.
50. Warburg, *Aufzeichnungen*, p. 6.
51. Gay, *Freud*, pp. 127–28.
52. Warburg, *Aufzeichnungen*, pp. 10–11, 15; see also pp. 6–11; see Attali, *Siegmund G. Warburg*, pp. 63–66.
53. See Attali, *Siegmund G Warburg*, pp 68–69, 85.
54. See Flechtner, *Carl Duisberg*, pp. 231–32, 291–92.

name and believed he was under the obligation at least to equal our father's achievements."[55]

The three sons of the very wealthy Hamburg merchant Ernst Schramm wanted to become architects. Only one of them, the eldest, Johann Gottfried Schramm (born 1894) was allowed to do so.[56] Carl Poensgen (born 1882), the fourth son of the industrialist of the same name, was allowed to study music, which he had learned to love at his mother's side. The eldest son took over the direction of the family business.[57.]

In a number of other cases, a son whose talents lay in the field of art or literature could be persuaded to become his father's successor, and the dream profession became an avocation. Did this lead to a deep sense of frustration? Was it the fate of Jewish businessmen's sons like Walther Rathenau to become businessmen out of a sense of duty while at the same time, as intellectuals looking at themselves from a distance, despising themselves as Jewish capitalists? This question also brings us back to Werner Mosse's ideas concerning the "Jewish psyche." We can examine these related themes on the basis of three Jewish and three non-Jewish businessmen's sons who had artistic or intellectual sensibilities.

Neurotics every bit as troubled as Rathenau could be found among non-Jews. The two examples here are of men born (like Rathenau) in the period before 1870. There are quite striking similarities between Rathenau and Friedrich A. Krupp (born 1854). Alfred Krupp, the founder of the firm, doubted whether his son, who was sickly, shy, and sensitive, would ever be able to take over the firm leadership. The father's method of child-raising has often been described as authoritarian. But Fritz (short for Friedrich) avoided collisions with his father and accepted his father's decision that he should become the head of the firm. However, he always felt more strongly attracted to science. He led the firm to some noteworthy accomplishments, but he took refuge in his natural science hobbies, and after the turn of the century he withdrew more and more from business in order to devote himself to those hobbies and in order to spend time in his villa on Capri. He died in 1905, probably a suicide, after being accused in Italy of pederasty.[58]

55. Duisberg, *Nur ein Sohn*, p. 13. Curt studied law after the First World War and was active in the management of I.G. Farben.
56. See Schramm, *Neun Generationen*, vol. 2, p 413.
57. See Hatzfeld, "Ernst Poensgen," p. 207.
58. See Menne, *Krupp*, pp. 173–74; Klass, *Die drei Ringe*, pp. 136–285; Berdrow, *Alfred Krupp*, pp., 190, 208; Boelcke, *Krupp*, pp. 152–54; Engelmann, *Krupp*, p. 291

In the case of Wilhelm von Siemens (born 1855) we again get the sense of how great a psychic burden the son of a world-famous firm founder bore. In 1873 he wrote in his diary: "I was sad this evening, always thinking about the future and fearing one day to be incompetent and to be the insignificant son of a great father." This problem deeply affected his personality: "What is the good of fighting against melancholy? Though I am free from it right now, it comes back at any moment on the proper occasion. It is almost my basic character trait." At one point it becomes clear how serious his problems were: "I am thinking about a quick end to my dreary life."[59] There are also indications of a rebellious streak, although not directed against his father. As a soldier (in 1875) he was punished more than once for lack of punctuality or for missing a formation. He was not even promoted to private first class. He would have liked to devote his life to scholarship but regarded it as his duty to take over the direction of the firm.

His brother-in-law understood Wilhelm's problems well: "He took up this career in order to carry on his father's work, and for the sake of the family's future, for it was his sacred duty, handed down to him by his father, selflessly to provide for the family's welfare." The brother-in-law assesses the psychic consequences of this act of renunciation as follows: "Life had placed him in a position that was not in accord with his innermost being and that demanded from him the sacrifice of his personal leanings. . . . His refined spirituality suffered from the brutal coarseness of the work that was demanded of him; he was a delicate instrument that prematurely became out of tune and worn out."[60]

Other sons were much better able to give up the dream of becoming a scholar or artist and adjust to a career in business. Three sons of Jewish businessmen are good examples here. Paul Wallich, whose amorous adventures were discussed in chapter 2, wanted for a time to become a philosopher. He was on the way toward developing along the same lines as Walther Rathenau: "When I arrived in Freiburg, I was an anti-Semite, more so than I have ever been since then."[61] He appears nonetheless to have gotten along quite well with his father during these years. During his time in the military it became clear to him that as a philosopher he would not be able to satisfy his ambitions. "It seemed to me that a

---

59. Quoted in Rotth, *Wilhelm von Siemens,* pp 11–12.
60. Harries, "Nachruf," p. 5. Siemens Archive
61. Wallich, "Lehr- und Wanderjahre," p. 161; see pp. 13–14.

person would not cut a very good figure standing next to a lieutenant of the Mounted Guards if as a philosopher one were not at least a full professor at the University of Berlin. In the regiment there had been some jokes about my being a philosopher, whereas my successes were due to my father's previous position as a bank director." Interestingly, he believed that the business world had greater prestige: "At a time when Georg von Siemens, shortly before his death, was being talked about as a future finance minister, a business career seemed to be the guarantee of the required future social status." Eventually, he became a banker and developed a positive attitude toward his Jewish origins.[62]

Hans Fürstenberg in his youth thought of becoming an architect. This inclination had nothing to do with rebellion. On his mother's as well as his father's side of the family there were numerous musicians, scholars, and writers. However, he was easily dissuaded by his parents: ". . . neither of them wanted to force their beloved son to do anything. So it remained at the level of gentle persuasion, which convinced me more and more of the attractiveness of a banking career."[63] After the final examination marking the completion of his secondary education, he was – as was customary – asked by his teacher what his professional goals were, and Fürstenberg replied that he wanted to go into banking. However, Fürstenberg believed that he had not abandoned the cultural and intellectual side of life: "I arranged things for myself in such a fashion that I avoided a one-sided decision and in the end combined the two great interests in my life."[64]

Wilfrid Israel (born 1899) had from childhood on a strong artistic bent that may have been awakened by his mother, Amy Israel. She cultivated friendships with musicians and actors and took him on a *Bildungsreise* – travels intended to educate – through northern Italy. In his youth he painted and wrote poetry. He later regretted not having studied at an academy of art. During the First World War he was a pacifist and would have become a conscientious objector if his parents had not arranged for a doctor's certificate in order to prevent this. During the Weimar Republic he took a position in the N. Israel Department Store.[65]

Some were able from the beginning to distinguish between their artistic hobbies and their professional goals. Ernst Poensgen, the

---

62 Ibid., pp. 186–87
63 H. Fürstenberg, *Erinnerungen*, p. 18; see pp 16–18.
64 Ibid., p. 18; see p. 19.
65. See Shepherd, *Wilfrid Israel*, pp. 22–25.

eldest son of the heavy industrialist Carl Poensgen and a Protestant, went through a period of search for identity without – as far as is known – ever seriously considering withdrawing from the world of business. (It should be remembered that his brother Carl studied music.) He is described as having been a "bookworm" and an enthusiastic theater-goer. He would have liked to become a scientist but regarded it as his duty to become the head of the company. His flawless curriculum vitae shows that he always kept this goal in mind: university studies in mathematics, chemistry, and metallurgy, then apprenticeship, and finally employment in the *Düsseldorfer Rohren-und-Eisenwalzwerken* (pipe and iron mills) before his twenty-fifth birthday.[66]

But the dream of a life devoted to the "nobler" things in life haunted even the most successful businessmen. Robert Bosch (born 1861) once talked of retiring from business at age fifty-five in order to devote himself to his hobbies (botany, zoology, and biology). He did not act on this dream. His son was also interested in the natural sciences, but was being groomed as his father's successor at the time of his premature death.[67]

In sum, most of the evidence discussed here contradicts Hellige's thesis of "the 'critical German puberty' of the imperial period," involving "open revolt, despairing withdrawal, cynical resignation to the point of self-surrender, adaptation to the world of the parents, and finally the assumption of the father's role"[68] – which is essentially a description of the reproduction of the authoritarian personality. The more successful rebellions of Weisbach and Borchardt were also not the norm. The dream of a life as a gentleman-scholar or actor only rarely went hand-in-hand with anti-capitalism or anti-Semitism. The intellectual activities of a number of businessmen's sons such as Aby Warburg and Max von Oppenheim were not directed against their class or origins in any way. In most cases, a love of art history or philosophy did not involve rebellion against an authoritarian father. Rather, such interests usually originated in the family. Further explanations for the attraction to art, music, literature, and scholarship lie in the traditional German ideal of humanist education, transmitted through the humanist *Gymnasium* that more and more businessmen's sons attended, as well as in the post-materialist values of a generation

66. See Hatzfeld, "Ernst Poensgen," pp. 209–11.
67. See Heuss, *Robert Bosch*, pp. 184–85, 263. Theodor Heuss knew Bosch personally.
68. Hellige, "Rathenau," p. 31.

that had grown up in affluence. In the context of German culture of the late nineteenth and early twentieth centuries, these values were not primarily anti-bourgeois.

By the turn of the century, career choice in this class usually involved a late crisis of adolescence that helped a young man in his twenties to break out of patriarchal structures and define himself as an individual. This individualistic ideal, born of the Enlightenment and Romanticism, did not come to fruition in the business elite until the late nineteenth century, in part the result of the declining economic role of the business family. Growing individualism did not, however, spell the decline of the business class. It is striking that in most cases the son who turned his back on the business world had a brother who followed in his father's footsteps. If he did not, the son often felt duty-bound to take the helm. Wilhelm von Siemens is a good example of this.

Among those businessmen's sons who gave up their intellectual interests to run the family firm, there certainly were some who had psychological problems – Wilhelm von Siemens, Rathenau, F.A. Krupp. But we do not find a typical pattern (postulated by Hellige) of forced renunciation leading to neurosis. There is also scant evidence of the kind of Jewish neurosis described by Mosse, induced by anti-Semitism. Paul Wallich overcame his "Jewish self-hate," became convinced that he would have more opportunities for self-realization as a businessman than in other professions, and found his way back to his class of origin. Hans Fürstenberg did not feel that his parents had coerced him into going into banking, and he was perfectly content to make art his hobby. Wilfrid Israel was somewhat more unhappy to give up a career in art. However, his pacifism shows that his independence of spirit had certainly not been broken. In general, we find only occasional evidence in this class of the kind of broken spirit characteristic of an authoritarian upbringing.

Businessmen's Sons in Aristocratic Professions

Aristocratization, at its most extreme, meant abandoning the business world and seeking acceptance as a pseudo-noble (usually adorned with a new title of nobility) in a traditionally aristocratic profession: as an officer, a diplomat, a big landowner, or a *Landrat*. Proponents of the feudalization thesis thought this to have been a widespread phenomenon, which it was not. About twelve percent of the sons of the wealthiest millionaires listed in the *Yearbook of Millionaires* pursued aristocratic professions, becoming big landowners, gentleman farmers, or military officers for the most part. In most of these cases, assimilation into the nobility began long before 1890 and was part of an agenda set by the family (usually one of the very wealthiest families).[69] A title of nobility generally belonged to this program. Thus, every fifth son of a newly ennobled family entered a traditionally aristocratic profession, as against every twelfth commoner's son.

One reason is that such professions were largely closed to the bourgeoisie. High positions in the Prussian diplomatic service and civil service were largely reserved for members of the military and bureaucratic nobilities. It was quite difficult even for the sons of recently ennobled men to gain admittance to the Foreign Service, and they were discriminated against when it came to promotions.[70] For most families, it was too expensive to purchase a landed estate in order to provide a son with a field of activity. When the army expanded in the 1860s, it was to a certain extent opened up to the bourgeoisie. Between 1903 and 1913, about fifteen percent of the newly commissioned officers were the sons of merchants and manufacturers, but a rigid ideological selectivity was applied. The businessmen's sons who took up the career of military officer came primarily from East Prussia, West Prussia, and Brandenburg. Thus recruitment was largely restricted to bourgeois groups that had grown up in the old Prussian traditions.[71] Even so, a businessman's son who became a career officer was often discriminated against. One of the sons of Fritz von Dippe, a nursery owner who in 1910 was ennobled and in 1913 was the richest man in Saxony, entered a military career. He was assigned to a second-rate – i.e., bourgeois – regiment.[72]

69. For example, among the businessmen in this study were three members of the Stumm family whose principal occupation was army officer or diplomat and whose sons followed such professions. A second example would be the Silesian industrialist Eugen von Kulmiz. His father was ennobled as early as 1867, and Eugen married Maria von Moltke. All three sons were landowners The eldest, Karl-Adolf, was also a lieutenant in the elite Cuirassier Guard Regiment No. 1 in Breslau. Thus, in these cases there was no youthful rebellion.

Aristocratization, as measured by the profession of the son, was somewhat more widespread among the families in the upper half of the wealth pyramid than among those in the lower half.

70. See Cecil, *German Diplomatic Service*, pp. 63–64.

71. But between one-fourth and one-third of the newly commissioned officers of the navy in the pre-war period were the sons of merchants and factory owners See Bald, *Der Deutsche Offizier*, esp. pp. 38–48, 69, Detlef Bald, "Die Revolution von 1848 und ihre Auswirkungen auf Bildungssystem und Sozialstruktur der preußischen Armee," in: *Acta 11* (1988) (The latter according to the author.)

72. On the relative status of the regiments, see Endres, "Soziologische Struktur," p. 296.

Jews faced almost insurmountable hurdles. In Prussia, a Jew could not become a military officer, and it was difficult for a baptized Jew to do so. In Bavaria, conditions were somewhat more liberal. In Prussia, Jews could also not join the diplomatic corps.[73] They could at most become landowners.[74]

However, it would be patently false to conclude from this that the wealthy businessmen's sons in this study did not enter aristocratic professions because they did not have the opportunity to do so. For one, the path of pseudo-aristocratization lay open to them, usually involving early retirement from business and a life of idleness. For example, the sons of Gerson Bleichroder (born in the 1850s and 1860s) "never learned to work" and turned over the management of their father's bank to others.[75] Willy Liebermann von Wahlendorf, who came from a Saxon textile manufacturing family, bore the title Ritter (roughly equivalent to "Sir") and lived as a rentier. His father had not prepared him and his brother for the management of their wealth. When their father died in 1893, they were helpless: "Though we were about thirty years old, we had remained real children." In retrospect Liebermann recognized that "a human being is formed by life and a profession and not by the unworldly concepts of honor on which we were raised. At that time money seemed like *nothing* to me and my brothers."[76] Only one percent of the sons of business millionaires in the *Yearbook of Millionaires* became rentiers.

Did the pre-industrial elite reject the sons of the business elite or the other way around? To answer this question, we must look at the motivations of sons who wanted to enter these professions, as well as at the attitude of those sons who had no inclinations in this direction. Of particular interest are not those families that had been drifting off into the aristocratic world for two or three generations, but rather cases of aristocratization in the Wilhelmine period. Youthful rebellion could, of course, play a role here.

Why might a businessman's son find a military career appealing? For Baron Simon Moritz von Bethmann (born 1887), scion of an old Frankfurt banking family, it seems to have been a way of lessening the psychological burden of the heir, the fear of losing one's

73. See Richarz, *Jüdisches Leben*, pp 32, 39

74 See Rosenberg, "Die Pseudodemokratisierung," pp. 289–94.

75. Stern, *Gold and Iron*, p 546; see p. 485 Also, see Landes, "Bleichröders," esp. pp. 101–3.

76 Liebermann von Wahlendorf, *Erinnerung*, pp. 103–4. Liebermann traveled and hunted frequently and left the management of his wealth to others His fortune quickly melted away. See p. 109.

freedom, and the fear of failure. The idea of being thrust into a pre-determined role did not appeal to him, and during his military service he enjoyed the "simple life" greatly. In the army he was thrown together with the sons of peasants and workmen, and he spent his time in riding, gymnastics, and marksmanship, ". . . and that is why the world suddenly seemed so simple, so natural, so solid."[77] In this situation he did not realize that objectively as an officer he would have much less freedom than as a businessman. However, after his father's death, his mother found the arguments that persuaded him to take over the direction of the family bank: "This wise woman told her children unequivocally that in their case, the adoption of a new profession, as a diplomat or an officer, would by comparison be easier, that the path laid out by a family rich in tradition does not lead to a comfortable life of happiness but rather to a life of exertion, because the family's traditional goals must be pursued with new means in full view of those who are envious and those who are enemies. She made it clear to her sons that the lifetime objectives worth striving for are not the easy ones but the hard ones. So she persuaded her sons to make the continuation of the banking business their personal responsibility, their future."[78]

Willy Liebermann von Wahlendorf for a short while entertained the desire to become an active cavalry officer. What appealed to him were "the beautiful horses, breaking them in, the outdoor life, the blue and yellow uniform, the sporting attitude of the lieutenant in charge of recruits, the favor of women, etc." However, he soon underwent a change of attitude: "It soon became clear to me that I was at heart only a rider, not a military man, and that the officer's subjection to higher authority would have gone against the grain."[79]

Though Hans Adt (born 1888) found military life appealing and enjoyed socializing with noblemen, he was remarkably single-minded in his pursuit of a career in business. During his time as a university student, he joined a student corps. (These organizations were often dominated by aristocrats, or at least pseudo-aristocrats.) He interrupted his studies to perform compulsory military duty, serving in a distinguished hussar regiment with a good friend. "Those were glorious times," he writes.[80] Later on he maintained

77. Quotation out of Bethmann's unpublished memoirs as cited in Heym, "Simon," pp. 260–61.
78. Ibid., p 258.
79. Liebermann von Wahlendorf, *Erinnerung*, p. 56.
80 Adt, *Leben*, pp. 142, 147.

friendships with several old fraternity brothers, regimental comrades, and other reserve officers. However, he does not in any way indicate that this phase of his life represented anything other than the golden days of youth. He did not serve in the military longer than required, and returned to Berlin to complete his studies, avoiding the corps in his last semesters ". . . because I had had enough of beer-drinking parties in Munich."[81] Later he joined the family firm.

Most businessmen's sons found the prospect of a military career singularly unappealing, Paul Wallich, for example (who nonetheless was interested in becoming an officer of the reserve because of the social status this conferred).[82] Concerning his cavalry captain he wrote, "My military duties consisted more and more of carrying around cigarettes for him, a heavy cigarette smoker." His remarks concerning his lieutenant are even more critical: "His motto was 'strict but just,' but he often carried the strictness to the point of brutality, and the justness disappeared in the process." He was a "gambler (of course), a drinker, and a woman-chaser par excellence." Wallich's lieutenant "no longer regarded anti-Semitism as a question of religion. He was not satisfied until he was assured of my praiseworthy intention of giving up my race and my Asiatic culture. As a human being, this little alcoholic was surely the best-natured and most tender-hearted member of the regiment."[83]

One recognizes a deep and mutual antipathy between the officer corps and the propertied bourgeoisie in Wallich's memoirs, an aversion to the rigid discipline and coarseness of the officers and their anti-Semitism. For the most part, military service is not even mentioned in the autobiographies of very wealthy businessmen and their sons. These were two worlds that hardly touched one another. For the son of a middle-class businessman, the fact that even a lowly lieutenant had the right to make an appearance at the imperial court might carry considerable weight, but the son of a big businessman had other means at his disposal to advance socially.

Data on the Sons' Professions

Of the 443 sons on whom information is available, fifty-four percent became big businessmen and sixteen percent businessmen

81. Ibid., p. 142. See pp. 139–61.
82. See P. Wallich, *Lehr- und Wanderjahre*, pp. 167–68.
83. *Ibid*, pp. 169–70, 172–75.

Table 5. Professions of the Sons of the Wealthiest Businessmen[a]
(in %)

OCCUPATIONAL GROUP

Pre-industrial elite (without civil servants)	12.2
Upper civil servants	4.3
Professionals, academics[b]	5.4
Big businessmen	54.4
Businessmen: status unknown	16.0
Lower middle class	6.1
Other[c]	1.6
Total (in %)	100.0
Total (absolute)	443

[a] Excluding eighteen businessmen who belonged to the aristocracy or whose families had been integrated into the aristocracy. Only cases with information. Data were available on the sons of 249 businessmen; data were available on *all* sons of 182 businessmen.

[b] Universities, college preparatory schools, and school administration.

[c] Rentiers; upper class, profession unknown.

whose status cannot be determined. (See table 5.) Thus a large majority of the sons remained in the propertied bourgeoisie. About twelve percent pursued aristocratic professions, and four percent became high government officials. About five percent can be counted among the educated bourgeoisie, while at most seven percent entered creative or scholarly fields.[84] This is very much in line with the findings of other studies.[85]

Were the sons able to maintain the social status bequeathed them? Only six percent of the sons belonged unequivocally to the lower middle class (and none to the lower class). An additional sixteen percent were businessmen who cannot be neatly categorized. Moreover, the indicator used is the last occupation up to 1918. The class of the businessman is determined by the status of the company or companies he headed during the imperial period. It is possible that more sons declined socially during the Weimar period. It must in particular be assumed that some of their companies

84. If one lumps together university professors, heads of scholarly institutions, the higher free professionals, teachers, private scholars, and free professionals in the artistic and literary fields.

85. See Kaelble, "Sozialstruktur," p. 172, Stahl, *Elitenkreislauf,* pp. 281, 306–7.

lost their dominant position after 1918. For this reason, no firm conclusions can be drawn with regard to social mobility.

As might be expected, inheritance of the father's profession was more frequent among the sons of the owners of private companies than among the sons of top managers in joint stock companies, while the percentage that entered the traditional ruling class, the educated bourgeoisie, or the lower middle class, was higher among the sons of the heads of joint stock companies. Just over half of the sons of managers and "entrepreneurs" in joint stock companies pursued a business career.[86] Connections and wealth undoubtedly smoothed the way for these sons. It can be assumed that they often held large blocks of stock in the companies they later headed.

The eldest son was still regarded as the "natural" successor of the father. Almost two-thirds of them became big businessmen – usually in the father's company. An additional eight percent were active in large- or middle-sized businesses. Thus a total of about seventy percent became businessmen. The second son became a businessman exactly as often as the eldest, but not as often in the father's company. A somewhat smaller percentage of those born later chose a business career, but it was still sixty percent. The percentage of those who entered the traditional ruling class rose as one went down the age ladder in the family. Once the succession in the business was assured, younger sons had more freedom to go into a traditionally aristocratic profession. The figures for the other occupational groups show no clear pattern.

The percentage of sons becoming businessmen increased from fifty-eight percent (for the 1830-to-39 cohort) to seventy-six percent (for the 1860-to-69 cohort). Unfortunately, we cannot exclude the possibility that this is due to a distortion of the data: in order to confine our conclusions to the imperial period, those sons who were born after 1900 were excluded from the tables. Thus a number of late-born sons of businessmen of the cohorts born between 1850 and 1869 are not included. We know that the older sons were the most likely to become businessmen.

86 Wilhelm Stahl's data on the sons of businessmen listed in the *Neue Deutsche Biographie* who were born in the eighteenth and nineteenth centuries differ considerably from mine. According to him, ninety-eight percent of the fifty-six sons of business owners were themselves businessmen. The percentages for the 124 sons of managers were: big landowners and military officers, eleven percent; government officials, eight percent, the remainder of the educated bougeoisie, sixteen percent; businessmen, forty-eight percent; lower middle class, two percent; rentiers, two percent; graduates from secondary school with a major related to business (profession unknown), ten percent; chemists and physicists, three percent See Stahl, *Elitenkreislauf,* pp 281, 306–7. His main source, correspondence with the descendents, is somewhat biased.

In view of the discrimination against Jews in the traditionally aristocratic professions, it is not surprising that substantially fewer businessmen's sons of Jewish origin are to be found in this category of professions. However, the percentage of government officials was equally low among Christians and Jews.[87] Jews traditionally regarded the free professions as a potential alternative. The Prussian universities were also not completely closed to Jews. (In 1909, ten percent of the instructors, seven percent of the assistant professors, and two percent of the full professors were Jews. However, the percentages would undoubtedly have been substantially higher had there been no discrimination.[88]) However, the sons of the wealthiest Jewish businessmen are not encountered more frequently in the free and academic professions than non-Jewish businessmen's sons. (The thesis of a unique relationship between the Jewish bourgeoisie and the arts and scholarship cannot be substantiated here either.) Instead, they became big businessmen in larger numbers. This was possible because in the Jewish families there were fewer sons. In other words, instead of seeking alternative professions to which less prestige was attached, the Jewish families limited the number of children.

Regional differences, particularly those in the aristocratization rate, are surprisingly small. However, sons of businessmen in the Hanseatic cities tended to become part of the educated bourgeoisie (including civil servants) more often (in seventeen percent of the cases) than elsewhere (ten percent in Berlin and Rhineland-Westphalia). This results from the fact that in Hamburg, Lübeck, and Bremen, the business elite was an integrated part of a patrician class that included professionals, academics, and civil servants.

The statistical breakdown by area of economic activity shows that the transmission of profession from father to son was unusually low (fifty-six percent) among the sons of heavy industrialists. As will be shown in the following section, preferential treatment of a principal heir occurred most frequently among the heavy industrialists. Nonetheless, the percentage of their sons who pursued traditionally aristocratic professions was barely higher than in other industries. On the other hand, higher government officials, the educated bourgeoisie, and rentiers were overrepresented. This contradicts the thesis that heavy industry was more highly aristocra-

---

87 There was discrimination against Jews in the civil service. Jews were to be found in the greatest numbers among judges of lower courts, making up 4.3 percent of all Prussian judges in 1907. See Richarz, *Jüdisches Leben*, p. 33.

88. See ibid., p. 32; David L Preston, "German Jews," pp 99–116

150

tized than other industries. Only two-thirds of the sons of businessmen in the growth industries became businessmen, whereas they became military officers or landowners in greater numbers. This is an unexpected finding, since the growth industries are thought to be especially "modern." One explanation is that the growth industries were given preference in the conferment of titles of nobility because of their significance for the German economy. Many of these families were then accepted by the nobility. The only son of Walther von Rath, chairman of the board of the *Hoechst Farbwerke* (a chemical company) and of the *Lahmeyer Elektrische Gesellschaft* (an electric company), became an attaché. The only son of Herbert von Meister, managing director of the *Hoechst Farbwerke*, turned to large-scale farming. A second explanation is that the businessmen in a growth industry more frequently headed a joint stock company. In general, the sons of top managers became businessmen more rarely; they often sought an alternative profession in the traditionally aristocratic sector. On the other hand, the sons of bankers and wholesale merchants in our study were especially strong in their bourgeois orientation.

Who Shall the Successor Be?

How was succession determined when more than one son wanted to go into business? In the older nobility around the turn of the century, inheritance was still governed by a system of primogeniture under which the eldest son inherited the bulk of the fortune, but was morally – though not legally – bound to distribute a part of the estate among his younger brothers and sisters. Rudolf Martin asserts that in Cassel and Essen (a heavy industrial area) there was in effect among the wealthy bourgeoisie a similar principle of inheritance by which the principal heir inherited five-sixths while the other family members shared the remainder.[89] Alfred Krupp placed the wealth of his company in an entail. His son, F.A. Krupp, accumulated a private fortune separate from the entail so as to be able to bequeath a part of his fortune to his wife and to his second daughter, Barbara. The elder daughter, Bertha, inherited the firm. In 1903, at the wish of her deceased father, she converted the family business into a joint stock company, and in return she acquired all but four shares of the stock.[90] Joseph Hirsch, who was

89. See Martin, *Jahrbuch der Millionäre Deutschlands*, vol. 12, p. 76; vol. 10, pp 100–1.
90. See Borchardt, "Der Unternehmerhaushalt," pp. 13–14.

the third son of the wholesale merchant Benjamin Hirsch and was born during the imperial period, was excluded from the management of the firm his brothers headed.[91] Hugo Stinnes wanted to give preference to his second son, but his widow nullified his plans.[92] The reaction of the eldest son, Edmund, shows that in this period such provisions were regarded as unjust.[93]

In most families the estate of the deceased was presumably divided equally among the children. This appears to have been the case in Thyssen's agreement with his wife.[94] The industrialist Leopold Hoesch stipulated that each of his three sons should acquire his own area of activity. Wilhelm (born 1845) became owner of the firm Eberhard Hoesch and Sons and chairman of the board of the Hoesch Corporation (iron and steel works). Albert (born 1847) became director of the Hoesch Corporation. Leopold bought a paper mill for his third son Hugo.[95] Wilhelm Merton prepared three of his sons for positions in his firm. (It is not clear whether the fourth son, who was killed in the First World War, was also destined for participation in the business.) They shared equally in the inheritance. At first Walther Merton was the head of the corporation, but in 1910 he moved over to the *Berliner Handels-Gesellschaft*. After the death of the father in 1916, Alfred and Richard Merton headed the firm. "One can only conclude, from correspondence Wilhelm Merton carried on toward the end of his life with his two sons, that he trusted them and was in agreement with them to an equal degree."[96] After the unexpected death of Franz Carl Guilleaume, his factories in Cologne and Mülheim an der Ruhr were legally separated in order to facilitate the succession. The youngest son, Arnold, received the hemp spinning mill, while Max and Theodor took over the direction of the *Carlswerk* as equal partners.[97] Rudolf Martin estimated the wealth of the three as about equal. The Berlin wholesale merchant Philipp Freudenberg headed the firm Hermann Gerson together with his two brothers. Philipp's four sons (born from 1866 on) became co-owners.[98]

91. See Mosse, *German-Jewish*, p. 86.

92. See Kohlschütter, *Ein Genie*, pp. 59–61.

93. See also Davidoff/Hall, *Family Fortunes*, p. 206.

94. See Treue, *Die Feuer*, p. 166.

95. See Hashagen, *Geschichte*, vol. 2, part 2, pp. 568–69.

96. Achinger, *Richard Merton*, p. 370; see p. 205. Also, see Achinger, *Wilhelm Merton*, p. 322.

97. See Wessel, "Die Unternehmerfamilie," pp 59, 63, 78. After the firm was converted to a joint stock company in 1899, the family's share in the capital declined See pp. 69–73.

98. StA Potsdam, Pr.Br.Rep. 30 Berlin C Tit. 94 Nr. 10265 passim.

There is considerable evidence of harmonious collaboration between brothers inside the same firm. The classic example is the Siemens family. Werner von Siemens shared the direction of the firm with two brothers. Werner died in 1883 and left the company to his brother Carl (who shortly thereafter retired) and to his sons Wilhelm and Arnold. (Werner stipulated in his will that his share of the partnership should be shared equally by three of his children. The four younger children were to be only sleeping partners.) Wilhelm, the younger of the two, played the leading role. Arnold was described by a relative, Georg Siemens, as a person who shied away from personal contacts and conflicts. He concerned himself primarily with matters relating to personnel, administration, and social policy.[99] A sister reported that Arnold was completely "free of any jealousy" toward his brother.[100] Carl Friedrich, another brother, who was seventeen years younger, spent many years preparing to take over the direction of the company, which occurred in 1919. Other relatives had top management positions in the Siemens Corporation. In addition, many members of the family were stockholders in Siemens and Halske.

The four Mannesmann brothers demonstrated excellent teamwork in the invention of seamless piping and in the founding and direction of the German-Austrian *Mannesmannröhren* Works (pipe factories) in Berlin.[101] There was also a harmonious division of labor in the *Brockhaus Verlag* (publishing house). Until 1895 the brothers Eduard and Rudolf Brockhaus headed the firm. One was responsible for the book-marketing side of the business, the other for the technical (printing) side. They took one another's place during absences. From 1895 to 1905 Eduard's son Albert and Rudolf's son Rudolf Jr. directed the company. Albert, the older of the two, took over the management, the finances, and personal contacts with authors and editors. Rudolf, who was responsible for retail trade, the second-hand book business, commission sales and bookkeeping, left the firm in 1905. Albert then brought in his brother Fritz as partner.[102] Three of the seven sons of industrialist Karl Röchling were active in their father's company. Louis, who interrupted his chemistry studies in order to come into the business at his father's request, took over sales management. The tech-

99. See Siemens, *Carl Friedrich von Siemens*, pp. 15, 23. Also, see Siemens, *Geschichte*, vol. 1, p, 192.

100. See Goetzeler and Schoen, *Wilhelm und Carl*, p. 31.

101. See Bauert-Keetmann, *Deutsche Industriepioniere*, pp 233–34.

102. See Brockhaus, *Die Firma*, pp. 283–84, 301, 345, 351, 360.

nical director was first Richard, who died young, and then Hermann.[103] Three Berlin department stores were headed by brothers during the Wilhelmine period and afterwards: Berthold and Hermann Israel; Georg, Franz, and Wilhelm Wertheim; and Georg and Martin Tietz.[104] Three brothers participated in the direction of the Borsig Works from 1895 on.[105]

One brother often played a dominant role. Theodor Guilleaume apparently did not want to work on the basis of equality with his brother Max, and he succeeded in having his own way. He had certain prerogatives, for example, in the signing of contracts.[106] Josef Thyssen concerned himself with daily administrative matters in a position decidedly inferior to that of his brother August.[107] Max Warburg was the real head of the Warburg bank.[108] A police report on the Pintsch brothers (Richard, Julius, Oskar, and Albert) whose firm (J. Pintsch AG) produced gas appliances, stated, "The four brothers share the management of the business in admirably harmonious collaboration." However, Richard is described here as the dominant figure. "Oskar, who lacks broad business vision, is concerned with the construction of fine mechanical instruments, lives only for this practical activity, and does not want to assert himself."[109]

Wolf Wertheim left the Wertheim Corporation because of personal conflicts and founded a competing business.[110] The Stinnes family broke apart. But it is amazing how seldom power struggles occurred in these families. Family solidarity, which was the life-blood of a family business, was still strong among the Wilhelmine business elite. Werner Mosse is mistaken in his assumption that collaboration between brothers was typical only of the Jewish community.[111]

103. See Nutzinger, *Karl Röchling*, p. 117.
104. On the Israels, see StA Potsdam, Pr.Br.Rep. 30 Berlin C Tit. 94 Nr. 10848 passim. On the Wertheims, see StA Potsdam, Pr.Br.Rep. 30 Berlin C Tit 94 Nr. 14311, Bl 18–19. A fourth brother had left the company. On the Tietz, see Tietz, *Hermann Tietz*, p. 150.
105 See Martius, *Erlebtes*, p. 30.
106. See Wessel, *Unternehmerfamilie*, pp. 78–81.
107. See Arnst, "August Thyssen," p 108.
108. See Rosenbaum, "M.M. Warburg," pp. 134–40.
109. Polizeipräsident Berlin an Handelsministerium, 1903, StA Potsdam, Pr.Br.Rep. 30 Berlin C Tit. 94 Nr. 12279, Bl. 68.
110. StA Potsdam, Pr Br.Rep. 30 Berlin C Tit. 94 Nr 14311 and 14340 passim.
111. "Indeed the joint activities of two or more brothers, or cousins, in the following generations were so widespread, at any rate in the nineteenth century, that they may be regarded as the typical form of Jewish economic organization at the level here considered. Impressionistically it would appear that such cooperation was considerably more common among Jews than among their Gentile counterparts." Mosse, *German-Jewish*, p. 96. The following businessmen's families mentioned above were not Jewish: Guilleaume, Hoesch, Siemens, Mannesmann, Röchling, Borsig, Thyssen, and Pintsch

Conclusion

Rebellion and a long phase of adolescence, lasting well into the twenties, had become typical for males in the wealthy business elite by the Wilhelmine period. As authoritarian family structures receded, young men were generally allowed a period devoted to fraternity life, drinking, bicycle racing, hunting, horseback riding, "driving around," swimming, traveling, or the cultivation of leftist political persuasions. Often, an identity crisis took place in which the businessman's son wrestled with the psychological burden of becoming his father's successor. This was sometimes magnified by cultural or intellectual interests, or awakened in the parents' home or at school. It would be false to ascribe these inclinations to anti-capitalist tendencies in pre-war German society. Rather, they grew out of a humanist educational ideal which had long served the purposes of the bourgeoisie and was an integral part of the middle-class mentality. Rarely were the intellectual and artistic activities of wealthy businessmen's sons anti-capitalist or anti-Semitic in nature. Seldom was the wealthy business elite infiltrated by the values of the traditional ruling elite – military values, for example. Thus, identity crises seldom took the form described by Hellige. Authoritarian family structures were far less common than Hellige believed, and bourgeois values far stronger, particularly in the German-Jewish business elite. Evidence of a typical Jewish neurosis could not be found.

The tradition in business was carried over to the next generation in the great majority of families. As a rule, the eldest son joined the management of his father's firm, especially if it was a private company. Here we find evidence that family solidarity continued to override individualism. We know from the autobiographical and biographical literature that fathers put a great deal of pressure on eldest sons and only sons to take over the family company. But it is also clear that most businessmen's sons eventually came to the conclusion that it was in their own best interests to follow in their fathers' footsteps. This is reflected in the fact that a majority of the younger sons and the sons of the heads of joint stock companies also entered a career in business, as well as in autobiographical accounts such as that of Paul Wallich. In many families, we find two or more brothers working together in the family company. Primogeniture was rare outside of heavy industry.

In this chapter, we found further evidence that aristocratization was largely limited to a small group of ennobled families, which had generally embarked on a program of assimilation with the nobility long before the 1890s. Aristocratization did not correlate with geographic regions and economic activity in expected ways. Few sons entered careers associated with the educated bourgeoisie (including civil service positions), except in the Hanseatic cities.

Chapter 5

Residential Patterns, Villas, and Landed Estates

Typical of the pretentiousness of the era, the Wilhelmine upper bourgeoisie lived in ever-growing luxury. After moving from a house by the factory to a mansion in an exclusive residential suburb, purchasing landed estates, and gaining entrance to aristocratic circles, the wealthy businessman had in large part lost contact with his middle-class roots. This reorientation has been seen by many as symptomatic of the decline of the German bourgeoisie, an interpretation that is based on a comparison with middle-class norms, values, and habits in the early nineteenth century. Friedrich Zunkel wrote, "Though the goal of working was the accumulation of money, it was not used to provide a pleasant and pleasurable life for oneself. Just as businessmen rejected any unproductive accumulation of dead capital, without putting it to work and accumulating interest, anything that did not contribute to realistic progress and financial security was foreign to his thinking." This attitude was the product not only of the Protestant work ethic but also economic necessity (i.e., the need for capital in the business enterprise). In the earlier part of the century, the homes of businessmen were large but decorated in a simple manner, their clothing elegant but plain, and their eating habits "moderate and modest." Luxury was frowned upon. Zunkel sees the gradual withering of traditional bourgeois values and the increasing imitation of aristocratic residential styles and social forms as symptoms of a growing feudalism.[1]

When, however, we place this re-orientation process within the

1. Zunkel, *Der rheinisch-westfälische Unternehmer*, esp. pp. 66–72, 110–12; quotation on p 71.

157

business community in a broader sociological context, other ways of looking at these changes come into focus. Of particular relevance is Thorstein Veblen's *Theory of the Leisure Class*, first published in 1899.[2] This was not only an exposé of social climbing in fin-de-siècle America, but also a work of considerable sociological merit. "In order to gain and to hold the esteem of men," he wrote, "it is not sufficient merely to possess wealth or power. The wealth or power must be put in evidence, for esteem is awarded only on evidence." According to Veblen, wealth and power are demonstrated primarily through conspicuous leisure and conspicuous consumption. The wife and household employees, by doing no productive work, show the world that the master of the house, a personage of high position, lives in affluence. Social status is also demonstrated through the use or consumption of the best (and most expensive) food. The process of social differentiation thus defines what is "good taste," and this applies not only to food, drink and life style but also to educational and cultural values. Beauty becomes a question of price. There is an entire range of standards of consumption that corresponds to social classification, and the standard rises almost automatically with increasing wealth: ". . .a fresh advance in conspicuous consumption is relatively easy; indeed it takes place almost as a matter of course. In the rare cases where it occurs, a failure to increase one's visible consumption when the means for an increase are at hand is felt in popular apprehension to call for explanation, and unworthy motives of miserliness are imputed to those who fall short in this respect. The motive is emulation – the stimulus of an invidious comparison which prompts us to outdo those with whom we are in the habit of classing ourselves."[3]

This provides an important explanation why the business elite imitated the aristocratic life style. Whereas the German business community in the middle of the nineteenth century was firmly anchored in the middle class, the Wilhelmine business elite, by virtue of its power and wealth, had risen into the highest ranks of society. The class with which it measured itself socially was the wealthiest, most powerful segment of the nobility. As Veblen would lead us to expect, competition took place partly at the level of taste and consumption. Spurred on by the "stimulus of invidious comparison," the business elite tried to demonstrate and legit-

2. Veblen, *Theory*
3. Ibid., pp. 42 and 81

158

imize its new social status through the accepted forms of display that were associated with the nobility.

However, the growing materialism of the bourgeoisie should also be understood as an outgrowth of the rising economic prosperity of the empire. The successes of capitalism led to the increasing social acceptance of the *nouveau riche* life style in certain circles. As the wealthiest businessmen moved into leading positions in society, the older middle-class patterns of behavior lost their validity.

Another factor must be taken into consideration. The rising European bourgeoisie, confronted with a society not organized according to the principle of achievement, but rather according to the principle of birthright, developed a code of values in opposition to those of the nobility. In mid-nineteenth-century Germany, these bourgeois values included rationality, punctuality, decency, honesty, frugality, and the strong ties of family and friendship.[4] The very rapid rise of the bourgeoisie in Germany did not extinguish this sense of being different from the pre-industrial elite. Thus, there was a tension between the old bourgeois values and the new tendency to "emulate the class next above it in the social scale," the aristocracy, or to be more exact, the wealthiest segment of the aristocracy.

Warren Breckman has shown what impact these forces had on the debate about luxury in Germany.[5] Up through the mid-nineteenth century, the middle class primarily criticized aristocratic luxury. But as middle-class confidence grew, the discussion shifted to the effect of luxury on the middle class. Luxury was "recognized as inevitable," the product of hard work. However, it was felt that negative effects of growing luxury had to be fought: decadence, disinclination to continue to work hard, spiritual poverty. Breckman makes the point that middle-class concern with its own vitality reflects a sense of its own importance: ". . . we see at least a sector of the German bourgeoisie self-consciously proclaiming its distinct historical role and its leadership of society."[6]

The following discussion of values and life style will focus first on changing residential patterns and social segregation, the exodus to the suburbs and beyond, and the prevalence of the second

---

4. Admittedly, these values were not exclusively bourgeois. (For example, impoverished members of the German nobility made a virtue out of necessity by embracing frugality as a "higher value.") What is involved here is an ideal type of the bourgeoisie's self-image as formulated by Zunkel.

5. See Breckman, "Disciplining Consumption," pp. 485–505.

6. Ibid., p. 495.

home. An attempt will be made to decipher the "meaning" of the architecture of the businessman's villa and the significance of the purchase of castles, manors, and landed estates. In examining the layout of the villa and the choice between a residential suburb and a central residential location in the city, we shall inquire whether social life took precedence over family life.

Residential Patterns

In the nineteenth and early twentieth centuries, far-reaching changes took place in the social geography of the big German cities, coinciding with the social and economic rise of the business elite. Four overlapping stages in the residential patterns of the business elite can be identified. Originally the place of residence and the place of production or business were identical. Later the businessman lived in an urban "palace" or in a regal mansion in an exclusively residential area. In the third stage, some began to spend the winter in the city and the summer in the suburbs. The transition to year-round life in the suburbs took place in the fourth stage.

For much of the nineteenth century, a businessman's living quarters and his offices or factories were often located in close proximity to one another or even in the same building, though in some types of industries, such as mining and salt works, this was not possible.[7] This allowed the constant supervision of employees. "As in the villa of the renaissance, a protective girdle of gardens and groves of trees provided the necessary separation from the production areas without detracting from the impression of constant surveillance and the presence of power."[8] With the growing bureaucratization of business enterprises and the resulting weakening of patriarchal structures, management took over the function of direct supervision, thus allowing the owner of the company or head of the corporation to live elsewhere. Second, the expansion of factory installations and the resulting increase in noise, dirt, and stench made such a move desirable. The overall pollution levels in the cities were on the rise.[9] A third factor was a difference in outlook between the generation of founders and the generations of

7. See Grundmann, "Schlösser," p. 149.
8. Bentmann and Müller, *Die Villa*, p 121. Also, see Richter and Zännker, *Der Burgertraum*, p. 99.
9. On environmental pollution in Hamburg, see Evans, *Death*, pp. 109ff.

**Home of Conrad Niethammer (1863–1931) in Kriebstein, Saxony.
Note that his home was located next to his paper factory and down
the hill from a castle owned by an old baronial family.**

sons and grandsons. The generation that built up the company was
in many cases not used to middle-class comfort, and, after years of
struggle, could view with pride the smoke billowing out of the
smokestacks. The successors were more secure in their social position and were not content merely to make do. This transition
could take place within a single generation.

Wolfgang Brönner offers a fourth explanation for the origins of
the villa suburbs. According to Brönner the villa provided the
bourgeoisie with an escape from the world of business, a "house in
the countryside" where the private aspects of life could come fully
into play. The villa on the factory grounds fell far short of realizing
this bourgeois ideal. Brönner develops the thought that the bourgeois concept of an ideal dwelling place was closely linked to
nature and – under the influence of Romanticism – regarded the
Rhine valley as the ideal place of residence. As evidence of the link
to nature, he cites the importance given, in the choice of location,
to the panoramic view. For example, in the Bonn area, many villas
were located on the Drachenfels, overlooking the Rhine. "The
term 'villa', as it was used in the nineteenth century denotes not
only the antithesis of living in the city, but also a special manner of

161

living in the countryside. Meanwhile, the possibilities for realizing this villa ideal were quite limited. There was no second landscape in Germany that corresponded to the aspirations of that period to the same extent as the Rhineland."[10] However, the businessman saw himself compelled by the requirements of his professional life to choose a place of residence that was not ideal. The suburban villa was thus a compromise solution.

Knut Borchardt attributes the move to the suburbs largely to the aristocratic model. As a result of the move of the Krupps from a house next to the factory into the more remote Villa Hügel, ". . . the charisma of the Krupps was given an additional lift. The owner, by becoming more secretive, added a new dimension to his life." The model here, according to Borchardt, was the princely court. The ruler, in order to give his power mystical connotations, lived withdrawn from public view.[11] Borchardt has no empirical evidence that this is what the Krupps had in mind. There are much more obvious explanations – for example, foul air in Alfred Krupp's first mansion and the general trend among wealthy factory owners to move away from the factory grounds (for the reasons discussed above).

The separation of the home from the factory or office was a process that extended over the entire nineteenth century.[12] Accounts of moving to the outskirts of town are legion in autobiographies and biographies of members of the economic elite, peaking at around the turn of the century. In 1898 Karl Röchling, a heavy industrialist living in Saarbrücken, moved from a house in the center of town, in which there was also office space, to a home in the country. The cement factory owner Rudolf Dyckerhoff lived until 1889 in a house next to the factory in Amöneburg. "The immediate proximity to the factory was of course highly advantageous for Rudolf, since he was at all times close at hand. . . . How often he went at night up to the annular kilns to see whether the annealing process was being carried out according to his instructions and to observe the results of his experiments." In 1889 he bought a villa with a large garden on the Rhine below the castle in which Richard Wagner had composed "Die Meistersänger." August Thyssen lived for years in a house that was situated between the Thyssen-Werke, the railroad, and the Friedrich-

10 Bronner, *Die bürgerliche Villa*, p. 71; also, see pp. 68 and 70.
11. Borchardt, "Der Unternehmerhaushalt," p. 11.
12. Some of the early examples are the Borsig palace, the Rothschild villa in Frankfurt am Main, the palace of the Faber-Castells in Bavaria, and the Krupps' Villa Hügel. See Richter and Zännker, *Bürgertraum*, p. 121. Examples for Silesia in Grundmann, *Schlösser*, pp 149–62.

Wilhelms-Hütte. He described his motives for the purchase of Landsberg Castle in 1903 as follows: "Landsberg is the only estate one can reach by car from Mülheim. Besides it has finer woods and water. I am also pleased by the location in the mountains."[13] There was a similar development in merchant circles. The merchants of the Hanseatic cities lived, up into the nineteenth century, in houses in which living quarters, office space, and warehouse space were combined. Such bourgeois houses could also be found in Mainz. During the course of the nineteenth century these functions were separated; henceforth the businessman lived in a purely residential area, and the city house served only as a town business office.[14] There were similar developments in the banking sector. A prototypical Hamburg bank building around 1914 is described as follows: "The official residence of a director or senior bank officer, which previously was often housed in the second or third floor, has today had to give way almost everywhere to the increased need for business space. . . ."[15] However, this separation took place more slowly in banking than it did in commerce and industry. The big Berlin banks built between the 1870s and 1890s included apartments for the directors that were still used up until the First World War. There is clear evidence that some very wealthy directors and business owners such as Georg von Siemens, Adolf Salomonsohn, Herman Wallich, and Carl Fürstenberg had living quarters in bank buildings up to the 1880s and even beyond. However, the large number of bankers' villas in the Tiergarten section of Berlin indicates that this was more the exception than the rule. The Munich private banker Wilhelm von Finck lived in his bank during the Wilhelmine period.[16]

The physical separation of business and private life went hand-in-hand with the development of exclusive urban residential areas and suburbs. This was part of a process of social segregation that encompassed all segments of society and fundamentally altered the contours of the social geography of the big German cities. This segregation contributed to the decline of patriarchalism, which disturbed at least one contemporary: "When the masses of workers

13. See Nutzinger, *Karl Röchling*, pp. 151–53 Quotation concerning Dyckerhoff in Dyckerhoff Archive, Personalakte Rudolf Dyckerhoff, 26.4.48 Quotation of August Thyssen in Baumann, "August Thyssen," pp. 18–19.

14. On Hamburg, see Rudhard, *Das Burgerhaus*, esp. pp. 51–94, 101–2, 105–6. On Lübeck, see Hübler, *Das Bürgerhaus*, pp. 15–17; Niendorf, *Geschichte*, p. 37. On Mainz, see Stephan, *Das Bürgerhaus*, p. 107.

15 Anonymous, *Hamburg und seine Bauten*, vol. 1, p. 429.

16. See *Berlin und seine Bauten*, vols. 2 and 3, pp. 358–72; Helfferich, *Georg von Siemens*, vol. 3, p. 248; C. Fürstenberg, *Lebensgeschichte*, pp. 31, 132, 140, 504. On the Tiergarten, see Achterberg, *Berliner Hochfinanz*, pp. 43–46. On Finck, see Hoffmann, *Wilhelm von Finck*, p. 183.

come to work from the northern suburbs, the factory manager (or even the head of the corporation) from the Tiergarten, and the unmarried office worker from a furnished room in the middle of the city, and they are all together only by compulsion during the daily working hours, there can be no harmonious relationship between employer and employee, between owner and worker."[17]

The oldest exclusive residential areas were located in cities where commerce, or perhaps the finance sector, predominated. Whereas the proximity of the home to the industrial production facilities separated industrialists from one another, in the Hanseatic cities the places of business and the residences of the merchants were lined up in a row next to one another. Then in the nineteenth century, exclusive residential suburbs came into being in the Hanseatic cities.

Around 1800 the Tiergarten became the first Berlin residential suburb. In 1840 it contained only 118 built-up plots of land. By 1870 the number had risen to 336, but mansions stood on only eighty-four plots. (Sixty-nine percent of the buildings were apartment buildings.) During the imperial period, there was a marked increase in the construction of villas, the owners of which included not only wealthy businessmen but also diplomats and artists. However, around 1900 few villas were still being built in the city, and those were located primarily next to large park areas.[18] In Berlin multimillionaires also lived in apartment buildings. Of fifty-three Berlin businessmen who were among the 502 wealthiest in the *Yearbook of Millionaires*, twenty-four lived in their own houses, four in apartment buildings they owned, and twenty-five in rented apartments. These were magnificent dwellings that were comparable to mansions. Yearly rents fell between 5,000 and 15,000 marks. Most consisted of ten to fifteen rooms. Paul von Schwabach paid 30,000 marks a year for thirty rooms. At the other end of the scale Otto Gerstenberg, general director of Viktoria insurance company, rented a six-room apartment for 2,800 marks annually.[19]

17. E. Bruch, "Wohnungsnot und Hülfe," in *Berlin und seine Entwicklung, Jahrbuch fur Volkswirthschaft und Statistik*, vol. 6 (1872), pp. 50f. Cited according to Schwippe, "Prozeße," pp. 218–19; on social segregation in general, see pp. 195–224.

18. See Machule and Seiberlich, "Die Berliner Villenvororte," p. 95; Schmidt, *Das Tiergartenviertel*, part 1, pp 286 and 300; Posener and Bergius, "Individuell geplante Einfamilienhäuser," pp. 3–4.

19. My own calculation. Source: StA Potscam, Pr.Br.Rep. 30 Berlin C Tit. 94, passim. The fact that these are high for upper-class rental rates is confirmed by Clemens Wischermann's data on the Hamburg districts of Harvestehude and Rotherbaum, generally regarded as upper-class communities, where the average yearly rent in 1910 was about 1,500 marks. In Harvestehude the apartments consisted, on the average, of seven rooms (including the kitchen). See Wischermann, *Wohnen*, p. 318.

In Hamburg the long-established patricians and also some of the newly rich lived in the relatively centrally located residential areas of Harvestehude and Rotherbaum. In Harvestehude lived Albert Ballin, the shipping magnate Hermann Blohm, the Warburgs, the Godeffroys, the Berenberg-Goßlers, the Amsincks, the Petersens, the Rupertis, the Mercks, the Sievekings, and the Westphals – all of them members of the political or economic elite. Some members of the lower middle class lived in Harvestehude as well, though only the very wealthy lived directly on the Alster (a tributary of the Elbe, widened into a lake in downtown Hamburg). Very few Hamburg big businessmen lived in apartments. Schramm writes: "Surely none of the big German cities surpasses Hamburg in the cult of 'one's own home with a garden.'"[20]

Big businessmen also lived in centrally located sections of other cities. The business elite of Essen lived in the city. Cologne was the largest German city that retained its fortifications well into the nineteenth century, making it one of the most densely populated cities in Europe. In 1881, the walls were razed. Many of the wealthy bourgeoisie lived on the "Deutscher Ring." Ernst Wertheimber was not the only Frankfurt banker who lived in a palatial city home.[21]

For a growing number of businessmen, living in the city was restricted to the winter months. The townhouses of Hamburg were especially confining and unhealthy in the summer months, and in the first half of the nineteenth century the middle class began spending the summer months in the country. "Stately country homes" were beginning to appear around 1860. Elegant summer homes were also built in Bremen in the nineteenth century. There was a similar development in Lübeck. A typical example for the Wilhelmine period is that of the banker Albert Warburg, who spent the summer in Klein-Flottbek (and rode into the city every day). Several members of another branch of the family lived in houses that Moritz, also a banker, had built on a piece of land he had bought in 1896 in Kösterberg, a suburb of Hamburg. It was his intention to be able to assemble his children and grandchildren there for a few months every year. Although Kösterberg was not

---

20. Schramm, *Neun Generationen*, vol. 2, p. 421. Also, see Evans, *Death*, pp. 56–63; Wischermann, *Wohnen*, pp. 310–11, Rudhard, *Burgerhaus*, p. 98.

21. On businessmen in Essen, see Brandi, *Essener Arbeitsjahre*, p 15. On Cologne, see Ladd, *Urban Planning*, pp. 91, 108. For an example of a big businessman who lived on the Deutscher Ring, see Wessel, "Die Unternehmerfamilie," pp. 73–75. On Wertheimber, see Lanckoronska, *Li(e)ber Beda*, p. 22.

lacking in pastoral charm, it was closely tied to Hamburg: "The house was situated high above the Elbe. From the windows one had a view of the river and the opposite shore. All the steamships that sailed into or out of Hamburg harbor passed by our property. We could never get enough of that view."[22]

This development began somewhat later in Berlin. There were hardly any businessmen among the owners of summer houses that were built in the Tiergarten in the early nineteenth century. This was due to the economic structure of Berlin at that time. Before German unification, wealthy Berliners, including some businessmen, lived in the summertime in Charlottenburg, which at that time was still suburban in character. Berlin businessmen began building summer homes primarily in the late nineteenth century when the suburbs came into existence.[23]

Richard Evans graphically describes the effects that this summertime living in the country had on the social self-image and political attitudes of the business community: "Virtually all the nuisances which afflicted Hamburg, from rotten food and sour milk, smoke and dust, animal smells and ordure, vermin, parasites, and rats, were at their most unbearable in the summer months. The wealthiest taxpayers did little to improve the city's environment until they were forced to, because they could always escape from it when it became unbearable."[24]

The most striking development of the period around the turn of the century was the rapid growth of planned residential suburbs[25] and the transition to year-round living there. The motives for moving listed by Burkhard Hofmeister are only partially applicable to the business elite: "flight from inhuman housing conditions in the city; attachment to nature: verandas, terraces, gardens; withdrawal from the turmoil of city life; cultivation of family life; avoidance of property rental and attraction to ownership of real estate; small or non-existent local taxes."[26] In the first stages of many villa colonies, the owners lived there only during the summer months. Gradually more and more of them began living there year-round.

22. Warburg, *Aus meinen Aufzeichnungen*, p. 16. See Merck, *Vom gewesenen Hamburg*, p. 63; Rudhard, *Das Bürgerhaus*, p. 106; Stein, *Das Burgerhaus*, p. 119; Hübler, *Das Burgerhaus*, p. 88. On Ballin, see Cecil, *Albert Ballin*, p. 143. On the Warburgs, see Wenzel-Burchard, *Granny*, pp. 33–34; Attali, *Siegmund G. Warburg*, p. 71

23. See Machule and Seiberlich, "Berliner Villenvororte," p. 95; Gilbert, *Lehrjahre*, p. 12

24. Evans, *Death*, p. 126.

25 Exclusive residential suburbs were characterized by the detached houses, park-like surroundings, very broad streets, the architectural individuality of each house, and social exclusivity.

26 Hofmeister, "Wilhelminischer Ring," p. 114; see p. 109. See Maruhn, "Der Kolner Stadtteil," p. 131.

In Berlin, as in other cities, exclusive residential suburbs were laid out by developers along railroad lines built for military use and for freight. Police building regulations also encouraged this development. A regulation dated 5 December 1892 for the first time established zoning codes for Berlin suburbs that lay outside the city limits. Some areas were designated as residential areas for the construction of large country homes.[27] This government policy is astonishing when one considers the loss of local income tax resulting from the increasing migration of the wealthiest Berliners into suburbs located in the province of Brandenburg.[28] In the case of Grunewald, the explanation is that a deal was made. The developer, the Kurfürstendamm Gesellschaft, took on the obligation of expanding the Kurfürstendamm along the lines of the Paris boulevards, and in exchange was granted government permission to develop the Grunewald residential suburb.[29]

After 1885 there was a continuous growth of villa colonies including Westend, Herrstrasse, Grunewald, Dahlem, Friedenau, Zehlendorf, Nikolassee, and Frohnau. Berlin had the largest suburbs of any European city other than London.[30] After cheap commuter trains came into existence, people began to live in the suburbs in the winter as well. Among those buying property were businessmen, higher government officials, military officers, doctors, professors, artists, and rentiers. The wealthiest of the bourgeoisie built their villas primarily in Grunewald, which Alfred Kerr facetiously referred to as a "millionaires' shantytown." It was mostly businessmen who lived there but also a number of artists, scientists, writers, and musicians such as Fritz Kreisler, Gerhardt Hauptmann, Max Harden, and Fritz Haber.[31]

Marienburg was an exclusive residential suburb of Cologne. It

27. Later building regulations (introduced in 1894, 1897, 1903, etc.) reduced the areas provided for the construction of villas. However, there remained large areas for the construction of country homes. See Schwippe, "Prozeße," pp 213–17 For the criticism by the architect Muthesius of the police building regulations and the resulting creation of exclusive villa suburbs, see Muthesius, introduction to *Landhaus und Garten*, p XX. On the development of Berlin suburbs, see also Ladd, *Urban Planning*, p. 208.

28. In Prussia income taxes constituted a significant proportion of local taxes. Tax funds were not redistributed between local governments or between local, state, and federal governments. See Mulert, *Kommunalfinanzen*, pp 4–9, 58; Gerlach, *Die preußische Steuerreform*, esp. pp. 38–39 On the move of wealthy taxpayers to Grunewald, see Nagel, "Grunewald," p. 53

29. See Nagel, "Grunewald," p 43

30 On the history of the various suburbs, see Machule and Seiberlich, "Berliner Villenvororte," pp. 93 and 114; Posener and Bergius, "Individuell geplante Einfamilienhäuser," pp 1–42.

31. See Hofmeister, "Wilhelminischer Ring," pp. 109–11; Kerr, *Walther Rathenau*, pp. 34–35; Gläser, "Die Villenkolonie," pp. 63–93.

grew up outside the city gates from the 1870s on. Originally the wealthier citizens had lived in the older sections of Cologne. In the late nineteenth century they moved into a newer section of the city, but the lack of good building land there and the disagreeable aspects of city life increasingly caused them to move into the suburbs. Prior to the First World War the construction of homes in Marienburg was closely related to the expansion of the transportation network. During the first few years few people moved there, partly because the means of transportation to Cologne were inadequate. With the growing prospect of the streetcar line being extended to Marienburg, and especially after the laying of the rails, construction activity increased markedly.

The social profile of the residents of Marienburg in the year 1910 can be summed up as follows: fifteen percent of the heads of household were pensioners and rentiers; twenty-six percent merchants and manufacturers; eight percent engineers and professors; eleven percent lawyers, judges, architects, and building inspectors; fifteen percent domestic servants; and the remaining twenty-five percent was divided among various other professional groups. In 1910, forty-two percent of the inhabitants were Protestants, fifty-five percent were Catholics, and one percent Jews. Thus Protestants were present in greater numbers there than in the overall population of Cologne, due partly to their dominant role in the Cologne business community. In any event, Catholics were more likely to build in the suburban residential area of Lindenthal.[32] The social profile of Marienburg differed from that of Grunewald primarily in the fact that in Marienburg, various segments of the upper bourgeoisie lived together, while in Grunewald the residents were primarily businessmen with the exception of a few famous personalities from the intellectual-cultural world. Wealthy aristocrats seldom lived in these suburbs.

Businessmen moved to the outskirts of town in several regions, even where there were no residential suburbs. The tobacco industrialist Walther Böninger of Duisburg and Robert Bosch of Stuttgart moved into villas at the edges of their respective cities shortly after the turn of the century. Wealthy Bremen merchants moved out of the heart of the city after the walls were torn down in 1802. At first they lived next to the embankment. After 1849, when residents of the suburbs were given rights of citizenship and

---

32. See Maruhn "Kölner Stadtteil," pp. 131–47, Thomas and Trumper, *Bayenthal*, pp. 106–11.

the right of assembly, merchants built houses outside the old city limits, especially on the counterscarp (a part of the old fortifications), then in the suburbs where they made their permanent residences. In some areas the businessmen did not move to a suburb but into a nearby town. Thus some of the wealthy businessmen of Mannheim lived in Heidelberg, especially after 1900. Big businessmen from Frankfurt and Cologne built homes in the Rhine Valley. Some Hamburg businessmen lived on the Palmaille in neighboring Altona, where distinguished Altona families also had their palatial homes. Some Hamburg patricians lived in suburbs along the Elbe such as Gross-Flottbek, Othmarschen, and Blankenese. However, due to the geography of the city of Hamburg, the suburbs did not play as important a role there as they did in other cities.[33]

How did business families decide whether to live downtown or in the suburbs? Fürstenberg could never reach a definitive decision. From 1883 to 1889 he lived in the building where his bank was located. In 1889, when he married, he bought a house in the Tiergarten area. In 1897 he had a country home built in Grunewald where the family lived only in the summertime. After the turn of the century, when some of the children had left home, Fürstenberg sold the house in the Tiergarten. ("In the long run, it seemed to me too much to call two spacious homes my own. . . .") On a trial basis he spent a winter with his family in Grunewald. Apparently this experiment did not turn out completely successfully. "I could not seriously count on living permanently in Grunewald, because for my wife it would have meant a sort of unwanted banishment." So they again rented a centrally located apartment. In 1907 they moved into the new bank building. Finally, they seem to have lived mainly in Grunewald.[34]

Hildegard Wallich also commented on this subject in her memoirs. When her husband Paul became owner of the *Berliner Handels-Gesellschaft*, they had to look for a home in keeping with their social status. Paul wanted to take an old apartment like those available in the western part of the city. The reason: "He hated the modern Berlin apartments with their long hallways, where the din-

33. See Croon, "Die wirtschaftlichen Fuhrungsschichten," p 155 On Boninger, see Ring, *Geschichte*, p 282 (However, Boninger's house had been built much earlier by his father.) On Bosch, see Heuss, *Robert Bosch*, p. 190. On Bremen, see Stein, *Das Burgerhaus*, pp 119–23. On the Mannheimers, see Wachenheim, *Vom Großburgertum*, pp 1–2 On the Rhine valley, see Bronner, *Die burgerliche Villa*, p. 71 On the Palmaille the suburbs on the Elbe, see Gobert, *Die Bau- und Kunstdenkmale*, vol 2, pp 146–67, 189–242, Sloman, *Erinnerungen*, pp 86–87

34 See C Furstenberg, *Lebensgeschichte*, pp 231–33, 329, 450–51, 504.

**The home of Carl and Aniela Fürstenberg
at Viktoriastraße 7 in Berlin.**

ing room was always a passageway." They joined together two
adjacent apartments that were without central heating or water
heaters. The decisive factor in the decision to take this apartment
appears to have been a tour of the apartment of the artists Paul
Cassirer and Tilla Durieux, who lived in the same building.
Hildegard Wallich described that apartment as follows: "It was the
most beautiful apartment I had ever seen, very big, bright rooms,
beautifully decorated with marvelous pictures." For the apartment
above it, the Wallichs paid a yearly rent of 10,000 marks. In the
summertime they lived in a villa (which still stands) on the
Potsdam side of the Glienecke Bridge. Paul's father, who owned
the villa, thought they should move there permanently. Hildegard
resisted that idea because she was afraid she would become socially
isolated. The multimillionaire merchant Ernst Schramm wanted to
build a country home to live in year-round, but his wife kept him
from doing so because she did not want to live in such a remote
area. Quite a number of Berlin businessmen – for example, Paul
Schwabach and the Siemens brothers – lived in town in the winter
and in the country in the summertime.[35]

The case of the Fürstenbergs shows most clearly how one could

35 See H Wallich, *Erinnerungen*, pp 125–26, 129, 146; Schramm, *Neun Generationen*, p.
413

be torn between life in the city and life in the country. Living in a central location meant a short way to work and an active social life. Women were particularly reluctant to give up social contacts. Hildegard Wallich's remarks show that there was a refined style of living that could be found in the expensive residential areas of the city. There was also a special social prestige bound up in the purchase of the former city palaces of aristocrats in reduced circumstances who were forced to leave Berlin in droves.[36] On the other hand, life in the suburbs meant closeness to nature, tranquillity, and better air. For some the best solution was a summer home, since it was important to be in the city during the "season" (that is, in winter), while nature could best be appreciated in the warmer months. As more and more millionaires moved into Grunewald, its prestige rose, and it was possible to maintain intensive social contacts there also.

Some very wealthy businessmen had summer homes in the country, or in another town, or even in another country, such as the banker Fritz Andreae (on Lake Starnberg), Carl von der Heydt (in Godesberg), Georg von Siemens (on Lago Maggiore), Eduard Arnhold (one in Florence, one in Bavaria, as well as a small castle on a landed estate), Heinrich Ehrhardt (in his home town in Thuringia), the Essen banker Albert Müller (in Rapallo and Godesberg), Wilhelm Merton (on Lake Como), and Fritz Krupp (a hunting lodge in Sayn, and a second palace in Baden-Baden). A number of businessmen had second homes in Bavaria.[37] The purpose of these remote vacation homes was to provide personal comfort rather than to impress visitors and passers-by. This development reflects a change in the values of the German business community that increasingly permitted the enjoyment of the fruits of labor without detriment to the work ethic. For example, work papers were routinely taken along, business mail was forwarded and answered, and vacation stays were interrupted for business reasons.[38] This shows a marked tendency toward an elite life style that

36. Cecil, "Jew and Junker," pp. 54–55.
37. See Mangoldt, *Auf der Schwelle* (Weilheim, 1963), p. 56; Heydt, *Unser Haus,* p 43; Helfferich, *Georg von Siemens,* vol. 3, p. 251; Arnhold, *Eduard Arnhold,* p. 29; Bunsen, *Zeitgenossen,* p. 71; Ehrhardt, *Hammerschläge,* p. 70; Brandi, *Essener Arbeitsjahre,* p. 18; Achinger, *Wilhelm Merton,* p 243; Meisbach, *Friedrich Alfred Krupp,* pp. 16, 19. On Bavaria, see Martin, *Jahrbuch,* vol. 4; Ley, *Villa,* esp. pp. 95–160.
38. See, for example, Meisbach, *Krupp,* pp. 16, 19; Kohlschütter, *Ein Genie,* p. 44; Achinger, *Wilhelm Merton,* p. 247; Letter from Wilhelm von Siemens to Arnold von Siemens dated 1 July 1896, SAA Lr 563. The place of retirement, which of course was not limited to any specific location, is omitted from discussion here.

clearly distinguished the business elite from the rest of the bourgeoisie. The construction of homes far from the city increased after the First World War.[39]

Villas

The dwelling-place – whether it was a villa, a castle, a city palace, or just "our home" – was the most important status symbol of the Wilhelmine business elite and the most important investment for representational purposes. Schramm wrote concerning the businessman's villa of the Wilhelmine period: "If today one contemplates the dwelling-places in which the wealthy Berliners installed themselves around the year 1900, the palaces – modestly called 'villas' – of the 'magnates of the Ruhr district,' the pseudo-Gothic castles that the Rhineland industrialists caused to be constructed out of medieval ruins, then one shudders at the lack of moderation of the 'Wilhelminians.'"[40] The architect Hermann Muthesius found considerable differences between the externally simple English country home, which "does not pretend to be anything except a house to live in" and the German villa. He wrote, "If one compares these English houses with the pretentious façade that the house in our residential suburbs presents, the differences in the ways the German and English home owners think and feel immediately become clear. The villas are lined up on the street and try to surpass one another in architectural motifs and layout. . . . The only motive their creators appear to have had was to please the passers-by."[41]

In the Wilhelmine businessman's villa, various stylistic tendencies were interwoven that cannot be discussed in all their complexity here. In this study we can only point out the significance of aristocratic models and certain other influences on the bourgeois villa. From the eighteenth century on the castle served as a model for residences and factory buildings. However, the conclusions drawn from research by architects and art historians indicate that the bourgeois castle did not imply a symbolic feudalization but rather the use of certain elements of aristocratic style for bourgeois purposes. Hartwig Suhrbehr writes of the aristocratization of residen-

39. See, for example, Rudhard, *Das Burgerhaus*, p. 105.
40 Schramm, *Neun Generationen*, p. 426.
41 Muthesius, *Landhaus*, p XX.

tial style: "With his eyes firmly fixed on the social class above him, which still held a monopoly on political power, the businessman of the upper bourgeoisie used the architecture of the nobility as a model in erecting ostentatious dwellings as a manifestation of his claim to socio-political ranking."[42] Wolfgang Richter and Jurgen Zännker go further with the idea that the "bourgeois palace" combines the endeavor to gain social independence from the nobility with the attempt to expand authority over the working class: "The pretensions of the bourgeois palace fluctuate between these two ideas inasmuch as it tries on the one hand to surpass the nobility and on the other hand to imitate it by adopting its forms."[43]

During early industrialization, the factory acquired an aristocratic exterior that was designed to provide the business enterprise with prestige in a society in which pre-industrial values were still strong: "A conservative, impressive style of architecture was a better testimonial to the traditionalism, solidity, and integrity of a businessman than technical modernity could be. The architectural style of the nobility ennobled the businesses of the bourgeois parvenus who thought that with money they could buy anything, and with titles of nobility they could acquire aristocratic ways of life, reputations and credibility, which in turn could be converted into business advantage but also into a hedonistic enjoyment of life. The monied nobility tried to beat the nobility of birth at its own game by imitating it."[44] It has also been suggested that this was a way of demonstrating one's credit-worthiness.[45]

Andreas Ley has analyzed the building of castles for the bourgeoisie and for the nobility in the nineteenth century. Both the nobility, whose position in society was deteriorating, and the rising bourgeoisie made the palace an "architectonic manifestation of the claim to supremacy." The palace suggested established social status. In addition, the fortress-like appearance of these mansions, the turrets and parapets, were part of an almost crude demonstration of power.[46] The romantic image of the castle ruins, which was understood as the symbol of the evanescence of human endeavor

---

42. Suhrbier, "Abseits," p. 5.

43 Richter and Zännker, *Bürgertraum*, p. 87

44. Ibid., pp. 107–8, also, see p. 99.

45. Adorno, "Veblens Angriff," p. 88. Cited according to Goetz, "Schloß," p. 90. Adorno suggests that this is typical of periods of expansion, when credit is hard to come by

46 See Ley, *Villa*, pp. 27–36 The castle served as a legitimizing element for the nobility inasmuch as it was a part of an ostentatious life style, and underlined the age of the noble family by linking it to the architectural style of its ancestors. Examples for Silesia in Grundmann, "Schlößer," pp 149–62.

and of the power of nature, was also very appealing. In the nineteenth century the medieval period was regarded as a wholesome world, and the castle could also symbolize security and independence. In addition, German nationalism promoted the Gothic style as authentically German. Paradoxically, the enthusiasm for the Middle Ages could also be traced to English influences.[47]

The motives for buying "genuine" castles were basically the same.[48] Mention has already been made of August Thyssen's purchase in 1903 of Landsberg Castle (most of which was built in the seventeenth century). The aristocratic social world did not appeal to Thyssen, whose goals in life were centered almost exclusively on his company. His biographer Paul Arnst writes: "His purchase of the old feudal knightly castle and its authentic renovation were motivated less by a need for luxury than by the need to compensate for his lack of personal taste for ostentation by creating outward evidence of his standing in the world."[49] Though he was very frugal in private, "on the other hand he knew how to make a princely display," according to Hjalmar Schacht.[50] On the ground floor of the castle there were sumptuously decorated rooms where guests were received: the dining room, the garden room (where sculptures by Rodin were exhibited), and the drawing room (in which there was a piano). There were no separate family rooms there because Thyssen lived alone. The upstairs rooms used personally by Thyssen (bedroom, work room, etc.) were simply decorated. Noticeably more stylish was the guest room, next to which there was an art nouveau bathroom purchased at the Paris World's Fair.[51]

Gustav Adt, in whom a certain degree of enthusiasm for the Middle Ages can be detected, presents a different case. In 1886 he acquired the Castle Mount in Forbach, on which stood the ruins of an old castle, which he had reconstructed with the help of the assistant headmaster of a Forbach secondary school. The castle was not suitable for large social gatherings, since there was room for only thirty to thirty-five people in the drawing room. Adt appears to have brought in pseudo-feudal furniture and decorations on occasions when aristocrats were present. He invited military officers and old fraternity brothers to the hall of knights in

47 See Ley, *Villa*, pp. 37–58.
48 See Richter and Zannker, *Burgertraum*, pp. 120–21.
49. Arnst, *August Thyssen*, p. 70.
50 Schacht, *76 Jahre*, pp. 184–85
51 Private tour of the Landsberg castle, given by Dr Carl–Friedrich Baumann, Director of the Thyssen Archive See Baumann, "August Thyssen," p. 19.

174

Residential Patterns, Villas, and Landed Estates

the tower and had copies of hunting songs and the like printed for large parties.[52]

Another ingredient of the aristocratic residential style is the park. Almost every villa had a garden, but many mansions, especially those located in the suburbs, had a park.[53] The park of Hamburg merchant Robert Sloman included a peacock and greenhouses and was cared for by a chief gardener with two assistants and "several garden boys." August Thyssen also owned peacocks, and he employed a gamekeeper and a fishery attendant on a temporary basis. In the park of the Katharinenhof, Paul Reusch had the busts of "great Germans" exhibited, among whom there were several "great Swabians." (Reusch was a Swabian.) The model for this was the "German Honor Temple" that King Ludwig I of Bavaria had caused to be erected in the vicinity of Regensburg. This "Valhalla," erected during the First World War, should perhaps be regarded as a patriotic inspiration of amateur historian Reusch.[54]

Historical styles of the post-medieval period also had a major impact on Wilhelmine architecture. The villa in neo-Classical or neo-Baroque style contributed to the businessman's image as a cultivated person. As in the Renaissance, the aura of the villa as the ideal place for the pursuit of the arts, a world apart, was augmented by its location on high ground: "This villa paradise rises above the lowly aspects of ordinary existence, not only in the humanistic-literary sense, as a home of the muses and of letters, but also in a quite concrete and material sense."[55] Historicism was also an "architecture of domination." Renaissance copies of ancient villas advertised that their owners felt as mighty as the ruling class of ancient Rome and Greece; Wilhelmine copies of Renaissance villas had a similar function.[56]

52. See Adt, *Aus meinem Leben*, pp. 130, 144; Wilmin, *Die Familie*, pp. 57–58. However, assimilation into the nobility does not appear to have been his objective, for he rejected ennoblement, and there was never any question about his son Hans taking over the direction of the firm.

53 See Hammerbacher, "Die Hausgarten," pp. 293–398. For examples, see Kerr, *Walther Rathenau*, p 33 (on the Mendelssohns); Lanckoronska, *Li(e)ber*, p. 22 (on banker Ernst Wertheimer); Nutzinger, *Karl Rochling*, p 153 (on heavy industrialist Karl Rochling, Saarbrucken); Wenzel-Burchard, *Granny*, p 39 (on banker Albert Warburg); C. Furstenberg, *Lebensgeschichte*, p 323 (on Furstenberg and on the publisher August Scherl)

54. See Sloman, *Erinnerungen*, p. 88; Schacht, *76 Jahre*, p. 185; Maschke, *Es entsteht*, pp 37–38.

55. See Bentmann and Muller, *Die Villa*, esp. p. 121; quotation on pp 100, 102

56 Ibid., p. 93, also, see p. 121. This theory, first formulated by Veblen, is interpreted as follows by Adorno: "In Veblen's view these decorative elements, because of their similarity to ancient symbols of repression, become threatening. The features that he calls 'archaic' are at the same time symbols of looming calamity " Theodor Adorno, "Veblens Angriff auf die Kultur," in *Prismen, Kulturkritik und Gesellschaft* (Frankfurt am Main, 1955), pp. 88f Cited according to ibid , p 123

175

A love of nature also left its imprint on upper bourgeois concepts of the ideal residence. The anti-urban tendencies of the Wilhelmine period were a factor here, as they were in the Renaissance predilection for the villa.[57] Nevertheless, there was not necessarily a contradiction between nature and capitalism. On this point Rainer Goetz writes: " 'Nature' was. . . . the background against which one projected one's longings for freedom, open space, rest, relaxation, security, etc. The concept of 'nature' however, was bound up in a connotative network with other related concepts that fanned out into a remarkable spread of ideas such as pioneer spirit, adventure, risk-taking, and self-sacrifice, all the way to the concept of homeland – whereby one could close the circle all the way from the conventional perception of 'nature' to the 'marks of quality' of a newly strengthened business world."[58]

Technology could also be used symbolically in the design of the businessman's mansion. Robert Bosch saw to it that his house, built after the turn of the century, was technologically as up-to-date as possible. It contained a large number of bathrooms and toilets, which, though not unique, was certainly unusual for the period. Among the innovations in this mansion were not only a telephone, an elevator, and an electric intercom system, but also a modern system of ventilation, a central vacuum-cleaning system (with holes into which the hose could be inserted in most rooms), and a modern system for collection and use of rain water, which directed rain water to taps not used for drinking water.[59]

The magnificent mansions of the wealthy businessmen served as a backdrop for social life in this class. Nowhere is the connection between the villa and social and economic power as clear as in the case of the Krupp's Villa Hügel. The number of guest rooms and suites available was comparable to that of the palaces of Silesian or East Prussian magnates. In 1910 the villa administration employed 639 persons. The visitor ". . . received an impression that a century earlier could have been made only by a princely palace."[60] However, the legal status of the villa and the organization of the household management can be regarded as modern. Until 1903

57 See ibid., esp. pp. 95–125. The architect Hermann Muthesius championed a suburban ideology that was anti-urban in spirit. See Muthesius, *Landhaus*, pp. 1ff.

58. Goetz, "Das Schloß," p 90.

59. See Muller, *Das Robert-Bosch-Haus*, pp. 38–41.

60 Sturmer, "Alltag," p. 262; see p 257 See Borchardt, "Unternehmerhaushalt," p. 14

**The dining room in Walther Rathenau's home
in Grunewald (Berlin).**

the villa was a part of the factory property.[61] It had its own administrative staff. In 1877 and in 1882, house regulations were issued that
set down the areas of competence of the factory management and
the villa management rather precisely. In the 1870s a modern bookkeeping system was introduced.[62] In the words of Stürmer, "The
bourgeois way of living triumphed in substance, the *ancien régime*
survived in form."[63] The central role that the government played in
the Krupp concern meant that the Krupps had to court the pre-
industrial elite (especially high military officers and diplomats) and
gradually adapt to its life style. However, as Stürmer's own findings
and those of Borchardt show, every aspect of the Krupps' life was
directed toward public relations and business activity.

61. Friedrich Krupp wrote in 1898, "The Hügel property is a part of the assets of the factory
since this property constitutes an integral component of the factory because of its public relations function." Quoted in Borchardt, "Unternehmerhaushalt," p 12 After 1903 a distinction
was made in practice between the family's private property and the mansion. (See p 14.)

62. See ibid , pp. 14–19

63. Stürmer, "Alltag," p 256 Stürmer surprisingly contradicts himself on the same page. "It
is perhaps a manifestation of the tragedy of the German bourgeoisie that the spirit of self-assurance and rationality that originally characterized the villa was transformed into its opposite by
business success, by the power of the Empire and the splendor of its world-power status "

Even those villas that were more typical of the business elite than the Krupp villa were strongly oriented toward public relations. To whatever extent thriftiness still mattered to this class, it is almost never mentioned in autobiographies and biographies in connection with the home, and specific figures confirm the impression that a standard prevailed that was unthinkable in most of the middle class. In the sources there are only occasional mentions of expenditures for homes. Whereas the villa of the wealthy Cologne businessman Gustav von Mallinckrodt was assessed at only 222,000 marks in 1901, Gustav Adt spent more than one million marks for the restoration of a castle from 1911 to 1913. August Thyssen offered 300,000 marks for the Landsberg castle and 80,000 marks for the plot of ground on which it stood. How much he actually paid for it is not known. The granddaughter of Emil Rathenau wrote that he for a long time refused to move into his new home, built in 1912, because he was angry at having paid so much for its construction.[64] The value of the interior furnishings (including books and pictures) of Paul Reusch's Katharinenhof palace was estimated at 400,192 marks in 1917. Ernst Schramm had his dining room furnished for 40,000 marks. The renovation of Paul Wallich's apartment in Berlin cost over 10,000 marks.[65]

In his "Apologie" dated 1919, Walter Rathenau affirmed his work ethic, his lack of interest in luxury and display, and his simplicity: "My home is respectably bourgeois and is attended by two house companions with long years of service."[66] However, James Joll's opinion of this house, which was built in Grunewald in 1910 in accordance with Rathenau's own architectural plan, was as follows: ". . . his home, which he claims to be 'respectably bourgeois,' was in fact an example of that carefully cultivated simplicity and restrained elegance only available to the very rich."[67] Alfred Kerr wrote of Rathenau's city apartment in the Tiergarten: "Rathenau so often emphasized his simple requirements (a heavy industry Diogenes), but in his brain lurked an ineradicable passion for little palaces."[68]

The layout of the villa also tells us something about the relative

64. Cologne Municipal Archive: Abt. 1068 (Mallinckrodt), Kasten 77, Stadtarchiv Koln; Wilmin, *Familie Adt* , p 56, Thyssen Archive, A/9577, letter from August Thyssen dated 19 December 1902; Mangoldt, *Auf der Schwelle*, p. 18.

65 Haniel Archive, 400101290/249 On Schramm, see Schramm, *Neun Generationen*, vol. 2, pp 413, 423 On Wallich, see H Wallich, *Erinnerungen*, p 143.

66 Rathenau, *Schriften*, p 16

67 Joll, "Walther Rathenau," p. 57. Photos of the interior of the villa convey a similar impression. See Federn-Kohlhaas, *Walther Rathenau* and photo, p. 175 .

68 Kerr, *Walther Rathenau*, p. 27.

importance of family life and representational duties in the business elite. Brönner gives us a description of the typical villa of a wealthy businessman of the nineteenth century. On the lower floor were rooms where guests were received (entrance hall, waiting room, reception room, drawing room, and dining room), as well as rooms to which individual family members could withdraw or where family life took place (the husband's office, the wife's sitting room, the dining room again, and a living room). (Muthesius also mentions the music room as typical of upper-middle-class homes.) On the upper floor were the bedrooms, the children's room, the boudoir, and the bathroom. The principal rooms for family activities and for the entertainment of guests were generally on the ground floor, on the street side of the house. Typical for the entire nineteenth century was the separation between the living or family room and the drawing room, which parallels the separation between private and semi-public spaces.

Some houses had special rooms for the wife, others did not. These were often adjacent to the area where guests were received, otherwise they were upstairs, in the family's private domain. In some villas the husband's room and the wife's room were of the same size; in others the husband's room was substantially larger. According to Brönner, this was an indication as to whether the marriage was more of a partnership or a patriarchal arrangement. The floor plans in *Berlin und seine Bauten* show that the size and location of the wife's room varied considerably in the villas of Berlin businessmen of the Wilhelmine period.[69]

In many of the villas of the business elite there were rooms for large receptions. Villa Waldfried, which Carl von Weinberg, co-owner of Leopold Cassella (a chemical giant) had built in the vicinity of Frankfurt around the turn of the century, had huge rooms for social functions. Hans-Otto Schembs writes about this palatial home: "If today we want to form an idea of such a lordly residence, we must go to the Sonnenhof of the Rothschild family in Königstein or to the Friedrichshof palace of the Empress Victoria in Kronberg, both of which were built some years previously and, though of even greater dimensions, in an architectural form com-

---

69. See Brönner, *Die bürgerliche Villa*, pp 54–59, 83. The allocation of space in the city palace, which was not a villa but a town house, differed only slightly from that of the villa On Berlin, see Bergius and Posener, "Die Listen," pp 47–172. For an example of a rich businessman's family that spent evenings together in the living room, see von der Heydt, *Unser Haus*, p. 23 In contrast to the upper bourgeoisie, the petty bougeoisie had great difficulty in finding space in their smaller houses and apartments for both family rooms and rooms for entertaining guests.

parable to that of the Weinberg villa."[70] In the Berlin villa of the banker Carl von der Heydt (built around 1860, now at Von-der-Heydtstrasse 18), there was a banquet hall surrounded by a series of rooms where guests could circulate. Large rooms where big receptions, balls, or banquets took place were to be found in many mansions, including those of the former director of the Deutsche Bank, Hermann Wallich (with four "giant" rooms), of Carl Fürstenberg (where hundreds of guests could be received simultaneously), of Hamburg banker Albert Warburg (with a banquet hall that could accommodate 100 visitors), of department store owner Oskar Tietz, and of Hamburg banker Max von Schinckel. The reception halls, decorated in Empire and Renaissance style, in the home of Emil Rathenau (on Viktoriastrasse) were described by his granddaughter as "cold magnificence." Family members were not allowed to use them except on social occasions. Unusual needs or desires for ostentation led to the construction of unusual homes. The "Golconda" of the Friedländer-Fulds on the Pariser Platz was among the most magnificent homes in Berlin. The "Villa Hügel" of the Krupps and the town "palace" of Albert Ballin on the Alster were undoubtedly built with the thought in mind of constructing ostentatious homes suitable for visits by the emperor.[71]

Public relations, but also the extensive demands of family members, required the employment of numerous household employees. According to Schramm, the service personnel in a household of the upper bourgeoisie in Hamburg typically included a children's maid, a cook, a cook's helper, a waitress, a lady's maid, and a chambermaid. In many homes a butler opened the door. Laundry was sent out to be washed. Men came in to shine shoes and tend to the heating. Usually, there was a gardener with a team of gardener's helpers and women who did the weeding. From time to time, window washers and floor polishers were brought in. "Looking back, it is a puzzle to me why so many service personnel were employed in my parent's home and an even greater puzzle how it was possible to keep them busy six days a week."[72]

The number of servants in most elite business households was

70. Schembs, "Die Frankfurter Familie," p. 56. The entrance hall occupied approximately 150 square meters, the large dining room 100 square meters. Frankfurt Municipal Archive. S2/10305 Familie Weinberg, p. 16

71 See Heydt, *Unser Haus*, pp. 21–23; H. Wallich, *Erinnerungen*, p. 109; C. Fürstenberg, *Lebensgeschichte*, p. 504, Wenzel-Burchard, *Granny*, p. 18; Tietz, *Hermann Tietz*, p. 118; Rohrmann, *Max von Schickel*, p. 78; Mangoldt, *Auf der Schwelle*, p. 53; Sturmer, "Alltag," p 257; Borchardt, "Unternehmerhaushalt," pp 11–19, Cecil, *Albert Ballin*, p. 107.

72 Schramm, *Neun Generationen*, p. 422; see p. 421

impressive, especially when one considers that enumerations of household employees in businessmen's biographies and autobiographies include only permanent full-time employees, since stokers, weeders, and the like seldom appear in such listings. The Warburgs had two male house servants, a coachman, a gardener, a lady's maid, a cook, a scullery maid, a laundress, and a maid to do the ironing. In Carl Duisberg's home in Leverkusen a nursemaid, two house maids, a cook, two butlers, a gardener, and a chauffeur were employed. If there were small children present, there were usually servants to take care of them. As a baby, the daughter of Ernst Wertheimber was cared for by a German wet nurse and an English nurserymaid; later a governess was hired for her. Aniela Fürstenberg had (presumably in addition to numerous servants) a housekeeper and later a secretary. Some households no doubt got along with substantially fewer personnel. The banker Hermann Wallich and his wife had only a cook, a scullery maid, a house maid, and a lady's maid. August Thyssen is said to have had only four household employees, but it should be remembered that he lived alone.[73] Veblen was of the opinion that household employees had fewer and fewer real duties, because their principal duty was to demonstrate the waste ("conspicuous leisure" or "wasted effort") that his class could afford.[74] Which is not to say that servants did not really work: they were occupied with endless tasks that in most societies would be considered useless, such as dusting and cleaning huge quantities of superfluous ornamentation.[75]

One school of architecture strongly disliked the emphasis placed on entertaining in this class and its impact on house design. Hermann Muthesius's criticisms of the typical suburban villa of circa 1900 are interesting because they tell us a good deal about the function of the villa: "In designing the floor plan, emphasis is placed on the way the main living areas fit together for the purposes of social entertainment. How many people can sit in the dining room, where the guests go after leaving the table, how they circulate after they get there, those are the main considerations in drawing up the floor plan. . . . The country home must above all have a magnificent salon, if possible two stories high." Muthesius advocated life in the suburbs as an escape from unhealthy living condi-

---

73. See Wenzel-Burchard, *Granny*, p 18; Duisberg, *Nur ein Sohn*, pp 17, 20; Lanckoronska, *Li(e)ber*, pp. 9, 15; C. Furstenberg, *Lebensgeschichte*, p. 505; H. Wallich, *Erinnerungen*, p. 135, Arnst, *August Thyssen*, p. 71.
74. See Veblen, *Theory*, esp pp. 52–55
75. For a description of such tasks, see Meyer, *Das Theater*.

tions in the city and a return to nature and privacy. The villa was not suited to suburban life as he visualized it: ". . . the villa dweller has not yet given up the vices that life in a big city flat has bred into him. Though he has moved out into the country, he does not want to give up the ostentatious rooms. In a little one-family home he demands the same five-meter-high rooms and the gigantic dining room he had in the city flat. The joys of life in the country and the deepening influence of the country environment have not yet had enough lasting effect on him to wean him away from big city ostentation which exceeds the means of many of these people when they try to reproduce it in their own homes."[76]

Muthesius and others advocated the elimination of these ostentatious rooms in favor of rooms designed for private use. A first step in this direction is the "suburban villa," which differs distinctly from the city villa. "The house in Grunewald, though pretentious in its external form . . . has to a great extent abandoned the idea of interconnected rooms. . . . This means that people can withdraw, can get away from one another. . . . The city villa is still planned for social life, the villa in Grunewald more for family life." This tendency is accentuated in the country home (*Landhaus*),[77] which became quite popular after 1905: "Its floor plan was specifically designed with the daily life of the family in mind, of course without eliminating the possibility of 'refined sociability.' Its rooms were substantially more individualized [than in the suburban villa] and even less interconnected. Every room turned its back, so to speak, on the other rooms and opened onto its own part of the garden."[78]

The country home movement found adherents primarily in the educated bourgeoisie, but top businessmen also built houses in this style. It is an expression of the desire for more comfortable living, which was becoming more widespread at that time. But did this have a real impact on social life? Did it bring about a reorientation from a life style geared primarily to sociability to one that centered on family life? At least for the business elite, this was not the case. The family rooms were of course larger than those in a city villa, but the country homes built by Muthesius for rich businessmen

76. Muthesius, *Landhaus*, p. XXI

77. In Germany, the villa is defined as a free-standing house with garden for one family, with an impressive façade facing the street and a first floor above street level The "country home" (*Landhaus*), on the other hand, has a fairly modest façade; the ground floor is at street-level; and the rooms used on a daily basis are on the garden side of the house. See Machule and Seiberlich, "Berliner Villenvororte," p. 93.

78 Posener and Bergius, "Individuell geplante Einfamilienhauser," pp. 5, 11.

were so large that there was still space for rooms where a large number of guests could be entertained. An example is the country home of Wilhelm Merton, whose dining room now serves as a refectory for fifty-three deaconesses who live there.[79] Though the country home was not outwardly ostentatious, it still could serve representational purposes. Thus, this change of style did not so much entail a change in function as a change in fashion. The country home movement is frankly of greater interest to the history of architecture than to historical sociology.

Ownership of Landed Estates

Among the upper bourgeoisie the purchase of landed estates assumed notable proportions in the nineteenth century. The penetration of this elite into the class of estate owners is described in a classic study by Hans Rosenberg.[80] Almost one-fourth of the richest businessmen listed in the *Yearbook of Millionaires* were big landowners.[81] In chapter 4, it was shown that land ownership became the principal profession of very few of the sons. How many very wealthy businessmen abandoned their profession from 1890 to 1918 in order to live as feudal lords on their estates? Only six of the 502 businessmen in our quantitative study were active primarily as big landowners, among whom were Walter Naumann zu Königsbruck (1876–1944), Standesherr (peer) of Königsbruck and son of the sewing machine and typewriter manufacturer Bruno Naumann (Dresden); Paul Schottländer, son of Julius Schottländer, military supplies contractor and real estate speculator (Breslau); and James von Bleichröder (1861–1937), son of Gerson Bleichroder, who lived as an estate owner from 1886 on. These are classical cases of aristocratization. Max von Goldschmidt-Rothschild, a banker and owner of an entailed estate, also went into early retirement from business and probably lived on his estate.[82]

In autobiographies and biographies there are few examples of

79. See Posener and Bergius, "Listen," p. 143. See also listings for houses 1616 and 1691.

80. Rosenberg, "Die Pseudodemokratisierung," esp. pp 289–94.

81. My quantitative study Not counting eighteen heavy industrialists with older aristocratic stock, all of whom were part of the traditional elite and all of whom owned landed estates

82. Another two businessmen in the study were actually originally great noble landowners who married into business families without giving up their estates One is Baron Karl von Gamp-Massaunen (1846–1918), the ennobled son of an estate owner, who married Clara Bayer and became a member of the board of the Bayer Corporation He evidently sold stocks so as to be able to buy more land (See Martin, *Jahrbuch*, vol 16, p. 31.) Baron Friedrich von Gemmingen-Hornberg (1860–1924), of old aristocratic lineage, married Dora Siegle, a daughter of a co-founder of BASF. Gemmingen-Hornberg sat on several corporate boards, but continued to live in his castle; it is unclear if he was active in business.

active businessmen who withdrew to the country (except in old age) during the Wilhelmine period. One was Henry Brarens Sloman, who went to Chile as a young man and then returned to Germany a wealthy man in 1898. He bought a noble estate in 1909. His biographer writes: "He was never attracted to city life. His dream was to own an estate, to improve it, expand it, and work it as he had been accustomed to do all his life."[83]

The great majority of wealthy businessmen who owned large estates lived there only on weekends or during a part of the year. The way such businessmen saw their roles as landowners varied considerably. The wealthy Gilka family of Berlin, who owned distilleries, did not belong exclusively to either the business world or the landowner class. Arthur Gilka, who had studied agriculture and commerce, was active primarily on his Kartzow estate, although he traveled three or four times a week to the distillery to attend to business. His brother Albert was the owner of the Basthorst estate in Mecklenburg but was also active in the management of the firm.[84]

Other businessmen, though not living primarily on their estates, still became enthusiastic farmers and applied to agriculture the same rational methods that they employed in business. Munich banker Wilhelm von Finck, who began in the 1890s to invest a greater and greater share of his fortune in land, wrote in 1892: "I also admit that the acquisition of these run-down properties was stimulating for me inasmuch as I hoped to find in them a satisfying field of activity." However, he lived in his bank building in Munich and only traveled out to his estate on Sundays.[85]

The Siemens family presents an interesting case, since one branch had been involved in farming for generations. Georg von Siemens, a director of the *Deutsche Bank*, was deeply interested in farming. He rounded off the Ahlsdorf estate, which he had inherited from his father, by buying up adjacent properties in order to increase profitability and making his estate into a "model enterprise." In 1884 he commented in a letter to his wife on the importance of Ahlsdorf in his life: "Though it is true that one can earn money and live more comfortably in the city, one should not overlook the fact that only a fixed piece of property (and indeed a property in the country) gives one a certain feeling of being on home ground. This continual concentration of interest on a specific

83 Marchtaler, *Die Slomans*, p. 231

84. This information was obtained in a conversation with Dr. Gerhart Gilke, a son of Arthur Gilka

85. See Hoffmann, *Wilhelm von Finck*, pp. 172, 183; quotation on p. 101.

place also will give the family cohesion later on when the children get married and move off into different locations. Ahlsdorf is one of the worst financial investments in existence, but I gladly forgo the profits, though I could use them (and would at the same time be free of a lot of annoyances), in order to hold on to this satisfying awareness of my right, and that of the children, to a piece of home turf [*Heimat*]."[86] This feeling of being on one's own home ground is perhaps closest to the feelings of a peasant for his home and land.

The attitude of the Jewish merchant Eduard Arnhold about his estate – judging from a passage in a book published by his wife – is somewhat more anti-urban (and by implication anti-modernist) in tone: "The ownership of the estate meant far more [than just being a professional farmer]; it meant – to put it dramatically – a link to the forces of the earth, to the soil, that this elemental man did not want to abandon for the bustle of the great city."[87] The inclinations of Alfred Ackermann (born 1857), head of the B.G. Teubner publishing house in Leipzig, were decidedly neo-feudal. His wife wrote about his relationship with the farm workers on the Gundorf estate: "He also tries sincerely to strengthen the bonds between employer and employees and to keep the relationship between them pure and on a lofty plane." The family anniversaries celebrated on the estate also had a patriarchal character: "The congratulatory plaques that were given to us on these occasions will for all time remain precious proofs of the loyal attachment of our dear Gundorf people."[88]

In general, however, more pragmatic attitudes prevailed among the business elite. Wealthy businessmen regarded their estates primarily as vacation homes, a status symbol or an investment. Wilhelm von Siemens regarded his Biesdorf estate in the vicinity of Berlin (which he had not bought himself but had taken over from his father) primarily as a place for rest and relaxation. It was near enough to Berlin so that the family was not socially isolated. They invited guests to come to Biesdorf for hunting. "Everyone was happy to come out and enjoy the hospitality of the big house where there were overnight accommodations for a remarkable number of them if they missed their return trip connections."[89] Another member of the family, who was also named Georg Siemens, wrote about Wilhelm's estate and Arnold's house at

---

86 Quoted in Helfferich, *Georg von Siemens*, vol 3, pp. 320–21; see p 251
87 Arnhold, *Eduard Arnhold*, p. 36.
88 Quoted in Schulze, *Geschichte*, pp 126–27.
89. Harries, "Nachruf," p 9

Wannsee: "Such a place represented the permanent commitment of a sizable portion of their wealth, and at a time when only a stable currency seemed conceivable, this was regarded as an uneconomical luxury. But the Siemens brothers thought they could afford this luxury and derived a lot of pleasure from it."[90]

According to Hildegard Wallich, it was fashionable for a Berlin banker to own an estate: "In those days it was customary for the bank directors to purchase an estate or a country home where they spent the summer and could invite guests." These properties were also purchased "partly as capital investments." She also wrote about the criteria applied by her parents-in-law, the bank director Hermann Wallich and his wife, in their search for an estate: "He would have preferred to include a practical purpose and wanted to buy an estate that would also bring in a profit. But Mama [Frau Wallich] wanted it to be close enough to Berlin so that guests would not have to spend the night there. The house also had to be comfortable and 'high-class' with a beautiful park, as befitted a bank director." They finally agreed on the Jerchel estate, which was located at a distance from Berlin but was quite beautiful. The soil was relatively poor, and the estate was managed by an overseer.[91] Fritz von Friedländer-Fuld's "Lanke" estate, which featured "country living in the English style," and Paul von Schwabach's "Kerzendorf" served as a backdrop for elegant social events. Kerzendorf was only thirty kilometers away from Schwabach's office. Both families lived in the country only in the summertime.[92] Arthur von Gwinner, director of the *Deutsche Bank*, wrote about the decision of his family to buy an estate: "We finally became tired of vacation trips and of staying in overfilled hotels, and we longed for a place of our own." They found an estate they liked: "It was Krumbke, which has become dear to the hearts of all of us, and it was its magnificent park and beautiful woods that convinced us that we should take it."[93]

Conclusion

For the business elite, the villa was both the most important instrument used to demonstrate and attain social stature and the most coveted !uxury item for the satisfaction of material desires. The

90 Siemens, *Carl Friedrich von Siemens*, p. 77 See Rotth, *Wilhelm von Siemens*, p. 105.

91. H. Wallich, *Erinnerungen*, pp 111–12, also, see p. 137.

92. See Horstmann, *Unendlich viel*, pp. 11–12. Quotation on life in a country home in C. Furstenberg, *Lebensgeschichte*, p 399.

93. Gwinner, *Lebenserinnerungen*, p. 109.

typical large villa of this period did not represent a new development, although it was more widespread than in earlier times because the ranks of the wealthy bourgeoisie had greatly swelled in number. It owed its size primarily to the fact that rooms for formal occasions required considerable space. On the other hand, the size of the villa also demonstrated the power and wealth of the owner. Other elements of ruling-class architecture (which was not always identical with the architecture of the homes of the German nobility) were employed: the historicist style, the monumentality, the park, the valuable and luxurious decorations, the location. The observer, at whom these symbols were directed, was usually an upper-class guest but might also be an employee or worker of the owner's company. As a participant in some special reception that might take place in the businessman's home (such as a company anniversary celebration), as a messenger, or even as a passerby or newspaper reader, he or she was supposed to be overawed by this symbol of the employer's powerful position.

The businessman's villa displayed a number of elements that in Germany were associated with the aristocratic residential style. These suggested that the owner was a legitimate member of the upper classes, a message directed above all to high-born guests. To explain this phenomenon primarily in terms of aristocratization is to miss the central point: that a new elite was trying in a traditional manner to convert power and wealth into social prestige, which was not an end in itself, but a necessary prerequisite for business activities. There could hardly be an industrialist more bourgeois in orientation and more fixated on his work than August Thyssen, and yet even he purchased a castle.

Residential style in the business elite cannot, however, be reduced to a façade intended for the outside world. The mansion was also a home intended for private use – and this is especially true of English-style country houses built in the suburbs. Going far beyond the middle-class ideal of a home of one's own, wealthy men's villas and summer houses were the ultimate luxury in this class. The prevalence of the summer residence, be it on a landed estate or elsewhere, was part of an elite life style virtually unknown even in the German upper middle class. This elite life style meant that very wealthy business families were cut off from the life of the masses in a way their middle-class forebears were not.

In only a few cases did the businessman who purchased a landed estate integrate himself with the landed nobility or adopt aristocratic values (as in the case of Ackermann). It is not at all clear whether Arnhold's almost mystic conception of closeness to the earth, Georg von Siemen's enthusiasm for farming, and the "home instinct" of Finck and Siemens can be regarded as aristocratization. They suggest ties more typical of the peasant class. For the most part, however, the ownership of a landed estate was designed to demonstrate wealth and social position in a traditional way. However, the majority of the wealthiest businessmen were not owners of large estates. For example, Hugo Stinnes considered buying a landed estate in Thuringia but came to the conclusion that he could not afford it.[94]

Typical of the Wilhelmine period was the move from the factory grounds to planned suburbs or to some other exclusive residential area. The motives were a flight from dirt and noise and the love of nature. The separation of workplace and residence was made possible by the increasing bureaucratization of the factory organization that substantially reduced the necessity for continuous control and supervision or transferred these responsibilities to the managers. This development is related to the decline of patriarchal structures in the factory and residential patterns: the boss's absence undermines his authority. The move to the suburbs did not mean a withdrawal into privacy, because the business families living in the suburbs also carried on an active social life. One's neighbors, whether in Grunewald (Berlin) or Marienburg (Cologne), were generally upper middle class, often fellow business families.

The alternative to the exclusive suburb was the city apartment or town house. Living in a central location meant a shorter way to the workplace and a more intensive social life. The quality of life in expensive residential areas such as those on the Alster (Hamburg) was not necessarily worse than in the suburbs. The social composition of these areas is also interesting. In the Tiergarten (Berlin) lived a number of bankers. In Harvestehude (Hamburg) there was a mixture of upper bourgeoisie and the broader middle class. The wealthy could combine the advantages of urban and suburban living if they spent the winter in the city and the summer in a country home. However, the constánt expansion of the transportation network induced many to move out of the city permanently. A snowball effect can also be observed once it became common to live in the suburbs.

94. Kohlschutter, *Ein Gente*, p 37.

Chapter 6

Wealthy Business Families
in High Society

The pomp and pageantry that we have come to associate with "Wilhelmianism" reached out beyond parades and public ceremonies. This spirit of grandeur and vacuous formality found its way into the drawing rooms, dining halls and ballrooms of the upper bourgeoisie. Wealthy Germans plunged themselves into an orgy of luxury, much encouraged by the emperor's own attitudes: "The Emperor's broadness of view resulted in Berlin becoming like Paris, the only passport being the possession of an unlimited amount of money and perfect knowledge of the art of spending it with advantage to oneself and to others."[1] In the imperial capital, hostesses vied nightly for the attention of high society, sparing no expense in the effort to impress. Regal in demeanor, these women left no doubt that their families had won a place in most exalted realms of society.

Mosse asserts that female vanity impelled these women to seek a coveted place for their family at the pinnacle of high society.[2] Lamar Cecil, on the other hand, interprets the social swirl of the capital as evidence that wealthy Jews were willing to go to any length to gain the acceptance of the very Junkers who despised them.[3] In their courtship of the Junkers, Jews supposedly shunned other Jews and adopted aristocratic habits, spending large amounts of money on entertainment, clothing, and mansions. Jews sought marriage alliances and noble pedigrees. According to Cecil, they even went so far as to renounce their political and religious identity, converting to Christianity and conservative politics, or at least

1. Schwering, *Berlin Court*, pp. 254–55.
2. See Mosse, *German-Jewish*, pp. 97, 110–16.
3 See Cecil, "Jew and Junker."

political quietism. But their social ambitions remained unfulfilled. Members of the nobility were willing to visit Jews, but seldom returned the invitation. Jews were excluded from student corps and aristocratic clubs. The recalcitrant blue bloods clung to their anti-Semitic and anti-capitalist attitudes to the end.

Mosse and Cecil fail to perceive that these social connections were instrumentalized by business families to advance their business interests. When the business family courted an aristocrat, it was usually because he was a power broker. It made little difference whether the business family was Jewish or Christian: in such social relationships, class predominated over ethnicity. Certainly an important aspect of what was going on here is captured by "networking," a term of recent vintage usually understood to mean the purposeful building up a panoply of social contacts that socially define an individual and place him or her in a position of power. The implication is not one of cultivating ties with specific people for specific purposes, but of establishing a network that can be activated (to promote professional, social, economic, or political interests) at some indeterminate point in the future. The Wilhelmine business elite organized its social life around such networks, to which businessmen, but also government officials, belonged. Though autobiographies are frustratingly vague concerning the details of what was discussed at social events, there is a sense that they promoted consensus-building.

The term "networking" also implies the formation of a group to which an individual can belong on a basis of equality and within which a set of reciprocal relations can be established. It is quite different from patronage, which is based on an unequal relationship. In the Wilhelmine business elite, networking went on among businessmen or in other groups that possessed a sense of solidarity – the Hamburg patrician class, for example. In a city like Berlin, businessmen seem to have sought specific favors, momentary advantages in their relationships with bureaucrats, military men, or diplomats. Social relations between businessmen and government officials were more sporadic and discontinuous and generally did not lead to a sense of group solidarity.

Pre-war Germany lacked the vocabulary to honestly discuss such power relations. In the nineteenth century, authors of autobiographies were not very forthcoming regarding the way in which they instrumentalized friendships. Typically, they made rather promiscuous use of the term "friend," obscuring the difference between close business associates and people with whom they had close emotional ties. For our purposes, the most useful contemporary concept is that of *Repräsentation*, which roughly means the social representation (for example in entertaining, conspicuous consumption, or architecture) of real social or economic power.

Berlin was not Germany, and in this chapter we will look at social life in several regions. The Hanseatic cities – Hamburg, Lübeck, and Bremen – form an interesting counterpoint to Berlin. They seem to symbolize bourgeois society as it might have been in Germany as a whole: self-assured, liberal, and anti-aristocratic. Historians are generally in agreement with Richard J. Evans in his assertion that "neither the economic activity nor the social world nor finally the political beliefs and actions of the Hamburg merchants corresponded to anything that has ever been defined, however remotely, as 'feudal.'"[4] However, a comparison of Hamburg and Berlin reveals important parallels that have often been overlooked. Wealthy businessmen used social relations to further their business interests in a very similar way in the two cities. The feudalization thesis also rests on evidence from Rhineland-Westphalia, the third region to be discussed. Finally, we will examine the west and southwest of Germany.[5]

The Hanseatic Cities: A Bourgeois Model?

In Hamburg, a city that had for centuries been ruled by a bourgeois ruling class and that had no indigenous nobility, social status depended much more on wealth than on title. In fact, its citizens traditionally had an aversion toward titles of nobility. The social circles of Hamburg businessmen were almost purely bourgeois. Richard J. Evans has pointed out the significance in Hamburg social life of the "*Herrendiners*," all-male dinner table gatherings at which wholesale merchants, high city officials, local government leaders, representatives from the citizens' assembly, and a few clergymen, academics, and artists were present. A syndic of the Hamburg senate named Buehl described the function of these dinners as follows: "An advantage of this institution was that it often afforded the opportunity to deal with difficult official or political problems. These were much easier to decide at the dinner-table

4 Evans, *Death*, p. 559.

5. The available source material was insufficient to include other regions in this part of the analysis.

than they were at the committee table." These dinners contributed not only to the solution of concrete problems, but also to the formation of a general consensus within the elite.[6] The big businessmen of the Hanseatic cities were also anxious to establish relationships with the emperor and his ministers. Heinrich Wiegand, the director of the Norddeutscher Lloyd, (steamship line), was on friendly terms with Admiral Tirpitz and other high imperial officials and met with the emperor several times. The bankers Max Warburg and Max von Schinckel also had that honor. A good deal is known about the friendship of Albert Ballin with the emperor.[7]

Cultural activities also contributed to the social life of the elite. The patricians of Bremen, for example, gathered together on Sundays at the galleries of the *Kunstverein* (art society). These were more in the nature of social gatherings than cultural affairs. Wiegand and some others in 1904 organized a cultural tour of Greece in which about eighty individuals participated, including the mayor of Bremen.[8]

Friendships between businessmen were of key importance in the Hanseatic cities. Wiegand for years maintained friendly relations with Ballin in order to minimize competition between the Norddeutscher Lloyd and HAPAG (another steamship line), and presumably in order to make it possible to arrive at agreements. At first this relationship was in some respects a personal one, but it soured and deteriorated into an "amicable utilitarian association."[9] Hamburg businessmen met together daily, for example, at the Alster-Pavilion. The members of the Union Club were primarily wholesale merchants. The *Bund Elektra* was a club composed of the members and former members of the chamber of commerce.[10]

Hamburg lacked a native aristocracy, and so it is not surprising that members of the nobility played a very minor role in these exclusive circles. The Slomans, who belonged to the best circles, mingled socially, for example, with the older Hamburg families such as the Ohlendorffs, the Amsincks, and the Berenberg-Gosslers, but also with Max von Schinckel, the industrialist Rechberg, an English ship-owner, a member of the Stumm family, and ship captains. However, one of the regular guests of the

6 Evans, *Death*, pp. 21–22; Buehl quoted according to Evans.

7 On Wiegand, see Petzet, *Heinrich Wiegand*, pp. 211, 291. On Ballin, see Cecil, *Albert Ballin*.

8 See Petzet, *Heinrich Wiegand*, pp. 273–75, 280–81.

9. On the friendship between Wiegand and Ballin, see ibid., p. 291. This was a period of widespread cartel formation in Germany.

10. See Cecil, *Albert Ballin*, pp. 37; Rohrmann, *Max von Schinckel*, p. 186.

Slomans was the Count zu Inn und Knyphausen. Hunting – regarded as aristocratic in most of Germany – was known, though not popular, in Hanseatic business circles.[11] It is possible that in these cities, hunting was associated with England rather than with the German nobility.[12] Regarding the social profile of guests at parties in bourgeois circles, Schramm writes: "One seldom saw military officers, because the seventy-sixth infantry regiment was looked down on, and the Wandsbeker Hussars were suspected by the fathers of being after rich heiresses. Hamburg 'society' was regarded as exclusive; and in fact, few people showed up that one did not know."[13]

In Hamburg society, social status was by no means based solely on individual achievement. There were also social divisions within the bourgeoisie. The old established patricians to a large extent shut themselves off from the "new money," though there was some tendency to allow in some new faces around the turn of the century. Schramm describes the attitude of Anna Jencquel, whose family was one of the most respected in Hamburg:

> And if one had asked her what she honestly thought about the O'Swalds, the Rupertis, the Woermanns, the Webers, the Nottebaums, and other families that had come to Hamburg between 1815 and 1840 and had subsequently overshadowed the Jencquels, she would probably have said: yes, those are capable people, but one cannot count them among the best society, at least there are, among the really good families, some that are substantially "better." This concept of "society" dominated social life up to the First World War. One person belonged to it and another did not, and the one might be a newcomer and the other a native of long standing.[14]

According to Schramm, these ideas began to crumble even before the First World War. Even Anna Jencquel associated with two Jewish women before 1914, though she (patrician that she was) had "reservations" about doing so.

Perhaps the most prominent example of aristocratization among Hamburg businessmen is that of a Protestant social climber. Even as an important banker and son of a rich merchant, Max von

---

11 Examples in Sloman, *Erinnerungen*, pp. 89–90; Ropers, *Vom Geldwechsler*, p 39; Rohrmann, *Max von Schinckel*, p 19.

12 The fact that in England hunting was also an aristocratic activity is irrelevant because no power relationship existed between Hamburg merchants and the English aristocracy.

13. Schramm, *Neun Generationen*, vol. 2, p. 425. On the Slomans, see Sloman, *Erinnerungen*, pp. 84, 90, 92.

14 Schramm, *Neun Generationen*, p. 417; also, see p. 407

Schinckel did not penetrate into the "best circles" until he married Olga Berckmeyer, of an old patrician family, in 1882. Perhaps this is the explanation for the unusual pattern of his social life. He cultivated acquaintanceships with the nobility, in some cases the upper nobility, and with members of Berlin society. As president of the Hamburg Racing Club, he came into constant contact with aristocrats. A biographer, Elsabea Rohrmann, comments on ". . . his extreme eagerness to enumerate noble acquaintanceships, especially in the retrospect of his memoirs, where he represents a long list of barons, counts, princes and dukes as 'personally acquainted' with him, 'closely tied' to him, 'good friends' of his."[15] She sees a close connection between his political attitudes and his social attitudes: "Schinckel was not a representative of the traditional bourgeois Hanseatic spirit of the 'Free and Hanseatic City' of Hamburg. He was rather an 'imperial Hanseatic' patrician with aristocratic inclinations which lifted him out of Hamburg society and immediately placed him on the level of the specifically national – or it might better be called 'Wilhelmine' – social class."[16]

The Warburgs, a very important Jewish banking family, had a different position in Hamburg society. Military officers and assistant judges were well represented at their parties and balls. We know that Max Warburg was a friend of Albert Ballin (who was also Jewish), but the Warburgs were fully integrated into the Hamburg patrician community. Ballin was also fully a part of the best circles in Hamburg, in part because of his friendship with the emperor. He was on friendly terms with the Laeisz, Burchard, and Woermann families – some of the best names in the city. He showed little interest in army officers, government officials, and the higher nobility.[17]

In general, it appears that in Hamburg, Jews were allowed to participate fully in business and politics, but not in high society. In the private sphere, Jews lived in a world apart, strictly separated from non-Jews.[18] Jews and non-Jews had business dealings with one another at the Hamburg stock exchange, but after the exchange closed in the evening, they sat at separate tables in the

15. Rohrmann, *Max von Schinckel*, p. 289; see pp. 19, 75, 186, 286–87
16. Ibid., pp. 287–88.
17. On the Warburgs, see Ron Chernow, *The Warburgs* (New York, 1993).. On Ballin, see Cecil, *Albert Ballin*, pp. 37, 108–10
18 According to Jules Huret, the best social circles in the more pronouncedly bourgeois cities such as Hamburg, Bremen, Aachen, and Frankfurt were less accessible to the Jewish bourgeoisie than those in Berlin, where the nobility set the tone See Huret, *En Allemagne. Berlin*, pp. 347–49.

Alster-Pavilion. When Paul Wallich completed a training course in banking in Hamburg, because of his Jewish origins he was only invited to the homes of businessmen who had business dealings with his father (Hermann Wallich, director of the *Deutsche Bank*).[19]

During the imperial period, and especially from the 1890s on, Hamburg and Bremen society adopted a new style. An active social life requiring considerable expenditures became the norm. This development is probably due primarily to an assimilation with the bourgeoisie in other parts of the empire, which came about as a result of the economic and political integration of the Hanseatic cities into the empire, the expanding transportation and communications networks, and the influx of wealthy outsiders.[20] Second, the rapid increase in wealth made extravagance possible. A third explanation lies in the growing competition between established families and social newcomers,[21] who had a special need to document their social status through conspicuous consumption.

The social life of Hamburg wholesale merchants and bankers was characterized by the frequency of social events, lavish expenditures, luxury, and social sophistication. Balls for more than one hundred guests were not a rarity, and they were held in private homes. Balls, masquerade balls, soirées, and dinner parties were often given at the home of Albert and Gerta Warburg. In addition, the lady of the house had an "at-home" day for receiving polite calls.[22] Mary Sloman, who had married into a shipping family, says of her representational duties: "In the ancestral home of my husband I now became acquainted with a luxurious life style, in constant contact with many people. One was required to take part in everything."[23] As early as the 1870s and 1880's, the very wealthy Bremen merchant family, the Melchers, entertained guests almost every day. Only the most carefully selected and expensive dishes were served: "The best vintages of the noblest Bordeaux wines . . . truffles from Périgord, rice birds from Canton. On one occasion a special courier was sent by train to Moscow in order to bring some sterlet, a fish considered to be the greatest delicacy in the world, back to

19. See Cecil, *Albert Ballin*, p. 37; Evans, *Death*, pp. 392–93; P. Wallich, *Lehr- und Wanderjahre*, p. 227.
20. See Evans, *Death*, pp. 560–62.
21. These newcomers were mostly either transplants from outside or individuals who had climbed out of the upper middle class into the elite.
22. See Schramm, *Neun Generationen*, pp. 425–26. On the Warburgs, see Wenzel-Burchard, *Granny*, pp. 16, 20.
23. Sloman, *Erinnerungen*, p. 91.

Bremen completely fresh."[24] At the "*Herrendiners*" described by
Evans, six to eight courses were customary, each served with a different type of wine.[25] According to Schramm, caviar, *paté de foie
gras*, ice cream, and champagne were served at a typical supper in
wealthy bourgeois circles. "In short, a lavish life style, a luxurious
manner of living, much money spent on social entertainment." But
he says that the style of the west German industrialists was even
more illustrious.[26]

Material simplicity – much vaunted in earlier times – was still
preached to children,[27] but had essentially lost its centrality in the
way Hanseatic patricians presented themselves to the world. One of
the few cases in which it is mentioned in the literature involves Gerta
Warburg ("Granny," born 1856). Originally she had no objections
to make-up and jewelry, according to her granddaughter. "But after
it occurred one day to the cartoonist Oberländer to portray 'Frau
Geheimer Kommerzienrat' (wife of a privy commercial councillor)
dripping in diamonds, Granny put all of her jewelry into a safe and
never wore it again."[28] The vehemence of her reaction was undoubtedly due to the anti-Semitic tenor of this caricature.

The wealthy businessman no longer acted as a defender of bourgeois morality but rather as a man of the world. Albert Ballin
embodied this new type to perfection. He was regarded as a
charming host. Cecil describes him as ". . . intelligent and well-
informed, a marvelous host, an imaginative raconteur, and a
knowledgeable *Feinschmecker* (gourmet)." He gave magnificent
parties on board HAPAG ships: "His entertainments aboard these
floating palaces were sumptuous affairs, the refinements and grace-
ful execution of which did not escape the Kaiser's discriminating
eye." Prince Bernhard von Bülow and Count Johann Heinrich
Bernstorff were impressed by Albert Ballin's self-assured manner.
"A figure of considerable sartorial fashion, from formal attire to
yachting dress, Ballin wore his clothes with a knowing grace and
mixed easily with men of high station. He wrote and spoke in a
facile style; his letters which have survived are short and persuasive,

24. Melchers, *Erinnerungen*, p. 76. Unfortunately, these memoirs do not cover the period
after 1888. However, it is most instructive to discover that in this earlier period, which for
Bremen is considered to be more bourgeois than the Wilhelmine, such pretentious style prevailed.

25. See Evans, *Death*, p. 21.

26. Schramm, *Neun Generationen*, pp. 425–26.

27. See Hauschild-Thiessen, *Bürgerstolz*, p. 30. On the importance of frugality in the rearing
of children, see chapter 3.

28. Wenzel-Burchard, *Granny*, p. 24.

sometimes witty, almost never contrived. Ballin's manners were faultless, and he possessed an intuitive sense of appropriateness of this gesture or that remark. Here was a man of elegance and refinement, at home in society, though of humble lineage."[29]

The social life of Lübeck was different in style. The millionaire merchant Emil Possehl considered the city "narrow and lacking in energy," and participated very little in its social life. His few guests included relatives and employees of his firm. He did appear occasionally in public at events organized by merchant groups and by nationalistic societies. In 1910 he wrote to his old friend Curtius that he would have preferred to live in Hamburg or Düsseldorf, where he could associate with big businessmen. "I know I would fit in well there and would not have to put up with petty matters for which I am not suited by temperament. Here I do not have any close contacts, any friend to whom I could talk freely."[30] The comparison to Hamburg makes it clear how much social life depended on the size of the wealthy business community and of the upper bourgeoisie as a whole.

Berlin: The Aristocratic Model?

Does Berlin really represent the pinnacle of feudalization? Thanks to the high intellectual level of the Berlin bourgeoisie and the resulting enthusiasm for the written word, a wealth of material on Berlin social life exists that makes it possible to study this question in considerable detail. In this section, we will look first at social contacts within the business elite and the bourgeoisie, then at those with the emperor, court society, and the nobility, followed by a discussion of ties with the cultural sphere. Finally, we will turn to the style of social life.

SOCIAL CONTACTS WITHIN THE BUSINESS ELITE
AND WITHIN THE BOURGEOISIE

In Berlin businessmen spent more time with one another than with members of any other social group. The everyday life of Berlin businessmen was generally characterized by daily contacts with

29. Cecil, *Albert Ballin*, pp. 29, 103, 27–28. Cecil discounts the role of Ballin's wife in all of this· "Retiring by nature, she did not enjoy the role which Ballin's prominence thrust upon her. But she was pleasant, kindly, and devoted to her husband, and she performed her social obligations, if not with éclat, assuredly with dignity" (pp. 29–30).

30. Niendorf, *Geschichte*, p 134; see pp. 35, 133.

other businessmen.[31] They met for lunch at the Club of Berlin, which acquired the nickname "Millionaires' Club," or at certain restaurants. Jews and non-Jews mixed at these business lunches.[32]

Perhaps the most important source on social life in Berlin is the autobiography of Carl Fürstenberg, especially since he and Aniela Fürstenberg, his wife, were very prominent socially.[33] At their home, a focal point of Berlin society, the Berlin business world met and mixed with high society. Their "friends" included bankers from Berlin, France, and Italy; Emil and Walther Rathenau, the mine owner and coal dealer Fritz von Friedländer-Fuld, August Thyssen, Albert Ballin, AEG Director Felix Deutsch, and the owner of the *Frankfurter Zeitung* (a prominent newspaper), Thérèse Simon-Sonnemann. He was also acquainted with the western German heavy industrialists Haniel, Stumm, Stinnes, and Krupp.[34]

Some of these were intimate friendships. Hans Fürstenberg regarded Ballin and Thérèse Simon-Sonnemann as his father's closest friends. The three traveled together every year to the spa at Kissingen. Their main topic of conversation was politics.[35] Carl Fürstenberg wrote about Ballin: "This peculiar little man had a woman's charm and, what may seem even more remarkable, the sensitivity of a woman. . . . I have seldom had such a close friend." Fritz von Friedländer-Fuld had business relations with Fürstenberg but asked his advice when he was unable to find a suitable wife. An argument about business affairs led to the break-up of their friendship. Fürstenberg commented, "What pained me the most deeply was the personal loss of a friend to whom I had been loyally devoted for so long a time."[36] This may show that there were limits to a "sentimental friendship" between businessmen, but it also shows how personal feelings and business relationships mixed with one another in such friendships. Like many other close friends of Fürstenberg, Ballin, Simon-Sonnemann, and Friedländer-Fuld were Jewish.

31. In many autobiographies and biographies, they were not emphasized as much as contacts with well-known personalities from other fields, such as government ministers or artists, because they were far less sensational.

32. On restaurants, see C. Fürstenberg, *Lebensgeschichte*, p. 397. On the Club of Berlin, see Gwinner, *Lebenserinnerungen*, pp. 54–56; Wolff, *Club*, esp. pp. 20–29, 89, 99, P. Wallich, *Lehr- und Wanderjahre* , pp. 352–53.

33. C. Furstenberg, *Lebensgeschichte* Hans Furstenberg claims in his autobiography to have been the ghost writer of his father's autobiography, basing the book on conversations and his father's notes. See H Fürstenberg, *Erinnerungen*, p. 16.

34. See C. Furstenberg, *Lebensgeschichte* passim.

35. See H Furstenberg, *Erinnerungen*, p. 15.

36. C. Furstenberg, *Lebensgeschichte*, pp. 436, 497.

Turning first to Jewish businessmen, Eduard Arnhold, the department store owners Berthold Israel and Oskar Tietz, the bankers Paul Wallich and Valentin Weisbach, and Walther Rathenau had numerous (mostly Jewish) friends in the business world, though they also had important social connections to other professional groups.[37] Typically, wealthy Jewish business families had relatives abroad, and thus they possessed a network of social and business contacts that was international in scope. A man whose orientation was strongly bourgeois was Adolf Salomonsohn, managing director of the Berlin *Disconto-Gesellschaft*, who rose from a modest, provincial background. Among his closest friends were fellow managing directors of the *Disconto-Gesellschaft*, and Emil Kirdorf.[38] At a reception given by Adolph von Hansemann, chief managing director of the Disconto-Gesellschaft, at which military officers and dignitaries were present, Salomonsohn is reported to have said, "Actually I am the most distinguished person present, because I am respected even though I do not have a single decoration on my frock coat."[39]

Willy Liebermann von Wahlendorf conveys the image of a Jewish elite that was held together by a complex network of family ties, marriages, and friendships. It had a strong tendency to exclude the *nouveaux riches*. ". . . these circles were so exclusive that when a certain man moved into Berlin who had a lot more money than any of them, they spoke contemptuously – and as I later learned, unjustly – about the money he made in the war of 1870 and the amount of interest he earned by investing it, and none of these houses were opened to receive him, though the emperor had conferred high titles on him."[40] Social integration

37. Arnhold had as friends Gustav Krupp von Bohlen und Halbach, the industrialist Isidor Loewe, the banker Eugen Gutmann, the chairman of the board of the Berlin *Kassen-Verein* Ernst Meyer, the Rathenaus, Albert Ballin, Heinrich Wiegand, and Fritz Andreae, co-director of the *Berliner Handelsgesellschaft*. The banker Paul Wallich had personal contacts in Berlin between 1910 and 1912 with the directors of the Berliner *Handelsgesellschaft*, including Hermann Rosenberg and his daughter Ilse, whose husband, Hermann Dernburg, was a building contractor and brother of a state secretary; also with directors of the *Deutsche Bank*, the merchant James Simon, and the bankers (and later rentiers) Hugo and Eugen Landau and Felix Schwabach. Wallich was baptized; Weisbach, Israel, Tietz, Arnhold, and Rathenau were not.

On Arnhold, see Arnhold, *Eduard Arnhold*, pp. 43 and Mosse, *German-Jewish*, pp. 131–32. On Israel, see Shepherd, *Wilfrid Israel*, pp. 20–21. On Tietz, see Tietz, *Hermann Tietz*, p. 49. On Wallich, see P. Wallich, *Lehr- und Wanderjahre*, pp. 343–45. On Weisbach, see Weisbach, *Und alles*, p. 109. On Rathenau, see Berglar, *Walther Rathenau*, p. 311.

38. This is an example of friendships between Jews and non-Jews in this class.

39. Solmssen, *Gedenkblatt*, p. 19; see pp. 10–12

40. Liebermann von Wahlendorf, *Erinnerung*, p. 84. I assume that the man involved was Siegmund Aschrott See Polizeipräsident an Handelsministerium, StA Potsdam, Pr.Br.Rep 30 Berlin C Tit. 94, Nr. 8795 passim.

between these Jewish patricians and the non-Jewish business elite was quite limited, as Werner Mosse illustrates with a number of examples.[41]

Of the three non-Jewish Berlin businessmen on whose circles of friends and acquaintances good source material is available, the first, the banker Carl von der Heydt, had some ties with bankers although they were not particularly strong. A large percentage of the guests of the second, Wilhelm von Siemens, were big business-men, while the third, the banker Georg von Siemens, was some-thing of a non-Jewish equivalent of Salomonsohn, avoiding con-tact with the aristocracy as much as possible.[42]

All in all, the social relationships of the wealthy Berlin business-men with one another were rather close. Social ties with prominent artists and intellectuals were strong. Wealthy businessmen also socialized a good deal with high government officials, consisting in Berlin mainly of aristocrats but possessing a distinct group profile and mentality. In Berlin, this was a distinct group that straddled the pre-industrial elite and the bourgeoisie, belonging in a sense to neither. On the other hand, like Fontane's Jenny Treibel,[43] Berlin businessmen only seldom associated with socially somewhat inferi-or segments of the educated bourgeoisie (teachers, clergy, and the like). Their employees and middle-class businessmen do not appear among the friends and acquaintances mentioned in autobiogra-phies and biographies. The lower middle class is hardly represented at all. As in the case of the Hamburg business elite, it can be seen that in Berlin the wealthy businessmen had to a great extent cut themselves off from the middle class and had risen into an upper bourgeoisie that was, however, split according to religion. A good example of this trend can be observed in the family of the depart-ment store owner Oskar Tietz, who had begun his business career as an owner of a small shop, and by 1911 was worth about twenty-five million marks. During the 1890s a change took place in the social contacts of the now well-to-do family that moved first into a genteel neighborhood in Munich, and then to Berlin. Whereas the family had previously entertained visiting manufacturers and poor Jewish students and soldiers, it was now associating with politi-cians, lawyers, big industrialists, bankers, and journalists.[44]

41. Mosse, *German-Jewish*, pp. 117–33, 207–13.

42. On von der Heydt, see Heydt, *Unser Haus*, pp. 29–30, 35–37. On Wilhelm von Siemens, see Harries, "Nachruf," p. 9. On Georg von Siemens, see Helfferich, *Georg von Siemens*, vol. 3, p. 240.

43. Fontane, *Frau Jenny Treibel*.

44. See Tietz, *Hermann Tietz*, p. 49.

Hildegard Wallich (née Rehrmann, born 1887), the daughter of the headmaster of a cadet academy and the wife of Paul Wallich, briefly describes in her autobiography the impressions that she and her parents gathered at her engagement party with regard to her future husband's social circles: "It was something like running the gauntlet in front of the critical members of west Berlin, but . . . it turned out to be not as bad as I had expected. . . . It was simply another world with which we were not familiar and had to learn to understand."[45] Especially the second statement shows that there was a clear divide between the business elite and the educated bourgeoisie.

Lamar Cecil places considerable importance on the fact that wealthy Berlin Jews had social contacts primarily in the upper echelons of society but seldom entertained other Jews, and that exceptions were made "only" for Jews that were as powerful as their hosts. He implies that the explanation for this behavior lies in Jewish self-abasement, over-eagerness to assimilate, and aristocratization.[46] As Veblen points out, all social groups tend to turn their backs on their social origins when they rise socially. It is not surprising that the wealthy Jews of Berlin had almost no contact with the Jewish middle class. The Jewish business elite of Berlin, like the German business elite in general, associated almost exclusively with groups of equal economic status, including Jews. Social exclusivity had nothing to do with "Jewish self-hate."

THE EMPEROR AND COURT SOCIETY

Businessmen who had personal contacts with the emperor had at their disposal special channels that could be used to exert political influence. Werner Mosse regards the close relationship of Jewish businessmen with the emperor as a sort of tutelage: "They would thus perpetuate, if in a somewhat different setting, the traditional client-patron relationship of 'court Jew' and prince. Could the more sensitive among the Jewish partners be wholly unaware of a certain lack of dignity in such a relationship?"[47] First, it should be pointed out that powerful non-Jewish businessmen like Krupp and Stumm were also on friendly terms with the emperor. Second, in the late nineteenth century businessmen in other European countries also withdrew from their respective parliaments and increas-

45. H. Wallich, *Erinnerungen*, p. 113
46. See Cecil, "Jew and Junker," pp 49–50.
47. Mosse, *German-Jewish*, p. 353.

201

ingly established personal relationships with the heads of government in order to gain direct influence on the political decision-making process.[48]

Numerous businessmen had at least some personal contact with the emperor.[49] Isabel Hull is of the opinion that Krupp and Ballin exercised considerable influence on the emperor: "The Kaiser regarded Krupp as his industrial counterpart, a kind of bourgeois king whose meaning to Germany's strength, internal and external, was practically as important as his own."[50] Michael Stürmer terms the meetings of Krupp with the emperor as an encounter between business interests and *raison d'état*. According to Willi Boelcke, this friendship ". . . had no comparable parallel in the history of other countries."[51] F.A. Krupp established an entire network of social contacts in order to further his interests. In an interview with Jules Huret, the arms manufacturer Heinrich Ehrhardt severely criticized this Krupp strategy: "Krupp fought us with the most odious weapons. It was within his power to form a circle around the emperor that was impenetrable for us. All the military officers in the entourage of the emperor were relatives or friends of Krupp's senior employees."[52] The subsequent head of the Krupp Concern, Gustav Krupp von Bohlen und Halbach, like F.A. Krupp, was on close friendly terms with the emperor.[53]

A personal relationship with the emperor did not necessarily bring with it access to court society. Admiral Fritz Hollmann, state secretary in the Admiralty, was one of the few court officials who

48. See Cassis, "Wirtschaftselite," p. 31

49. These include Max Warburg, Max von Schinckel, Heinrich Wiegand, and Richard Krogman, all from Hamburg; Richard Roesicke, owner of the Berlin Schultheiss Brewery; Emil and Walther Rathenau, Fritz von Friedländer-Fuld; Berlin bankers Franz von Mendelssohn, Paul Schwabach, Arthur von Gwinner, Georg von Siemens, and Carl Fürstenberg; Berlin wholesale merchants James Simon and Eduard Arnhold, industry magnates Prince Egon Fürstenberg, Prince Pless, Count Scholto von Douglas, and Prince Guido Henckel von Donnersmarck; the Berlin machine and arms manufacturer Isidor Loewe; and Ziese, the director of the Schichau shipyards Businessmen who were regarded as especially important personal friends or advisers of the emperor were the heavy industrialist Baron Carl Ferdinand von Stumm-Halberg, Albert Ballin, and Friedrich Alfred Krupp. See Attali, *Siegmund G. Warburg*, p. 83; Petzet, *Heinrich Wiegand*, p. 211; Rohrmann, *Max von Schinckel*, p 190; Art'l, *Richard Roesicke*, p. 25; Feder, "James Simon," p. 6; Stern, *Gold and Iron*, p. 544; Arnhold, *Eduard Arnhold*, pp. 45–46; C. Fürstenberg, *Lebensgeschichte*, p 439; Hellwig, *Carl Ferdinand*, pp. 429, 515; Cecil, *Albert Ballin* passim; Jaeger, *Unternehmer*, pp. 171–83.

50. Hull, *Entourage*, pp. 159–60; also, see pp 157–74.

51 See Stürmer, "Alltag," p. 266. Boelcke, *Krupp*, p. 108. However, Lamar Cecil mentions similar examples for England. See Cecil, *Albert Ballin*, p. 98.

52. Jules Huret, *In Deutschland*, part 1. *Rheinland und Westfalen*, p. 279. On preferential treatment accorded the Krupps, see Jaeger, *Unternehmer*, p 176.

53. See Jaeger, *Unternehmer*, p. 175.

really liked to associate with businessmen. Jewish businessmen met Wilhelm II at hunting parties and lunches or received visits from the emperor but were not invited to court receptions and parties.[54] A non-Jewish ennobled businessman such as the banker Carl von der Heydt, who lived in Berlin, could also encounter insuperable obstacles: "As members of the bourgeoisie we were excluded from the court, which also meant that we could not belong to court society, by which is to be understood that exclusive circle assembled around the court, consisting of the higher nobility, the diplomatic corps, the highest court officials, and some very wealthy noble families."[55] Hans Fürstenberg even advanced the theory that up to the First World War the chasm between the bourgeois society of Berlin and the court society was growing.[56]

However, individual businessmen were accepted in these circles. During the "season" Frau Krupp held balls in Berlin that the court, and sometimes even the emperor, attended. The home of the senior managing director of the *Disconto-Gesellschaft*, Adolph von Hansemann, ". . . was the center of a glittering social life that embraced the court and the top leaders of the country, and its importance grew along with that of the *Disconto-Gesellschaft* as the latter more and more took a leading role in the development of the Fatherland."[57] Theodor Guilleaume of Cologne stood at the fringes of court society; he was on friendly terms with state secretaries Stephan and Podbielski, he was presented to the emperor, and he received visits from Crown Prince Wilhelm and other members of the imperial family. As the director of the Norddeutscher Lloyd (steamship line), Heinrich Wiegand conducted negotiations with the director of the office of internal affairs, with state secretaries and other high officials, and with Bernhard von Bülow and Alfred von Tirpitz; as time went on, these relationships assumed more and more the character of friendships. There were also contacts with the courts in states outside of Prussia. Alfred Ackermann, head of the B.G. Teubner publishing house in Leipzig, for example, entertained Saxon princes as guests at his home.[58] Behind these formal contacts, one can assume there was an attempt to penetrate into the centers of power.

54. See Cecil, *Albert Ballin*, p. 99. On Hollmann, see Hull, *Entourage*, pp. 161–62.
55. Heydt, *Unser Haus*, pp. 30–31.
56. See H. Fürstenberg, *Carl-Furstenberg-Anekdoten*, pp. 14.
57. Solmssen, *Gedenkblatt*, pp. 23–24; see Huret, *In Deutschland*, part 1, p. 356.
58. See Wessel, "Die Unternehmerfamilie," pp. 73, 81; Petzet, *Heinrich Wiegand*, p. 211; Schulze, *Geschichte*, pp. 128.

Perhaps the most astonishing case of acceptance of a business-man into court circles was that of Walther Rathenau, son of the founder of the AEG, and an unconverted Jew. Around 1900, Rathenau sought and obtained access to the refined salons, "more European than bureaucratic in nature," where the circle around the Empress Augusta met and "set the tone" for the court society.[59] Count Kessler, who was a friend of Rathenau, thought that an exception was made in Rathenau's case because of his social and intellectual talents, whereas Rathenau's friend Alfred Kerr attributed it to his wealth.[60] Both factors probably helped.

Social Ties with the Pre-industrial Elite

A businessman could seek social relationships with the nobility for quite varied reasons. Within the Berlin business elite there were indeed cases of full-blown aristocratization, attempts to integrate into the nobility and to shed one's bourgeois identity. However, this was rare. More commonly, aristocratic guests fulfilled a decorative function: "Some people get an especially exalted sensation by surrounding themselves with bright-colored jackets and noble personages. It flatters one's vanity to have Prince X and Count Y in one's home. . . . Still others use military officers as a filler, as decorative trimming. They invite them because they are clever people and dance well."[61] Wealthy businessmen's wives would invite two or three officers to a ball out of a desire to appear socially superior.[62]

However, the Berlin business elite cultivated contacts with the pre-industrial elite primarily in order to be able to advance its own business and political interests.[63] This can be seen in the high offices that most of these aristocratic guests held. The basis for these contacts becomes all the more clear if, instead of focusing on ethnicity – Cecil's research is on Jewish businessmen – we look at the area of economic activity involved. For among the wealthy businessmen of Berlin there were many bankers who headed very large banks with international connections. These banks were particularly dependent on the state for business and for inside infor-

---

59. Kessler, *Walther Rathenau*, pp. 55–56.
60. See ibid. p. 56; Kerr, *Walther Rathenau*, p. 92.
61. Zobeltitz, *Chronik*, vol. 2, p. 210.
62. See Huret, *En Allemagne. Berlin*, pp. 346–47. Huret specifies "Jewish businessmen's wives," but we can assume that non-Jewish businessmen's wives did the same.
63. See Jaeger, *Unternehmer*, esp. p. 171.

mation on affairs at home and abroad. They also had to cultivate good relations with foreign governments. Political motives may also have played a role. The wealthier and more powerful segments of the bourgeoisie had little interest in promoting liberalism and mass political participation, but rather in reinforcing the government's conservative, nationalistic interpretation of the interests of the economy and the nation. An intimate of the emperor has written that the interest of the bourgeois elite in politics increased during the Wilhelmine period, ". . . partly because it [the elite] did not quite trust the emperor, and partly because it felt that things had changed; Germany was getting so prosperous that it behooved everybody to watch carefully all that was being done to safeguard the interests and the integrity of the Fatherland."[64]

The Fürstenbergs associated with Imperial Chancellor Bernhard von Bülow, numerous government officials (in areas such as colonial affairs, international commercial policy, and foreign affairs), generals, diplomatic representatives of the various German states with which his bank maintained business dealings, and German diplomats.[65] As the director of one of the most important banks of the imperial capital, Fürstenberg needed to maintain relationships not only with the bank's customers, other bankers, and government leaders, but also with groups such as military generals who were, to be sure, of no direct interest to the bank but were a part of an elite network that as a whole constituted a powerful force.

Lamar Cecil somewhat inaccurately characterizes two additional wealthy Jews – Paul Schwabach and Fritz von Friedländer-Fuld – as examples of feudalization. In actual fact, they socialized with some of the politically best-informed aristocrats in the capital – ministers, state secretaries, ambassadors. The information they picked up undoubtedly helped them to keep an eye on events at home and abroad that could have a major impact on their business ventures.[66] Friedländer-Fuld and Schwabach would not have been able to express any controversial political opinions in these circles if

---

64 Schwering, *Berlin Court*, p. 255.

65. See C. Fürstenberg, *Lebensgeschichte* passim.

66. Among Schwabach's acquaintances were Baroness Spitzemberg, Alfred von Kiderlen-Wächter (who from 1910 on was the state secretary of the Foreign Office), Baron von Holstein (a high official – *Vortragender Rat* – in the Foreign Office), Holstein's friend, Helene von Lebbin (an intimate friend of von Bülow's), and Count Bogdan von Hutten-Czapski (a member of the Prussian ruling family) Frequent guests of Friedlander-Fuld were Prince Heinrich, brother of the emperor, Prussian Finance Minister von Rheinbaben, Kiderlen-Wächter, Ambassador Count Anton von Monts, State Secretary Wilhelm Solf, and the French Ambassador Cambon See Vierhaus, *Das Tagebuch*, esp. pp. 456, 475, Rheinbaben, *Viermal Deutschland*, p. 76; Mosse, *German-Jewish*, pp , 192–197.

they had wanted to: "The Friedländer salon, which carefully avoided the appearance of being a political salon, was a neutral ground on which the most diverse leading personalities met. . . ."[67] It seems doubtful, however, that Schwabach and Friedländer-Fuld sacrificed deeply-felt political beliefs to the god of social ambition. They were hardly radicals: the former was conservative, the latter more of a National Liberal.

If anything, through their social relationships they had an opportunity to influence the political and diplomatic decision-making process. Both met with the emperor and had something of a role in diplomacy. Schwabach reported to the Foreign Ministry what he learned from business contacts regarding French and British foreign policy. He was assigned minor diplomatic missions. This was not an isolated instance – other businessmen were accorded a small role in diplomacy in this period. Talks between the German diplomat Alfred von Kiderlen-Wächter and the French diplomat Paul Cambon took place on Friedländer-Fuld's estate. Through Kiderlen, Friedländer-Fuld's wife, Milly, became involved: ". . . when he [Kiderlen] was traveling abroad and even when he was in Berlin, he carried on an extensive correspondence with Frau Friedländer, whose political tact and widely ramified connections with her relatives and friends in Holland and Paris were often useful to him."[68] Here we have a reciprocal relationship, not one of patronage.

Admittedly, social ambitions and a certain degree of aristocratization were at work here as well. Among the guests of the Friedländer-Fulds were also officers and the scions of the great Silesian landowning families – nobles whose friendship may or may not have furthered business interests. (It is not known whether the Silesian estate owners in question were – as was typical in this period – also involved in mining operations, and therefore of interest as business contacts.) At first anti-Semitism constituted a great obstacle. A contemporary, Lady Susan Townley, writes of Milly von Friedländer-Fuld's unfulfilled social aspirations: "But she could not force the portals of Berlin society, not even though she added a covered tennis-court and a riding-school to the already numerous amenities of her beautiful house in the Pariser Platz. She

67. Hutten-Czapski, *Sechzig Jahre*, vol. 2, p. 63.

68 Ibid , p 63. On Schwabach, see Jaeger, *Unternehmer*, p. 181. On the political attitudes of the two, see Polizeiprasident Berlin an Handelsministerium, 1902, StA Potsdam, Pr.Br Rep. 30 Berlin C Tit. 94 Nr 13431 and Polizeiprasident Berlin an Handelsministerium, 1901, StA Potsdam, Pr. Br.Rep. 30 Berlin C Tit. 94 Nr 9940

climbed and climbed, but when I left Berlin she had not succeeded in reaching the top, although to accomplish her end she had recourse to all sorts of expedients."[69] In any event, she reached her goal prior to the First World War, at the time of her daughter's debut, because many families hoped for the marriage of a son to the sole heiress of the Friedländer-Fulds. "It soon became 'the thing' to go to the Friedländers," wrote a confidant of the emperor.[70] After repeated attempts, Milly von Friedländer-Fuld succeeded in inducing the British Ambassador to accept her invitations, "and this gave the final *cachet* to their social aspirations." One of the very few people who would not visit her home was the wife of the chief marshal of the imperial court.[71] However, Fritz von Friedländer-Fuld had no intention of leaving the world of business. Hans Fürstenberg writes: "Along with all these successes outside his profession, this smart man never for one moment forgot his coal business."[72]

We know all too little about the social relationships of other Jewish businessmen with the pre-industrial elite. Among the guests at the home of Eduard Arnhold (along with industrialists and artists) were ambassadors, government ministers, "dukes," and "princes." Eugen Gutmann gave ". . . frequent big parties at which military officers are always represented." The Israels associated with diplomats and businessmen, the Weisbachs with high officials, scientists, artists, and bankers.[73]

The social profile of the guests of some of the non-Jewish Berlin businessmen follows a similar pattern. The speculator Max Esser had a large circle of acquaintances among government officials, military officers, and merchants.[74] A review of a sampling of visiting cards reveals the following picture of the visitors at the home of Wilhelm von Siemens: among the visitors were eleven German big businessmen, two foreign businessmen, ten university professors, one medical superintendent, one engineer, one Reichstag delegate, three high government officials, and four military officers or

69. Townley, *"Indiscretions"*, pp 45–46.

70. Schwering, *Berlin Court*, p 217; see Buchanan, *Ambassador's Daughter*, pp. 45–46

71. See Huret, *En Allemagne. Berlin*, p. 348; quotation in Gleichen, *Guardsman's Memories*, p 276.

72. Fürstenberg, *Erinnerungen*, p. 128

73. On Arnhold, see Arnhold, *Eduard Arnhold*, pp. 43, 197, 218 and Bunsen, *Zeitgenossen*, p. 72. On Gutmann, see Polizeipräsident Berlin an Handelsministerium, 1898, StA Potsdam, Pr Br Rep. 30 Berlin C Tit 94 Nr. 10239. On the Israels, see Shepherd, *Wilfrid Israel*, pp. 20–21 On Weisbach, see Weisbach, *Und alles*, p 109.

74. Polizeipräsident Berlin an Handelsministerium, 14.2 1896, StAPotsdam, Pr.Br.Rep. 30 Berlin C Tit. 94 Nr. 9748

aristocrats whose profession was not indicated.[75] It is also known that around the turn of the century, Wilhelm von Siemens invited government ministers, scientists, doctors, artists, high government officials, and military officers to his hunting estate for a *battue* hunt. His brother Arnold and the latter's wife Ellen had social relationships with Bernhard von Bülow, General Field Marshal Helmuth von Moltke, Rudolf von Delbrück, and Count Otto Schlippenbach, whom they regarded as a family friend.[76]

Lucy Siemens wrote the following tongue-in-cheek comments on the aristocratization of the family's social contacts in a letter to her brother-in-law Wilhelm von Siemens:

> Your little one has written to us that you have gotten into a frightfully aristocratic circle and are going around with countesses, princes, etc. I am delighted to hear this, because in my opinion it will be good for you to get out of your bourgeois atmosphere and be among people in whose veins flows sky-blue blood, which is always a rare phenomenon in the life of humankind. Besides, the favor of princes should never be underestimated, and I advise you always to control your impulses and never, in a moment of poetic inspiration in the presence of your eminent new friend, sing the popular ditty: "Princely blood shall flow to drench the roots of the German Republic."[77]

Here we see that the family by no means approached the nobility with reverence; rather, it cultivated such relationships for pragmatic reasons, but did not lose the sense of its own identity in the process.

The banker Carl von der Heydt represents a clearer case of aristocratization. He moved to Berlin in the 1890s to take over a branch office of the Elberfeld banking firm, which was under the direction of his relatives. Von der Heydt formed friendships with a few bankers, but they did not constitute the "main thrust" of his social life. And he seldom entertained aristocrats, senior military personnel, and diplomats. He associated primarily with government ministers, state secretaries, a few Reichstag delegates, and military officers. The latter were not members of the elite mounted guard regiments, which consisted exclusively of members of court society. However, almost all of the male dancers at balls in his

75. SAA 4/LC 999; SAA 4/LC 999 This enumeration omits family members, factory employees, and persons whose profession could not be determined.
76. On Wilhelm, see Harries, "Nachruf," p 9. On Arnold, see Bunsen, *Zeitgenossen*, pp 42–44.
77. Letter dated 17 August 1881, SAA Lr 567.

home were officers. Von der Heydt was generous in his praise for the officer corps that he regarded as a "force for good breeding." "With regard to these young gentlemen, looking back over twenty years of experience, I must say that I have never seen a more well-bred, more modest group of young people, so completely free of any class arrogance."[78]

ANTI-SEMITISM AND JEWISH ETHNICITY

If social contact between business and noble families was limited in scope, could this be because of the social exclusivity of the nobility and anti-Semitism? There is little doubt that anti-Semitism was widespread in the Prussian nobility. In the Jewish autobiographies of the empire period studied by Monika Richarz, anti-Semitism arose primarily in connection with school, university, and the army.[79] It is not a coincidence that these were avenues of social advancement. The same tendency appears in the autobiographies and biographies analyzed in the present study. Especially children and young people were faced with discrimination. In the words of Walther Rathenau, "In the youthful years of every German Jew there comes a painful moment which he remembers for the rest of his life: when he for the first time becomes fully aware that he has come into the world as a citizen of second class and that no amount of ability and no degree of merit can free him from this situation."[80] Werner Weisbach, the son of a Berlin private banker, Georg Tietz, a member of the family of a department store owner, Walther Rathenau and his sister Edith, and Paul Liebermann von Wahlendorf, who came from a family of Saxon textile industrialists, were all subjected to the discrimination of their schoolmates, ranging from exclusion to harassment. On the other hand, Hans Fürstenberg, the baptized son of Carl, speaks only of a happy childhood.[81]

At the university, the sons of Jewish big businessmen were above all confronted with anti-Semitism in the student corps (fraternities) and students' associations. Paul Wallich described these social

78. Heydt, *Unser Haus*, pp. 29–30, 35–37. For another example of non-Jewish aristocratization, see Reibnitz, *Gestalten*, pp. 124–25.

79. See Richarz, *Jüdisches Leben*, vol. 2, p. 38. See also Kaplan, *Making*, pp. 148–52.

80 Rathenau, "Staat und Judentum," pp. 188–89.

81. See Weisbach, *Und alles*, p. 53; Tietz, *Hermann Tietz*, p 64; Mangoldt, *Auf der Schwelle*, pp. 23–24; Hellige, "Rathenau und Harden," p 32, Liebermann von Wahlendorf, *Erinnerung*, p. 34; H. Furstenberg, *Erinnerungen*, p. 1. Of these, only Weisbach later converted to Christianity

209

dividing lines in detail in his autobiography. During his attendance at Freiburg University, he tried to avoid fellow students from Jewish families and gain entrance to one of two exclusive circles, one consisting of wealthy aristocrats, the other of wealthy, mostly ennobled, Christian sons of the bourgeoisie, each of which was further divided into corps. He would have been accepted into the Jewish group or into one of the students' associations (which were far less exclusive than the corps), but that was what he did not want. On one occasion when Wallich was supposed to introduce one of his few Jewish friends, Walter Levy, to a group of non-Jewish students, he mumbled the name so as to make it incomprehensible. A young count, with whom Wallich went riding and drinking, did not keep Wallich away from his circle of acquaintances, but neither did he try to help him gain acceptance in it. The result of Wallich's snobbery and Jewish self-hatred was that "my entire stay in Freiburg was ruined by my attempt to direct the greater part of my social activity into Aryan channels. As a result I was closer to having no social activity at all."[82]

Willy Liebermann von Wahlendorf, son of an ennobled Saxon textile industrialist and a cousin of Walther Rathenau and the great painter Max Liebermann, became a corps member at the University of Würzburg in the mid-1880's, and then was accepted into the *Starkenburger*, an aristocratic fraternity, at the University of Giessen. Connections played a role in this. At the Jewish dances in Würzburg he was "certainly the only fraternity member." During his time at Giessen, a member of an allied fraternity came to Giessen to "remove the two Jews" (Liebermann and a friend), but it did not come to this.[83] In 1896 the national assembly of *Burschenschaften* (German student associations) passed a resolution no longer to accept Jews. Thereafter, the Jewish students streamed into the allied independent clubs.[84]

During military service, many of the sons of the wealthy Jewish bourgeoisie suffered under the open anti-Semitism of some of the officers, and under social segregation among the recruits or officers. This was the case especially in Prussia, although conditions were somewhat better in Bavaria, where unbaptized Jews could become officers. (However, this meant little to most Jews, first because the Bavarian army was much smaller than the Prussian

82 Wallich, *Lehr- und Wanderjahre*, p. 162, see pp. 160–63. Wallich does indeed use the term "Aryan" (as an adjective) here.
83 See Liebermann von Wahlendorf, *Erinnerung*, pp 40–43.
84. See Richarz, *Jüdisches Leben*, pp 39–40.

army, second because most Jews lived in Prussia, not Bavaria.) Wallich's experiences in the Prussian military were quite varied; he became friends with two officers, and snubbed Jewish comrades and those of the petty bourgeoisie in order to improve his chances of becoming a reserve officer. The experiences of Liebermann von Wahlendorf in the army were predominantly of a negative nature, and Werner Weisbach had only superficial relationships with his comrades. Rathenau developed a close relationship with his comrades in the aristocratic cuirassier guard regiment. One of the greatest disappointments of his life was that he was not allowed to remain in the military as an active officer.[85]

Such experiences, coupled with the legal discrimination against the Jews, could deeply embed in the mind of an individual Jew the consciousness of being "different," leading in some cases to Jewish self-hatred. In the case of Walther Rathenau, one senses a deep inner discord, an irreconcilable inconsistency, alongside the consciousness of belonging to a minority that been persecuted for centuries. However, Rathenau's neuroses and self-hatred were by no means typical of the Jewish business community of the Wilhelmine era. Discrimination often muted or snuffed out admiration for the nobility. Georg Tietz spoke out as a student against the authorization of student associations at his university.[86] The frustration of Paul Wallich's lofty social ambitions, directed toward the nobility, drove him back into the arms of his own class and ethnic group. This reorientation was much more than an admission of defeat. Wallich, though baptized, ended up rediscovering his ethnic Jewishness and a sense of belonging in the wealthy Jewish bourgeois milieu. In retrospect, the Jewish circles at the university, for example, seemed to him to have been the "most intellectual and the most genial." The uncompromisingly self-critical tone of his memoirs testifies to his inner rejection of an earlier reverence for the nobility and to his success in overcoming his Jewish self-hatred.[87]

Even in the case of Rathenau, there is evidence of turning against the nobility. In his description of the typical careerist (*"Patentschiesser"*) he reveals an antipathy, not entirely uncommon

---

85 On Wallich, see P. Wallich, *Lehr- und Wanderjahre*, pp. 169–178; on Liebermann von Wahlendorf, see Liebermann von Wahlendorf, *Erinnerung*, pp. 55–57; on Weisbach, see Weisbach, *Und alles*, p. 172. On Rathenau, see Kessler, *Walther Rathenau*, p. 32, Hellige, "Rathenau und Harden," p. 35.

86. See Tietz, *Hermann Tietz*, p. 85.

87. See P. Wallich, *Lehr- und Wanderjahre*, esp. pp. 163, 219ff., 343ff Since we do not know when Wallich wrote his memoirs, it is not clear at what stage of his life this reorientation process began.

in bourgeois circles, against the coarse, militarized, rural Prussian Junker: "Puffed-up fellows, insolent and cynical in manner, with pasted-down hair, welted faces, tight-fitting pant-legs, snarling voices imitating the tone of an officer giving orders. . . . Such characters were tolerated, even accepted; they were destined to take their place among those who rule, judge, teach, cure and cultivate the people."[88]

Thus, rejection did not just work in one direction. In fact, it is questionable that the bulk of the bourgeoisie – whether Jewish or non-Jewish – really longed to be accepted into aristocratic circles. How many businessmen would have felt at ease in the Union Club where gambling was the principal occupation? The dull, narrow atmosphere that prevailed in the casino on the Pariser Platz also corresponded very little with the mentality of the bourgeoisie or the newly wealthy. The attitudes of the older members of the club has been described as follows: "They regarded the club as an officers' casino and they did not want any innovations to be introduced. They had already experienced with great annoyance the installation of a bowling alley on the lawn."[89]

As an adult, a very wealthy Jewish businessman encountered anti-Semitism of a subtle kind in Berlin society. Lamar Cecil points out various kinds of social barriers encountered by Berlin Jews. Members of the nobility invited Jews much more rarely than the reverse. Jews were not accepted into certain clubs. Moreover, in the writings of various aristocrats, anti-capitalist and anti-Semitic views are expressed.[90] Baroness Spitzemberg reported that Albert von Goldschmidt-Rothschild, diplomat, banker, and son of a Rothschild, ". . . came out here this winter . . . was royally entertained in shifts, was exploited and then shamefully treated."[91] Jews like the Friedländer-Fulds, who wanted to be accepted in the very best society, needed to have "thick skin."[92]

On the other hand, it should not be forgotten that the Jewish upper bourgeoisie chalked up some great social triumphs during the imperial period. The most important representatives of the government and of the diplomatic corps were entertained at the homes of the Friedländer-Fulds and the Fürstenbergs. The journal-

88. Walther Rathenau, *An Deutschlands Jugend* (Berlin, 1918), p 19. Quoted (without indication of page) in Kessler, *Walther Rathenau*, p. 54.

89. Brauer, *Im Dienste*, p. 213. On the Union Club, see Schwering, *Berlin Court*, pp 228 ff.

90. See Cecil, "Jew and Junker," esp. pp. 53–56.

91. Vierhaus, ed., *Das Tagebuch*, p. 446, cited according to Mosse, "Die Juden," p. 89.

92. Gleichen, *Guardsman's Memories*, p. 276.

ist Jules Huret writes that Jews were victorious in their "assault" (an unkind term) on the aristocratic salons. This did not mean, naturally, that attitudes towards Jews had changed, but merely that the nobility hoped to gain something from the acquaintanceship. Schwering writes ironically about Fritz von Friedländer-Fuld: "His Jewish origin was not allowed to weigh in the balance against his millions."[93] Young aristocrats went to the parties of wealthy Jews in hopes of finding a wife with a sizable dowry. Willy Liebermann von Wahlendorf attended balls in Baden-Baden (where the nobility of all Germany gathered) and was graciously received by aristocratic ladies who thought he was wealthier than he actually was.[94] Beneath the surface ran an undercurrent of ugly prejudice. An acquaintance of Jules Huret described the attitude of the Prussian nobility as follows: "Here people think they need to make excuses if they are entertained in Jewish homes. 'It is really sad' – they say when they are alone among themselves – 'a bad sign of the times' . . . [but] how can one in the long run escape from people who try so hard to get one? One sighs and – goes back again."[95] Despite the obvious survival of prejudice, one should not overlook the trend (most evident in intermarriage) in the direction of the social acceptance of Jews, a trend that was broken off during the First World War.

One can only speculate where the anti-bourgeois attitudes of the nobility ended and its anti-Semitism began. Liebermann von Wallendorf was convinced that members of the Christian upper bourgeoisie were not welcomed into the aristocratic circles (coming from all over Germany, including Prussia) that he had access to in Baden-Baden.[96] Though this may be an exaggeration, it is certainly clear that the exclusivity of the aristocracy also applied to non-Jewish businessmen. One finds evidence of this, for example, in Heydt's remarks about the closed nature of court society and in Wallich's description of the social circles at the university. In the following passage regarding the attitude of the officer corps, Baron von Rheinbaben does not distinguish between Jews and non-Jews: "It was always a major subject of conversation whether the 'Guards' should accept invitations to this or that home of a wealthy

93. Schwering, Berlin Court, p. 218· see Huret, En Allemagne Berlin, p. 346.

94. See Liebermann von Wahlendorf, Erinnerung, p 116. On dowry-chasing, see Huret, En Allemagne. Berlin, pp 346–47.

95. See Huret, En Allemagne Berlin, pp. 347–49.

96 See Liebermann von Wahlendorf, Erinnerung, p. 116 On dowry-chasing, see Huret, En Allemagne. Berlin, pp. 346–47

banker, a well-to-do industrialist, or some newly ennobled honorary consul general, etc."[97] If these impressions are typical, then the Jewish and non-Jewish segments of the German business elite were not in an entirely dissimilar situation vis-à-vis the nobility. Even if this theory is correct, it applies only to a very small, wealthy, and privileged group of Jews, some of whom were baptized, and especially those of Berlin.[98] Thus, this elite held a social position that was unique for German Jews of the Wilhelmine period. This position received special confirmation by the emperor, who maintained personal relationships with a number of Jewish businessmen. Here lies the explanation for why the wealthy Jews of Berlin thought that they were playing a leading role in society – they were.[99]

Why are these findings so different from Cecil's? One reason is that Cecil relies primarily on the observations of aristocrats and makes little use of the autobiographies and biographies of Jewish businessmen. In the view of Junkers and English nobility, the highest goal of all wealthy Jews was social acceptance by the nobility. These aristocrats had little conception of the autonomous bourgeois orientation that prevailed within the upper-middle-class Jewish community. Moreover, they had little opportunity to see Jewish businessmen who did not move about in aristocratic circles. It should also be pointed out that Cecil did not have a control group. He treats Jewish behavior as unique. However, the results of research on non-Jewish businessmen indicate that among them, tendencies were to be found that were similar to those in the Jewish business elite. Third, Cecil observes wealthy Berlin Jews as actors on the social stage and not as businessmen, and thereby overlooks the practical advantages that accrued to them from social contact with the nobility.

SOCIAL CONNECTIONS WITH THE WORLD OF CULTURE

The social relationships of the business elite with representatives of the world of art and learning were closer in Berlin than in other

---

97. Rheinbaben, *Viermal Deutschland*, p. 76.

98. According to Huret, the nobility in other parts of Germany – including Frankfurt – was much more rejecting of the Jewish bourgeoisie. See Huret, *En Allemagne. Berlin*, pp. 347–49.

99. Peter Gay writes, "For German Jews anxious to live and work in peace, as Germans, the persistence of exclusive organizations, outbursts of hostility, and anti-Semitic publicists appeared as depressing survivals. The centers of darkness and animosity still scattered across the social landscape seemed so unpleasant precisely because so much had happened in the way of liberalization and enlightenment. But the main point was that much *had* happened." Gay, *Freud*, p. 93.

parts of Germany. Carl Fürstenberg writes that his wife Aniela ". . . came as close to establishing a salon as was possible in Berlin at that time." She attached ". . . great importance to the formation of acquaintanceships and friendships with the most diverse and most interesting people possible, so that along with industrialists, bankers, and diplomats, a large number of artists and scholars also figured in our narrower circle."[100] Even before their marriage, Fürstenberg had been on friendly terms with the chief editor of the satirical political weekly *Kladderadatsch*, Ernst Dohm, and his wife Hedwig Dohm, a well-known writer and feminist. Fürstenberg first met his wife Aniela Treitel, née Natanson, in the social circle of theater critic Paul Lindau and his brother Rudolf, who was press officer of the Foreign Office and a writer. In this salon, writers, artists, and diplomats mingled with one another. After her marriage to Carl Fürstenberg, Aniela Fürstenberg was anxious to maintain relationships with artists, composers, musicians, writers, architects, and scientists. "From Richard Strauss and Max Reinhardt to Gerhart Hauptmann and the great bacteriologist Koch, many of the greatest figures of Germany of that time honored us with their acquaintanceship."[101] Aniela Fürstenberg tried to stimulate conversations on art, literature, and music at formal dinners by inviting outstanding conversationalists, such as the writer Gabriele Reuter, and by placing scholars, journalists, and artists next to industrialists and government officials at the table. This may have helped to mediate between the very disparate value systems and conventions of the bourgeois and noble guests. Since she also maintained friendships with controversial figures of the Wilhelmine period such as Gerhart Hauptmann and the pacifist and women's rights advocate Bertha von Suttner, one can conclude that more was at stake for her than merely decorating her table with famous people.[102] It is surprising, then, that Mosse advances the theory, based on assertions by Ballin, that Aniela Fürstenberg broke off the relationships with intellectuals that her husband had cultivated because her social ambitions were aimed more toward high society.[103]

The writer Maximilian Harden was Fürstenberg's closest friend.

100. Fürstenberg, *Lebensgeschichte*, pp. 399, 334.
101. See ibid., pp 95, 99–100, 216–17; quotation on p. 398
102. See ibid., pp. 142, 317, 398
103 "In fact, not only did the sociable Aniela soon expand her social activities but she also, to some extent, changed their character What had been the meeting place of a cultured intelligentsia was turned into one for ʼhigh societyʼ and a forum of social snobbery " Mosse, *German-Jewish*, p. 113; see pp 110–33 Neurotic, jealous Ballin can hardly be regarded as an impartial observer.

Werner Mosse, who has studied the extensive correspondence between Harden and Fürstenberg, believes that there was a strongly emotional, even "erotic" side to this friendship. Mosse argues rather convincingly that the Fürstenberg of the autobiography is a mask and that the real person speaks in Fürstenberg's letters to Harden.[104] Like the Fürstenbergs, the Schwabachs cultivated an intellectual style in their social life. A contemporary wrote about Léonie Schwabach: "She was extraordinarily intelligent, and at a time when it was not easy to find an intellectual salon in Berlin, hers was a place where one could talk of everything that was going on in the world of literature and art, with a sprinkling of politics now and then to give zest to the conversation."[105]

A number of additional cultivated businessmen's homes might be mentioned. The music world of Berlin gathered at the home of the owner of the *Frankfurter Zeitung* newspaper, Thérèse Simon-Sonnemann. AEG director Felix Deutsch and his wife were themselves musicians. "The most interesting people of Berlin met in the Deutsch home," Walther Rathenau among others.[106] The musical tradition of the Mendelssohn family was carried on by members of the family who were actively engaged in the banking business. For example, Franz von Mendelssohn was an excellent violinist, a pupil of the violin virtuoso Josef Joachim; his brother Robert was a good cellist; Robert's Italian wife, Giulietta, was a pianist; and the three of them played at social gatherings with professional musicians, some with famous names. Franz von Mendelssohn was a friend of Josef Joachim and his divorced wife, the singer Alma Weiss. The actress Eleonora Duse stayed at the home of Robert and Giulietta von Mendelssohn when she was in Berlin. The composers Engelbert Humperdinck and Ruggiero Leoncavallo, as well as the "Secession" painters, were frequent guests at the home of the Mendelssohns. Ernst von Mendelssohn Bartholdy and his wife welcomed into their home a number of illustrious guests: Adolphe Thiers (a statesman, journalist, and historian), Honoré de Balzac, Theodor Mommsen (a historian), Hermann von Helmholtz (a scientist and professor), Ferdinand Gregorovius (a historian), Richard Wagner, and Franz von Lenbach (a painter).[107]

104. Ibid., pp. 117–22. Also, see details in C. Furstenberg, *Lebensgeschichte*, pp. 416–19, 425–26
105. Schwering, *Berlin Court*, p. 220.
106. See C. Fürstenberg, *Lebensgeschichte*, p. 512, quotation on p. 492.
107. See Treue, "Das Bankhaus," pp. 54–55, 57–58; Lowenthal-Hensel, "Franz von Mendelssohn," p. 259; Gilbert, *Bankiers*, p. 229, Gleichen, *Guardsman's Memories*, pp. 277; Huret, *En Allemagne. Berlin*, p. 348, Schwering, *Berlin Court*, pp. 222–23.

In Berlin, a center of art patronage, many wealthy patrons also had private social relations with artists. "It was thanks to these circles that artists from all parts of Germany came to Berlin."[108] Jewish businessmen played an especially important role as patrons of the arts in Berlin.[109] Artists and well-to-do members of the bourgeoisie met at the homes of the artists Reinhold and Sabine Lepsius, Eduard and Johanna Arnhold, bank director Stern, and Félice Bernstein, widow of an economics professor. The banker Hermann Rosenberg placed a country home in Grunewald at the disposal of the painter Walther Leistikow and his wife for the summer months. Among the friends and acquaintances of Fritz Andreae were Gerhart Hauptmann, the writer Hugo von Hofmannsthal, the poet Karl Gustav Vollmoeller, and Max Liebermann. Andreae was a prominent patron of the arts and a Goethe scholar. Carl von der Heydt was an art collector, and among his guests were artists, scientists, and writers, such as Rainer Maria Rilke, the writer Hermann Sudermann, the sculptor Georg Kolbe, and the museum director Wilhelm von Bode.[110]

English-born Amy Israel (née Salomon), wife of the department store owner Berthold Israel, maintained social relationships with actors, musicians, and intellectuals. This well-read merchant's wife "terrified the more sedate wives of businessmen by quoting from contemporary French poets; she signed herself 'Aimée.'" Her son Wilfrid was often a guest at the home of Albert Einstein, who moved to Berlin in 1914.[111] Paul Wallich had social relationships with Fritz von Unruh, who was a military officer and poet, the daughter of Max Liebermann, several actors, Hedwig Dohm, and Katja Mann (the wife of Thomas Mann). Artists were among the guests of Valentin Weisbach and Rudolph Mosse.[112]

The cultivation of ties with the leading intellectual and literary circles was a professional necessity for the publisher Samuel

108. Lepsius, *Ein Berliner Kunstlerleben*, p. 157

109. A few examples are James Simon, Eduard Arnhold, Eugen Gutmann, Oskar Hainauer, Julius Freund, Franz and Robert von Mendelssohn, Oskar Huldschinsky, Marcus Koppel, and publisher Rudolph Mosse.

110. On the Lepsius circle, see Lepsius, *Berliner Kunstlerleben*, pp. 175, 177–78. On the Bernstein salon and on Rosenberg, see Weisbach, *Und alles*, pp. 367, 370–72. On the Arnholds, see Wirth, "Juden," p. 36; Arnhold, *Eduard Arnhold*, pp. 43, 197, 218. On Stern, see Bunsen, *Zeitgenossen*, p. 70. On Andreae, see Otto Hintner, "Franz Friedrich Andreae," in *Neue Deutsche Biographie*, vol. 1 (Berlin, 1953), p. 280. On von der Heydt, see Heydt, *Unser Haus*, pp. 29–30.

111 See Shepherd, *Wilfrid Israel*, pp 20–21, 24–25.

112. On Wallich, see P. Wallich, *Lehr- und Wanderjahre*, pp. 343–45. On Weisbach, see Weisbach, *Und alles*, p 109. On Mosse, see Mosse, "Rudolf Mosse," pp. 250, 253.

Fischer. Hedwig Fischer, his wife, was responsible for the organization of a very active social life. Her daughter has written about her:
"For many years she was the heart of that great publishing house
which was at the center of the intellectual and artistic life of Berlin.
Her accomplishments and her radiant personality may have been
similar to those of the famous women of the Romantic period,
who for her still lived as her ideal. Our home in the Erdenerstrasse
thus became a home for the family of writers."[113]

Emil Rathenau grew up in the upper-bourgeois Jewish circles of
Berlin characterized by "elegance," "active social life," and "culture." Rathenau turned away from this world, and from the 1880s
on, when he was building up the AEG, had hardly any time for
activities outside his business. His wife Mathilde (née Naumann)
came from a background similar to his, was interested in art and
music, and suffered greatly from her husband's one-sidedness. Her
granddaughter has written that Mathilde Rathenau ". . . went
through all the stages of embitterment, loneliness, and despair."[114]
Their son Walther in a sense returned to the world of his grandpar-
ents, but developed far beyond that world and became a unique
figure in Wilhelmine society, a businessman-intellectual who, as an
unbaptized Jew, gained great recognition at court, in business, and
among intellectuals. He had an "almost limitless" circle of friends.
His "daily rounds" consisted of contacts with his cousin Max
Liebermann (one of the greatest painters of his age), journalist
Maximilian Harden, theater director Max Reinhardt, writer Frank
Wedekind, Hugo von Hofmannsthal, poet Richard Dehmel,
Gerhart Hauptmann, poet Rudolph Alexander Schröder, the
Krupp director Eduard Bodenhausen (a man with considerable cul-
tural interests), architect Henry van de Velde, painter Edvard
Munch, and actress Tilla Durieux.[115] In addition, Rathenau had an
entrée to court society,[116] and had widespread contacts in business
circles. Also connected to Rathenau was the circle around
Maximilian Harden, which came into being largely on Rathenau's
initiative. Carl Fürstenberg, Fritz Andreae (a banker at Hardy &
Co.), Felix and Lili Deutsch, and Hermann Rosenberg belonged
to it. Emil Kirdorf, Hugo Stinnes, and Albert Ballin also maintained contact with Harden.[117]

113. Fischer, *Sie schrieben*, p. 40.
114 Mangoldt, *Auf der Schwelle*, p. 12; see Kessler, *Walther Rathenau*, pp. 9–12, 18;
Federn-Kohlhaas, *Walther Rathenau*, p. 24.
115 See Bottcher, *Walther Rathenau*, p. 37, Kessler, *Walther Rathenau*, p. 59.
116. See Jaeger, *Unternehmer*, pp. 171–83.
117. See Hellige, "Rathenau," p. 146.

The general intellectual and cultural level that prevailed in Berlin business circles should not, however, be overestimated. According to Hans Fürstenberg, court gossip and foreign policy were among the main topics of conversation at bourgeois parties in Berlin. Business could not be discussed. "Art and literature were topics more for the ladies and were regarded as somewhat effeminate."[118]

Nevertheless, it is astonishing what a high regard the arts and intellectual life enjoyed in the wealthy business bourgeoisie in Berlin. One partial explanation is that Berlin was becoming a cultural center. However, it is striking that with few exceptions the culturally and intellectually interested businessmen of Berlin were Jewish. Ethnically molded cultural models and educational traditions played a role in this. Kaplan has shown that the ideal of *Bildung* was very important to middle-class Jews because it helped them to be both Jews and Germans.[119] There were also conscious links with the Berlin salon culture of the early nineteenth century, in which Jews played an important part.[120]

THE STYLE OF SOCIAL LIFE

Throughout Germany, a very formal, expensive style prevailed in clothing, household furnishings, and entertainment in the Wilhelmine period. Marie von Bunsen writes that into the early 1880s guests were served simple food, and that it was customary to visit acquaintances without advance notice. "Then the formal dinner party became obligatory; as a rule, professional cooks and waiters were brought in, always a sumptuous and expensive overabundance, for the saying was, 'that is what is required nowadays.'"[121] Around the turn of the century, a society matron told Huret that the German upper class was spending three times as much on travel, pleasure, comfort, and dress as it had ten or fifteen years earlier. The life style of wealthy Berlin businessmen must be viewed in this context. Léonie Schwabach had an annual budget of 70,000 marks for her clothing.[122]

Milly von Friedländer-Fuld wore long strings of pearls and used

118. Fürstenberg, *Anekdoten*, pp. 14–15.
119. See Kaplan, *Making*, esp. pp. 8–10. As Kaplan explains, the German concept of *Bildung*, which originated in the Enlightenment, meant not only education and culture, but also refinement and character formation.
120. See Gay, *Freud*, esp. pp. 93–188; Hertz, *Jewish High Society*; Kaplan, *Making*, pp. 8–10.
121. Bunsen, *Die Welt*, p. 185. Bunsen's comments relate to the bourgeoisie as well as the pre-industrial elite.
122. See Huret, *En Allemagne. Berlin*, p. 104.

gold flatware when entertaining members of royal families or other important personalities. The wedding of her daughter was reported to be ". . . one of the most splendid parties ever given in Berlin outside of the imperial court."[123] The reaction of Berlin society to the life style of the Friedländer-Fulds was divided, judging from two contradictory reports. According to Schwering, "It soon became 'the thing' to go to the Friedländers', and, thanks to the luxury they displayed at the entertainments they gave so frequently during the winter season, their house became a social center without rival in Berlin." On the other hand, Hans Fürstenberg wrote in his memoirs: "Frau Milly filled it [the Friedländer-Fuld palace] with guests of high rank, though this rapid rise did not always go smoothly, because in the circles of court society, Berlin was still very conventional and was not accustomed to so much splendor."[124]

When Eduard Arnhold invited guests to breakfast, he used the finest porcelain. "The best of the best was brought to the table, heavy old wines." During the breakfast an orchestra played Johann Strauss waltzes.[125] At the home of the Israels the entertainment of guests took place in a luxurious setting: "No quiet bluestocking, Amy had no compunction about displaying the Israels' great wealth . . . the Israels entertained in the formal style which Berlin Jewry believed was English, with a butler and a team of other servants. Artists, opera singers and diplomats, as well as business friends, were always Amy's guests on her birthday, 1 January, when she wore her favorite emerald necklace."[126]

This style was cultivated not only in the families of Jewish businessmen. Schwering writes about Ellen von Siemens, wife of Arnold von Siemens: "She is one of Berlin's greatest *élégantes* and is to be met in the most fashionable circles of the capital. Her pretty, smart figure can be seen on the race-courses and on first nights at fashionable theatres as well as at court balls, where she was admitted by the special order of the emperor, with whom she was a great favorite. Mrs. Siemens gives receptions that are considered as events of the winter season."[127] Not only Milly von Friedländer-Fuld but also Ellen von Siemens and some of the aristocratic ladies

123 Rheinbaben, *Viermal Deutschland*, p 76. Also, see Schwering, *Berlin Court*, pp. 218–19.
124. Schwering, *Berlin Court*, p. 217; H. Furstenberg, *Erinnerungen*, p. 128.
125. Bunsen, *Zeitgenossen*, pp. 72–73.
126 Shepherd, *Wilfrid Israel*, pp. 20–21
127. Schwering, *Berlin Court*, p. 221.

followed Paris fashions. Huret's account does not imply that Jews made a greater effort socially than others.[128]

In the Berlin business elite it was customary every evening either to entertain guests or to go out to someone's house. Businessmen sometimes found these social obligations burdensome, as for example Carl Fürstenberg: "In Berlin the custom of the dinner party prevailed, and I am sorry to say that it began to become an unfortunate custom. . . . Though we tried to avoid some of these parties, it soon got to the point that for every evening during the winter months we received a dinner invitation and usually several, and every day we attended such a party. At eight o'clock one ate a ceremoniously served meal that by today's standards was incredibly long and not always satisfying from a culinary point of view, and at nine-thirty one rose overfed from the table. . . . All that was often more tiring than stimulating, and it incidentally kept me away from my children and my home to an unwarranted degree."[129] A contemporary wrote concerning Arnold von Siemens, "He was polite and friendly toward all guests, but he seemed to get little pleasure out of visitors."[130] Siemens wrote to his brother on one occasion, "Nothing exciting is going on here. The social season is in full sway, fortunately interrupted for the moment by the court mourning for the King of Denmark. To be sure, the young girls think differently about that."[131] Elly von Siemens, wife of Wilhelm, hosted "large social gatherings and drinking parties" that her husband considered "distressing" since he allowed himself to be ". . . impressed by people whose inner worth was not commensurate with their surface cleverness."[132]

The life style of the Berlin elite was in part a manifestation of the crass materialism of the period, an indication that capitalist values had at least partially gained acceptance in Germany. The new rules of the game of course brought great advantages to the bourgeois millionaires of Berlin because many government officials and military officers of necessity still lived in "old Prussian simplicity."[133] Some rejected this new luxury, as can be seen in the quotation

---

128. See Huret, *En Allemagne. Berlin,* pp. 97–99, 105.

129. Fürstenberg, *Lebensgeschichte,* p. 396. On the other hand, his son writes: "My father sometimes grumbled, but actually he greatly enjoyed this almost continuous partying. He was a tireless conversationalist and always an interesting one." H. Furstenberg, *Erinnerungen,* p. 8.

130. Bunsen, *Zeitgenossen,* p. 43.

131. Letter from Arnold von Siemens to Wilhelm von Siemens dated 3 February 1906, SAA Lr 563.

132. Harries, "Nachruf," p 6; Harries was the brother-in-law of Wilhelm von Siemens.

133. See Brauer, *Im Dienste,* p. 212

from Hans Fürstenberg. The Berlin business elite was successful in its attempts to compete with the wealthiest aristocrats. Pushing their way into the upper echelons of society, these business families took up the battle of social competition with the "crème de la crème." Berlin had seen a similar period a hundred years earlier. During the period from 1780 to 1806, wealthy bankers met with big landowners and intellectuals in the great salons on the basis of equality. It was no coincidence that these groups had in common an expensive, ostentatious life style: ". . . wealth was surely necessary for the cultural acculturation and social integration of the Jewish elite in Berlin."[134]

Social competition had grown quite keen in the imperial capital. Large-scale capitalists had to stay on a social merry-go-round that was turning fast and faster or risk losing business connections and influence on decision-making. Not all of them considered this life style merely an obligation, however. Many greatly enjoyed the luxury and the "gay parties." In his autobiography, an acquaintance of Fritz von Friedländer-Fuld commented on the latter's "extroverted and social inclinations" and his "enjoyment of an elegant life."[135] In this class means for such pleasures were abundantly available.

To be sure, not every Berlin businessman wanted to be part of high society. Georg von Siemens, a director of the Deutsche Bank and a relative of the heads of Siemens & Halske, was not a sociable person even before his marriage: ". . . the lack of hospitality in his parents' home, and his own lack of domestic instincts, and not least of all the peculiarities and gruffness that he displayed with a certain deliberation before his marriage – none of these things were exactly conducive to the development of pleasant social relationships."[136] After his marriage he changed his behavior but he retained a traditional bourgeois aversion toward a pattern of living strongly oriented toward ostentation, as can be seen from the following lines addressed to his daughter, who was visiting at the home of Sir Ernest Cassel:

> I am greatly pleased that you are seeing such a pretentious house. In doing so one learns that pretentiousness usually is destructive of a feel-

134. Hertz, *Jewish High Society*, p. 47; see pp. 3–36 "The public happiness created by the Jewish salonières was based on defiance of the traditional boundaries separating noble from commoner, gentile from Jew, man from woman" (pp. 3, 7). The old social barriers were reestablished during the Restoration.

135. Liebermann von Wahlendorf, *Erinnerung*, p. 84.

136. Helfferich, *Georg von Siemens*, vol. 3, pp. 245–46.

ing of warm hospitality and that it is difficult to have both at the same time. From your letter I take it that you would choose the warm hospitality. I am deeply pleased by that, because such a feeling of hospitality can be created with modest means, simply through the inner qualities of those involved. The first prerequisite is the affability of the host. In the so-called pretentious homes everyone present plays a role as in the theater; where a warm hospitality prevails, everyone gives of himself; and even in those cases where that is not worth the trouble, still it is much more pleasant than a bad comedy. So be friendly, be nice, be modest (that is usually the rarest and therefore the most highly appreciated form of behavior in homes such as that one). Observe well and come back home healthy in heart and soul.[137]

The publisher August Scherl can be cited as an extreme example of a businessman who lived withdrawn from social life. As the owner of the largest newspaper company in Germany, he was worth an estimated seventeen million marks in 1911 according to Martin. Carl Fürstenberg, who was one of the few people who had ever been a guest in Scherl's home, related that the latter shut himself off more and more from human society. "However, in the case of August Scherl, it was not a matter of insanity. When important decisions had to be made, Scherl was on the spot, and his publishing company was constantly moving ahead. . . ."[138] Carl Klönne, a director of the Deutsche Bank, also did not participate in the social swirl of the capital. He was described as follows in a biographical sketch: "Coming from a family of modest means, he always remained frugal and undemanding, without any outside interests and had a passion only for business."[139]

Adolf and Sara Salomonsohn, both of whom came from modest provincial backgrounds, personified, in the opinion of their son, the old bourgeois virtues, which contrasted sharply with the grand bourgeois style otherwise prevalent in Berlin. "From it [the privation of their early years] came a tendency toward thriftiness, respect for the penny, the appreciation of wealth as reward for accomplishment and as a basis for outward freedom, and an abhorrence of thoughtless squandering of that which one had laboriously accumulated." Sara Salomonsohn is described as follows by her son: ". . . though she was proud of the position her husband had

---

137. Ibid., pp. 336–337 (out of a letter dated 12 January 1892).

138. Fürstenberg, *Lebensgeschichte*, p. 321, quotation on pp. 322–23. No attempt was made, for the purposes of this study, to evaluate a semi-fictional work: Hans Erman, *August Scherl Dämonie und Erfolg in wilhelminischer Zeit* (Berlin, 1954).

139. Achterberg and Müller-Jabusch, *Lebensbilder*, p. 244.

gradually attained, and though she made great sacrifices daily to maintain that position, at the same time she was above all the surface tinsel and trifles with which the rest of the world is so intoxicated, and she was completely free of the arrogance and conceit that all too often attend success."[140] The fact that Emil Rathenau also had a deep aversion to extravagance, pleasures, and social life, is amply confirmed in the autobiography of his granddaughter, who describes him as "puritanical."[141] A biographer writes: "He had no needs, he had no appreciation of luxurious living. Though he was not completely free of ambition and the need for recognition, he had no desire to play a pretentious role in social life."[142]

How can such variations be explained? The need for public relations was apparently greater for some firms (such as the large Berlin banks) than it was for others (such as the Scherl company), and this depended, among other things, on how important customers were to the company, whether the firm received government contracts or needed to negotiate with government agencies over laws and regulations, whether good relations with foreign governments were important to the firm, and what stage of development the firm had reached. (In the consolidation phase, relations with the outside world were probably more important than in the expansion phase, at least in industry.) In some companies there was apparently a sort of division of labor, whereby one or another of the co-owners or directors was more concerned with public relations. Who took over what role depended on the social skills of the individuals concerned, or, more accurately, their wives, but it also depended on the value systems of those individuals. An explanation for the tendency of some people to cling to earlier bourgeois standards lies primarily in social origins. Klönne, Salomonsohn, Scherl, and in a certain sense Emil Rathenau, were self-made men.[143]

The wealthy of Berlin for the most part appeared in society as socially skilled, cultivated individuals. In one police file, Max Esser was described as "a genuine epicure." Walther Rathenau was described by various contemporaries as the prototype of a man of the world. Carl Fürstenberg liked to see himself in the role of a

140. Solmssen, *Gedenkblatt*, pp. 3, 25. Georg Solmssen was their son.
141. See Mangoldt, *Auf der Schwelle*, esp. pp. 10–19.
142. Pinner, *Emil Rathenau*, p. 361.
143. Rathenau's father lost the family fortune. Besides, Emil Rathenau was under great pressure to rebuild the AEG (electric company) after the crisis of the founding years. See Riedler, *Emil Rathenau*, p. 188; Schulin, *Walther Rathenau*, p. 12.

charming host.[144] On the other hand, aristocratic prototypes seldom appear among the business elite.[145] Particularly striking is the
key role of the wife in shaping social life within this class, a role
that finds outward expression in the character of the *"grande
dame."* An aristocrat described Léonie von Schwabach as "the
most charming of the women." She wrote: "Thanks to her [L. von
Schwabach], he [Paul von Schwabach] has made a conquest of a
part of this society. That couple has gained entrance by a secret
door into a certain number of homes, for the most part the homes
of foreigners, and one must admit that the tact, the spiritedness,
and the manners of Madame Schwabacher [*sic*] are not out of place
in any of them."[146] Schwering writes about her: ". . . she treated
other women with extreme politeness, but with a mixture of disdain and contempt that was most interesting to watch."[147] The
social talents of Milly von Friedländer-Fuld have already been
described in detail. In a police file it was reported: "Frau
Friedländer is an elegant, sophisticated lady, charming – when it
suits her; she comes close to being haughty, but she knows how to
captivate her guests."[148]

Aniela Fürstenberg, Amy Israel, Ellen von Siemens, and Hedwig
Fischer were also among the great hostesses of Berlin. They shaped
the social life in their homes with originality and creativity. Aniela
Fürstenberg maintained extensive contacts with intellectuals in
whom she was interested, and took delight in organizing social
functions that bore the stamp of her personality. Born a Pole, she

144. On Esser, see Politische Polizei, 3. Abt. an Handelsministerium, 22.12.1898 (Vermerk
auf Bericht vom 21.12.1898) StA Potsdam, Pr.Br.Rep. 30 Berlin C Tit. 94 Nr. 9748. On
Rathenau, see Weisbach, *Und alles*, p. 385. On Fürstenberg, see C. Fürstenberg, *Lebensgeschichte*, passim.

145. An example would be Rudolf Mosse. Theodor Herzl became acquainted with Rudof
Mosse and his wife in 1903 at the home of the Jewish banker Baron Simon Alfred von
Oppenheim in Cologne. Herzl describes Oppenheim as "a good but somewhat affected copy of
a Prussian Junker," and he added: ". . . also Herr and Frau Mosse, of a Berlin advertising
agency, who regard Oppenheim as distinguished. What an effort these Jews make to play comi-
cal roles." Th. Herzl, *Gesammelte zionistische Werke*, 3rd ed. (Tel Aviv, 1934), vol. 4 (paperpack
ed., vol. 3), pp. 400–1, cited according to Mosse, "Rudolf Mosse," pp. 249–50. (On
Oppenheim, see Stürmer, Teichmann, and Treue, *Wägen und Wagen*.) However, genuine
members of the nobility appear not to have belonged to Mosse's circle of acquaintances.
Interestingly enough, Mosse rejected a title of nobility offered him by the emperor. See Mosse,
"Rudolf Mosse," pp. 253, 250.

146. Vasili, *La Société*, p. 160. It is clear from the context that he meant "Madame
Schwabach." According to Cecil, Vasili is a pseudonym for Princess Catherine Radziwill. See
Cecil, "Jew."

147. Schwering, *Berlin Court*, p. 220.

148. Polizeipräsident Berlin an Handelsministerium, 1901, StA Potsdam, Pr.Br.Rep. 30
Berlin C Tit. 94 Nr. 9940.

introduced into her circle the custom of the "open house": "On the covered veranda of her home in Grunewald, starting in the late afternoon, there usually stood a simmering samovar, so that any arriving guest would not have to wait for his or her tea."[149] Amy Israel was an eccentric who openly displayed her education and wealth. Thus, in addition to fulfilling an important function, the women in this class enjoyed a degree of independence and public visibility that was quite atypical for Germany in this era.

The Rhineland and Westphalia

In the Rhineland and Westphalia, the wealthy propertied bourgeoisie was socially isolated to a greater extent than in either Berlin or Hamburg. In most places, the relatively new wealth generated by industry did not propel the wealthy into a local patrician class, if one existed. Social relations with politicians or government officials were of less importance than in Berlin and were different in nature. For one, the most important political and administrative elites, at both the state (Prussian) and the national level, resided in Berlin, not in Essen or Elberfeld. Moreover, due to the economic structure of Rhineland-Westphalia, businessmen had far less reason to court the regional or local political-bureaucratic elite. Apart from the munitions manufacturers, the businessmen of this area, among whom industrialists predominated, were not as dependent upon the government as, for example, the owners and directors of the big Berlin banks. And those provincial and municipal officials with whom Rhineland and Westphalian businessmen socialized were on the whole firmly rooted in the bourgeoisie.

The industrialists of Rhineland-Westphalia socialized almost exclusively within bourgeois circles, and especially business circles. Paul Reusch, the director of the *Gutehoffnungshütte* (mining company), had a large circle of acquaintances, as shown by his extensive correspondence. Out of forty-eight congratulatory and condolence messages Reusch received on various occasions prior to 1914, thirty-two of the senders were businessmen, many of them heavy industrialists, two were high government officials, one a chief mayor, two legislators, one an architect, three university professors, and seven engineers or miscellaneous salaried industrial employees.[150] Out of six-

---

149. Fürstenberg, *Erinnerungen*, p. 8.

150. Organizations and unidentifiable persons were not counted. None of the senders–and none of the unidentifiable persons–had a title of nobility. Haniel Archive 3001938/0 und 40010128/52.

teen (identifiable) addressees of letters indicating a personal relationship, eleven were businessmen, two high government officials,
two professors, and one an engineer.[151] At a dinner given on 31
January 1914, five businessmen were present, three government
mining officials and one assistant, and twelve engineers.[152] The
engineers may have been businessmen or businessmen's sons.
Among Reusch's closest friends were Robert Bosch, the historian
Oswald Spengler, the businessman and founder of the *Deutsches
Museum* (a museum for technology) Oskar von Miller, and (only
from 1931 on) Theodor Heuss. Reusch traveled every year with
the electrical engineer Dr. Gustav Schwabe to the spa at
Karlsbad.[153]

Close friends of August Thyssen were the banker Carl Klönne,
heavy industrialist Peter Klöckner, and Edmund Stinnes, son of
heavy industrialist Hugo Stinnes. Thyssen's associate Conrad
Verlohr was also an intimate. When the journalist Jules Huret was
a guest at Thyssen's home, others present were mine owners,
directors of joint stock companies, engineers, and bankers. Peter
Klöckner was a friend of businessmen and high government officials. A close personal friend was the chief mayor of the city of
Duisburg. The guest book of Emil Kirdorf contains names from
industry, politics, and government. The mine director Bruno
Schulz Briesen counted a number of heavy industrialists among his
friends. The general director of the Bayer company, Carl Duisberg,
had social relations with Bayer's son and son-in law, with scientists,
with the board of directors member Carl Hauptmann, and with
industrialists such as Paul Silverberg, Gustav Krupp von Bohlen
und Halbach, and Albert Vogler.[154]

There were also certain tendencies toward exclusivity in the business elite of Rhineland-Westphalia. Whereas the older business
families of the Rhineland (such as the vom Rath family of sugar
industrialists) belonged to the local patrician class, even the very
wealthiest of the newer businessmen's families were accepted only

151. Haniel Archive 30019390/0b, 30019390/36, 30019390/51, 400101290/160,
400101290/159.
152. Haniel Archive 400101294/0.
153 See Maschke, *Es entsteht*, p. 39; Haniel Archive 40010128/52.
154 On Thyssen, see Treue, *Die Feuer*, pp. 109, 161; Huret, *In Deutschland*, part 1, pp.
253–54; Winschuh, "Der alte Thyssen," pp. 109, 113; Henle, *Weggenosse*, pp. 67–68;
Kohlschutter, *Ein Genie*, p. 254. On Klöckner, see Henle, *Weggenosse*, p. 225; Reichert, "Peter
Klöckner," pp. 101–2. On Kirdorf, see Bacmeister, *Emil Kirdorf*, p. 160. On Schulz-Briesen,
see Schulz-Briesen, "Bruno Schulz-Briesen," pp. 129, 131. On Duisberg, see Duisberg, *Nur
ein Sohn*, pp. 15, 21–22.

gradually in such circles. Carl Duisberg wrote the following about the position of his parents in the society of Elberfeld: "It was a closed world. It is true that my parents did not belong to the old high society of Elberfeld which distinguished between the 'blue bloods' and 'those people.' Even today I am not sure whether my parents originally were counted as 'those people' and later as 'blue bloods'; in any event their social relationships were limited. . . ."[155] A certain amount of discrimination could also be observed with respect to Jewish businessmen. The Jewish banker Louis Levy, son of a middle-class banker, was baptized in connection with his marriage to a Catholic, and he took Hagen, the name of his father-in-law, a metal dealer and manufacturer, who introduced him into Cologne society and especially into businessmen's circles. Louis Hagen's success in these circles should, however, not be overestimated. One of the documents submitted in connection with the proposed granting of the title of Commercial Councillor stated that Hagen held a "not particularly prominent position" in society.[156]

The social life of the Krupps was strongly influenced by the fact that as arms manufacturers they were dependent upon government contracts. Among their most prominent guests, along with the emperor and members of court society, were generals, admirals, ministers, state secretaries, and German and foreign diplomats. People who could be considered personal friends of Friedrich Alfred Krupp (1854-1902) included the Prussian minister of Public Worship and Education, a major, an admiral, and an assistant judge. In his wider circle of acquaintances were numerous businessmen. Guest lists for the great balls (studied by Stürmer) reveal that members of the higher Rhineland nobility were often invited but often declined. Bankers who were invited also frequently declined. The majority of the guests were military officers, high government officials, engineers, jurists, directors, and other businessmen. Thus the social profile of the guests in the Krupp home reflected to an extraordinary degree the almost unique importance of the government to the firm. During the "interregnum" period when F.A. Krupp's wife Margarete, a general's daughter, headed the firm, there was a decided shift in favor of the military officers

---

155. Duisberg, *Nur ein Sohn*, pp. 14–15.

156. See Kellenbenz, "Louis Hagen," p. 140; Central State Archives of the G.D.R., Merseburg: Zentrales Staatsarchiv, Dienststelle Merseburg, Geheimes Zivilkabinett, 2 2.1. Nr. 1596, Bl. 5.

and to the disadvantage of the engineers, a shift that cannot be explained in terms of the company's interests, but rather reflects admiration for the military.[157]

Heinrich Ehrhardt, the founder of "Rheinmetall," regularly entertained the duke of Saxe-Coburg-Gotha. On the other hand, he did not have the kind of social connections with the military, the bureaucracy, and the diplomatic corps that the Krupps possessed, and therefore did not receive the government support that they enjoyed.[158] A further example of social contacts between the nobility and the world of big business is the Rodensteiner Society in the Saarland. Its members were primarily members of the nobility, including generals, but also included bankers and industrialists such as the Röchlings (who were involved in heavy industry) and high government officials.[159]

In the Rhineland and Westphalia the links with artistic and intellectual circles found in Berlin were largely missing. The Krupps were patrons of the arts, but they hardly invited representatives of the worlds of science, literature, the theater, and art to parties at the Krupp villa.[160] Paul Reusch's friendship with Oswald Spengler remained an exception.[161]

In the autobiographies and biographies of the region's businessmen, there is ample evidence of conspicuous consumption, especially in connection with entertaining. The figure of the sophisticated host or hostess who possessed social skills and enjoyed entertaining was not uncommon. Reusch, for example, loved "good company, a cultivated conversation, a good wine and a strong cigar."[162] Carl Duisberg on occasion served his guests delicacies brought from Berlin or Hamburg. Max Liebermann, who painted a portrait of Duisberg, wrote that Duisberg was ". . . a rarity in Germany . . . not only a professional but also an Epicurean."[163] The Duisburg tobacco manufacturer Arnold Böninger (1825-1905) was quite gregarious: "Arnold Böninger attached impor-

157. See Boelcke, *Krupp*, p. 109, Meisbach, *Friedrich Alfred Krupp*, pp. 14, 16, Stürmer, "Alltag," pp 263–64; Huret, *In Deutschland*, part 1, pp. 355–56.

158. See Ehrhardt, *Hammerschläge*, p. 176. Also, see comments in section on "The Emperor and Court Society."

159. See Wilmin, *Die Familie Adt*, p. 58.

160. See Kühne-Lindenlaub, "Private Kunstförderung," pp 55–82; Sturmer, "Alltag," pp 263–64

161. Even this friendship did not begin until shortly after the First World War. Reusch had no other personal friendships with intellectuals, unless Oskar von Miller can be counted as one See Herzog, "Die Freundschaft," pp. 77, 81–82; and Maschke, *Es entsteht*, passim.

162. Maschke, *Es entsteht*, p. 55.

163. See Flechtner, *Carl Duisberg*, pp. 171. (No source named for Liebermann quotation.)

tance to the pleasurable aspects of life. He knew how to give lively parties and he enjoyed doing so. One of his sayings was 'Cooking is an art.' Because of his, elegant appearance he was called 'Marquis.'"[164] Hugo Stinnes, according to his son, was a connoisseur of wine, and could be a charming host. Hunting, which enjoyed a growing popularity among the business elite of Rhineland-Westphalia, was also an element of the new style.[165]

After his divorce, August Thyssen lived in relative seclusion, and was often alone in the evening. Winschuh makes the following judgment of Thyssen's outside contacts: "What was August Thyssen's attitude toward the other industrialists in the region? Did he feel himself to be a part of a community with them? Hardly. He remained a sharp-edged loner who felt no desire for socializing or for working in collaboration with others, and least of all for dependency on others." Once on close terms with Kirdorf, he quarreled with him and they parted.[166] Nonetheless, Thyssen realized the need to keep up social contacts. He felt obliged to do some formal entertaining, and he spared no expense on these occasions.[167] A brunch at his home included caviar, soup, salmon, ham with asparagus spears, roast beef with salad, and a compote with pineapple ice cream. Though it was a spring day, his male guests (mainly businessmen) wore tails, his female guests embroidered crêpe de chine, tulle, sequined dresses, and a great deal of jewelry.[168]

The Krupp family can be cited as an extreme example of the magnitude that public relations requirements could attain in the wealthy Wilhelmine bourgeoisie. At Villa Hügel the entire course of the day was governed by the professional and social duties of the family. Guests were received every day. The breakfast hour was intended as a time in which the family could be alone, undisturbed, but sometimes breakfast guests were present. Even when the family was alone, no private conversations took place; instead, Krupp discussed with his wife the seating arrangements, the order of courses, and the choice of wines for the evening, along with

164 Ring, *Geschichte*, pp. 278, 382. However, Böninger lived too early to be of great interest here

165. On Stinnes, see Kohlschütter, *Ein Genie*, pp. 32, 42. Examples for hunting enthusiasm in Klass, *Die drei Ringe*, p. 69; Bacmeister, *Gustav Knepper*, p. 86; Hashagen, *Geschichte*, vol. 2, part 2, pp. 535–72.

166 Winschuh, "Der alte Thyssen," p. 113; see Treue, *Die Feuer*, pp. 109, 161; Henle, *Weggenosse*, pp. 67–68, Huret, *In Deutschland*, part 1, p. 253.

167. Schacht, *76 Jahre*, pp. 184–85. Thyssen's frugality is affirmed in numerous anecdotes. See Baumann, "August Thyssen," pp. 15–16.

168. Huret, *In Deutschland*, part 1, pp. 253–54.

other arrangements. In the afternoon when F.A. Krupp came home from the office, there were already guests present, who had mostly business affairs to discuss with him.

Villa Hügel resembled a court household organized around the flawless management of lavish social events. According to an employee of Villa Hügel, an unavoidable escalation of entertainment duties took place during the time of F.A. Krupp: "A consequence of the visits of kings and princes was that a princely household was created, more magnificent and wealthier than the court household of some of the royal houses. But this enormously increased the social demands on the owner of the Krupp works, and it required of him an expenditure of energy and a suppression of his own inclinations that were highly admirable, but in any event this has to be regarded as an extraordinarily strenuous and exhausting form of activity."[169]

However, F.A. Krupp has been called a "master in the art of living, with an artistically schooled eye and a refined taste" who tried to offer his guests every possible amenity.[170] Above all he enjoyed the more informal small parties and casual conversations with entertaining people.[171] There was a change in style when Gustav Krupp von Bohlen und Halbach took over the direction of the company. Dinner parties became stiff, formal affairs at which courses were served in rapid succession. As a host he performed well in his prescribed role, but he had no real "feel" for it. "In all seriousness and devotion to duty, he knew how to be charming and obliging when appropriate, in this respect a diplomat of the old school."[172] As Knut Borchardt points out, *Repräsentation* became the central role of the family, much as in the princely court in the nineteenth century.[173] The explanation for this lies, in my opinion, not so much in an imitation of the princely rulers, but rather in the extreme ambition of this and other business families, and in the necessity for carrying out public relations in a way typical not only of the German nobility, but also of the upper bourgeoisie.

In Rhineland-Westphalia, as in other regions, the wife played a special role in the social sphere. Klöckner's son-in-law wrote, "My mother-in-law was impressive in appearance and manner, just as

169. Meisbach, *Krupp*, p. 15; see p. 11; see Klass, "Bertha Krupp," p. 9; Klass, *Die drei Ringe*, p. 230.

170. Meisbach, *Krupp*, p. 12.

171. Berdrow, *Alfred Krupp*, p. 208.

172. Klass, *Die drei Ringe*, pp. 325, 324.

173. Borchardt, "Der Unternehmerhaushalt," pp 11, 12.

she was in her entire being; she incorporated most completely what one conceives a *'grande dame'* to be."[174] Clara Poensgen, wife of the Düsseldorf heavy industrialist Carl Poensgen, is an example of a businessman's wife who maintained a certain independence in her social life. She was deeply interested in the women's issues of her time and repeatedly held women's conferences in her home.[175]

There were business families in the Rhineland and Westphalia whose lives did not revolve around public relations. The social life of the Duisbergs, for example, was not as active as that of the Berlin monied elite, and the family often spent evenings at home alone.[176] Older patterns of social behavior survived in the Rhineland and Westphalia just as they did in other regions. Karl Röchling, a Saarbrücken heavy industrialist, is described by his children's tutor as a "man of the old school who has a respect for tradition," and "an advocate of the simple, solid way of life." With regard to Röchling's leisure activity he wrote, "Sometimes he allowed himself an hour of relaxation, of quiet contemplation. Sometimes after finishing work at the office he went to a neighborhood café to play a game of billiards with acquaintances, and then he left business behind and was a human being among other human beings. Or when he went to the swimming pool operated by an old Saarbrücken character named Latte and took a swim in the cold pool and all the while chatted with Latte in a genuine Saarbrücken dialect, then all the folksiness of his homespun nature came tumbling out."[177] However, Röchling also took part in the social life of the business elite of the region. He was a member of Saarland's "Rodensteiner-Gesellschaft," and he was a regular guest at the Mannheim home of big businessman Carl Reiss and his sister Anna Reiss.[178]

Gustav Knepper, the director of the coal mines of the German-Luxembourg Mining and Foundry Corporation, sang in a men's chorus in his leisure hours and played cards with business friends. His biographer, who conducted interviews with Knepper, does not mention any other social contacts.[179]

Thus, for this region, we have three examples of businessmen who largely led simple, private lives: Knepper, Duisberg, and

174. See Henle, *Weggenosse*, p. 52.
175. See Hatzfeld, "Ernst Poensgen," p. 207.
176. See Duisberg, *Nur ein Sohn*, p. 22.
177. Nutzinger, "Karl Rochling," pp 84, 148, 151.
178. Mannheim Municipal Archive: guest book in: Nachlaß Carl und Anna Reiß, Nr 11, Stadtarchiv Mannheim.
179. See Bacmeister, *Gustav Knepper*, p. 32.

Röchling. The main explanation for this is that they lived in relatively small towns: Elberfeld and Leverkusen (Duisberg), Saarbrücken (Röchling), and Bochum (Knepper). An additional factor in the case of Knepper was that he was a social newcomer who started his career as a miner. These cases are an exception to the general pattern in this region. On the whole, the business elite of Rhineland and Westphalia spent much time and money on entertainment. Even a businessman like Thyssen, who apparently had little inclination in this direction, adhered to the new upper-bourgeois standard.

Further examples of private thrift coupled with public luxury can be found for the western provinces. The Krupp children were raised in frugality.[180] Hugo Stinnes gave his children small allowances and was parsimonious in his personal expenditures. His autos were not particularly big, and he never used special trains. "He always ate the same things – fried eggs with bacon about three times a day." His clothes were "cheap" and "old-fashioned." His son thinks the reason for this behavior was ". . . that in earlier days things did not by any means go as splendidly for my father in business as they did later. Before he spent fifty marks, he thought twice about it. Every penny was urgently needed in the business. Then when my younger brothers and sisters were growing up, he was much more generous in the matter of pocket money."[181]

The West and Southwest of Germany

The cities of Hesse, Baden, Wurttemberg, and Lorraine are too diverse to permit any generalizations applicable to the entire area. A wide variety of social attitudes prevailed.

We turn first to Frankfurt am Main and Wiesbaden, located in the part of Hesse that was annexed by Prussia in 1866. Frankfurt was then, as now, a great banking center. Carl von Weinberg (co-owner of Leopold Cassella & Co.) cultivated friendships that furthered his business interests.[182] There were close social interrelationships within the monied elite. For example, a hunting club was formed by a group of rich Frankfurt businessmen that included

180. See Klass, *Die drei Ringe*, pp. 301, 322–24; Klass, "Bertha Krupp," p. 3; Manchester, *Arms*, p. 226.

181 Kohlschütter, *Ein Genie*, pp. 37, 39, see also pp. 44, 51

182 See "Carl von Weinberg," *Frankfurt - Lebendige Stadt*, issue no. 3, 1961, p 27, out of the collection of the Municipal Archive of Frankfurt (Stadtarchiv Frankfurt).

several bankers and industrialists.[183] "In accordance with the bourgeois custom of that time," the Frankfurt banker Daniel Weismann (partner in the banking house of Bethmann Brothers from 1903 to 1916) went on Saturdays with a group of friends to Hotel Union in Frankfurt, where a table was permanently reserved for them.[184]

The friendships of Wilhelm Merton were closely related to his business activities but also to his welfare activities and his efforts in behalf of the advancement of science and education. An acquaintance of Merton remarked later: "The great hospitality of his home was genuine, but for Merton it was only a part of his continuous involvement in business or civic-minded enterprises."[185] He was a friend of the Rathenaus, Carl Fürstenberg, the Siemens, the Roesslers, and other heads of companies including foreign companies with which the *Metallgesellschaft* had business dealings. He also associated with his own employees. Probably his closest friend was Frankfurt's Mayor Adickes. This friendship was closely bound up with Merton's non-professional activities. A letter from Merton to Adickes, which relates to an argument between the two of them over plans for an academy of social and commercial studies, gives insight into the emotional as well as the practical dimensions of this friendship: "The last day of the year just ended was for me the saddest in a year that brought me many gloomy days because of the words that I heard from you on that day indicating that the esteem in which you previously held me has turned into precisely the opposite." A certain orientation toward the artistic elite can also be observed. The violinist Joseph Joachim stayed at the Merton home during his annual visits to Frankfurt, and he played for invited guests at the home of Merton or Merton's father-in-law, the banker Emil Ladenburg. Merton's wife was said to be "musical – like all the Ladenburgs."[186]

Networking does not seem to have occupied an important place in the lives of the Dyckerhoff family, cement industrialists who lived in Amöneburg and Bieberich (in the vicinity of Wiesbaden). Their social connections were limited to bourgeois circles. The close friendship of the older generation of the family with the Kalle

183. These were Karl Borgnis, Heinrich Hauck, Peter Karl von Grunelius, Simon Moritz von Bethmann, Walther von Rath, and Carl Schmidt-Polex. See Klötzer, "Wilhelm Daniel Weismann," p. 249.

184. See ibid., p 254

185 Achinger, *Wilhelm Merton*, p 247

186. See ibid , pp. 245–47, 250, 259; quotation from Merton's letter to Adickes on pp. 266–67.

234

and Albert industrialist families of Bieberich was maintained by the younger generation.[187] However, a case of aristocratization is encountered in the person of a younger member of the Albert family, Ernst Albert (a chemical industrialist), who adapted to the social ambitions of his wife Katharina. The couple had social relations with the grand duke of Hesse, and the czar and czarina of Russia were once guests at their home.[188]

We now turn to Baden and Wurttemberg. The best friend of Robert Bosch, a Wurttemberg businessman, was Paul Reusch, who wrote about their friendship: "At an early age – I was then a young university student – I felt strongly attracted by the pronounced individuality of the man. Not that I always shared his opinions. On the contrary! But the passionate and convincing way he expressed his views, which often deviated from the conventional, made a deep impression on me, seven years his junior."[189] Bosch apparently maintained no relationship with the pre-industrial elite, especially none with the officer corps: "Bosch is known to be no friend of the military and to harbor a deep mistrust of everything connected with militarism."[190] Bosch had social relationships in circles with which hardly any other wealthy businessman of the Wilhelmine period had personal contact, such as his acquaintanceship with the socialist Karl Kautsky, who for a time lived in the same building, and Klara Zetkin – an important leader of the Social Democratic women's movement – and her husband, F. Zundel, a painter who was also a socialist, and who painted a portrait of Bosch's daughter.[191]

Like the banker Karl Borgnis, Bosch was an enthusiastic hunter, and in this he was not in any way emulating aristocratic behavior. He regarded hunting primarily as a sport. His main criterion in issuing invitations to his hunting grounds was ability as a hunter. "Even in cases where the hunt might be considered a piece of public relations, he did not consider rank or position but only sporting reputation, and many a man counted in vain on a second invitation."[192] For twenty-five years Bosch went hunting with Franz Scholl, a ". . . farm boy from the Allgau who had a real passion for

---

187. Dyckerhoff Archive: biographical sketch on Rudolf Dyckerhoff dated 26 April 1948, pp. 2–4 in: Personalakte Rudolf Dyckerhoff, Dyckerhoff-Archiv.
188. See Kardorff-Oheimb, *Politik*, p. 54.
189. Reusch and Bücher, *Robert Bosch*, pp. 12, 14
190. Matschoß and Diesel, *Robert Bosch*, p. 15.
191. See Heuss, *Robert Bosch*, pp. 188–89, 535.
192. Ibid., p. 559; see pp. 551–58. The author conducted interviews with friends of Bosch. On Borgnis, see Klötzer, "Karl Borgnis," p. 249.

hunting." Added to this was the male-bonding aspect of the hunting experience. Hermann Bucher, who went along a few times, described the mood of these outings as follows: "Hunting in the mountains makes people dependent upon one another and brings them together in a man-to-man relationship. What binds them together is dependability and loyalty."[193] Bosch nonetheless sometimes carried on important business negotiations during the hunts.[194] Thus, he apparently used hunting to establish a feeling of personal trust.

Mannheim society was dominated by old, patrician families that were slow to admit outsiders. Many important decisions were made in middle-class clubs there.[195] At the center of Mannheim society were the Reiss siblings. Anna Reiss, "the uncrowned grand duchess of Mannheim," ran the household of her widowed brother Carl, who headed two banks and an insurance company. The family had belonged for generations to the best society of Mannheim. Their circle of friends included business families such as the Engelhorns (chemical industrialists), the Bassermanns, the Röchlings, and the Ladenburgs. Their links with the pre-industrial elite were not insignificant. Military officers were often among their guests. Among forty-nine entries in their guest book were nine people with titles of nobility.[196] Brother and sister also moved about in musical circles and corresponded with personalities such as the writer Ludwig Ganghofer and the composer Hugo Wolf. Anna's strong ties to the theatrical world can be explained by the fact that in her younger years she was a singer, and her cousin August Bassermann was general manager of the national theater.[197]

A certain degree of aristocratization can be observed in the Adt family of Lorraine. Gustav Adt had social relations with army officers stationed in Forbach and with old fraternity brothers. At his home he also frequently entertained city officials and notables, two of his cousins, senior company employees, and Baron von

193. Reusch and Bucher, *Robert Bosch*, p. 42; see p. 39.

194. See Heuss, *Robert Bosch*, p. 559.

195. See Gall, *Bürgerliche Gesellschaft*, esp. pp. 413–14.

196. Mannheim Municipal Archive: guest book in Nachlaß Carl und Anna Reiß, Nr 11, Stadtarchiv Mannheim.

197. On the social structure of their social circle, see Ludwig W. Böhm, "Carl und Anna Reiß," *Mannheimer Hefte*, vol. 1 (1954), pp. 18–19; "Geheimrat Dr. Karl Reiß zu seinem 70. Geburtstag," in. *NBLZ*, 13 February 1913; Juliana von Stockhausen, "Erlebnis mit Anna Reiß in der Rheinstraße," *Mannheimer Morgen*, 30 March 1962, p. 24. All out of the collection of the Mannheim Municipal Archive. Mannheim Municipal Archive: Nachlaß Carl und Anna Reiß, Nr 33, 44, Stadtarchiv Mannheim.

Gemmingen-Hornberg, an intimate friend who was chief magistrate and later president of the administrative district. Gustav's son Hans was, at the pre-school stage, friendly with children who received student grants from the Adt company, including the sons of a foreman, a master locksmith, and a Jewish banker. Later he became a friend of the children of Gemmingen-Hornberg, and at age sixteen he formed friendships with Fritz Melsheimer (later a vineyard owner) and Hans Steuer (later a state's attorney), both from non-Jewish bourgeois families. The intervention of the parents was apparently not necessary in order to bring about this change in social relationships. The friendship with Melsheimer had a strong emotional content. Adt has written: "Fritz Melsheimer became the most loyal friend of my entire life." As youths they were "inseparable friends" who frequently visited one another's homes and sometimes spent their vacations together. Then their paths parted, ". . . but we resolved to stay together later on in life."[198]

We find various patterns in the south and southwest of Germany – a business-centered sociability in Frankfurt that reminds us of Rhineland-Westphalia; in Mannheim, a society dominated – as in Hamburg – by a patrician class, but not averse to social contact with the nobility. As in other regions, social relationships and even close friendships with high government officials were not unusual. One might recall the friendships between Merton and Adickes and between Adt and Gemmingen-Hornberg. Merton and Adt also had social contacts with employees of their companies. Links with other segments of the bourgeoisie appear to have been as rare in the south and southwest as in most other regions.

The upper-bourgeois life style observed in other regions could also be found in southwestern and western Germany. Katharina Kardorff-Oheimb, wife of the Bieberich chemical industrialist Ernst Albert, described the period after the turn of the century as follows: "Nowadays one can no longer imagine the freedom from care and the joyousness of the life – I could almost say life of luxury – of that period and, to be sure, its materialism." For a ball she had a dress made in Paris for 1,300 marks. Later, as a memento of her first flight in a balloon she received from her husband a diamond-studded cigarette case.[199]

198 Adt, *Aus meinem Leben*, p 146; see pp. 134, 138, 144–45; see Wilmin, *Familie Adt*, p. 58.

199. Kardorff-Oheimb, *Politik*, p 54; see p 57. See also Lanckoronska, *Li(e)ber Beda*, pp 18–19

In general, there was somewhat more restraint. Wilhelm Merton's biographer, Hans Achinger, writes: "Merton's style of living was, to be sure, a generous one, but it was governed by ingrained habits and fixed limits, as was the case in many other Frankfurt homes of that time." Merton's wife, Emma, cultivated an elegant appearance. But, like other society ladies, she wore no jewelry on the street. "Merton himself was quite careful about his appearance, but it was his greatest concern not to overstep the boundaries of convention." Achinger attributes this attitude to English influence. (Merton was originally English.)[200] The Frankfurt banker Daniel Weismann consciously adopted the English style in dress and manner during a stay in England.[201]

Ostentatious entertainment played a major role in Frankfurt and Mannheim. Social competition in these two cities expressed itself in lavish expenditures and in the frequency of social affairs. The Mertons often gave parties, large or small. Anna Reiss gave the largest parties and balls in Mannheim, sometimes in banquet halls. "Nobody knew how to celebrate and entertain the way she did."[202] Gustav Adt organized big parties from time to time. He had booklets printed and distributed that contained hunting and homeland songs, party songs, and sometimes the program for a theatrical play. The hospitality of the Adt home is illustrated by an anecdote. When he was a child, Hans Adt one day invited fifty-six schoolmates to come to his home to play on the palace grounds. "My mother and grandmother hastily bought candy and cakes at the confectioner's shop, and everyone was served lemonade. Some of the boys played on the see-saw, others smeared themselves with food, and finally one of them even fell into the pond. It was a great party."[203] This is an interesting example of how children were introduced into social life. Carl von Weinberg ". . . maintained a magnificent household and took personal pleasure in doing so, and he was a master at the art of creating the atmosphere of an intimate social group." His brother Arthur von Weinberg and sister-in-law had far fewer outside contacts. They tended to invite over smaller groups of people, to musical soirées and afternoon teas for example.[204]

200 Achinger, *Wilhelm Merton*, pp. 243–44, 246.
201 See Klotzer, "Wilhelm Daniel Weismann," p. 254
202 Bohm, "Carl und Anna Reiß," p. 19. (Out of the collection of the Mannheim Municipal Archive) On the Frankfurt bourgeoisie, see ibid , p 254 On the Mertons, see Achinger, *Wilhelm Merton*, p 245
203 Adt, *Aus meinem Leben*, p 136; see Wilmin, *Die Familie Adt*, p. 57.
204 See "Carl von Weinberg," p. 27, out of the collection of the Frankfurt Municipal Archive, Schembs, "Die Frankfurter Familie," p. 58.

Most members of the Dyckerhoff family lived in relative seclusion, undoubtedly due to the fact that they lived in the somewhat remote towns of Amöneburg and Bieberich. Only Alfred Dyckerhoff and his wife, who were childless, often entertained guests; their garden and tennis court were a "favorite meeting-place for many."[205] An active social life was not the rule in the smaller towns.

Conclusion

The abandonment of middle-class forms of social life in the Wilhelmine propertied bourgeoisie was indicative neither of aristocratization nor of a merger of nobility and bourgeoisie. This class – with the exception of a few newcomers whose self-image was still very middle class – presented itself to society as an elite, documenting its advance into the upper echelons of society with a new upper-bourgeois life style. Frenzied social life and the ostentatious consumption that accompanied it were also an outgrowth of the search for useful connections, social competition, the rapid growth of large fortunes that made this extravagance possible in the first place, and, most importantly, new societal attitudes towards wealth. By the turn of the century, the business elite had succeeded in making Germany the most dynamic major economy in Europe. In an era that greatly admired these successes, moral scruples concerning self-gratification and the exhibition of wealth lost their significance. Encouraged by the emperor, a *nouveau riche* enthusiasm for luxury became widespread. The Wilhelmine era was the golden age of the parvenu.

The wealthy business elite rose into the highest echelons of society. Whereas in Hamburg or cities such as Elberfeld and Mannheim the wealthy business elite was largely integrated into a broader patrician class, in Berlin it maintained social ties with the traditional ruling classes without merging with them. The inadequacies of the aristocratization model became very much apparent in the analysis of Berlin society. It is true that social ties between the wealthy bourgeoisie and the nobility were closer than in the Hanseatic cities, but this results from the fact that in Hamburg, Bremen, and Lübeck political power was in the hands of the bour-

205. Dyckerhoff Archive: Funeral oration, held by Hans Dyckerhoff on 25 June 25 1965 (Trauerrede, gehalten von Herrn Dr. Hans Dyckerhoff am 25 Juni, 1965), p. 3, in Personalakte Alfred Dyckerhoff, Dyckerhoff-Archiv.

geoisie while in Berlin it was not. Wealthy Berlin business families were on the whole not interested in courting members of old aristocratic families as such, but in building up a network of contacts with the political and administrative elites that could be activated to gain access to insider information, influence the formulation of government policy and bureaucratic regulations, and to win state contracts. The same phenomenon could be observed in the case of the Krupps.

Wealthy business families formed an exclusive elite within which there was a high degree of social cohesion. Business and personal relationships were often interwoven, as for example in the friendships between Fürstenberg and Friedländer-Fuld and between Reusch and Bosch. The emotional ties of male friendship could create a basis for trust that could be highly useful for business relationships. This "male bonding" in the bourgeoisie also indicates a strong personal identification with the propertied bourgeoisie and a merging of personal and professional ambitions and desires. Social life centered on networking in wealthy business circles. The scope of these networks was national or even international, especially in the case of Jewish families.

What lines of separation existed inside the big business community? Within the Hamburg patrician class, there were hardly social divisions between bankers, merchants, shipping magnates, and industrialists.[206] Not every very wealthy businessman was accepted into this elite, however. Jews and self-made men were generally excluded. (Ballin is an exceptional case.) The heavy industrialists of Rhineland-Westphalia formed a clearly delineated social circle without excluding representatives of other economic sectors. The same is true of Berlin banking families, which for the most part lived in the vicinity of one another in the Tiergarten. Nevertheless, there is considerable evidence of social relationships between bankers and industrialists in Berlin and Rhineland-Westphalia as well as in Frankfurt and Mannheim (an outgrowth of bank financing of industry).

Though highly cohesive, there were ethnic divisions within the business elite. A few Jews, such as Carl Fürstenberg, Albert Ballin, and Wilhelm Merton, had intimate non-Jewish friends, but most Jews were poorly integrated into the business elite. One reason is anti-Semitism. But these patterns of sociability also reflect the fact that most Jews of the upper bourgeoisie wanted to associate with Jews.

206. See Evans, *Death*, p 559.

240

The highly exclusive monied elite of Wilhelmine Germany only socialized with those who belonged to the loftiest spheres of society. It hardly had contact with the bulk of the middle class. The business elite of Berlin associated only with the upper segment of the educated bourgeoisie, and especially with prominent writers, musicians, artists, intellectuals, and scholars. In Berlin and Hamburg wealthy business families did not mix with company employees and less successful businessmen. On the other hand, engineers and company employees were accepted to a limited extent in the social circles of the heavy industrialists of the Rhineland and Westphalia and in the homes of Wilhelm Merton and Gustav Adt. This should probably not be regarded so much as a regional difference as one related to the area of economic activity. It is probably due to the patriarchal structure of heavy industry, which was conducive (within narrow class-defined roles) to social relations between employers and employees.

It has often been overlooked (by Cecil, for example) that in this elite, class interests predominated over ethnicity. Very wealthy Jewish business families patterned their social lives in accordance with their economic interests, cultivated the same useful connections with diplomats or government ministers as Protestant businessmen, and demonstrated – despite anti-Semitism – a remarkable self-assurance. It is true that one encounters identity crises and admiration for the nobility in the cases of certain wealthy Jewish businessmen such as Walther Rathenau and the youthful Paul Wallich. However, both overcame their self-hatred (Wallich more successfully than Rathenau) and turned away from aristocratic models of behavior. It is actually astonishing how seldom business families allowed anti-Semitism to intrude upon their lives.

Within this class there are a number of examples of strong personalities – Jewish and non-Jewish – who presented themselves to society with great self-assurance. Among them were the *grandes dames* of Berlin society, who could deal socially with leading figures of any professional group, but another such strong personality was the "ordinary citizen" Salomonsohn, who held on to his own value system. Jewish businessmen also demonstrated a strong sense of their own identity in maintaining old ties to the artistic-intellectual world and thus to Jewish cultural traditions. Liebermann von Wahlendorf's comments on the Jewish monied elite of Berlin tells a great deal about its self-image: "Nowhere could one detect a trace of snobbishness, arrogance, or parvenu behavior, because

241

none existed; among these people there *was* culture, there *was* refinement, coupled with good upbringing, education to a greater or lesser degree, and high Jewish ethical standards."[207]

The sense of self that one encounters among the Jewish business elite is of course based on ethnicity rather than religion, because in this class many converted to Christianity. Their sense of ethnic identity was essentially based on cultural and educational ideals (*Bildung*), success in business, and social integration into the Jewish upper bourgeoisie. The first two of these elements meshed quite well with the mentality of the German business elite and were part of the economic and social successes of the Jewish elite. Underlying Jewish self-esteem and pride was the conviction that anti-Semitism was on the wane and that the position of wealthy Jews in German society would improve. On this subject Peter Gay writes: "It is easy now to ridicule them [German Jews] for thinking that if they behaved as Germans they would be treated as Germans – easy, but unhistorical in the extreme. However self-deluded it may now appear, in the 1890s this was a reasonable reading of their situation."[208]

Women played a major role in the social advancement of the wealthy business elite, a fact that has not been fully appreciated by historians such as Werner Mosse. It was the businessman's wife who for the most part did the organizational work involved in networking and cultivating useful contacts.[209] She defined who belonged to her social circle and who did not, and what social circles her family should try to become part of. Women presented an image, a social persona that stood for the wealthy bourgeosie's new place in the upper ranks of society. The manner in which the wives worked for the social rise of their families was just as legitimate (or illegitimate, for that matter) as the manner in which their husbands worked for the interests of their families in the realm of business.

207. Liebermann von Wahlendorf, *Erinnerung*, p. 49.
208 Gay, *Freud*, pp 165–66; see also pp. 93–95, 162–70
209. See chapter 3.

❀

Conclusion

As a sector of the business elite rose into the upper echelons of Wilhelmine society, a relatively superficial process of assimilation with the pre-industrial elite took place. More significantly, a new upper-bourgeois mentality emerged, as the class that had turned Germany into the most economically dynamic nation in Europe claimed its place in the German ruling class. This reorientation involved the abandonment of some middle-class virtues, the adoption of a life style geared more to social life than to family life, and conspicuous consumption on a grand scale. Admittedly, the often bombastic, pretentious style associated with the Wilhelmine period is in part the product of an imitation of the aristocracy. This is not necessarily indicative of fusion with the nobility, however. Status symbols and styles heretofore regarded as aristocratic were employed because they spoke a language generally understood in German society. Behind this behavior lies the parvenu attitude that anything can be bought – even the respectability and power of the nobility.

The new bourgeois social forms and participation in high society grew out of social competition in the big cities, which arose because businessmen cultivated business connections and relations with political and administrative elites within a private setting. The international successes of the German economy – publicly celebrated on many occasions by the emperor – lent a mark of respectability to *nouveau riche* life styles. The growing hedonism of the age also reflects the declining influence of religion. It should also not be forgotten that the number of businessmen who could afford to spend large amounts of money for conspicuous consumption was substantially larger around the turn of the century than ever before. The business elite presented itself to society as an elite,

243

sparing no expense on entertainment, and cultivating an image as *grande dame*, connoisseur, or "man of the world." The business families who did not go along with these changes generally fall into at least one of four categories: they lived in small towns where there was hardly anyone worth influencing; they were social newcomers; they were involved in an economic activity or company in which public relations were unimportant; or there were others in their company who took care of networking.

Far from being the product of women's vanity, a socially oriented life style promoted the economic and political interests of this elite. Networking and the cultivation of useful connections dominated the wealthy business family's social life. The business elite sought connections with the power elite – be it bourgeois as in the Hanseatic cities or dominated by the Prussian nobility as in Berlin. The heads of the big Berlin banks associated with high government officials, ministers, and diplomats because they needed reliable sources of information and wanted to promote business in foreign countries. To be sure, social ambitions played a role for a small minority, and it is in such cases that one can speak of genuine aristocratization. Less than one-tenth of the investigated businessmen married into aristocratic circles, but one-fourth of their sons and one-third of their daughters did so. While this did not weaken the position of business families in the business world – enough sons followed their fathers' footsteps – intermarriage did create real links with the pre-industrial elite.

However, these links were largely concentrated in a small number of families, often those with the largest fortunes and with a noble pedigree. Some historians have argued that aristocratization, along with the granting of titles and decorations, cut the head off the body of the bourgeoisie. Yet is this what we see here? It is clear that over the course of time – especially *before* the era of dynamic economic growth in the late nineteenth and early twentieth centuries – a small number of families dropped out of the business elite entirely. As was the case much earlier with the great Fuggers, so, too, in the imperial period did the Stumms, the Liebermann von Wahlendorfs, and other families largely (though not entirely) turn their backs on the business world. Their number was small in the Wilhelmine period, as the life histories of the wealthiest businessmen and their sons show. Very few of the investigated businessmen and less than one-third of their sons abandoned the world of business. Most of the aristocratization picked up by the indicators used in this study – connubium and social ties with the nobility, ennoblement, the purchase of landed estates – was to be found in families still actively engaged in business. For example, leading Hamburg banking families did not seek the title of baron so as to gain the acceptance of the nobility, but rather so as to preserve and promote their position in the business world as well as in the patrician ruling class of the city. Most of these superficially aristocratized business families were fully integrated into the business elite. Not only did they conduct business and socialize with the less aristocratized members of the monied bourgeoisie, but they had strong, intimate, emotional ties to the business class, as the friendship between Friedländer-Fuld and Fürstenberg attests. While the former chased after titles, decorations, an aristocratic son-in-law, and aristocratic friends, the latter eschewed titles, and worked to motivate his sons to pursue a career in the corporate world, though of course he did nonetheless cultivate connections in government and diplomatic circles dominated by the nobility. Thus, what took place in Germany was the partial, superficial aristocratization of a small group of very wealthy businessmen who by and large remained an integral part of the bourgeoisie. A more thorough process of assimilation of the bourgeoisie to the nobility, a true feudalization in the sense of a real subordination of the bourgeoisie to the aristocracy or a fusion of the two classes, failed to take place.

These findings are important because we have every reason to think that the group under study was among the most aristocratized in that period. Multimillionaires had easier access to aristocratic circles than less wealthy businessmen, since wealth "ennobled," and allowed one to acquire the status symbols of the upper class. In addition, since in most cases it took time to accumulate such fortunes, the very age of their wealth had a legitimizing effect in the eyes of the nobility.

The industrial and pre-industrial elites failed to merge because their values were too different. Certainly, the aristocracy resisted bourgeoisification and segregated itself socially, but the wealthy business class also largely resisted feudalization. First, only in isolated cases is there evidence of courting of the aristocracy per se. When wealthy business families socialized with government officials of noble descent or pursued titles and decorations, they were generally trying to establish links with the state. Second, for many wealthy businessmen, the nobility represented a world whose values and standards they in the final analysis rejected. Sons seldom found a military career appealing. Few became rentiers or aspired to the life of a landed grandee. Landed estates were generally purchased as vacation homes, as model farms where modern business techniques could be tried out, as status symbols, or as a place to receive upper-class guests. A few businessmen seem to have been seeking their peasant "roots," real or imagined. Third, the tremendous upsurge in materialistic values set the business elite apart from the aristocracy. Fourth, ties within the propertied bourgeoisie had a strong emotional underpinning, as evidenced in close friendships and even romances, such as that between Carl and Aniela Fürstenberg. Fifth, the self-confident manner in which these businessmen and their wives presented themselves to society is indicative of a strong collective sense of self-assurance.

The wealthy propertied bourgeoisie formed a distinct social entity that was relatively closed in its recruitment pattern and socially cohesive. The overwhelming majority of the businessmen under study were the fathers and sons of businessmen. In fact, the majority of sons of the directors and chairmen of the board of joint stock companies and of younger sons followed business careers. Socialization in the family usually strongly motivated the sons in this direction. They were constantly exposed to their fathers' professional preoccupations and were "taught the value of money," often by imposed frugality. The social lives of these families centered on business circles. And two-thirds of the businessmen in this study married into business families, though only half of their sons and one-third of their daughters did so. The businessman himself was more likely than his son to marry a businessman's daughter because the family's rise into the business upper class often took place in the earlier generation when it was necessary to build up capital by means of a dowry and to expand business connections through intermarriage. In some cases the businessman became the head of the firm that belonged to his father-in-law. But in the next generation, marriage alliances with other business families were of less importance. This relates to the declining importance of the family in the pooling of financial, managerial, and political resources.

Very wealthy businessmen generally had little to do with small businessmen and white-collar workers, even managers of their own companies. The industrialists of Rhineland-Westphalia and the Frankfurt industrialist Merton were the exception here. This phenomenon is possibly related to patriarchal structures in industry.

The move to the exclusive residential suburbs loosened the ties between employer and employee and caused the business elite to have less and less contact with the lower and middle strata of the population. In Hamburg not even all of the wealthy bourgeoisie was socially accepted by the patricians. Jews were admitted only with reluctance, but wherever there was a large concentration of well-to-do Jews – especially in Berlin – very exclusive Jewish social circles came into being. It was only in the small towns that a very rich businessman (such as Gustav Knepper) would associate socially with members of the lower middle class. Possehl, who resided in Lübeck, lived withdrawn from society because there were hardly any prominent business families there.

The wealthy propertied bourgeoisie had much in common with the educated bourgeoisie. The educational and cultural ideals of the latter influenced the former. This led to growing similarities in child-rearing practices and career patterns, to a similarly long period of career moratorium, dependence, and adolescent search for identity, as well as to common values and interests. We find evidence of this in leisure activities, social ties with the world of learning and culture, and the sons' interest in professions in this area. Wealthy businessmen also sought honors – those granted by universities in particular – that technically placed them on a par with academics and professionals. The villa was the typical bourgeois home of this period. Its architecture contained elements that signaled that its owner – whether professor or businessman – was a cultivated person. Increasingly, the businessman's villa was not located next to his factory or offices, but in an exclusive residential suburb where a cross section of the upper bourgeoisie lived.

Intermarriage with the educated bourgeoisie was nevertheless somewhat rarer than with the pre-industrial elite, even if we count government bureaucrats as members of the educated bourgeoisie. Social ties with the educated bourgeoisie were strongest in the Hanseatic cities where a patrician ruling class existed that consisted of various segments of the bourgeoisie. Such ties were also to be found to a certain extent in Rhineland-Westphalia and the southwest and west of Germany. In Berlin, on the other hand, the only representatives of the educated bourgeoisie that were likely to grace the drawing rooms of wealthy businessmen were prominent scholars, artists, writers, and the like. The bourgeois friends of wealthy businessmen were upper middle class, and often quite prominent. On the other hand, ties with the lower middle class had been cut off. And the business elite drew a sharp distinction between itself and the rest of the bourgeoisie by buying second villas and country estates, which only the very wealthy could afford. The wealthy business elite no longer belonged to the middle class, but had "arrived" socially, becoming part of the upper echelons of society.

In the elite business family of the Wilhelmine era patriarchal structures were beginning to crumble, making room for growing individualism. Only among the Jews and the patrician class of the Hanseatic cities did arranged marriages and closed marriage circles still prevail. Otherwise, the "love marriage" became the norm, though men had greater latitude in spouse selection than women. The main reason for this is that the dowry had lost its importance in the accumulation of capital. In addition, the young man was usually in a better position than his parents to find a woman capable of satisfying the increasing demands that were being placed on the wife in this class. As a rule the parents could depend on his "falling in love" with a woman who possessed an optimal set of characteristics. The emotional life of people of this class was generally guided by their economic interests. The son's embarkation on a professional life was also generally dealt with in a flexible manner. As a result, adolescence (which often lasted into the mid-twenties) became a stage of "self-discovery" that in the end usually brought the son back to the "right path." The prevalence of authoritarian family structures have been greatly overestimated by Hellige and others. Especially among sons growing up in the imperial period an authoritarian upbringing was regarded as abnormal and increasingly led to rebellion or failure rather than conformity.

With the help of her husband, or at least of his money, the wife in this class was freed from the constant care of the children, was treated as a companion (though seldom an equal) by her husband, and was able to assume responsible duties, make semi-public appearances, and in rare cases even flout bourgeois standards of behavior (in matters of sexuality or in the formation of friendships with critical intellectuals and the like). The prominent hostesses of this class appeared in society with great self-assurance. To fulfill their assigned roles, women needed education and a sense of self. Thus, conditions for women in this class were more conducive to the development of women's personality and abilities than in most of the middle class. This had an impact on the rearing of daughters, foreshadowing future developments in this direction.

In the business elite, family members enjoyed growing opportunities for personal growth, and were not asked to sacrifice themselves to family interests as much as in earlier times – for example, with regard to equal inheritance. A total breakdown of family solidarity did not take place, however. Sons still felt obliged to take over the family firm. In cases in which two or more brothers ran the family firm together, young businessmen were often called upon to subordinate their own desires and ambitions to family interests. Thus, even in this age of corporate capitalism and growing individualism, the family continued to perform (if in diminished form) economic functions as described by Kocka for the period of early industrialization.

In its family life, the wealthy propertied bourgeoisie had a fair amount in common with the middle class. Children led very sheltered lives and were inculcated with bourgeois values such as self-discipline and the work ethic. Gender roles corresponded to middle-class notions of separate spheres. The most important differences lay in the loss of intimacy in the family of the business elite, its greater openness to the outside world, and in the potential for development enjoyed by wives and daughters.

Some of the most important findings of the present study are in regard to the significance of ethnicity in the wealthy business elite. Little evidence was found to support the old conceptions of Jewish "overcompensation" or capitulation to the Junkers (Cecil). As far as relations with other classes go, class interests tended to override ethnic differences. If Jews are particularly well known for courting the nobility, then it is only because they predominated in the group – Berlin bankers – that geographically had the best access to the highest ranks of government and diplomacy, and that was very much needed to influence these elites. If Jewish business families sought to conquer a place in Wilhelmine high society, so did non-Jews such as the Krupp and Siemens families – and for much the same reasons. If the German-Jewish monied elite broke off ties with middle-class Jews, it was not because the latter were Jewish but because they were not their social equals. Wealthy Protestants behaved in a similar manner.

Jews did not imitate or court members of the nobility to a greater extent than non-Jews. The results of the quantitative study indicate that intermarriage with the pre-industrial elite was no more frequent among the wealthiest Jewish businessmen's families than among the non-Jewish. Wealthy Jews for the most part want-

249

ed to socialize with and marry members of the upper bourgeoisie. Sons overwhelmingly pursued careers in business. Self-hatred was not unknown in this class, but negative experiences during youth could lead not only to disillusionment with the "aristocratic model," but also to identification with the Jewish bourgeoisie. Neurosis does not seem to have been any more typical of Jewish families than of non-Jewish ones. It is actually astonishing how little Jews allowed themselves to be beaten down by anti-Semitism and with what self assurance they claimed a place for themselves at the pinnacle of society. Hindsight has led some historians to falsely condemn this class for not having an inkling of the ultimate fate of German Jewry, but that was not foreseeable in the pre-war period.

Ethnicity molded the lives of members of wealthy Jewish business families in subtle ways. The arranged marriage was more common, the age at marriage higher, the difference in age between man and wife greater, and the percentage of unmarried people higher among the Jews in the present study. This strategy was in part a reaction to anti-Semitism, which limited the professional opportunities and marriage choices of young Jews. However, it probably also reflects the difficulties in finding suitable partners encountered by those who wanted to marry within the Jewish faith. Granted, for every Friedländer-Fuld who sought a Jewish spouse, there was a (baptized) Paul Wallich, who specifically wanted a non-Jewish bride. Wealthy Jewish business families tended to socialize primarily with Jews of their own class, and friendships with other Jews tended to be more emotionally intense. Social cohesion was both the product of anti-Semitism (stronger in Hamburg than in Berlin) and Jewish ethnicity (something to be found even among baptized Jews such as Wallich). Jewish ethnicity often expressed itself in educational, intellectual, and cultural ideals and achievements. On the one hand, this was a way of acculturating to German society and of opening professional opportunities to the younger generation. On the other hand, this reflects both traditional Jewish attitudes towards education and traditional links between wealth and learning in Jewish communities.

Volkov's notion that Jewish ethnic characteristics were particularly "modern" was shown to be an oversimplification. Arranged marriages and the pattern of gratification postponement or gratification denial found in low nuptiality rates, high average age of marriage, and large differences in age between husbands and wives are indicative of the persistence of patriarchal structures. On the other hand, Jews were more modern than non-Jews in their pro-motion of education and a low fertility rate. And we certainly find many examples of growing individualism in the German-Jewish monied elite (for example, love matches).

Regional diversity had long been thought to be a major force in German nineteenth-century history, its proponents ranging from traditionalists who believe in the existence of typical regional char-acter to modern scholars conducting *Historische Regionalforschung* (historical region research) who empirically study regional differ-ences, analyzing the impact of diverse patterns of social, economic, and political development on historical processes of all sorts. The present study, which unlike most studies looked at a group that was national in scope, pointed up unexpected similarities in the wealthy business elites of the major regions. A similar percentage of businessmen were ennobled in the three most important regions – the Hanseatic cities, Berlin, and Rhineland-Westphalia. Titles of nobility – although not the Commercial Councillor title – became a status symbol in Hamburg, where titles of nobility traditionally had been shunned. Networking in business circles was similar across Germany, though more intense in urban centers.

Regional differences in social relations with political and admin-istrative elites can be explained in terms of the geographical distrib-ution of national, provincial, and local elites and of businesses that needed contacts in government (such as banking and arms manu-facturing). Berlin businessmen did not court the Junkers as such, but rather power brokers of the same sort that Hamburg business-men pursued. The difference was that in Hamburg businessmen were integrated into a patrician class, whereas in Berlin business-men sought useful connections but did not become part of the rul-ing class. The extravagance connected with entertaining members of the upper class was the same in Berlin, the Hanseatic cities, and Rhineland-Westphalia. The degree to which business families were oriented to family life as opposed to social life depended much more on the size of the town where they lived than on the region. Correspondingly, wealthy businessmen's wives were more active outside of the family in the big cities. The emotional dynamics and power relations in wealthy business families were not subject to regional variation, either. The leveling of regional differences in this class is rooted in the growing economic, political, and social ties to a united Germany (particularly to Prussia), in the impact of wealth on social behavior, in the dictates of capitalist development, and in the emergence of an urban culture molded less and less by regional traditions.

The contrasting of top corporate managers, "entrepreneurs," and owners provided some insight into the social impact of the rise of corporate capitalism, one of the minor themes of this study. One might have expected to find in the ranks of top corporate management a large number of men of lower-middle-class and lower-class background, men who would perhaps be less tradition-al in outlook and less likely to seek assimilation with the aristocra-cy. In fact, the corporate elite was hardly more open to social new-comers and men of non-business background than the family-run private companies. The explanation for this lies in the educational requirements and professional connections necessary to a successful corporate career. Aristocratization – as measured by ennoblement, the sons' choice of profession, and social circle – was, if anything, somewhat stronger in the families of heads of corporations, proba-bly because they were among the very wealthiest, but also because sons could not inherit their father's company and might therefore enter a traditionally aristocratic profession.

The growth industries (chemicals, electricity, and machinery), which have been regarded as especially "modern" (because busi-nessmen in this sector were newcomers), had the highest rates of aristocratization in terms of ennoblement and the sons' choice of profession. Again, many of the firms in growth industries were joint stock companies, so that the sons were more frequently com-pelled to seek other professions. Another explanation lies in the fact that the government gave preference to growth industries in the granting of titles. This could lead to genuine aristocratization and permanent withdrawal from industry.

On the other hand, very little evidence was found that supported the thesis that the more politically conservative element in indus-try, particularly heavy industry, tended towards feudalization. The percentage of ennoblements among heavy industrialists was not above average, and their sons were not especially prone to take up traditionally aristocratic professions. (The rate of transmission of profession from father to son was, however, lower than it was in other types of business, probably because in the families of heavy industrialists, primogeniture was more widespread.)

Segmentation within the business elite was less than has been generally supposed. Very wealthy managers were easily integrated into the monied elite. Among Berlin bankers or industrialists in

Rhineland-Westphalia, for example, there do not appear to have been social barriers between owners and top corporate managers. Granted, the concept of a "business elite" did not exist in pre-war Germany. Far more usual were terms such as "merchant," denoting any prosperous businessman in the Hanseatic cities, and elsewhere "finance people" or "industrialist," depending on the main economic activity of the region. Nonetheless, as a result of bank financing of industry there were close social ties between bankers and industrialists in most of Germany. In Hamburg what mattered was not whether a family was engaged in banking, industry, commerce, or shipping, but whether it belonged to the patrician ruling class. Those shunned by the patrician elite were generally integrated into national social networks. Ethnicity constituted the most important division within the monied elite. In Berlin Jews and non-Jews of the upper bourgeoisie mixed socially, though Jews constituted a distinct social group. In other cities, Jews enjoyed less social acceptance but constituted (except in Frankfurt) a small minority of the business elite. As would be expected anywhere around 1900 (due to the state of transportation systems), social circles were largely regional rather than national in scope. But what was different in Germany is that there was no center and no one regional elite that was recognized as socially preeminent – no equivalent of the London City.

Thus, the wealthiest businessmen of Wilhelmine Germany formed part of a cohesive elite,[1] bound together by social and family networks that were usually regional but sometimes national or even international in scope. It encompassed and integrated managers and owners and businessmen of all sectors and industries. We do not find a business elite divided into hostile camps, one politically conservative and feudalized, the other liberal and bourgeois. Representatives of the more modern, export-oriented sector of the economy – the chemical, machinery, and electrical industries – actually showed a greater predilection for ennoblement and ties with the aristocracy than heavy industry, which was supposedly more pro-Junker. The wealthiest businessmen listed in the *Yearbook of Millionaires* were not politically fragmented, either. In their education and social background, the members of this elite were relatively homogeneous. No more than subtle shifts in mentality were to be found between different generations. Social new-

---

1. An elite displaying a high degree of moral solidarity and social integration See Giddens, *Class Structure*, pp. 120–21.

comers were few in number and they did not form a faction with a will to take on the establishment in any sense. Business families living in small towns did not fully participate in the life of the elite, but these were isolated individuals who hardly had any social or political impact. Though Jewish ethnicity was alive in this elite, it did not create a different attitude towards the aristocracy, a different life style, or a different sense of class identity. Similarly, though regional pride lived on, regional disparities in social behavior were very much on the decline.

The mentality and life style of this elite was molded above all by its great wealth and economic power. Surging forward into the highest echelons of society, the business elite broke with its middle-class past and became very socially exclusive – a class of parvenus and patricians. If a "classless society of *Bürger*" (Gall) had ever existed in Germany, it had certainly broken apart by 1900. The fact that the middle class "lost its leadership" has been made out to be a German peculiarity, and yet this also took place in France, Britain, and the United States. This development is not indicative of the decline of the bourgeoisie, but rather of its rise. It is also not indicative of a failure of nerve or a lack of modernity. The wealthy business elite of Wilhelmine Germany did not subordinate itself to the aristocracy, and in embracing certain elements of the norms and habits of the pre-industrial elite so thoroughly redefined them that they took on a new meaning. The outlook and behavior described in this study was characterized by an ongoing modernization, notably the gradual breakdown of patriarchal structures.

Fusion with the nobility only took place in the cases of a very few families. Their number was too small for a conservative "feudal-capitalistic ruling class" to come into existence. Nor did a merger of bourgeoisified nobility and aristocratized bourgeoisie take place as in England. Moreover, links between the educated bourgeoisie and the wealthy propertied bourgeoisie were weak. Thus, neither a coherent upper class nor a cohesive upper bourgeoisie came into existence in pre-war Germany.

Bibliography

I. Archives

BASF-Archiv (Archive of the BASF)

W1 Brunck:

–Begleitschrift betreffend ein Projekt in Erbauung eines Familienhauses für Herrn Dr. Brunck

–Vertrag über Festlegung und Auszahlung des Pflichtteilanspruchs

–Schloß Kirchheimbolanden (Grundriß)

–Daten zum Brunck´schen Schloßgarten in Kirchheimbolanden (21.5.80/bo)

Newspaper Clippings

–A. Bernthsen, "Heinrich von Brunck 26.3.1847–4.12.1911," *Chemiker Zeitung* 1911, issue no. 149.

–Walter Voigtländer Tetzner, "Heinrich von Brunck 1847–1911."

–"Das Kirchheimbolander Schloß," *Zeitbilder zugleich Illustrierte Zeitschrift für den Fremden- und Familienverkehr in der Pfalz*, Sunday magazine section of the *Pfälzischen Presse*, 29 October 1911, pp. 141–42.

–"Geheimer Kommerzienrat Ritter Dr. Heinrich von Brunck," *Zeitbilder zugleich Illustrierte Zeitschrift für den Fremden- und Familienverkehr in der Pfalz*, Sunday magazine section of the *Pfälzischen Presse*, 17 December 1911, p. 161.

–Otto N. Witt, "Heinrich von Brunck," offprint out of *Chemischen Industrie*, issue no. 24, 1911.

–C. Glaser, "Heinrich von Brunck. Nachruf," offprint out of *Berichte der deutschen Chemiken Gesellschaft*, vol. 46 (1913).

Dyckerhoff-Archiv (Archive of the Dyckerhoff Corp.)

Personalakte Alfred Dyckerhoff:

–Trauerrede, gehalten von Herrn Dr. Hans Dyckerhoff am 25.6.1965

Personalakte Rudolf Dyckerhoff:

–August an Rudolf Dyckerhoff, 10.11.1907

–26.4.1948 (Kurzbiographie)

Personalakte Karl Dyckerhoff:
–Vize-Präsident Dr. Wilhelm Dyckerhoff: Trauerrede für Commer-
zienrat Karl Dyckerhoff (13.9.1869–10.12.1938)

Haniel-Archiv [vorm. Historisches Archiv der Gutehoffnungshütte] (Archive
of the Haniel Corp., former Archive of the Gutehoffnungshütte)

Bestand Paul Reusch:
3001938/0, 30019390/0b, 30019390/36, 400101290/115, 159, 160:
Private Korrespondenz, 1903–1916
40010128/52:
–Glückwunschschreiben zur Verleihung des Kommerzienrats-Titels
1910
40010128/60:
–Inventar des Katharinenhofs (1917)
400101294/0:
–Abendessen am 31. Januar 1914 abends 8 Uhr (Gästeliste)
400101299/58:
–Haushaltsbücher, Katharinenhof: Weihnachtsgelder (1909)

Historisches Archiv der Stadt Köln (Historical Archive of the City of
Cologne)

Nachlaß Mallinckrodt (Abt. 1068)
Kasten 73:
–Erinnerungen der Tochter Mathilde
Kasten 77:
–Briefwechsel zwischen Wilhelm von Mallinckrodt und Gustav von
Mallinckrodt
Kasten 82:
–Fotographie des Hauses Sachsenring 77

Institut zur Erforschung historischer Führungsschichten (Institute for the
Research of Historical Ruling Classes), Bensheim (Archive director:
Friedrich Wilhelm Euler)
Genealogische Sammlung, A–Z

Landesarchiv Saarbrücken (State Archive of the Saarland, Saarbrücken)
Abt. D, Korrespondenz des Familie Stumm:
–Carl Ferdinand an Ferdinand von Stumm-Halberg, 28.11.1860
Rheinisch-Westfälisches Wirtschaftsarchiv zu Köln (Economic Archive of
Rhineland-Westphalia, Cologne)

1. Nachlaß Eugen Langen:

7–9–4, 7–9–5: Schriftwechsel (1884–1894)
7–9–9: (undatiertes) Manuskript einer Biographie über Eugen Langen von
Bruno Kuske (1969 eingegangen)

2. Nachlaß Wilhelm Scheidt:

60-12-8: Zeichnung zu baulichen Änderungen im Hause des Herrn
  Wilhelm Scheidt

Siemens-Archiv (Archive of the Siemens Corp.): SAA

Wilhelm von Siemens:
4/Lb 843: Notizen und Reflexionen, Aufzeichnungen aus verschiedenen
  Gebieten
4/Lc 999: Sammlung von Visitenkarten
4/Ld 151: Schriftstücke betr. Rittergut Biesdorf (1889–1928);
  Schriftwechsel (1908–1930)
4/Lk 72: Schriftwechsel betr. Familienangelegenheiten (1884–1908)
4/Lr 507: Biographisches Material (1855–1919)
4/Lr 562: Familienbriefe: Arnold und Wilhelm an ihren Onkel Carl
  Siemens (1893–1904)
4/Lr 563: Familienbriefe: Arnold an Wilhelm von Siemens (1872–1916),
  Wilhelm an Arnold von Siemens (1868–1906), Carl Friedrich an
  Wilhelm von Siemens (1901–1911), Arnold und Wilhelm an Carl
  Friedrich von Siemens (1894–1908)
4/Lr 566: Familienbriefe. . .an Wilhelm von Siemens (1869–1919)
4/Lr 567: Familienbriefe. . .an Wilhelm von Siemens

Carl Dietrich Harries, "Nachruf für Wilhelm von Siemens," offprint out of
  Wissenschaftliche Veröffentlichungen aus dem Siemens-Konzern, vol. 1,
  issue 1.

Staatsarchiv Dresden (State Archive, Dresden)

Ministerium des Innern:
Nr. 4967, 4968, 4974, 4990, 4991: Auszeichnungen, Orden pp. (1890/
  1896/1903–1906)
Nr. 5012, 5014, 5031, 5081–5088: Sächsische Auszeichnungen
  (1898/1906–1918)

Staatsarchiv Potsdam (Sanssouci - Orangerie) (State Archive, Potsdam)

Polizeipräsidium Berlin, Pr. Br. Rep. 30 Berlin C Tit. 94:
Acta des Polizeipräsidii Berlin betreffend:
Nr. 8654: Eduard Arnhold
Nr. 8795: Sigmund Aschrott
Nr. 8953: Edwin, Carl und Hans Bechstein
Nr. 8968: Georg Büxenstein
Nr. 9047: Rudolf Blanckertz
Nr. 9128: James Bleichröder
Nr. 9310: Sigmund Bergmann
Nr. 9650: Ludwig Delbrück
Nr. 9662: Ludwig Darmstädter
Nr. 9748: Max Esser

Nr. 9929: Carl Fürstenberg
Nr. 9940: Fritz Friedländer (Fritz von Friedländer-Fuld)
Nr. 9977: Georg Fromberg
Nr. 9990: Hermann Ernst Frenkel
Nr. 10123: Arthur und Albert Gilka
Nr. 10124: Gelpcke
Nr. 10125: Moritz, Louis, Julius Gerson
Nr. 10141: Ludwig Max Goldberger
Nr. 10239: Eugen Gutmann
Nr. 10265: Philipp Freudenberg
Nr. 10348: Otto Gerstenberg
Nr. 10520: Oskar Huldschinsky
Nr. 10522: Wilhelm Herz
Nr. 10547: Georg Heckmann
Nr. 10594: Walter Kyllmann
Nr. 10606: Wilhelm von Siemens
Nr. 10608: Theodor Hildebrandt
Nr. 10619: Engelbert und Gustav Hardt
Nr. 10620: Emil Hecker
Nr. 10676: James Hardy
Nr. 10686: Karl von der Heydt
Nr. 10699: Georg Haase
Nr. 10746: Georg Haberland
Nr. 10848: Berthold Israel
Nr. 10937: Adolf Jandorf
Nr. 11075: Rudolf von Koch
Nr. 11077: Wilhelm von Krause
Nr. 11146: Wilhelm Kopetzky
Nr. 11199: Karl Klönne
Nr. 11253: Leopold Koppel
Nr. 11299: Markus Koppel
Nr. 11595: Georg Liebermann
Nr. 11596: Karl Hagen [Karl Levy]
Nr. 11764: Rudolf Mosse
Nr. 11791: Robert und Franz von Mendelssohn
Nr. 11792: Paul von Mendelssohn-Bartholdy, Arthur Fischel
Nr. 11832: Alexander Karl von Martius
Nr. 11868: Paul Mankiewitz
Nr. 11880: Waldemar Mueller
Nr. 11893: Moritz Manheimer
Nr. 12081: Hugo Oppenheim
Nr. 12237: Joseph Pinkuß
Nr. 12279: Albert und Richard Pintsch
Nr. 12414: Albert Pinkuß
Nr. 12623: Louis Ravené

Nr. 12674: Hermann Rosenberg
Nr. 12685: Emil Rathenau
Nr. 12723: Max Richter
Nr. 12749: Jakob Riesser
Nr. 13190: Eduard Simon
Nr. 13236: August Scherl
Nr. 13247: Max Steinthal
Nr. 13410: Emil Sauer
Nr. 13424: James Simon
Nr. 13431: Paul von Schwabach
Nr. 13432: Arnold von Siemens
Nr. 13461: Max Schlesinger
Nr. 13470: Hans Schlesinger
Nr. 13496: Walter Sobernheim
Nr. 13596: Georg Solmssen
Nr. 13810: Oskar Tietz
Nr. 14107: Hermann Wallich
Nr. 14287: Maximilian Weigert
Nr. 14311: Franz, Wilhelm und Georg Wertheim
Nr. 14340: Wolf Wertheim

Stadtarchiv Frankfurt (Frankfurt Municipal Archive)

S1/6, Nr. 2: Heinrich Roessler
S1/6, Nr. 10: Fritz Roessler
S2/221: Weinberg
S2/379: Merton
S2/789: Arthur von Weinberg
S2/10305: Familie Weinberg

Stadtarchiv Mannheim (Mannheim Municipal Archive)

1. Nachlaß Carl und Anna Reiß:
Nr. 4: Programmhefte
Nr. 11: Gästebuch
Nr. 15: Dr. Karl Reiss zum 70. Geburtstag am 14. Februar 1913
Nr. 33: Korrespondenz
    –Ludwig Ganghofer an Carl Reiss, 18.6.1903
Nr. 44: Korrespondenz
    –Hugo Wolf an Anna Reiß, 21.4.1897
    –Hugo Wolf an Anna Reiß, 17.5.1897

2. S1/631: Collection of newspaper clippings:
    –Hans Forth, "Vorbild lebendigen Bürgersinns. Erinnerungen an das Geschwisterpaar Anna und Carl Reiß," *Rhein-Neckar-Zeitung*, 1 September 1970.
    –Ludwig W. Böhm, "Carl und Anna Reiss," *Mannheimer Hefte*, vol. 1/54, pp. 16–20.

–"Gehiemrat Dr. Karl Reiß zu seinem 70. Geburtstag," *NBLZ*,
13 February 1913.
–Juliana von Stockhausen, "Erlebnis mit Anna Reiß in der
Rheinstraße," *Mannheimer Morgen*, 30 March 1962.
Thyssen-Archiv (Archive of the Thyssen Corp.)

Familie Thyssen:

A/886: In Sachen August Thyssen jun. gegen August Thyssen sen. wegen
Pflichtteilsentziehung: Briefwechsel der Parteien.
A/1769: Hermann Jungbluth, Stammtafel der Familie Thyssen,
Privatdruck Aachen 1934.
A/1788: Manuskript einer Biographie August Thyssens von Walther
Däbritz.
A/3614: Stellungnahme des Oberpräsidenten bezüglich August Thyssens
geplante Berufung ins Herrenhaus.
A/9577: Korrespondenz August Thyssen (1895–1911).

Magazine and newspaper collection:
Der Roland von Berlin, 24 November 1904; 8 December 1904; 12
January 1905; 2 March 1905; 13 July 1905.
Rheinisch-Westfälische Zeitung, 10 November 1906.
Berliner Morgenpost, 29 January 1905.
Unsere ATH. Werkzeitschrift der August Thyssen-Hütte AG, issue 12
(1966) (articles: "Begründer der Verbundwirtschaft in der Stahl-
industrie," pp. 14–15; "'Schlicht und einfach, wie er gelebt. . .'", p.
16; "August Thyssen und Auguste Rodin," pp. 20–21).

Photographs: F 412, F 4042, F 403

Westfälisches Wirtschaftsarchiv (Westphalian Economic Archive)

F 17: Dresler, D: Nachlaß H.A. Dresler:
Nr. 485: Ms., Ansprache d. Superintendenten Hubbert bei der Trauerfeier
für Clementine Dresler geb. Klein. 1925 Dez. 31.
Nr. 488: Ansprache (Schwiegersohn Alfred Niederstein) bei der
Trauerandacht für Heinr. Adolf Dresler. 1929 März 2.
Nr. 489: Nachruf (Stahl und Eisen). 1929.
Nr. 490: J. Vorlaender, Zur Erinnerung an Adolf Dresler. Für seine Kinder
und Enkel, Anverwanten und Freunde, Privatdruck Hilchenbach, o.J.
Nr. 491: Korrespondenzen zur öffentlichen Tätigkeit (1870–1920).

Zentrales Staatarchiv Merseburg (Central State Archives of the G.D.R.,
Merseburg)

1. Geheimes Zivilkabinett, 2.2.1.

Akten betr. die Verleihung des Adelstitel:
Nr. 1018: Baum (1910–13)

Nr. 1036: Beit von Speyer (1909–1910)
Nr. 1048: Berenberg-Goßler (1889–1914)
Nr. 1340: Koch (1915–1916)
Nr. 1473: Scheibler (1869–1909)
Nr. 1516: Wassermann (1910)

Akten betr. die Verleihung des Titels Kommerzienrat und Geheimer Kommerzienrat, Nr. 1590–1597 (1897–1918)

Akten betr. die Verweigerung der Annahme von Titeln und Orden, Nr. 1836 (1867–1917)

2. Ministerium für Handel und Gewerbe, Rep. 120, A IV

Nr. 5, Bd. 9–17, 20, 21: Titel- und Ordensverleihungen an Kaufleute und Gewerbetreibende in der Provinz Brandenburg, 1867–1876/ 1878–1880.
Nr. 5a, Bd. 1, 4: Titelverleihungen an Kaufleute und Gewerbetreibende in Berlin, 1880–1885/1900–1901.
Nr. 5b, Bd. 1, 5, 6: Titelverleihungen an Kaufleute und Gewerbetreibende in Berlin, 1881–1885/1894–1898.
Nr. 9, Bd. 3–4: Titel- und Ordensverleihungen an Kaufleute und Gewerbetreibende in der Provinz Schlesien, 1861–1868.
Nr. 11b, Bd. 1: Titelverleihungen an Kaufleute und Gewerbetreibende in der Provinz Sachsen, 1881–1896.
Nr. 12b, Bd. 2: Titel- und Ordensverleihungen an Kaufleute und Gewerbetreibende in der Provinz Westfalen, 1900–1901.
Nr. 13b, Bd. 2–4: Titel- und Ordensverleihungen an Kaufleute und Gewerbetreibende in der Rheinprovinz, 1890–1899.

II. Other Unpublished Sources: Letters

Friedrich Wilhelm Euler, director of the Institut zur Erforschung historischer Führungsschichten, letters to the author, dated 28 August 1985 and 13 January 1988
Countess Sibylle von Hardenberg, granddaughter of banker Emil Hecker, letter to the author, dated 25 November 1985
Dr. Hofmeister, of the State Archive, Bremen, letter to the author, dated 18 January 1988
Prof. Dr. Frank Lerner, letter to the author, dated 11 October 1985
Werner E. Mosse, Leo Baeck Institute (London), letter to the author, dated 30 August 1986
Dr. Müller, director of the State Archive, Bremen, letter to the author, dated 30 September 1985
Friedrich August Nebelthau, grandson of the merchant Friedrich Wilhelm Nebelthau, letter to the author, dated 18 February 1986
Werner Pfeiffer, banker in the firm Wilhelm Ahlmann in Kiel (his wife is

the great-granddaughter of banker Wilhelm Ahlmann), letter to the author, dated 30 May 1987

Ernst-Ludwig Raab, descendent of the mine-owner Joseph Raab, undated letter to the author (received on 31 September 1985)

Dr. Rothe, director of the Central Office for Geneology of the G.D.R., letter to the author, dated 22 September 1986

Hermann Segnitz, grandson of the merchant Fritz Segnitz, letter to the author, dated 28 May 1986

Municipal Archive of Frankfurt, letter to the author, dated 25 September 1985

III. Sources for Quantitative Study, Autobiographies and Biographies

Achinger, Hans. *Richard Merton*. Frankfurt am Main, 1970.

Achinger, Hans. *Wilhelm Merton in seiner Zeit*. Frankfurt am Main, 1965.

Achterberg, Erich. *Berliner Hochfinanz. Kaiser, Fürsten, Millionäre um 1900*. Frankfurt am Main, 1965.

Achterberg, Erich. *Frankfurter Bankherren*, 2nd ed. Frankfurt am Main, 1971.

Achterberg, Erich and Maximilian Müller-Jabusch. *Lebensbilder Deutscher Bankiers aus fünf Jahrhunderten*, 2nd ed. Frankfurt am Main, 1964.

Adolph, Rudolf. *Hans Fürstenberg*. Aschaffenburg, 1960.

Adt, Hans. *Aus meinem Leben und aus der Geschichte der Firma Gebr. Adt. Autobiographische Aufzeichnungen*. Private print, Bad Orb, 1978.

Allgemeine Deutsche Biographie. Leipzig, 1875–1912. 56 vols.

Arnhold, Johanna, ed. *Eduard Arnhold. Ein Gedenkbuch*. Private print, Berlin, 1928.

Arnsberg, Paul. *Die Geschichte der Frankfurter Juden seit der Französischen Revolution*. Frankfurt am Main, 1983, vol. 3: *Biographisches Lexikon*.

Arnst, Paul. "August Thyssen. 1842–1926." *Rheinisch-Westfälische Wirtschaftsbiographien*. Münster, Westphalia, 1934, vol. 2/1.

Arnst, Paul. *August Thyssen und sein Werk*. Leipzig, 1925.

Art'l, H.S. *Richard Roesicke. Sein Leben und Wirken dem Volke dargestellt*. Berlin, 1904.

Ascher, Abraham. "Baron von Stumm, Advocate of Feudal Capitalism." *Journal of Central European Affairs*, vol. 22 (1962), pp. 271–85.

Attali, Jacques. *Siegmund G. Warburg. Das Leben eines großen Bankiers*, trans. Hermann Kusterer. Düsseldorf and Vienna 1986.

Bachfeld, Hanns-Ludwig. "Hanns Jencke." *Rheinisch-Westfälische Wirtschaftsbiographien*. Münster, Westphalia, 1983, vol. 11, pp. 163–94.

Bacmeister, Walter. *Emil Kirdorf. Der Mann. Sein Werk*, 2nd ed. Essen, 1936.

Bacmeister, Walter. *Gustav Knepper: Das Lebensbild eines großen Bergmannes*. Essen and Rüttenscheid, 1950.

Bauert-Keetmann, Ingrid. *Deutsche Industriepioniere.* Tübingen, 1966.

Baum, Marie Luise. "Conrad Albert Ursprung, 1856–1932." *Wuppertaler Biographie,* vol. 11 (1973), pp. 80–84.

Baumann, Carl-Friedrich. "August Thyssen – Ein Bürger Mülheims." *Zeitschrift des Geschichtsvereins der Stadt Mülheim a.d. Ruhr,* vol. 61 (1989), pp. 7–26.

Baumgart, Waldemar. *Der zündende Funke. Weg, Wesen und Werk des Robert Bosch.* Zeulenroda, 1944.

Behrend, M., ed. *Magdeburger Großkaufleute. Lebensbilder, ed. zur Einweihung des Hauses der Handelskammer, Alter Markt 5 und 6, am 19. Mai des Jahres 1906.* Private print, Magdeburg, 1906.

Berck, Marga. *Aus meiner Kinderzeit. Bremer Erinnerungen 1881–1891.* 1957; reprint Bremen, 1979.

Berdrow, Wilhelm. *Alfred Krupp und sein Geschlecht. Die Familie Krupp und ihr Werk von 1787–1940 nach den Quellen des Familien- und Werksarchivs geschildert.* Berlin, 1943.

Berglar, Peter. *Walther Rathenau. Seine Zeit. Sein Werk. Seine Persönlichkeit.* Bremen, 1970.

Boelcke, Willi A., ed. *Krupp und die Hohenzollern in Dokumenten. Krupp-Korrespondenz mit Kaisern, Kabinettschefs und Ministern 1850–1918,* 2nd ed. Frankfurt, 1970.

Böttcher, Helmuth M. *Walther Rathenau. Persönlichkeit und Werk.* Bonn, 1958.

Borchardt, Knut. "Der Unternehmerhaushalt als Wirtschaftsbetrieb." *Villa Hügel. Das Wohnhaus Krupp in Essen,* ed. Tilmann Buddensieg. Essen and Berlin, 1984, pp. 10–31.

Brandi, Paul. *Essener Arbeitsjahre. Erinnerungen des Ersten Beigeordneten Paul Brandi.* Essen, 1959.

Brauer, Arthur von. *Im Dienste Bismarcks: Persönliche Erinnerungen.* Berlin, 1936.

Bremische Biographie 1912–1962. Bremen, 1969.

Brinckmeyer, Hermann. *Die Rathenaus.* Munich, 1922.

Brockhaus, Heinrich Eduard. *Die Firma F.A. Brockhaus von der Begründung bis zum hundertjährigen Jubiläum. 1805–1905.* Leipzig, 1905.

Buchanan, Meriel. *Ambassador's Daughter.* London, 1958.

Buddensieg, Tilmann. "Einleitung." *Villa Hügel. Das Wohnhaus Krupp in Essen.* Essen and Berlin, 1984, pp. 7–9.

Bunsen, Marie von. *Die Welt in der ich lebte. Erinnerungen aus glücklichen Jahren 1860–1912,* 3rd ed. Leipzig, 1929.

Bunsen, Marie von. *Zeitgenossen die ich erlebte 1900–1930.* Leipzig, 1932.

Cecil, Lamar. *Albert Ballin. Business and Politics in Imperial Germany, 1888–1918.* Princeton, 1967.

Croon, Helmuth. "Die wirtschaftlichen Führungsschichten des

Ruhrgebiets in der Zeit von 1890 bis 1933." *Blätter für deutsche Landesgeschichte*, vol. 108 (1972), pp. 143–59.

Deutsches Geschlechterbuch (Genealogisches Handbuch bürgerlicher Familien). Glücksburg, etc., 1889–1982. 187 vols.

Dietz, Alexander. *Geschichte der Familie Andreae Frankfurter Zweig*. Frankfurt am Main, 1923.

Dietz, Alexander. *Stammbuch der Frankfurter Juden*. Frankfurt am Main, 1907.

Dresdner Molkerei Gebrüder Pfund Dresden 1880–1910. Berlin, 1910. Out of the collection of the Dresden Municipal Archive.

Duisberg, Curt. *Nur ein Sohn. Ein Leben mit der Großchemie*. Stuttgart, 1981.

Eckert, Christian. *J.H. Stein, Werden und Wachsen eines Kölner Bankhauses in 150 Jahren*. Berlin, 1940.

Ehrhardt, Heinrich. *Hammerschläge. 70 Jahre deutscher Arbeiter und Erfinder*. Leipzig, 1922.

Ehrhardt, Heinrich. *Kreuz- und Querfahrten eines Mechanikers und Arbeiters, eines Waisenkindes*. Düsseldorf, 1920.

Ellenbeck, Hans, August Dresbach, and D. Traub. *Erinnerungen an Kommerzienrat Bernhard Krawinkel 1851–1936*. Gummersbach, 1937.

Emrich, Wilhelm and Manfred Linke. "Lebenschronik." *Carl Sternheim Gesamtwerk*. Neuwied and Darmstadt, 1976, vol. 10/II.

Engelmann, Bernt. *Krupp. Legende und Wirklichkeit*. Munich, 1969.

Engelmann, Bernt. *Das Reich zerfiel, die Reichen blieben. Deutschlands Geld- und Machtelite*, 5th ed. Munich, 1981.

Erman, Hans. *August Scherl. Dämonie und Erfolg in wilhelminischer Zeit*. Berlin, 1954.

Euler, Friedrich Wilhelm. "Bankherren und Großbankleiter nach Herkunft und Heiratskreis." *Bankherren und Bankiers. Büdinger Vorträge 1976*, ed. Hanns Hubert Hofmann. Limburg an der Lahn, 1978, pp. 85–144.

Eynern, Gert von. *Die Unternehmungen der Familie vom Rath. Ein Beitrag zur Familiengeschichte*. Bonn, 1930.

Eynern, M. von, ed. *Walther Rathenau. Ein preußischer Europäer. Briefe*. Berlin, 1955.

"Familie Raab (Joseph und Ludwig). Ihre Bedeutung für den Eisenbergbau in Wetzlar." *Wetzlaner Heimathefte*, vol. 12 (1963), pp. 51–55.

Feder, Ernst et al. "James Simon. Industrialist, Art Collector, Philanthropist." *Leo Baeck Institute Year Book*, vol. 10 (1965), pp. 3–23.

Federn-Kohlhaas, Etta. *Walther Rathenau. Sein Leben und Wirken*, 2nd ed. Dresden, 1928.

Festschrift zum 50-jährigen Bestehen der Firma Ernst Grumbt. Dampfsäge- und Hobelwerke Dresden. Schluckenau in Böhmen. Sahland an der Spree.

Without place of publication, 1914. From the collection of the Municipal Archive of Dresden.

Fischer, Brigitte B. *Sie schrieben mir oder was aus meinem Poesiealbum wurde.* Stuttgart and Zurich, 1978.

Flechtner, Hans-Joachim. *Carl Duisberg. Eine Biographie.* 1960; reprint Düsseldorf, 1981.

Freundt, F.A., ed. *Emil Kirdorf. Ein Lebensbild. Zum fünfzigjährigen Gedenktage seines Eintritts in den Ruhrbergbau.* Essen, without date of publication.

Fritsch, Baron Thomas von. *Die Gothaischen Taschenbücher, Hofkalender und Almanach.* Limburg an der Lahn, 1968.

Fuchs, Konrad. "Guido Georg Friedrich Graf Henckel von Donnersmarck. 1830–1916." *Wirtschaftsgeschichte Oberschlesiens 1871–1945. Aufsätze.* Dortmund, 1981, pp. 76–91.

Fuchs, Max. *Max Steinthal zu seinem achtzigsten Geburtstag am 24. Dezember 1930. Eine Festschrift.* Berlin, 1930.

50 Jahre Seidel & Naumann. Dresden, 1918. From the collection of the Municipal Archive of Dresden.

Fürst, Artur. *Emil Rathenau. Der Mann und sein Werk.* Berlin, 1915.

Fürstenberg, Carl. *Die Lebensgeschichte eine deutschen Bankiers, 1870–1914,* ed. Hans Fürstenberg. Berlin, 1931.

Fürstenberg, Hans. *Carl-Fürstenberg-Anekdoten. Ein Unterschied muß sein.* Düsseldorf and Vienna, 1978.

Fürstenberg, Hans. *Erinnerungen. Mein Weg als Bankier und Carl Fürstenbergs Altersjahre.* Düsseldorf and Vienna, 1968.

Carl Funke und seine Werke. Essen, 1914.

"Karl Funke 1855–1912." *Der Bergbau,* vol. 25 (25 April 1912), pp. 235–37.

Gantzel-Kress, Gisela. "Noblesse oblige. Ein Beitrag zur Nobilitierung der Mendelssohns." *Mendelssohn-Studien,* vol. 6 (1986), pp. 163–81.

Genealogisches Handbuch des Adels:

Fürstliche Häuser, Glücksburg an der Ostsee and Limburg an der Lahn, 1951–1987, vols. 1–13;

Gräfliche Häuser A. Glücksburg an der Ostsee and Limburg an der Lahn, 1952–1973, vol. 1–7;

Gräfliche Häuser B. Glücksburg an der Ostsee and Limburg an der Lahn, 1953–1983, vols. 1–11;

Freiherrliche Häuser A. Glücksburg an der Ostsee and Limburg an der Lahn, 1952–1986, vols. 1–14;

Freiherrliche Häuser B, Glücksburg an der Ostsee and Limburg an der Lahn, 1954–1982, vols. 1–8;

Adelige Häuser A. Glücksburg an der Ostsee and Limburg an der Lahn, 1953–1985, vols. 1–18;

Adelige Häuser B. Glücksburg an der Ostsee and Limburg an der Lahn, 1954–1986, vols. 1–17.

Genealogisches Taschenbuch der adeligen Häuser Österreichs. Vienna, 1912/13, vol. 5.

Gesellschaft von Berlin. Hand- und Adreßbuch für die Gesellschaft von Berlin, Charlottenburg und Potsdam. Berlin, 1891–1892, vol. 2.

Geßner, Gerhard, ed. *Deutsches Familienarchiv*. Neustadt an der Aisch, 1952/53–1989, vols. 1–104.

Gilbert, Felix. *Lehrjahre im alten Europa. Erinnerungen 1905–1945*. Berlin, 1989.

Gilbert, Felix, ed. *Bankiers, Künstler und Gelehrte. Unveröffentlichte Briefe der Familie Mendelssohn aus dem 19. Jahrhundert*. Tübingen, 1975.

"Paul Girardet." *Lebensbilder aus dem rheinisch-westfälischen Industriegebiet*. Vol. for 1968/1972, pp. 64–66.

Gleichen, Lord Edward. *A Guardsman's Memories. A Book of Recollections*. Edinburgh and London, 1932.

Goetzeler, Herbert and Lothar Schoen. *Wilhelm und Carl Friedrich von Siemens. Die zweite Unternehmergeneration*. Stuttgart, 1986.

Gothaischer Genealogischer Hofkalender nebst diplomatisch-statistischem Jahrbuch. Gotha, 1871–1919, vols. 108–156.

Gothaisches Genealogisches Taschenbuch der briefadeligen Häuser. Gotha, 1907–1919, vols. 1–13.

Gothaisches Genealogisches Taschenbuch der freiherrlichen Häuser. Gotha, 1871–1942, vols. 21–92.

Gothaisches Genealogisches Taschenbuch der gräflichen Häuser. Gotha, 1871–1942, vols. 44–115.

Gothaisches Genealogisches Taschenbuch der uradeligen Häuser. Gotha, 1907–1919, vols. 8–20.

Grünfeld, Margarete. *Alte unnennbare Tage. Erinnerungen*. Private print, London, 1958.

Gwinner, Arthur von. *Lebenserinnerungen*, ed. Manfred Pohl. Frankfurt am Main, 1975.

Haberland, Georg. *Aus meinem Leben*. Private print, without place of publication, 1931.

Ham, Hermann van. "Rudolf Böcking." *Rheinisch-westfälische Wirtschaftsbiographien*. Münster, Westphalia, 1932, vol. 1, pp. 298–317.

Handbuch der deutschen Kommerzienräte, II. Ausgabe 1911/12. Berlin, 1911.

Handelskammer zu Frankfurt a. Main, ed. *Geschichte der Handelskammer zu Frankfurt a. Main (1707–1908). Beiträge zur Frankfurter Handelsgeschichte*. Frankfurt am Main, 1908.

Hansabund, ed. *Handbuch wirtschaftlicher Vereine und Verbände des Deutschen Reichs*. Berlin and Leipzig, 1913.

Harries, Carl Dietrich. "Nachruf für Wilhelm von Siemens." Reprint from *Wissenschaftliche Veröffentlichungen aus dem Siemens-Konzern*, vol. 1.

Harttung, Arnold, ed. *Walther Rathenau, Schriften*, 2nd ed. Berlin, 1981.

Hashagen, Justus. *Geschichte der Familie Hoesch.* Cologne, 1916, vol. 2: *Vom Zeitalter der Religionsunruhen bis zur Gegenwart,* part 2.

Hatzfeld, Lutz. "Ernst Poensgen (1871–1949)." *Rheinische Lebensbilder.* Cologne, 1977, vol. 7, pp. 203–25.

Helbing, Claus. *Die Bethmanns. Aus der Geschichte eines alten Handelshauses zu Frankfurt am Main.* Wiesbaden, 1948.

Helfferich, Karl. *Georg von Siemens. Ein Lebensbild aus Deutschlands großer Zeit.* Berlin, 1923, vol. 3.

Hellige, Hans Dieter. "Rathenau und Harden in der Gesellschaft des Deutschen Kaiserreichs." *Walther Rathenau-Gesamtausgabe.* Munich and Heidelberg, 1983, vol. VI: *Walther Rathenau. Maximilian Harden. Briefwechsel 1897–1920,* pp. 15–299.

Hellwig, Fritz. *Carl Ferdinand Freiherr von Stumm-Halberg 1836–1901.* Heidelberg and Saarbrücken, 1936.

Henle, Günter. *Weggenosse des Jahrhundert. Als Diplomat, Industrieller, Politiker und Freund der Musik.* Stuttgart, 1968.

Herzog, Bodo. "Die Freundschaft zwischen Oswald Spengler und Paul Reusch." *Spengler-Studien. Festgabe für Manfred Schröder zum 85. Geburtstag,* ed. Anton Mirko Koktanek. Munich, 1965, pp. 77–97.

Herzog, Bodo. "Paul Reusch und das Deutsche Museum in Munich. Zum 100. Geburtstag von Paul Reusch." *Deutsches Museum. Abhandlungen und Berichte,* vol. 35 (1967), pp. 5–37.

Heuss, Theodor. *Robert Bosch, Lebens und Leistung,* 5th ed. Tübingen, 1946.

Heydt, Carl von der. *Unser Haus.* Private print, without place of publication, 1919.

Heyl, Gertraut. "August Thyssen, eine Unternehmergestalt." Dr. phil. diss., Berlin, 1950.

Heym, Heinrich. "Simon Moritz H.A. Freiherr von Bethmann." *Bankiers sind auch Menschen. 225 Jahre Bankhaus Gebrüder Bethmann,* ed. Johann Philipp Frhr. von Bethmann. Frankfurt am Main, 1973, pp. 257–70.

Hintner, Otto. "Franz Friedrich Andreae." *Neue Deutsche Biographie.* Berlin, 1953, vol. 1, pp. 280.

Hoffmann, Bernhard. *Wilhelm von Finck. 1848–1924. Lebensbilder eines deutschen Bankiers.* Munich, 1953.

Horstmann, Lali. *Unendlich viel ist uns geblieben.* Munich, 1954.

Huldermann, Bernhard. *Albert Ballin,* 6th ed. Oldenburg, 1921.

Huret, Jules. *En Allemagne. Berlin.* Paris, 1909. [German: *Berlin um Neuzehnhundert,* trans. Nina Knoblich. 1909; reprint Berlin, 1979.]

Huret, Jules. *In Deutschland,* trans. E. von Kraatz. Leipzig, Berlin, and Paris, 1907, vol. 1: *Rheinland und Westfalen.*

Hutten-Czapski, Bogdan Graf von. *Sechzig Jahre Politik und Gesellschaft.* Berlin, 1936, 2 vols.

Jacobson, Jacob, ed. *Die Judenbürgerbücher der Stadt Berlin 1809–1851.* *Mit Ergänzungen für die Jahre 1791–1809.* Berlin, 1962.

Joll, James. "Walther Rathenau – Intellectual or Industrialist?" *Germany in the Age of Total War, Essays in Honour of Francis Carsten,* eds. Volker R. Berghahn and Martin Kitchen. London and Ottowa, 1981, pp. 46–62.

Jüdisches Adressbuch für Groß-Berlin, Ausgabe 1929/30. Berlin, 1929; *Ausgabe 1931.* Berlin, 1931.

Kaiserliches Statistisches Amt, ed. *Statistik des deutschen Reichs. Berufs- und Betriebszählung vom 12. Juni, 1907.* Berlin, 1909, vol. 218: *Gewerbliche Betriebsstatistik, Abt. VI: Kleinere Verwaltungsbezirke; Preußen.*

Kardorff-Oheimb, Katharina von. *Politik und Lebensbeichte,* ed. Ilse Reicke. Tübingen, 1965.

Kaznelson, Siegmund, ed. *Juden im deutschen Kulturbereich. Ein Sammelwerk,* 2nd ed. Berlin, 1959.

Kellenbenz, Hermann. "Louis Hagen. insbesondere als Kammer-präsident." *Rheinisch-Westfälische Wirtschaftsbiographien.* Münster, Westphalia, 1974, vol. 10, pp. 138–95.

Kellenbenz, Hermann. "Paul Silverberg." *Rheinisch-Westfälische Wirtschaftsbiographien.* Münster, Westphalia, 1967, vol. 9, pp. 103–32.

Kelleter, Heinrich and E. Poensgen, eds. *Die Geschichte der Familie Poensgen.* Düsseldorf, 1908.

Kerr, Alfred. *Walther Rathenau. Erinnerungen eines Freundes.* Amsterdam, 1935.

Kessler, Harry Graf. *Walther Rathenau. Sein Leben und sein Werk.* Berlin, 1928.

Kessler, Harry Graf. *Tagebücher, 1918–1937,* ed. Wolfgang Pfeiffer-Belli. Berlin, Darmstadt, and Vienna, 1961.

Kirchholtes, Hans-Dieter. *Jüdische Privatbanken in Frankfurt am Main.* Frankfurt am Main, 1969.

Klass, Gert von. "Bertha Krupp von Bohlen und Halbach." *Beilage zu den Krupp-Mittelungen,* 29 March 1956, pp. 1–16.

Klass, Gert von. *Die drei Ringe. Lebensgeschichte eines Industrie-unternehmens.* Tübingen and Stuttgart, 1953.

Klass, Gert von. *Hugo Stinnes.* Tübingen, 1958.

Klötzer, Wolfgang. "Karl Borgnis." *Bankiers sind auch Menschen. 225 Jahre Bankhaus Gebrüder Bethmann,* ed. Baron Johann Philipp von Bethmann. Frankfurt am Main, 1973, pp. 247–49.

Klötzer, Wolfgang. "Wilhelm Daniel Weismann." *Bankiers sind auch Menschen. 225 Jahre Bankhaus Gebrüder Bethmann,* ed. Baron Johann Philipp von Bethmann. Frankfurt am Main, 1973, pp. 250–56.

Kohlschütter, Andreas, ed. *Ein Genie in chaotischer Zeit. Edmund H. Stinnes über seinen Vater Hugo Stinnes (1870–1924).* Berlin, 1979.

Kraft, Werner. *Rudolf Borchardt. Welt aus Poesie und Geschichte.* Hamburg, 1961.

Kupferberg, Herbert. *Die Mendelssohns. Three Generations of Genius.* New York and London, 1972.

Lanckoronska, Maria. *Li(e)ber Beda. Memoiren einer Individualistin.* Frankfurt am Main, 1977.

Landes, David S. "Bleichröders and Rothschilds. The Problem of Continuity in the Family Firm." *The Family in History,* ed. Charles E. Rosenburg. Philadelphia, 1975, pp. 95–114.

Lepsius, Sabine. *Ein Berliner Künstlerleben um die Jahrhundertwende.* Munich, 1972.

Lerner, Franz, ed. *Das tätige Frankfurt im Wirtschaftsleben dreier Jahrhunderte (1648–1955) zugleich ein Handbuch der Altfrankfurter Firmen.* Frankfurt am Main, 1955.

Liebermann von Wahlendorf, Willy Ritter. *Erinnerung eines deutschen Juden 1863–1936,* ed. Ernst Reinhard Piper. Munich and Zurich, 1988.

Löbe, Karl. *Die vom Löwenhof. Geschichte des Bremer Weinimporthauses A. Segnitz & Co.* Bremen, 1984.

Lowenthal, Ernst G. *Juden in Preußen. Biographisches Verzeichnis. Ein repräsentativer Querschnitt.* Berlin, 1981.

Lowenthal-Hensel, Cécile. "Franz von Mendelssohn." *Mendelssohn-Studien,* vol. 6 (1986), pp. 251–65.

Manchester, William. *The Arms of Krupp. 1587–1968.* Boston and Toronto, 1968.

Mangoldt, Ursula von. *Auf der Schwelle zwischen Gestern und Morgen. Begegnungen und Erlebnisse.* Weilheim, 1963.

Marchtaler, Hildegard von. *Die Slomans. Geschichte einer Hamburger Reeder- und Kaufmannsfamilie.* Hamburg, 1939.

Martin, Rudolf. *Das Jahrbuch der Millionäre Deutschlands.* Berlin, 1911–1914. 19 vols.

Martin, Rudolf. *Das Jahrbuch des Vermögens und Einkommens der Millionäre in Preußen.* Berlin, 1912.

Martius, Lilli. *Erlebtes den Verwandten und Freunden erzählt.* Private print, Kiel, 1970.

Maschke, Erich. *Es entsteht ein Konzern. Paul Reusch und die GHH.* Tübingen, 1969.

Matschoß, Conrad, ed. *Werner Siemens. Ein kurzgefaßtes Lebensbild nebst einer Auswahl seiner Briefe.* Berlin, 1916, vol. 2.

Matschoß, Conrad and Eugen Diesel, eds. *Robert Bosch und sein Werk.* Berlin, 1931.

Meisbach, Julius. *Friedrich Alfred Krupp, wie er lebte und starb.* Cologne, 1903.

Melchers, Gustav Adolf. *Erinnerungen aus meiner Jugendzeit. Geschrieben für meine Kinder, Enkel und Urenkel.* Private print, Leipzig, 1940.

Menne, Bernhard. *Krupp. Deutschlands Kanonenkönige.* Zurich, 1937.

Merck, Heinrich. *Vom gewesenen Hamburg. Nach eigenen Erinnerungen aufgezeichnet.* Hamburg, 1953.

Milkereit, Gertrud. "Carl Spaeter." *Rheinisch-Westfälische Wirtschafts-biographien.* Münster, Westphalia, 1974, vol. 10, pp. 78–115.

Möring, Maria. *A. Kirsten Hamburg.* Hamburg, 1952.

Mosse, Werner E. "Rudolf Mosse and the House of Mosse 1867–1920." *Leo Baeck Institute Year Book,* vol. 4 (1959), pp. 237–59.

Mühlen, Norbert. *Die Krupps,* trans. Walter Purgleitner. Frankfurt am Main, 1960.

Müller, Rainer. *Das Robert-Bosch-Haus.* Stuttgart, 1988.

Muthesius, Volkmar. *Peter Klöckner und sein Werk,* 2nd ed. Essen, 1959.

Neue Deutsche Biographie. Berlin, 1953–1982. 13 vols.

Niendorf, Helmuth. *Geschichte des Handelshauses Possehl 1847–1919.* Lübeck, 1962.

Nutzinger, Richard. *Karl Röchling 1827–1910. Das Lebenswerk eines Großindustriellen.* Völklingen and Saarbrücken, 1927.

Perlick, Alfons. *Oberschlesische Berg- und Hüttenleute. Lebensbilder aus dem Oberschlesischen Industrierevier.* Kitzingen am Main, 1953.

Petzet, Arnold, ed. *Heinrich Wiegand. Ein Lebensbild.* Bremen, 1932.

Pierson, Kurt. *Borsig – ein Name geht um die Welt. Die Geschichte des Hauses Borsig und seiner Lokomotiven.* Berlin, 1973.

Pilet, Otto. *Ein Rückblick auf mein Leben insbesondere auf die Entwicklung des Handels in den letzten 50 Jahren.* Private print, Magdeburg, 1900.

Pinner, Felix. *Deutsche Wirtschaftsführer,* 15th ed. Charlottenburg, 1925.

Pinner, Felix. *Emil Rathenau und das elektrische Zeitalter.* Leipzig, 1918.

Präser, Friedrich. "Die Vietor aus und in Bremen." *Niedersächsische Lebensbilder.* Hildesheim, 1971, vol. 7, pp. 311–29.

Pudor, Fritz, ed. *Lebensbilder aus dem rheinisch-westfälischen Industrie-gebiet.* Düsseldorf, 1960–1962, vols. for 1952–54, 1955–57, 1958–59.

Pudor, Fritz, ed. *Nekrologe aus dem Rheinisch-Westfälischen Industriegebiet.* Düsseldorf, 1955, vol. for 1939–52.

Quadt, Ernst. *Deutsche Industrie-Pioniere. Der Anbruch des technischen Zeitalters.* Berlin, 1940.

Raphael, Gaston. *Hugo Stinnes. Der Mensch – Sein Werk – Sein Wirken,* trans. not named. Berlin, 1925.

Raphael, Gaston. *Krupp et Thyssen.* Paris, 1926.

Rathenau, Walther. "Gedächtnisrede für Emil Rathenau. Gehalten am Tage der Beisetzung 23. Juni, 1915 in Oberschöneweide." *Gesammelte Schriften.* Berlin, 1918, vol. 5: *Reden und Schriften aus Kriegszeit,* pp. 9–21.

Rathenau, Walther. "Staat und Judentum. Eine Polemik." *Gesammelte Schriften,* Berlin, 1918, vol. 1, pp. 183–208.

Rathenau, Walther. "Zur Kritik der Zeit." *Walther Rathenau-Gesamtausgabe*, eds. Hans Dieter Hellige and Ernst Schulin. Munich and Heidelberg, 1977, vol. 2: *Hauptwerke und Gespräche.*

Reh, Theodor. "Friedrich Lenz." *Pommersche Lebensbilder.* Stettin, 1934, vol. 1, pp. 322–35.

Reibnitz, Baron Kurt von. *Gestalten rings um Hindenburg. Führende Köpfe der Republik und die Berliner Gesellschaft von Heute.* Dresden, 1928.

Reichert, Jakob. "Peter Klöckner." *Rheinisch-Westfälische Wirtschafts-biographien.* Münster, Westphalia, 1960, vol. 7, pp. 85–104.

Reichshandbuch der deutschen Gesellschaft. Das Handbuch der Persönlichkeiten in Wort und Bild. Berlin, 1931. 2 vols.

Reissner, H.G. "The Histories of 'Kaufhaus N. Israel' and of Wilfrid Israel." *Leo Baeck Institute Year Book*, vol. 3 (1958), pp. 227–56.

"Paul Reusch. Der Unternehmer, Kunstfreund und Mensch. 1865–1956." *Praktikus, 1958. Oberhausener Haus- und Heimatfreund,* pp. 25–37.

Reusch, Paul and Hermann Bücher. *Robert Bosch aus alter und neuer Zeit.* Private print, Berlin, 1931.

Rheinbaden, Baron Werner von. *Viermal Deutschland. Aus dem Erleben eines Seemanns, Diplomaten, Politiker 1895–1954.* Berlin, 1954.

Riedler, Alois. *Emil Rathenau und das Werden der Großwirtschaft.* Berlin, 1916.

Ring, Walter. *Geschichte der Duisberger Familie Böninger.* Duisberg, 1930.

Rohrmann, Elsabea. *Max von Schinckel, hanseatischer Bankmann im wilhelminischen Deutschland.* Hamburg, 1971.

Ropers, Julius W. *Vom Geldwechsler zur Großbank. Ein Rückblick auf die Entwicklung eines bremischen Bankhauses.* Bremen, 1937.

Rosenbaum, Eduard. "M.M. Warburg & Co. Merchant Bankers of Hamburg." *Leo Baeck Institute Year Book*, vol. 7 (1962), pp. 121–49.

Rosenbaum, Eduard and A.J. Sherman. *Das Bankhaus M.M. Warburg and Co. 1798–1938.* Hamburg, 1976.

Rotth, August. *Wilhelm von Siemens. Ein Lebensbild. Gedenkblätter zum 75-jährigen Bestehen des Hauses Siemens und Halske.* Berlin and Leipzig, 1922.

Sächsische Lebensbilder. Leipzig, 1930–1941. 3 vols.

Salin, Edgar. "Paul Reusch." *Lynkeus – Gestalten und Probleme aus Wirtschaft und Politik*, ed. Edgar Salin. Tübingen, 1963, pp. 51–57.

Saling's Börsen-Papiere. Zweiter (finanzieller) Teil. Saling's Börsen-Jahrbuch für 1911/1912. Ein Handbuch für Bankiers und Kapitalisten. Berlin, Leipzig, and Hamburg, 1911.

Schacht, Hjalmar. *76 Jahre meines Lebens.* Bad Wörishofen, 1953.

Schembs, Hans-Otto, ed. *Bibliographie zur Geschichte der Frankfurt Juden. 1781–1945.* Frankfurt am Main, 1978.

Schembs, Hans-Otto. "Die Frankfurter Familie von Weinberg." *Kleine Möbel*, ed. Georg Himmelheber. Munich, 1979.

Schramm, Percy Ernst. *Neun Generationen. Dreihundert Jahre deutscher "Kulturgeschichte" im Lichte der Schicksale einer Hamburger Bürgerfamilie (1648–1948)*. Göttingen, 1964, vol. 2.

Schroeder, Hiltrud, *Sophie & Co.: bedeutende Frauen Hannovers*. Hannover, 1990.

Schümann, Carl-Wolfgang. "'Die Pfalz der Stahlkönige' Das Innere der Villa Hügel im Wandel." *Villa Hügel. Das Wohnhaus Krupp in Essen*, ed. Tilmann Buddensieg. Essen and Berlin, 1984, pp. 275–309.

Schulin, Ernst. "Die Rathenaus. Zwei Generationen jüdischen Anteils an der industriellen Entwicklung Deutschlands." *Juden im Wilhelminischen Deutschland, 1890–1914*, eds. Werner E. Mosse and Arnold Paucker. Tübingen, 1976, pp. 115–42.

Schulin, Ernst. *Walther Rathenau. Repräsentant, Kritiker und Opfer seiner Zeit*. Göttingen, Zurich, and Frankfurt am Main, 1979.

Schulz-Briesen, Max. "Bruno Schulz-Briesen." *Rheinisch-Westfälische Wirtschaftsbiographien*. 1941; reprint Münster, Westphalia, 1974, vol. 4, pp. 119–32.

Schulze, Friedrich, ed. *Geschichte der Familie Ackermann aus Gödern*. Private print, Leipzig, 1912.

Schwann, Mathieu. *Leonhard Tietz. Ein Wort über ihn und sein persönliches Werden*. Private print, Cologne, 1914.

Schwering, Count Axel von (pseud.). *The Berlin Court under William II*. London, New York, Toronto, and Melbourne, 1915.

Selve, Walther von. *Selve. Seinen Kindern gewidmet*. Without place of publication (Braunschweig?), 1923.

Selve, Walther von. *Treue um Treue*. Zurich and Leipzig, 1941.

Serlo, Walter. *Rheinisch-Westfälische Wirtschaftsbiographien*. 1936; reprint Münster, Westphalia, 1974, vol. 3: *Bergmannsfamilien in Rheinland und Westfalen*.

Shepherd, Naomi. *Wilfrid Israel. German Jewry's Secret Ambassador*. London, 1984.

Siebertz, Paul. *Ferdinand von Steinbeis. Ein Wegbereiter der Wirtschaft*. Stuttgart, 1952.

Siemens, Georg. *Carl Friedrich von Siemens. Ein großer Unternehmer*. Munich, 1960.

Siemens, Georg. *Geschichte des Hauses Siemens*. Munich, 1947–1951. 3 vols.

Siemens, Werner von. *Lebenserinnerungen*, 3rd ed. Berlin, 1901.

Sigilla Veri (Ph. Stauff's Semi-Kürschner). Lexikon der Juden, Genossen und Gegner aller Zeiten und Zonen, insbesondere Deutschlands, der Lehren, Gebräuche, Kunstgriffe und Statistiken der Juden sowie ihrer Gaunersprache, Trugnamen, Geheimbünde, usw., 2nd ed. Erfurt, 1929. 4 vols.

Sloman, Mary Amelie. *Erinnerungen.* Hamburg, 1957.

Solmssen, Georg. *Gedenkblatt für Adolf und Sara Salomonsohn zum 19. März, 1931.* Private print, Berlin, 1931.

Statistik der preußischen Einkommenssteuer-Veranlagung für das Steuerjahr, 1914 und der Ergänzungssteuer-Veranlagung für die Steuerjahre, 1914/16. Berlin, 1914.

Statistisches Handbuch für das Großherzogtum Hessen, 2nd ed. Darmstadt, 1909.

Stern, Fritz. *Gold and Iron. Bismarck, Bleichröder and the Building of the German Empire.* New York, 1977.

Stürmer, Michael. "Alltag und Fest auf dem Hügel." *Villa Hügel. Das Wohnhaus Krupp in Essen,* ed. Tilmann Buddensieg. Essen and Berlin, 1984, pp. 256–73.

Stürmer, Michael. Gabriel Teichmann, and Wilhelm Treue. *Wägen und Wagen. Sal. Oppenheim jr. & Cie. Geschichte einer Bank und einer Familie.* Munich, 1989.

Thyssen, Fritz, *I Paid Hitler.* New York and Toronto, 1941.

Tietz, Georg. *Hermann Tietz. Geschichte einer Familie und ihrer Warenhäuser.* Stuttgart, 1965.

Townley, Lady Susan. *"Indiscretions" of Lady Susan.* New York, 1922.

Treue, Wilhelm. "Das Bankhaus Mendelssohn als Beispiel einer Privatbank im 19. und 20. Jahrhundert." *Mendelssohn Studien,* vol. 1 (1972), pp. 29–80.

Treue, Wilhelm. *Die Feuer verlöschen nie. August Thyssen-Hütte. 1890–1926.* Düsseldorf and Vienna, 1966.

Treue, Wilhelm. "Henschel & Sohn – Ein deutsches Lokomotivbau-Unternehmen 1860–1912, Tl. II." *Tradition,* vol. 20 (1975), pp. 3–23.

Treue, Wilhelm. "Max Freiherr von Oppenheim – Der Archäologe und die Politik." *Historische Zeitschrift,* vol. 209 (1969), pp. 37–74.

Vagts, Alfred. "M.M. Warburg & Co. Ein Bankhaus in der deutschen Weltpolitik, 1905–1933." *Vierteljahrschrift für Sozial- und Wirtschaftsgeschichte,* vol. 45 (1958), pp. 289–388.

"Vasili, Paul Comte" (pseudonym for Catherine Princess Radziwill). *La Société de Berlin,* 12th ed. Paris, 1884.

Venzmer, Wolfgang. "Hermann Bahlsen und die Kunst." Rudolf Hillbrecht, Wolfgang Venzmer, and Eberhard Hölscher, *Hermann Bahlsen.* Hannover, 1969.

Verhandlungen, Mittheilungen und Berichte des Centralverbandes deutscher Industrieller, vols. 29–131 (1884–1918).

"Verzeichnis des Vorstandes, des Großen Ausschußes des Bundes der Industriellen und der ihm angeschlossenen Körperschaften und Verbände." *Veröffentlichungen des Bundes der Industriellen,* vol. 3 (November, 1912), pp. 37–51.

Vierhaus, Rudolf, ed. *Das Tagebuch der Baronin Spitzemberg, geb. Freiin von Varnbüler. Aufzeichnungen aus der Hofgesellschaft des Hohenzollernreiches*, 3rd ed. Göttingen, 1963.

40 Jahre Fabrikationsgeschichte der Firma Seidel und Naumann Dresden 1868–1908. Berlin, 1908. Out of the collection of the Dresden Municipal Archive.

Voelcker, H. *Geschichte der Familie Metzler und des Bankhauses B. Metzler seel. Sohn & Co. zu Frankfurt am Main 1674 bis 1924*. Frankfurt am Main, 1924.

Wachenheim, Hedwig. *Vom Großbürgertum zur Sozialdemokratie. Memoiren einer Reformistin*. Berlin, 1973.

Wätjen, Hans. *Weißes W im blauen Feld. Die bremische Reederei und Überseehandlung D.H. Wätjen & Co. 1821–1921*. Wolfsburg, 1983.

Wallich, Hermann. *Aus meinem Leben*. Private print, Berlin, 1929.

Wallich, Hildegard. *Erinnerungen aus meinem Leben*. Altenkirchen, 1970.

Wallich, Paul. "Lehr- und Wanderjahre eines Bankiers." *Zwei Generationen im deutschen Bankwesen 1833–1914*. Frankfurt am Main, 1978, pp. 159–426.

Walther, Heidrun. *Theodor Adolf von Möller 1840–1925. Lebensbild eines westfälischen Industriellen*. Neustadt an der Aisch, 1958.

Walther, Heidrun, ed. *Aus dem Leben von Theodor Adolf von Möller. Nach unvollendet hinterlassenen Aufzeichnungen über die Jahre 1840–1890*. Neustadt/Aisch, 1958.

Warburg, Max M. *Aus meinen Aufzeichnungen*. Private print, New York, 1952.

Weimarer historisch-genealoges Taschenbuch des gesamten Adels jehudäischen Ursprunges (Semi-Gotha). Weimar, 1912; 2nd ed. Munich, 1913.

Weisbach, Werner. *"Und alles ist zerstoben". Erinnerungen aus der Jahrhundertwende* (Vienna, Leipzig and Zurich, 1937).

Wenzel, Georg, ed. *Deutscher Wirtschaftsführer. Lebensgänge Deutscher Wirtschaftpersönlichkeiten* (Hamburg, Berlin, and Leipzig, 1929).

Wenzel-Burchard, Gertrud. *Granny. Gerta Warburg und die Ihren. Hamburger Schicksale*. Hamburg, 1975.

Wessel, Horst A. "Die Unternehmerfamilie Felten & Guilleaume." *Rheinisch-Westfälische Wirtschaftsbiographien*. Münster, Westphalia, 1986, vol. 13, pp. 3–112.

Westphal, Eberhard, *Ein ostdeutscher Industriepionier. Ferdinand Schichau in seinem Leben und Schaffen*. Essen, 1957.

Wiener Genealogisches Taschenbuch. Vienna, 1935–36, vol. 7.

Wilden, Josef. "Heinrich Ehrhardt." *Rheinisch-Westfälische Wirtschaftsbiographien*. 1941; reprint Münster, Westphalia, 1974, vol. 4, pp. 172–86.

Wilmin, Henri. *Die Familie Adt und ihre Industriebetriebe. Die Familie Adt in Forbach*, trans. Axel Polleti. Bad Orb, 1979.

Winschuh, Josef. "Der alte Thyssen." *Die heitere Maske im ernsten Spiel. Eine Freundesgabe für Volkmar Muthesius. Zum 19. März, 1960.* Frankfurt am Main, 1960, pp. 107–15.

Wolff, Emil, ed. *Zur Geschichte des Bierbrauergewerbes in Frankfurt am Main vom Jahr 1288 bis 1904. Aus Anlaß des X. Deutschen Brauertages in Frankfurt am Main, 1904.* Nürnberg, 1904.

Wolff, Heinz. "Hellmut Girardet, 1902–1973." *Wuppertaler Biographien*, vol. 12 (1974), pp. 22–27.

Wolff-Arndt, Philippine. *Wir Frauen von einst. Erinnerungen einer Malerin.* Munich, 1929.

Zielenziger, Kurt. *Juden in der deutschen Wirtschaft.* Berlin, 1930.

Zobeltitz, Fedor von. *Chronik der Gesellschaft unter dem letzten Kaiserreich.* Hamburg, 1922. 2 vols.

Zum Heimgang von Hugo Stinnes. Berlin, 1924.

Zypen, Ferdinand van der. *Um die Erde. Reisebriefe und Aufzeichnungen.* Private print, Cologne, 1898.

IV. Secondary Literature

Adelmann, Gerhard. "Führende Unternehmer im Rheinland und Westfalen 1850–1914." *Rheinische Vierteljahrsblätter*, vol. 35 (1971), pp. 335–52.

Adelmann, Gerhard. "Die wirtschaftlichen Führungsschichten der rheinisch-westfälischen Baumwoll- und Leinenindustrie von 1850 bis zum Ersten Weltkrieg." *Führungskräfte der Wirtschaft im neunzehnten Jahrhundert. 1790–1914. Büdinger Vorträge 1969–1970, T. II.*, ed. Herbert Helbig. Limburg an der Lahn, 1977, pp. 177–99.

Allen, Ann Taylor, *Feminism and Motherhood in Germany, 1800–1914.* New Brunswick, 1991.

Angress, Werner T. "Prussia's Army and the Jewish Reserve Officer Controversy before World War I." *Leo Baeck Institute Year Book*, vol. 17 (1972), pp. 19–42.

Ariès, Philipppe. *L'Enfant et la vie familiale sous l'ancien régime.* Paris, 1960.

Augustine, Dolores L. "Arriving in the upper class: the wealthy business elite of Wilhelmine Germany." *The German Bourgeoisie*, eds. David Blackbourn and Richard J. Evans. London, 1991, pp. 46–86.

Augustine, Dolores L. "The Banker in German Society." *Finance and Financiers in European History, 1880–1960*, ed. Youssef Cassis. London, 1991, pp. 161–185.

Augustine, Dolores L. "The Business Elites of Hamburg and Berlin." *Central European History*, vol. 24 (1991), pp. 132–46.

Augustine, Dolores L. "Die soziale Stellung jüdischer Unternehmer am Beispiel Berlin." *Jüdische Unternehmer in Deutschland im 19. und 20.*

Jahrhundert, eds. Werner E. Mosse and Hans Pohl, 64th special publication of *Zeitschrift für Unternehmensgeschichte*.

Augustine, Dolores L. "Very Wealthy Businessmen in Imperial Germany." *Journal of Social History*, vol. 22 (1988), pp. 299–321.

Augustine, Dolores L. *Die Wilhelminische Wirtschaftselite. Sozialverhalten, soziales Selbstbewußtsein und Familie*. Dr. phil. dissertation, Free University of Berlin, 1991.

Bald, Detlef. *Der Deutsche Offizier. Sozial- und Bildungsgeschichte des deutschen Offizierkorps im 20. Jahrhundert*, Munich, 1982.

Bald, Detlef. "Die Revolution von 1848 und ihre Auswirkungen auf Bildungssystem und Sozialstruktur der preußischen Armee." *Acta*, vol. 11 (1988). (according to author)

Bald, Detlef. *Vom Kaiserheer zur Bundeswehr. Sozialstruktur des Militärs: Politik der Rekrutierung von Offizieren und Unteroffizieren*. Frankfurt am Main and Bern, 1981.

Banks, Joseph Ambrose. *Prosperity and Parenthood: A Study of Family Planning among the Victorian Middle Classes*. London, 1954.

Banks, Joseph Ambrose. *Victorian Values: Secularism and the Size of Families*. London, Boston, and Henley, 1981.

Barkai, Avraham. *Jüdische Minderheit und Industrialisierung. Demographie, Berufe und Einkommen der Juden in Westdeutschland 1850–1914*. Tübingen, 1988.

Bauer, Franz J. *Bürgerwege und Bürgerwelten. Familienbiographische Untersuchungen zum deutschen Bürgertum im 19. Jh.* Göttingen, 1991.

Behrend, Hans-Karl. "Zur Personalpolitik des preußischen Ministeriums des Innern. Die Besetzung der Landratsstellen in den östlichen Provinzen 1919–1933." *Jahrbuch für die Geschichte Mittel- und Ostdeutschlands*, vol. 6 (1957), pp. 173–214.

Bentmann, Reinhard and Michael Müller. *Die Villa als Herrschaftsarchitektur. Versuch einer kunst- und sozialgeschichtlichen Analyse*. Frankfurt am Main, 1970.

Bergeron, Louis. "Familienstruktur und Industrieunternehmen in Frankreich (18. bis 20. Jahrhundert)." *Familie zwischen Tradition und Moderne. Studien zur Geschichte der Familie in Deutschland und Frankreich vom 16. bis zum 20. Jahrhundert*, eds. Neithard Bulst, Joseph Goy, and Jochen Hoock. Göttingen 1981, pp. 225–38.

Berghahn, Marion, *Continental Britons: German-Jewish Refugees from Nazi Germany*. 1984; reprint Oxford, Hamburg, and New York, 1988.

Bergius, Burkhard and Julius Posener. "Die Listen der individuell geplanten Einfamilienhäuser 1896–1918." *Berlin und seine Bauten*. Berlin, Munich, and Düsseldorf, 1970, part 4, vol. C, pp. 47–172.

Berlin und seine Bauten. Berlin 1896, vols. 2 and 3.

Berndt, Helga. "Die höheren Beamten des Ministeriums für Handel und Gewerbe in Preußen 1871 bis 1932. Eine Analyse und Dokumentation zu ihrer sozialen Zusammensetzung und Verflechtung." *Jahrbuch für Wirtschaftsgeschichte.* 1981/II, pp. 105–200.

Beutin, Ludwig. "Das Bürgertum als Gesellschaftsstand im 19. Jahrhundert." *Blätter für deutsche Landesgeschichte,* vol. 90 (1953), pp. 132–65.

Blackbourn, David and Geoff Eley. *The Peculiarities of German History.* Oxford and New York, 1984.

Blackbourn, David and Richard J. Evans. *The Germany Bourgeoisie.* London and New York, 1991.

Blosser, Ursi and Franziska Gerster. *Töchter der guten Gesellschaft. Frauenrolle und Mädchenerziehung im schweizerischen Großbürgertum um 1900.* Zurich 1985.

Bock, Gisela. "Geschichte, Frauengeschichte, Geschlechtergeschichte." *Geschichte und Gesellschaft,* vol. 14 (1988), pp. 364–91.

Böhme, Helmut. *Deutschlands Weg zur Großmacht. Studien zum Verhältnis von Wirtschaft und Staat während der Reichsgründungszeit 1848–1881.* Cologne and Berlin 1966.

Born, Karl Erich. "Der soziale und wirtschaftliche Strukturwandel Deutschlands am Ende des 19. Jahrhunderts." *Moderne deutsche Sozialgeschichte,* ed. Hans-Ulrich Wehler, 5th ed. 1977; reprint Königstein and Düsseldorf, 1981, pp. 271–84.

Born, Karl Erich. *Von der Reichsgründung bis zum Ersten Weltkrieg,* 5th ed. 1970; paperback Stuttgart, 1980.

Borscheid, Peter. "Geld und Liebe. Zu den Auswirkungen des Romantischen auf die Partnerwahl im 19. Jahrhundert." *Ehe, Liebe, Tod. Zum Wandel der Familie, der Geschlechts- und Generationsbeziehungen in der Neuzeit,* eds. Peter Borscheid and Hans J. Teuteberg. Münster, 1983, pp. 112–34.

Bourdieu, Pierre. *La distinction. Critique sociale du jugement.* Paris, 1979. German: *Die feinen Unterschiede. Kritik der gesellschaftlichen Urteilskraft,* trans. Bernd Schwibs and Achim Russer, 2nd ed. Frankfurt am Main, 1988.

Bramsted, E.K. *Aristocracy and Middle Classes in Germany. Social Types in German Literature 1830–1900.* Chicago and London, 1964.

Branca, Patricia. *Silent Sisterhood. Middle Class Women in the Victorian Home.* Pittsburgh, 1975.

Branca, Patricia. *Women in Europe since 1750.* New York, 1978.

Brandes, Erika. "Der Bremer Überseekaufmann in seiner gesellschaftsgeschichtlichen Bedeutung im 'geschlossenen Heiratskreis.'" *Genealogisches Jahrbuch,* vol. 3 (1963), pp. 25–52.

Braun, Rudolf. "Zur Einwirkung sozio-kultureller Umweltbedingungen auf das Unternehmerpotential und das Unternehmerverhalten." *Wirtschafts- und sozialgeschichtliche Probleme der frühen Industrialisierung,* Wolfram Fischer, ed. Berlin, 1968, pp. 247–84.

Breckman, Warren G., "Disciplining Consumption: The Debate about

Luxury in Wilhelmine Germany, 1890–1914." *Journal of Social History*, vol. 24 (1991), pp. 485–505.

Brinckmeyer, Hermann. *Hugo Stinnes*, 5th ed. Munich, 1921.

Brönner, Wolfgang. *Die bürgerliche Villa in Deutschland 1830–1890. Unter besonderer Berücksichtigung des Rheinlandes.* Düsseldorf, 1987.

Bruch, E. "Wohnungsnot und Hülfe." *Berlin und seine Entwicklung, Jahrbuch für Volkswirthschaft und Statistik*, vol. 6 (1872), pp. 50f.

Brüggemeier, Franz-Josef. "Der deutsche Sonderweg." *Bürgerliche Gesellschaft in Deutschland.* Frankfurt am Main, 1990, pp. 244–249.

Cassis, Youssef. *Les banquiers de la City à l'époque édouardienne, 1890–1914.* Geneva, 1984.

Cassis, Youssef. "Wirtschaftelite und Bürgertum. England, Frankreich und Deutschland um 1900." *Bürgertum im 19. Jahrhundert. Deutchland im internationalen Vergleich*, ed. Jürgen Kocka. Munich, 1988, vol. 2, pp. 9–34.

Castell, Countess zu. "Forschungsergebnisse zum gruppenspezifischen Wandel generativer Strukturen." *Sozialgeschichte der Familie in der Neuzeit Europas*, ed. Werner Conze. Stuttgart, 1976, pp. 161–72.

Cecil, Lamar A. "The Creation of Nobles in Prussia, 1871–1918." *American Historical Review*, vol. 75 (1970), pp. 757–95.

Cecil, Lamar A. *The German Diplomatic Service, 1871–1914.* Princeton, 1976.

Cecil, Lamar A. "Jew and Junker in Imperial Berlin." *Leo Baeck Institute Year Book*, vol. 20 (1975), pp. 47–58.

Chandler, A.D. and H. Daems. "Introduction." *The Rise of Managerial Capitalism*, eds. H. Daems and H. van der Wee. The Hague, 1974, pp. 1–34.

Claessens, Dieter und Karin. *Kapitalismus als Kultur. Entstehung und Grundlagen der bürgerlichen Gesellschaft.* Düsseldorf and Cologne, 1973.

Conze, Werner and Jürgen Kocka, eds. *Bildungsbürgertum im 19. Jahrhundert.* Stuttgart 1985, vol. 1: *Bildungssystem und Professionalisierung im internationalen Vergleich.*

Craig, John E. "Higher Education and Social Mobility in Germany." *The Transformation of Higher Learning 1860–1930*, ed. Konrad H. Jarausch. Stuttgart 1983, pp. 219–44.

Crew, David F. *Town in the Ruhr. A Social History of Bochum, 1860–1914.* New York, 1979.

Croon, Helmut. "Die wirtschaftliche Führungsschicht des Ruhrgebietes, 1850–1914." *Führungskräfte der Wirtschaft im neunzehnten Jahrhundert. 1790–1914. Büdinger Vorträge 1969–1970, T. II.*, ed. Herbert Helbig. Limburg an der Lahn, 1977, pp. 201–34.

Dahrendorf, Ralf. *Gesellschaft und Demokratie in Deutschland.* Munich, 1965.

Dammer, Susanna. *Mütterlichkeit und Frauendienstpflicht.* Weinheim, 1988.

Davidoff, Leonore. *The Best Circles. Women and Society in Victorian England.* Ottowa, 1973.

Davidoff, Leonore and Catherine Hall. *Family Fortunes: Men and Women of the English Middle Class, 1780–1850.* Chicago, 1987.

Demeter, Karl. *Das deutsche Offizierkorps in Gesellschaft und Staat 1650–1945,* 2nd ed. Frankfurt am Main, 1962.

Dietrich, Richard. "Die wirtschaftlichen Führungsschichten in Mitteldeutschland von 1850 bis zum Ersten Weltkrieg." *Führungskräfte der Wirtschaft im neunzehnten Jahrhundert. 1790–1914. Büdinger Vorträge 1969–1970, T. II.,* ed. Hebert Helbig. Limburg an der Lahn, 1977, pp. 109–43.

Doerry, Martin. *Übergangsmenschen. Die Mentalität der Wilhelminer und die Krise des Kaiserreichs.* Weinheim and Munich, 1986.

Eicke, Dagmar-Renate. *"Teenager" zu Kaisers Zeiten. Die "höhere" Tochter in Gesellschaft, Anstands- und Mädchenbüchern zwischen 1860 und 1900.* Marburg, 1980.

Elias, Norbert. *Über den Prozeß der Zivilisation,* 2nd ed. 2 vols. Bern and Munich, 1969.

Endres, Franz Carl. "Soziologische Struktur und ihr entsprechende Ideologien des deutschen Offizierkorps vor dem Weltkriege." *Archiv für Sozialwissenschaft und Sozialpolitik,* vol. 58 (1927), pp. 282–319.

Eulenburg, Franz. "Die Aufsichtsräte der deutschen Aktiengesellschaften." *Jahrbücher für Nationalökonomie und Statistik,* vol. 32 (1906), pp. 93–109.

Evans, Richard J. *Death in Hamburg. Society and Politics in the Cholera Years 1830–1910.* Oxford, 1987.

Faber, Karl-Georg. "Realpolitik als Ideologie: Die Bedeutung des Jahres 1866 für das politische Denken in Deutschland." *Historische Zeitschrift,* vol. 203 (1966), pp. 1–45.

Faulenbach, Bernd. "Die Herren an der Ruhr. Zum Typus des Unternehmers in der Schwerindustrie." *"Die Menschen machen ihre Geschichte nicht aus freien Stücken, aber sie machen sie selbst",* eds. Lutz Niethammer, Bodo Hombach, Tilman Fichter, Ulrich Borsdorf. Berlin and Bonn, 1984, pp. 76–88.

Faulenbach, Bernd. *Die Preußischen Bergassessoren im Ruhrbergbau. Mentalitäten und Lebensverhältnissen. Beispiele aus der Sozialgeschichte der Neuzeit. Rudolf Vierhaus zum 60. Geburtstag.* Göttingen, 1982, pp. 225–42.

Fenske, Hans. *Der liberale Südwesten. Freiheitliche und demokratische Traditionen in Baden und Württemberg 1790–1933.* Stuttgart, 1981.

Fischer, Wolfram. *Handbuch der europäischen Wirtschafts- und Sozialgeschichte.* Stuttgart, 1985, vol. 5.

Fischer, Wolfram. *Unternehmerschaft, Selbstverwaltung und Staat. Die Handelskammern in der deutschen Wirtschafts- und Staatsverfassung des 19. Jahrhunderts.* Berlin, 1964.

Fontane, Theodor. *Frau Jenny Treibel.* 1893; edition Munich, 1974.

Frevert, Ute. "Bewegung und Disziplin in der Frauengeschichte. Ein Forschungsbericht." *Geschichte und Gesellschaft,* vol. 14 (1988), pp. 240–62.

Frevert, Ute. "Bourgeois honour: middle-class duellists in Germany from the late eighteenth to the early twentieth century." *The German Bourgeoisie,* eds. David Blackbourn and Richard J. Evans. London and New York, 1991, pp. 255–92.

Frevert, Ute. "Bürgerliche Familie und Geschlechterrollen: Modell und Wirklichkeit." *Bürgerliche Gesellschaft in Deutschland.* Frankfurt am Main, 1990, pp. 90–100.

Frevert, Ute. *Ehrenmänner. Das Duell in der bürgerlichen Gesellschaft.* Munich, 1991.

Frevert, Ute. *Frauen-Geschichte. Zwischen Bürgerlicher Verbesserung und Neuer Weiblichkeit.* Frankfurt am Main, 1986.

Frevert, Ute, "Literaturbericht: Bürgertumsgeschichte als Familiengeschichte." *Geschichte und Gesellschaft,* vol. 16 (1990), pp. 491–501.

Frevert, Ute, *Women in German History: From Bourgeois Emancipation to Sexual Liberation.* Oxford and New York, 1989.

Fridenson, Patrick. "Herrschaft im Wirtschaftsunternehmen. Deutschland und Frankreich 1880–1914." *Bürgertum im 19. Jahrhundert. Deutchland im internationalen Vergleich,* ed. Jürgen Kocka. Munich, 1988, vol. 2, pp. 65–91.

Friedegg, Ernst. *Millionen und Millionäre. Wie die Riesen-Vermögen entstehen.* Berlin, 1914.

Fromm, Erich, *The Art of Loving.* New York, 1956.

Fuchs, Konrad. "Wirtschaftliche Führungskräfte in Schlesien 1850–1914." Konrad Fuchs, *Wirtschaftsgeschichte Oberschlesiens, 1871–1945. Aufsätze.* Dortmund, 1981, pp. 92–117.

Gall, Lothar. *Bürgerliche Gesellschaft in Deutschland.* Frankfurt am Main, 1990.

Gall, Lothar. "Die Stadt der bürgerlichen Gesellschaft – das Beispiel Mannheim." *Forschungen zur Stadtgeschichte. Drei Vorträge.* Opladen, 1986, pp. 55–71.

Gall, Lothar, *Stadt und Bürgertum im 19. Jh.* Munich, 1990.

Gay, Peter. *The Bourgeois Experience. Victoria to Freud.* New York and Oxford, 1984 and 1986, vol. 1: *Education of the Senses;* vol. 2: *The Tender Passion.*

Gay, Peter. *Freud, Jews and Other Germans. Masters and Victims in Modernist Culture.* New York, 1978.

Geeb, Hans Karl, Heinz Kirchner, Hermann, and Wilhelm Thiemann.

Deutsche Orden und Ehrenzeichen, 4th ed. Cologne, Berlin, Bonn, and Munich, 1985.

Gensel, Julius. *Der deutsche Handelstag in seiner Entwicklung und Tätigkeit 1861–1901*. Berlin, 1902.

Gerhard, Ute. *Verhältnisse und Verhinderungen. Frauenarbeit, Familie und Rechte der Frauen im 19. Jh.* Frankfurt am Main, 1978.

Gerlach, Otto. *Die preußische Steuerreform in Staat und Gemeinde*. Jena, 1893.

Giddens, Anthony. *The Class Structure of the Advanced Societies*. New York, 1973.

Gillis, John R. *Youth and History. Tradition and Change in European Age Relations, 1770 – Present*. Expanded revised ed., New York, etc., 1981.

Gläser, Helga. "Die Villenkolonie als kulturelles Zentrum." *100 Jahre Villenkolonie Grunewald 1889–1989*. Berlin, 1988, pp. 63–93.

Goetz, Rainer B. "Das Schloß." *Industriekultur in Nürnberg. Eine deutsche Stadt im Maschinenzeitalter*, eds. Hermann Glaser, Wolfgang Ruppert, and Norbert Neudecker. Munich, 1980, pp. 89–90.

Goodman, Katherine, *Dis/Closures: Women's Autobiography in Germany between 1790 and 1914*. New York, 1986.

Goody, Jack. "Bridewealth and Dowry in Africa and Eurasia." *Bridewealth and Dowry*, eds. Jack Goody and S.J. Tambiah. Cambridge, 1973, pp. 1–58.

Grebig, Helga. *Der "deutsche Sonderweg" in Europa 1806–1945. Eine Kritik*. Stuttgart, 1986.

Grundmann, Günther. "Schlösser und Villen des 19. Jahrhunderts von Unternehmern in Schlesien." *Tradition* 10. Jg. (1965), pp. 149–62.

Günter, Roland and Janne Günter. *Das unbekannte Oberhausen*. Wuppertal, 1983.

Haas, Rudolf. *Die Pfalz am Rhein. 2000 Jahre Landes-, Kultur- und Wirtschaftsgeschichte*. Mannheim, 1967.

Haltern, Utz. *Bürgerliche Gesellschaft. Sozialtheoretische und sozialhistorische Aspekte*. Darmstadt, 1985.

Hamburg und seine Bauten. unter Berücksichtigung der Nachbarstädte Altona und Wandsbek. 1914. Hamburg, 1914, vol. 1.

Hammerbacher, Herta. "Die Hausgärten." *Berlin und seine Bauten*. Berlin, Munich, and Düsseldorf, 1970, part 4, vol. C, pp. 293–398.

Handke, Horst. "Einige Probleme der Sozialstruktur im imperialistischen Deutschland von 1914." *Jahrbuch für Geschichte*, vol. 15 (1977), pp. 261–88.

Handke, Horst. "Soziale Annäherung und Verbindung von Adel und Bürgertum am Ende des 19. Jahrhundert. Ein Beitrag zur Herausbildung der Monopolbourgeoisie." Unpublished ms., Berlin (G.D.R.), 1987.

Haupt, Heinz-Gerhard, "Männliche und weibliche Berufskarrieren im deutsche Bürgertum in der zweiten Hälfte des 19. Jahrhunderts: Zum

Verhältnis von Klasse und Geschlecht." *Geschichte und Gesellschaft*, vol. 18, 1992, pp. 143–60.

Hauschild-Thiessen, Renate. *Bürgerstolz und Kaisertreue. Hamburg und das Deutsche Reich von 1871.* Hamburg, 1979.

Hausen, Karin, "Family and Role Division: The Polarisation of Sexual Stereotypes in the Nineteenth Century: An Aspect of the Dissociation of Work and Family Life," *The German Family*, eds. Richard J. Evans and W.R. Lee. London, 1981.

Hausen, Karin. "Die Polarisierung der 'Geschlechtscharaktere' – Eine Spiegelung der Dissoziation von Erwerbs- und Familienleben." *Sozialgeschichte der Familie in der Neuzeit Europas*, ed. Werner Conze. Stuttgart, 1976, pp. 363–93.

Hayes, Peter. "Industrial Factionalism in Modern German History." *Central European History*, vol. 24 (1991), pp. 122–131.

Heckel, Max von. "Vermögenssteuer." *Handwörterbuch der Staatswissenschaften*, 3rd ed., eds. J. Conrad, W. Lexis, L. Elster, E. Leoning. Jena, 1911, pp. 262–70.

Hellige, Hans Dieter. "Generationskonflikt, Selbsthaß und die Entstehung antikapitalistischer Positionen im Judentum. Der Einfluß des Antisemitismus auf das Sozialverhalten jüdischer Kaufmanns- und Unternehmersöhne im Deutschen Kaiserreich und in der K.u.K.-Monarchie." *Geschichte und Gesellschaft*, vol. 5 (1979), pp. 476–518.

Henning, Hansjoachim. "Soziale Verflechtung der Unternehmer in Westfalen 1860–1914." *Zeitschrift für Unternehmergeschichte*, vol. (1978), pp. 1–30.

Henning, Hansjoachim. *Sozialgeschichtliche Entwicklungen in Deutschland von 1815 bis 1860.* Paderborn, 1977.

Henning, Hansjoachim. *Das westdeutsche Bürgertum in der Epoche der Hochindustrialisierung 1860–1914. Soziales Verhalten und Soziale Strukturen.* Wiesbaden, 1972, vol. 1: *Das Bildungsbürgertum in den preußischen Westprovinzen.*

Herrmann, Ulrich. "Jugend in der Sozialgeschichte." *Sozialgeschichte in Deutschland. Entwicklungen und Perspektiven in internationalem Zusammenhang*, eds. Wolfgang Schieder and Volker Sellin. Göttingen, 1987, Bd. 4: *Soziale Gruppen in der Geschichte*, pp. 133–55.

Hertz, Deborah. *Jewish High Society in Old Regime Berlin.* New Haven and London, 1988.

Herwig, Holger H. *The German Naval Officer Corps. A Social and Political History 1890–1918.* Oxford, 1973.

Herzig, Arno. "Juden und Judentum in der sozialgeschichtlichen Forschung." *Sozialgeschichte in Deutschland. Entwicklungen und Perspektiven im internationalen Zusammenhang*, eds. Wolfgang Schieder and Volker Sellin, Göttingen, 1987, vol. 4: *Soziale Gruppen in der Geschichte*, pp. 108–132.

Hesselmann, Hans. *Das Wirtschaftsbürgertum in Bayern 1890–1914. Ein Beitrag zur Analyse der Wechselbeziehungen zwischen Wirtschaft und Politik am Beispiel des Wirtschaftsbürgertums in Bayern der Prinzregentenzeit.* Wiesbaden, 1985.

Hofmann, Hanns Hubert. *Adelige Herrschaft und Souveräner Staat. Studien über Staat und Gesellschaft in Franken und Bayern im 18. und 19. Jahrhundert.* Munich, 1962.

Hofmeister, Burkhard. "Wilhelminischer Ring und Villenkoloniengründung. Sozioökonomische und planerische Hintergründe simultaner städtebaulicher Prozesse im Großraum Berlin 1860 bis 1920." *Innerstädtische Differenzierungen und Prozesse im 19. und 20. Jahrhundert,* ed. Heinz Heineberg. Vienna, 1987, pp. 105–17.

Hübler, Hans. *Das Bürgerhaus in Lübeck.* Tübingen, 1968.

Huerkamp, Claudia. "Frauen, Universitäten und Bildungsbürgertum. Zur Lage studierender Frauen 1900–1930." *Bürgerliche Berufe. Zur Sozialgeschichte der freien und akademischen Berufe im internationalen Vergleich,* ed. Hannes Siegrist. Göttingen, 1988, pp. 200–22.

Hughes, Daniel J. "The Occupational Origins of Prussia's Generals 1872–1914." *Central European History,* vol. 13 (1980), pp. 3–33.

Hull, Isabel V. *The Entourage of Kaiser Wilhelm II, 1888–1918.* Cambridge, etc., 1982.

Izenberg, Gerald N. "Die 'Aristokratisierung' der bürgerlichen Kultur im 19. Jahrhundert." *Legitimationskrisen des deutschen Adels 1200–1900,* eds. Peter Uwe Hohendahl and Paul Michael Lützeler. Stuttgart, 1979, pp. 233–44.

Jacobi-Dittrich, Juliane. "Growing Up Female in the Nineteenth Century." *German Women in the Nineteenth Century. A Social History,* ed. John C. Fout. New York and London, 1984, pp. 197–217.

Jaeger, Hans. *Unternehmer in der deutschen Politik (1890–1918).* Bonn, 1967.

Jaide, Walter, *Generationen eines Jahrhunderts: Wechsel der Jugendgenerationen im Jahrhunderttrend: Zur Sozialgeschichte der Jugend in Deutschland, 1871–1985.* Opladen, 1988.

Jarausch, Konrad H. "Students, Sex and Politics in Imperial Germany." *Journal of Central European History,* vol. 17 (1982), pp. 285–303.

Jarausch, Konrad H. *Students, Society and Politics in Imperial Germany. The Rise of Academic Illiberalism.* Princeton, 1982.

Jarausch, Konrad H. *The Unfree Professions: German Lawyers, Teachers, and Engineers, 1900–1950.* New York, 1990.

Jarausch, Konrad H., ed. *The Transformation of Higher Learning, 1860–1930: Expansion, Diversification, Social Opening and Professionalization in England, Germany, Russia, and the United States.* Chicago, 1983.

Jarausch, Konrad H. and Geoffrey Cocks. *German Professions, 1800–1950.* New York, 1990.

John, Hartmut. *Das Reserveoffizierkorps im deutschen Kaiserreich 1890–1914. Ein sozialgeschichtlicher Beitrag zur Untersuchung der gesellschaftlichen Militarisierung im wilhelminischen Deutschland.* Frankfurt am Main and New York, 1981.

Kaelble, Hartmut. "Das aristokratiche Modell im deutschen Bürgertum des 19. Jahrhunderts: Ein europäischer Vergleich." Unpublished ms., Bielefeld, 1987.

Kaelble, Hartmut. *Berliner Unternehmer während der frühen Industrialisierung. Herkunft, sozialer Status und politischer Einfluß.* Berlin and New York, 1972.

Kaelble, Hartmut. "Französisches und deutsches Bürgertum 1870–1914." *Bürgertum im 19. Jahrhundert. Deutchland im internationalen Vergleich*, ed. Jürgen Kocka. Munich, 1988, vol. 1, pp. 107–40.

Kaelble, Hartmut. *Historische Mobilitätsforschung. Westeuropa und die USA im 19. und 20. Jahrhundert.* Darmstadt, 1978.

Kaelble, Hartmut. *Industrielle Interessenpolitik in der Wilhelminischen Gesellschaft. Centralverband Deutscher Industriellen. 1895–1914.* Berlin, 1967.

Kaelble, Hartmut. "Industrielle Interessenverbände vor 1914." *Zu soziologischen Theorie und Analyse des 19. Jahrhunderts*, eds. Walter Rüegg and Otto Neuloh. Göttingen, 1971, pp. 180–92.

Kaelble, Hartmut. "Long-Term Changes in the Recruitment of the Business Elite: Germany Compared to the U.S., Great Britain, and France since the Industrial Revolution." *Journal of Social History*, vol. 13/3 (1980), pp. 404–23.

Kaelble, Hartmut, *Nachbarn am Rhein. Entfremdung und Annäherung der französischen und deutschen Gesellschaft seit 1880.* Munich, 1991.

Kaelble, Hartmut. "Soziale Mobilität in Deutschland 1900–1960." *Probleme der Modernisierung in Deutschland*, eds. Hartmut Kaelble et al. Opladen, 1978, pp. 235–327.

Kaelble, Hartmut. *Social Mobility in the 19th and 20th Centuries: Europe and America in Comparative Perspective.* New York, 1986.

Kaelble, Hartmut. "Sozialer Aufstieg in Deutschland 1850–1914." *Vierteljahrschrift für Sozial- und Wirtschaftsgeschichte*, vol. 60 (1973), pp. 41–71.

Kaelble, Hartmut (assisted by Hasso Spode), "Sozialstruktur und Lebensweisen deutscher Unternehmer 1907–1927." *Scripta Mercaturae*, vol. 24 (1990), pp. 132–79.

Kaelble, Hartmut. "Wie feudal waren die deutschen Unternehmer im Kaiserreich? Ein Zwischenbericht." *Beiträge zur quantitativen vergleichenden Unternehmergeschichte*, ed. Richard Tilly. Stuttgart, 1985, pp. 148–71.

Kaplan, Marion A. "For Love or Money. The Marriage Strategies of Jews in Imperial Germany." *Leo Baeck Institute Year Book*, vol. 28 (1983), pp. 263–300.

Kaplan, Marion A. *The Making of the Jewish Middle Class. Women, Family, and Identity in Imperial Germany.* New York and Oxford, 1991.

Kaplan, Marion A. *The Marriage Bargain. Women and Dowries in European History.* New York, 1985.

Kaplan, Marion A. "Tradition and Transition. The Acculturation, Assimilation and Integration of Jews in Imperial German. A Gender Analysis." *Leo Baeck Institute Year Book*, vol. 27(1982), pp. 3–35.

Kaudelka-Hanisch, Karin. "Bielefelder Kommerzienräte. Wirtschaftliche Macht, Politischer Einfluss und Soziales Ansehen." *79. Jahresbericht des Historischen Vereins für die Grafschaft Ravensberg*, vol. 79 (1991), pp. 211–55.

Kaudelka-Hanisch, Karin. "Preußische Kommerzienräte in der Provinz Westfalen und im Regierungsbezirk Düsseldorf (1810–1918)." Dr. phil. dissertation, University of Bielefeld, 1989.

Kaudelka-Hanisch, Karin. "The titled businessman: Prussian Commercial Councillors in the Rhineland and Westphalia during the nineteenth century." *The German Bourgeoisie*, eds. David Blackbourn and Richard J. Evans. London and New York, 1991, pp. 87–114.

Kehr, Eckart. *Economic Interest, Militarism, and Foreign Policy: Essays on German History*, ed. Gordon A. Craig, trans. Grete Heinz. Berkeley, 1977.

Kehr, Eckart. "Das soziale System der Reaktion in Preußen unter dem Ministerium Puttkamer." *Die Gesellschaft*, vol. 6 (1929), pp. 253–74.

Kehr, Eckart. "Zur Genesis des Kgl. Preußischen Reserveoffiziers." *Die Gesellschaft*, vol. 5 (1928), pp. 492–502.

Klée Gobert, Renata, ed. *Die Bau- und Kunstdenkmale der Freien und Hansestadt Hamburg.* Hamburg, 1959, vol. 2: *Altona, Elbvororte.*

Knodel, John E. *The Decline of Fertility in Germany, 1871–1939.* Princeton, 1974.

Kocka, Jürgen. "Bildung, soziale Schichtung und soziale Mobilität im Deutschen Kaiserreich. Am Beispiel der gewerblich-technischen Ausbildung." *Industrielle Gesellschaft und politisches System. Beiträge zur politischen Sozialgeschichte. Festschrift für Fritz Fischer zum siebzigsten Geburtstag*, eds. Dirk Stegmann, Bernd-Jürgen Wendt, and Peter-Christian Witt. Bonn, 1978, pp. 297–314.

Kocka, Jürgen. "Bürgertum und bürgerliche Gesellschaft im 19. Jh. Europäische Entwicklungen und deutsche Eigenarten." *Bürgertum im 19. Jh. Deutschland im europäischen Vergleich*, Jürgen Kocka, ed. Munich, 1988, vol. 1, pp. 11–76. (English ed.: Jürgen Kocka and Allan Mitchell, eds. *Bourgeois Society in 19th Century Europe.* New York and Oxford, 1992.)

Kocka, Jürgen. "Der 'deutsche Sonderweg' in der Diskussion." *German Studies Review*, vol. 5 (1982), pp. 365–79.

Kocka, Jürgen. "Einleitung." *Bürger und Bürgerlichkeit im 19. Jh.*, ed.

Jürgen Kocka. Göttingen, 1987, pp. 7–20.

Kocka, Jürgen. "Familie, Unternehmer und Kapitalismus. An Beispielen aus der frühen deutschen Industrialisierung." *Zeitschrift für Unternehmergeschichte*, vol. 24 (1979), pp. 99–135.

Kocka, Jürgen. "Family and Bureaucracy in German Industrial Management, 1850–1914: Siemens in Comparative Perspective." *Business History Review*, vol. 45 (1971), pp. 133–56.

Kocka, Jürgen. "Family and class formation. Intergenerational mobility and marriage patterns in nineteenth-century Westphalian towns." *Journal of Social History*, vol. 17 (1984), pp. 411–34.

Kocka, Jürgen. "German History before Hitler. The Debate about the German 'Sonderweg.'" *Journal of Contemporary History*, vol. 23 (1988), pp. 3–16.

Kocka, Jürgen. *Unternehmer in der deutschen Industrialisierung.* Göttingen, 1975.

Kocka, Jürgen and Hannes Siegrist. "Die Hundert größten deutschen Industrieunternehmen im späten 19. und frühen 20. Jahrhundert." *Recht und Entwicklung der Großunternehmen im 19. und frühen 20. Jahrhundert,* eds. Norbert Horn and Jürgen Kocka. Göttingen, 1979, pp. 55–112.

Köhne-Lindenlaub, Renate. "Private Kunstförderung im Kaiserreich am Beispiel Krupp." *Kunstpolitik und Kunstförderung im Kaiserreich. Kunst im Wandel der Sozial- und Wirtschaftsgeschichte,* eds. Ekkehard Mai, Hans Pohl, Stephan Waetzoldt. Berlin, 1982, pp. 55–82.

Kößler, Gottfried. *Mädchenkindheiten im 19. Jh.* Gießen, 1979.

Kohli, Martin. "Die Institutionalisierung des Lebenslauf. Historische Befunde und theoretische Argumente." *Kölner Zeitschrift für Soziologie und Sozialpsychologie*, vol. 37(1985), pp. 1–29.

Kraul, Margret. *Das deutsche Gymnasium. 1780–1980.* Frankfurt am Main, 1984.

Küttler, Wolfgang and Gustav Seeber. "Forschungsprobleme der Geschichte des deutschen Bürgertums und der deutschen Bourgeoisie." *Zeitschrift für Geschichte*, vol. 28 (1980), pp. 203–22.

Kulemann, W. *Die Berufsvereine.* Jena, 1908. 3 vols.

Ladd, Brian, *Urban Planning and Civic Order in Germany, 1860–1914.* Cambridge, 1990.

Landes, David S. "The Jewish Merchant. Typology and Stereotypology in Germany." *Leo Baeck Institute Year Book*, vol. 19 (1974), pp. 11–30.

Leesch, Wolfgang. "Geschichte der Steuerverfassung und -verwaltung in Westfalen seit 1815." *Westfälische Zeitschrift*, vol. 131/132 (1981/1982), pp. 413–93; 133 (1983), pp. 233–336.

Lewis, Jane. *Women in England 1870–1950: Sexual Divisions and Social Change.* Brighton and Bloomington, 1984.

Ley, Andreas. *Die Villa als Burg.* Munich, 1981.

Lowenstein, Steven M., *The Mechanics of Change: Essays in the Social History of German Jewry*. Atlanta, 1992.

Lundgreen, Peter. "Bildung und Besitz – Einheit oder Inkongruenz in der europäischen Sozialgeschichte? Kritische Auseinandersetzung mit einer These von Fritz Ringer." *Geschichte und Gesellschaft*, vol. 7 (1981), pp. 262–75.

Lundgreen, Peter, Margret Kraul, and Karl Ditt. *Bildungschancen und soziale Mobilität in der städtischen Gesellschaft des 19. Jhs.* Göttingen, 1988.

McClelland, David C. *The Achieving Society*. Princeton, 1961.

Machtan, Lothar and Dietrich Milles. *Die Klassensymbiose von Junkertum und Bourgeoisie. Zum Verhältnis von gesellschaftlicher und politischer Herrschaft in Preußen-Deutschland 1850–1878*. Frankfurt am Main, Berlin, and Vienna, 1980.

Machule, Dittmar and Lutz Seiberlich. "Die Berliner Villenvororte." *Berlin und seine Bauten*. Berlin, Munich, Düsseldorf, 1970, part 4, vol. A, pp. 93–114.

Mann, Thomas. *Buddenbrooks*, trans. H.T. Lowe-Porter. New York, 1930.

Martin, G. *Die bürgerlichen Exzellenzen. Zur Sozialgeschichte der preußischen Generalität 1812–1918*. Düsseldorf, 1978.

Maruhn, Erwin. "Der Kölner Stadtteil Marienburg. Strukturwandel eines Villenvorortes von der Gründerzeit bis zur Gegenwart." *Jahrbuch des Kölnischen Geschichtsvereins*, vol. 52 (1981), pp. 131–90.

Mayer, Arno J. *The Persistence of the Old Regime. Europe to the Great War*. London, 1981.

Medick, Hans and David Sabean. "Emotionen und materielle Interessen in Familie und Verwandtschaft: Überlegungen zu neuen Wegen und Bereichen einer historischen und sozialanthropologischen Familienforschung." *Emotionen und materielle Interessen. Sozialanthropologische und historische Beiträge zur Familienforschung*, eds. Medick, Hans and David Sabean. Göttingen, 1984, pp. 27–54.

Mertes, Paul Hermann. "Zum Sozialprofil der Oberschicht im Ruhrgebiet. Dargestellt an den Dortmunder Kommerzienräten." *Beiträge zur Geschichte Dortmunds und der Grafschaft Mark*, vol. 67 (1971), pp. 165–226.

Meyer, Sibylle. *Das Theater mit der Hausarbeit: Bürgerliche Repräsentation in der Familie der wilhelminischen Zeit*. Frankfurt, 1982.

Meyer-Renschhausen, Elisabeth. *Weibliche Kultur und soziale Arbeit. Eine Geschichte der Frauenbewegung am Beispiel Bremens 1810–1927*. Cologne and Vienna, 1989.

Michels, Robert. *Umschichtungen in den herrschenden Klassen nach dem Kriege*. Stuttgart and Berlin, 1934.

Mielke, Siegfried. *Der Hansa-Bund für Gewerbe, Handel und Industrie. 1909–1914. Der gescheiterte Versuch einer antifeudalen Sammlungspolitik*. Göttingen, 1976.

Mitterauer, Michael. *Sozialgeschichte der Jugend*. Frankfurt am Main, 1986.

Mitterauer, Michael and R. Sieder. *Vom Patriarchat zur Partnerschaft. Zum Strukturwandel der Familie*. Munich, 1977.

Mosse, Werner. "Adel und Bürgertum im Europa des 19. Jahrhunderts. Eine vergleichende Betrachtung." *Bürgertum im 19. Jahrhundert. Deutschland im internationalen Vergleich*, ed. Jürgen Kocka. Munich, 1988, vol. 2, pp. 276–314.

Mosse, Werner. *The German-Jewish Economic Élite 1820–1935. A Sociocultural Profile*. Oxford, 1989.

Mosse, Werner. *Jews in the German Economy. The German-Jewish Economic Élite 1820–1935*. Oxford, 1987.

Mosse, Werner. "Wilhelm II and the Kaiserjuden. A Problematic Encounter." *The Jewish Response to German Culture: From the Enlightenment to the Second World War*, eds. Jehuda Reinharz and Walter Schutzberg. Hanover, N.H., 1985, pp. 164–94.

Mosse, Werner, ed. *Juden im Wilhelminischen Deutschland, 1890–1914*. Tübingen, 1976.

Mosse, Werner and Hans Pohl, *Jüdische Unternehmer in Deutschland im 19. und 20. Jahrhundert*. Special volume (*Beiheft*) 64 (1992) of *Zeitschrift für Unternehmensgeschichte*.

Mulert, O. *Kommunalfinanzen und Reichssteuerreform*. Berlin, 1925.

Muthesius, Hermann, ed. *Landhaus und Garten. Beispiele neuzeitlicher Landhäuser nebst Grundrissen, Innenräumen und Gärten*. 2nd ed. Munich, 1910.

Nagel, Thomas. "Grunewald: Von der Villenkolonie zum Ortsteil Wilmersdorf." *100 Jahre Villenkolonie Grunewald 1889–1989*. Berlin, 1988, pp. 36–62.

Nell, Adelheid von. "Die Entwicklung der generativen Strukturen bürgerlicher und bäuerlicher Familien von 1750 bis zur Gegenwart." Dr.phil. dissertation, University of Bochum, 1973.

Newby, Howard. "Paternalism and Capitalism." *Industrial Society. Class, Cleavage, and Control*, ed. Richard Scase. London, 1977, pp. 59–73.

Niemann, Hans-Werner. *Das Bild des industriellen Unternehmers in deutschen Romanen der Jahre 1890–1945*. Berlin, 1982.

Niethammer, Lutz et al. *Bürgerliche Gesellschaft in Deutschland: historische Einblicke, Fragen, Perspektiven*. Frankfurt, 1990.

Nipperdey, Thomas. "Verein als soziale Struktur in Deutschland im späten 18. und frühen 19. Jahrhundert. Eine Fallstudie zur Modernisierung." *Gesellschaft, Kultur, Theorie. Gesammelte Aufsätze zur neueren Geschichte*. Göttingen, 1976, pp. 174–205.

Nitschke, Kurt. *Einkommen und Vermögen in Preußen und ihre Entwicklung seit Einführung der neuen Steuern mit Nutzanwendung auf die Theorie der Einkommensentwicklung*. Jena, 1902.

Nussbaum, Helga. *Unternehmer gegen Monopole. Über Struktur und*

Aktionen antimonopolistischer Gruppen zu Beginn des 20. Jahrhunderts.
Berlin (G.D.R.), 1966.

Oberhänsli, Silvia. *Die Glarner Unternehmer des 19. Jahrhunderts.* Zurich,
1982.

Paulsen, Andreas. "Das 'Gesetz der dritten Generation.' Erhaltung und
Untergang von Familienunternehmungen." *Der praktische Betriebswirt.
Die aktive betriebswirtschaftliche Zeitschrift*, vol. 21 (1941), pp.
271–80. [not obtainable]

Peikert, Ingrid. "Zur Geschichte der Kindheit im 18. und 19. Jh. Einige
Entwicklungstendenzen." *Die Familie in der Geschichte*, ed. Heinz
Reif. Göttingen, 1982, pp. 114–36.

Petersen, M. Jeanne. *Family, Love and Work in the Lives of Victorian
Gentlewomen.* Bloomington and Indianapolis, 1989.

Pierenkemper, Toni. "Entrepreneurs in Heavy Industry: Upper Silesia and
the Westphalian Ruhr Region, 1852 to 1913." *Business History Review*,
vol. 53 (1979), pp. 65–78.

Pierenkemper, Toni. *Die westfälischen Schwerindustriellen 1852–1913.
Soziale Struktur und unternehmerischer Erfolg.* Göttingen, 1979.

Pilbeam, Pamela M., *The Middle Classes in Europe, 1789–1914: France,
Germany, Italy and Russia.* Houndmills, Basingstoke, Hampshire,
1990.

Pope, Barbara Corrado. "Angels in the Devil's Workshop: Leisured and
Charitable Women in Nineteenth-Century England and France."
Becoming Visible. Women in European History, eds. Renate Bridenthal
and Claudia Koonz. Boston, etc., 1977, pp. 296–324.

Posener, Julius and Burkhard Bergius. "Individuell geplante Einfamilienhäuser 1896–1968." *Berlin und seine Bauten.* Berlin, Munich, and
Düsseldorf, 1975, part 4, vol. C, pp. 1–42.

Preston, David L. "The German Jews in Secular Education, University
Teaching and Science. A Preliminary Inquiry." *Jewish Social Studies*,
vol. 38 (1976), pp. 99–116.

Prinz, Arthur. *Juden im deutschen Wirtschaftsleben. Soziale und
wirtschaftliche Struktur im Wandel, 1850–1914.* Tübingen, 1984.

Prüfer, Walter. *Methodologie zur Erforschung des Unternehmertums.*
Dresden, 1934.

Pulzer, Peter, *Jews and the German State: The Political History of a
Minority, 1848–1933.* Oxford and Cambridge, Mass., 1992.

Pulzer, Peter. "Die jüdische Beteiligung an der Politik." *Juden im
Wilhelminischen Deutschland, 1890–1914*, eds. Werner E. Mosse and
Arnold Paucker. Tübingen, 1976, pp. 143–239.

Rang, B. "Zur Geschichte des dualistisches Denkens über Mann und Frau,"
Frauenmacht in der Geschichte, eds. J. Dallrott et al. Düsseldorf, 1986.

Redlich, Fritz. *Der Unternehmer. Wirtschafts- und sozialgeschichtliche
Studien.* Göttingen, 1964.

Reif, Heinz. "Adelsfamilie und soziale Plazierung im Münsterland

1770–1914." *Familie und soziale Plazierung. Studien zum Verhältnis von Familie, sozialer Mobilität und Heiratsverhalten an westfälischen Beispielen im späten 18. und 19. Jahrhundert*, ed. Jürgen Kocka. Opladen, 1980, pp. 67–127.

Reif, Heinz. *Westfälischer Adel 1770–1860. Vom Herrschaftsstand zur regionalen Elite.* Göttingen, 1979.

Richarz, Monika, ed. *Jüdisches Leben in Deutschland.* Stuttgart, 1979, vol. 2: *Selbstzeugnisse zur Sozialgeschichte im Kaiserreich.*

Richter, Wolfgang and Jürgen Zännker. *Der Bürgertraum vom Adelsschloß. Aristokratische Bauformen im 19. und 20. Jahrhundert.* Reinbek, 1988.

Ringer, Fritz K. "Bildung, Wirtschaft und Gesellschaft in Deutschland 1800–1960." *Geschichte und Gesellschaft*, vol. 6 (1980), pp. 5–35.

Ringer, Fritz K. *The Decline of the German Mandarins: The German Academic Community, 1890–1933.* Cambridge (Mass.), 1969.

Ringer, Fritz K. *Education and Society in Modern Europe.* Bloomington and London, 1979.

Robertson, Priscilla. *An Experience of Women. Pattern and Change in Nineteenth-Century Europe.* Philadelphia, 1982.

Rosenbaum, Heidi. *Formen der Familie. Untersuchungen zum Zusammenhang von Familienverhältnissen, Sozialstruktur und sozialem Wandel in der deutschen Gesellschaft des 19. Jahrhunderts.* Frankfurt am Main, 1982.

Rosenberg, Hans. *Große Depression und Bismarckzeit. Wirtschaftsablauf, Gesellschaft und Politik in Mitteleuropa.* Berlin, 1967.

Rosenberg, Hans. "Die Pseudodemokratisierung der Rittergutsbesitzerklasse." *Moderne deutsche Sozialgeschichte*, ed. Hans-Ulrich Wehler. 5th ed. 1977; reprint Königstein and Düsseldorf, 1981, pp. 287–308.

Rothenbacher, Franz. "Soziale Ungleichheit des Wohnens in Deutschland im späten 19. und frühen 20. Jahrhundert." Unpublished ms., April 1985.

Rubinstein, William David. *Men of Property. The Very Wealthy in Britain since the Industrial Revolution.* London, 1981.

Rubinstein, William David, ed. *Wealth and the Wealthy in the Modern World.* London, 1980.

Rudhard, Wolfgang. *Das Bürgerhaus in Hamburg.* Tübingen, 1975.

Rürup, Reinhard. *Emanzipation und Antisemitismus. Studien zur "Judenfrage" der bürgerlichen Gesellschaft.* Göttingen, 1975.

Rumschöttel, Hermann. *Das bayerische Offizierkorps 1866–1914.* Berlin, 1973.

Schärl, Walter. *Die Zusammensetzung der bayerischen Beamtenschaft von 1806 bis 1918.* Munich, 1955.

Schenk, Herrad. *Freie Liebe – wilde Ehe. Über die allmähliche Auflösung der Ehe durch die Liebe.* Munich, 1987.

Schmelz, Usiel O. "Die demographische Entwicklung der Juden in Deutschland von der Mitte des 19. Jahrhunderts bis 1933." *Zeitschrift für Bevölkerungswissenschaft*, vol. 1 (1982).

Schmidt, Hartwig. *Das Tiergartenviertel. Baugeschichte eines Berliner Villenviertels.* Berlin, 1981, part 1: *1790–1870.*

Schramm, Percy Ernst. *Hamburg, Deutschland und die Welt. Leistung und Grenzen hanseatischen Bürgertums in der Zeit zwischen Napoleon I. und Bismarck.* Munich, 1943.

Schüren, R. *Soziale Mobilität. Muster, Veränderungen und Bedingungen im 19. und 20. Jh.* St. Katharinen, 1989.

Schütze, Yvonne. "Mutterliebe – Vaterliebe. Elternrollen in der bürgerlichen Familie des 19. Jahrhunderts." *Bürgerinnen und Bürger. Geschlechterverhältnisse im 19. Jahrhundert,* ed. Ute Frevert. Göttingen, 1988, pp. 118–33.

Schulte, Bernd Felix. *Die deutsche Armee 1900–1914. Zwischen Beharren und Verändern.* Düsseldorf, 1977.

Schumann, Dirk. "Bayerns Unternehmer in Gesellschaft und Staat, 1834–1914. Herkunft, Familie, Ämter und Auszeichnungen am Beispiel der Städte, Munich, Nürnberg, Augsburg, Regensburg und Ludwigshafen," Dr.phil. dissertation, University of Munich, 1990.

Schumann, Dirk. "Herkunft und gesellschaftliche Stellung bayerischer Unternehmer im 19. Jahrhundert – Eine Untersuchung mit Schwerpunkten in Augsburg und Nürnberg." *Lebensbilder aus der Frühzeit der Industrialisierung in Bayern,* ed. Rainer A. Müller. Munich, 1985, pp. 295–304.

Schumpeter, Joseph A. *Kapitalismus, Sozialismus und Demokratie,* trans. Susanne Preiswerk, 2nd ed. Bern, 1950.

Schumpeter, Joseph A. *Theorie der wirtschaftlichen Entwicklung. Eine Untersuchung über Unternehmergewinn, Kapital, Kredit, Zins und den Konjunkturzyklus,* 6th ed. Berlin, 1964.

Schwippe, Heinrich Johannes. "Prozesse sozialer Segregation und funktionaler Spezialisierung in Berlin und Hamburg in der Periode der Industrialisierung und Urbanisierung." *Innerstädtische Differenzierungen und Prozesse im 19. und 20. Jahrhundert,* ed. Heinz Heineberg. Vienna, 1987, pp. 195–224.

Sheehan, James J. "Conflict and Cohesion among German Elites in the 19th Century." *Modern European Social History,* ed. Robert J. Bezucha. Lexington (Mass.), Toronto, and London, 1972, pp. 3–19.

Sheehan, James J. "Political Leadership in the German Reichstag 1871–1918." *American Historical Review,* vol. 74 (1968), pp. 511–28.

Sholem, Gershom. "On the Social Psychology of the Jews in Germany 1900–1933." *Jews and Germans from 1860 to 1933: The Problematic Symbiosis,* ed. David Bronsen. Heidelberg, 1979, pp. 9–32.

Shorter, Edward. *The Making of the Modern Family.* London, 1976.

Sieder, Reinhard. *Sozialgeschichte der Familie.* Frankfurt am Main, 1987.

Siegrist, Hannes. *Bürgerliche Berufe. Zur Sozialgeschichte der freien und akademischen Berufe im internationalen Vergleich.* Göttingen, 1988.

Sloterdijk, Peter. *Literatur und Organisation von Lebenserfahrung.*

Autobiographien der Zwanziger Jahre. Munich, 1978.

Smith, Bonnie G. *Ladies of the Leisure Class. The Bourgeoises of Northern France in the Nineteenth Century*. Princeton, 1981.

Sombart, Werner. *Der Bourgeois. Zur Geistesgechichte des modernen Wirtschaftsmenschen*. Munich and Leipzig, 1913.

Sombart, Werner. *Die deutsche Volkswirtschaft im 19. Jahrhundert*. Berlin, 1903.

Sombart, Werner. *Die Juden und das Wirtschaftsleben*. Munich and Leipzig, 1920.

Spencer, Elaine Glovka. "West German Coal, Iron and Steel Industrialists as Employers, 1896–1914," Ph.D. dissertation, University of California at Berkeley, 1969.

Stahl, Wilhelm. *Der Elitenkreislauf in der Unternehmerschaft. Eine empirische Untersuchung für den deutschsprachigen Raum*. Frankfurt am Main and Zurich, 1973.

Steglich, Walter. "Beitrag zur Problematik des Bündnisses zwischen Junkern und Bourgeoisie in Deutschland 1870–1880." *Wissenschaftliche Zeitschrift der Humboldt Universiträt zu Berlin*, vol. 9 (1959–60), pp. 323–40.

Stegmann, Dirk. *Die Erben Bismarcks. Parteien und Verbände in der Spätphase des Wilhelminischen Deutschlands. 1897–1918*. Cologne and – Berlin, 1970.

Stegmann, Dirk. "Hugenberg Contra Stresemann: Die Politik der Industrieverbände am Ende des Kaiserreichs." *Vierteljahrshefte für Zeitgeschichte*, vol. 24 (1976), pp. 329–78.

Stegmann, Dirk. "Linksliberale Bankiers, Kaufleute und Industrielle 1890–1900. Ein Beitrag zur Vorgeschichte des Handelsvertragsvereins." *Tradition*, vol. 21 (1976), pp. 4–36.

Stein, Hans-Konrad. *Der preußische Geldadel des 19. Jahrhunderts. Untersuchungen zur Nobilitierungspolitik der preußischen Regierung und zur Anpassung der oberen Schichten des Bürgertums an den Adel*. Dr.phil. dissertation, Hamburg, 1982. 2 vols.

Stein, Rudolf. *Das Bürgerhaus in Bremen*. Tübingen, 1970.

Stephan, Ernst. *Das Bürgerhaus in Mainz*. Tübingen, 1974.

Stern, Fritz. "Prussia." *European Landed Elites in the Nineteenth Century*, ed. David Spring. Baltimore and London, 1977.

Stone, Lawrence and Jeanne C. Fawtier Stone. *An Open Elite? England 1540–1880*. London, 1984.

Suhrbier, Hartwig. "Abseits von Villa Hügel. Herrschaftsarchitektur im Ruhrgebiet." *Kritische Berichte*, vol. 4 (1976), pp. 5–14.

Taylor, Thomas William. "The Crisis of Youth in Wilhelmine Germany." Ph.D. dissertation, University of Minnesota, 1990.

Taylor, Thomas William. "Images of Youth and the Family in Wilhelmine Germany: Toward a Reconsideration of the German Sonderweg."

German Studies Review, special issue winter 1992, pp. 55–73.

Taylor, Thomas William. "The Transition to Adulthood in Comparative Perspective: Professional Males in Germany and the United States at the Turn of the Century." *Journal of Social History*, vol. 21 (1987/88), pp. 635–58.

Tenfelde, Klaus. "Die Entfaltung des Vereinswesens während der Industriellen Revolution." *Vereinswesen und bürgerliche Gesellschaft in Deutschland*, ed. Otto Daun. Munich, 1984, pp. 55–114.

Teuteberg, Hans-Jürgen. *Westfälische Textilunternehmer in der Industrialisierung. Sozialer Status und betriebliches Verhalten im 19. Jahrhundert.* Dortmund, 1980.

Thomas, Frank and Sofie Trümper. *Bayenthal-Marienburg. 150 Jahre Leben und Arbeiten am Rhein.* Cologne, 1985.

Toury, Jacob. *Die politischen Orientierungen der Juden in Deutschland. Von Jena bis Weimar.* Tübingen, 1966.

Treue, Wilhelm. "Unternehmer und Finanziers, Chemiker und Ingenieure in der chemischen Industrie im 19. Jahrhundert." *Führungskräfte der Wirtschaft im neunzehnten Jahrhundert 1790–1914, T. II. Büdinger Vorträge 1969–1976*, ed. Herbert Helbig. Limburg/Lahn, 1977.

Uhlhorn, Friedrich and Walter Schlesinger. *Die deutschen Territorien*, 5th ed. 1970; reprint Stuttgart, 1980.

Ullmann, Hans-Peter. *Der Bund der Industriellen. Organisation, Einfluß und Politik klein- und mittelbetrieblicher Industrieller im Deutschen Kaiserreich 1895–1914.* Göttingen, 1976.

Veblen, Thorstein. *The Theory of the Leisure Class. An Economic Study of Institutions.* 1899; reprint London, 1970.

Vogt, Marianne. *Autobiographik bürgerlicher Frauen. Zur Geschichte weiblicher Selbstbewußtwerdung.* Würzburg, 1981.

Volkov, Schulamit. "Jüdische Assimilation und jüdische Eigenart im Deutschen Kaiserreich. Ein Versuch." *Geschichte und Gesellschaft*, vol. 9 (1983), pp. 331–48.

Weber, Max. *Gesammelte politische Schriften*, 2nd ed. Tübingen, 1958.

Weber, Max. *Die protestantische Ethik*, ed. Johannes Winckelmann, 5th ed. 1920; reprint Tübingen, 1979, vol. 2: *Eine Aufsatzsammlung*.

Weber-Kellermann, Ingebord. "The German Family Between Private Life and Politics," trans. Mary Jo Maynes and Michelle Moutons. *Riddles of Identity in Modern Times*, eds. Antoine Prost and Gerard Vincents in *A History of Private Life*, gen. eds. Philippe Ariès and Georges Duby. Cambridge, 1991.

Weder, Dietrich. *Die 200 größten deutschen Aktiengesellschaften 1913–1962. Beziehungen zwischen Größe, Lebensdauer und Wettbewerbschancen von Unternehmern.* Dr.phil. dissertation, University of Frankfurt am Main, 1968.

Wehler, Hans-Ulrich, ed. *Klassen in der europäischen Sozialgeschichte.*

Göttingen, 1979.

Winkler, Heinrich A. "Der deutsche Sonderweg: Eine Nachlese." *Merkur* vol. 35 (1981), pp. 793–804.

Wirth, Irmgard. "Juden als Künstler und Kunstförderer in Berlin im späten 19. und 20. Jahrhundert." *Emuna*, vol. 9 (1974), pp. 31–38.

Wischermann, Clemens. *Wohnen in Hamburg vor dem Ersten Weltkrieg.* Münster, 1983.

Witt, Peter-Christian. "Der preußische Landrat als Steuerbeamter 1891–1918. Bemerkungen zur politischen und sozialen Funktion des deutschen Beamtentums." *Deutschland in der Weltpolitik des 19. und 20. Jahrhunderts*, eds. Imanuel Geiss and Bernd Jürgen Wendt. Düsseldorf, 1973, pp. 205–19.

Wolff, Max I. *Club von Berlin. 1864–1924.* Berlin, 1926.

Zapf, Wolfgang. *Wandlungen der deutschen Elite. Ein Zirkulationsmodell deutscher Führungsgruppen 1919–1961.* Munich, 1965.

Zorn, Wolfgang. "Die Sozialentwicklung der nichtagrarischen Welt (1806–1970)." *Handbuch der bayerishen Geschichte*, ed. Max Spindler, vol. 4: *Das Neue Bayern*, sub-vol. 2, pp. 846–82.

Zorn, Wolfgang. "Typen und Entwicklungskräfte deutschen Unternehmertums im 19. Jahrhundert." *Vierteljahrsschrift für Sozial- und Wirtschaftsgeschichte*, vol. 44 (1957), pp. 57–77.

Zunkel, Friedrich. "Beamtenschaft und Unternehmertum beim Aufbau der Rurhindustrie 1849–1880." *Tradition*, vol. 9 (1964), pp. 261–77.

Zunkel, Friedrich. *Der Rheinisch-Westfälische Unternehmer 1834–1879. Ein Beitrag zur Geschichte des deutschen Bürgertums im 19. Jahrhundert.* Cologne and Opladen, 1962.

Zwahr, Hartmut. "Zur Klassenkonstituierung der deutschen Bourgeoisie." Zwahr, Hartmut, *Proletariat und Bourgeoisie in Deutschland. Studien zur Klassendialektik.* Cologne, 1980.

Index

Blackbourn, David 4–5
Bleichröder, Else 85
Bleichröder, Gerson 72, 85, 145, 183
Bleichröder, James von 183
Blohm, Hermann 165
Blosser, Ursi 104
Bode, Wilhelm von 217
Bodenhausen, Eduard 218
Boelcke, Willi 202
Bohlen und Halbach, Gustav *see* Krupp
  von Bohlen und Halbach, Gustav
Böninger, Arnold 120, 229–30
Böninger, Walther 168
Borchardt, Knut 162, 231
Borchardt, Rudolf 135–6, 142
Borgnis, Karl 235
Bosch, Robert 119, 142, 168, 176,
  227, 235–6, 240
Botzow, Julius 75
Bötzow, Tutty (later von Siemens) 75
Bötzow Jr, Julius 57, 128
bourgeoisie 1–10
  aristocracy avoids 203, 213–14,
    240–1
  class identity and values 8–9
  homes 172–3
  rising 159
  social forms 242–7
  splendid style 219–6, 239
Brandes, Erika 76
Breckman, Warren 159
Bremen 27, 168–9, 192
Brennan, Marion 67, 68
Briesen, Bruno Schultz 227
Britain 28–30, 34, 104–5, 238
Brockhaus Verlag 153
Broich, Baron von 37
Brönner, Wolfgang 161, 179
Bucher, Hermann 236
Buddenbrooks (Mann) 125
Bülow, Prince Bernhard von 196, 203,
  205, 208
Bund Elektra 192
Bunsen, Marie von 219
Burchard family 194

Calvinism 32, 34
Cambon, Paul 206
capitalism 9, 15, 16
Cassella (Leopold) chemicals 179
Cassirer, Paul 170
castles *see* villas and castles
Catholics 49, 84, 89, 168
  profile of businessmen 32–5

Cecil, Lamar 10, 189–90, 201, 204,
  212, 214
  feudalization 205
Central Association of German
  Industrialists 30–1, 50
Chambers of Commerce 50
children and childhood 122–3, 125–7,
  248, 249 *see also* families;
  family-run businesses
  adolescence 91–2
  class differences 103
  data on sons' professions 147–51
  daughters 117–22, 246, 248
  frugal upbringing 233
  marriage and 85–8
  mother's role 110–12
  nobility 85
  rebellion 127–34
  sons 7, 51, 117–2, 125–34, 155–6,
    246, 248, 252
  transformation of attitudes 15
civil service 6, 9–10, 53, 144, 148
Claessens, Dieter 104
Claessens, Karin 104
class *see* aristocracy; bourgeoisie;
  residential patterns
Club of Berlin 198
Cologne 165, 167–9
Commercial Councillors 35–42, 47,
  59–60, 228
Conservative Party 49–50

Daelen, Felix 107
Davidoff, Leonore 14, 104–5
Decorations 35–48
Dehmel, Richard 218
Delbrück, Ludwig 21, 23
Delbrück, Rudolf von 208
Deutsch, Felix 198, 216, 218
Deutsch, Lili 218
Deutsche Bank 52, 222, 223
Deutscher Kaiser Mining Company 21
Deutz factory 129
diplomatic service 144, 145, 206
Dippe, Fritz von 144
Disconto-Gesellschaft 199, 203
Doerry, Martin 91
Dohm, Ernst 215
Dohm, Hedwig 215, 217
Duisberg, Carl 138–9, 181, 227–8, 229
  family 101, 112, 128
  social life 232–3
  titles and honors 37
Duisberg, Carl Ludwig 128, 138–9

296

Printed in the United Kingdom
by Lightning Source UK Ltd.
112001UKS00001B/2